At Home and Abroad

....
RELIGION, CULTURE, AND PUBLIC LIFE

RELIGION, CULTURE, AND PUBLIC LIFE

Series Editor: Matthew Engelke

The Religion, Culture, and Public Life series is devoted to the study of religion in relation to social, cultural, and political dynamics, both contemporary and historical. It features work by scholars from a variety of disciplinary and methodological perspectives, including religious studies, anthropology, history, philosophy, political science, and sociology. The series is committed to deepening our critical understandings of the empirical and conceptual dimensions of religious thought and practice, as well as such related topics as secularism, pluralism, and political theology. The Religion, Culture, and Public Life series is sponsored by Columbia University's Institute for Religion, Culture, and Public Life.

For a complete list of titles, see page 355.

At Home and Abroad

The Politics of
American Religion

Edited by
Elizabeth Shakman Hurd
and Winnifred Fallers Sullivan

Columbia University Press
New York

Publication of this book was made possible in part by funding from the Institute for Religion, Culture, and Public Life at Columbia University.

Columbia University Press
Publishers Since 1893
New York   Chichester, West Sussex
cup.columbia.edu

Copyright © 2021 Columbia University Press
All rights reserved

Library of Congress Cataloging-in-Publication Data
Names: Hurd, Elizabeth Shakman, 1970- editor. | Sullivan, Winnifred Fallers, 1950- editor.
Title: At home and abroad : the politics of American religion / edited by Elizabeth Shakman Hurd and Winnifred Fallers Sullivan.
Description: New York : Columbia University Press, 2021. | Series: Religion, culture, and public life | Includes bibliographical references and index.
Identifiers: LCCN 2020028011 (print) | LCCN 2020028012 (ebook) | ISBN 9780231198981 (hardback) | ISBN 9780231198998 (trade paperback) | ISBN 9780231552905 (ebook)
Subjects: LCSH: Religion and politics—United States.
Classification: LCC BL2525 .A88 2021 (print) | LCC BL2525 (ebook) | DDC 201/.720973—dc23
LC record available at https://lccn.loc.gov/2020028011
LC ebook record available at https://lccn.loc.gov/2020028012

Cover design: Milenda Nan Ok Lee

Contents

Acknowledgments ix

Introduction: Religion, Law, and Politics, American Style, by Elizabeth Shakman Hurd and Winnifred Fallers Sullivan 1

PART I
Making Religion American

1. A Home, Made Abroad: American Religion from Colonies Through the Civil War, by Evan Haefeli 19

2. "A Perfect, Irrevocable Gift": Recognizing the Proprietary Church in Puerto Rico 1898–1908, by David Maldonado Rivera 37

3. Home Rule: Equitable Justice in Progressive Chicago and the Philippines, by Nancy Buenger 51

4. America Is Hard to See,
by Courtney Bender   91

PART II
Making Ourselves

5. Homemaking in Palestine: Jessie Sampter,
Religion, and Relation, by Sarah Imhoff   115

6. On the Abroad of a Different Home: Muhammad Ali
in Micro-Scope, by M. Cooper Harriss   130

7. Domestic Bones, Foreign Land, and
the Kingdom Come: Jurisdictions of Religion
in Contemporary Hawaii, by Greg Johnson   148

8. "Legacy," by Matthew Scherer   167

PART III
Inside/Outside

9. The Rule of Law, by Winnifred Fallers Sullivan   183

10. Double Standards in a Tripartite World,
by Jolyon Baraka Thomas   196

11. The Cultural Politics of Yoga in India and
the United States, by Sunila S. Kale and
Christian Lee Novetzke   210

12. Border Religion, by Elizabeth Shakman Hurd   228

PART IV
Abroad

13. Established Authorities: Theology, the State, and the Apartheid Struggle, by Melani McAlister   249

14. In Search of Normcore? Religion at Home and Abroad in Norway, by Helge Årsheim   273

15. When Home Becomes Abroad, and Abroad Becomes Home: Thinking American Empire Through a New Sudan, by Noah Salomon   288

Afterword: Double Vision, Double Cross: American Exceptionalism, Borders, and the Study of Religion, by Pamela E. Klassen   304

....

Bibliography   315
List of Contributors   337
Index   339

Acknowledgments

This is the second in a pair of volumes developed under the auspices of the "Politics of Religion at Home and Abroad" project led by the editors with the generous support of the Henry R. Luce Initiative on Religion in International Affairs at the Henry Luce Foundation. We would like to take this opportunity to thank the Initiative not only for making this collaborative research project possible but also and more broadly for supporting new understandings of the intersections of religion, politics, and global public life for so many years under the creative intellectual leadership of Dr. Toby Volkman. We also would like to acknowledge the many contributions of Luce Postdoctoral Fellow Sarah Dees and editorial assistants Matthew Graham, Luca Fitzgerald, and Gina Giliberti, all of whom spent many hours ensuring that the wheels on this project kept turning. We are grateful to Pamela Klassen for offering a generous reading and response to the collection of essays, and to Columbia University Press, and in particular to Religion, Culture and Public Life series editor Matthew Engelke, whose support for this project as it approached publication gave us a boost. It was also a pleasure working with Wendy K. Lochner and Lowell Frye at the Press. Thanks to the Department of Religious Studies and the Center for the Study of Religion and the Human at Indiana University, and the Department of Political Science and the Weinberg College of Arts and Sciences at Northwestern University for their support of the collaborative intellectual work that went into this volume. Finally, to the contributors to this project, both those represented in these pages and others "at home and abroad," who contributed to the conversation over the past four years, thank you.

At Home and Abroad

Introduction

Religion, Law, and Politics, American Style

ELIZABETH SHAKMAN HURD AND

WINNIFRED FALLERS SULLIVAN

Is it, perhaps, possible that there are two kinds of Civilization—one for home consumption and one for the heathen market?

—Mark Twain, "To the Person Sitting in Darkness"

Religion has always been central to American self-understanding. But there is today and there always has been a difference in the United States between the domestic versions of religion and religious freedom and of those offered for export. This difference is not the result only of the different contexts but, more importantly, of the fact that the religion that is internal to American self-identity itself makes such a distinction. As with other aspects of the practices of American exceptionalism, religion—religion American style—is characterized by a curious inside/outside dynamic grounded in assumptions about our religious selves and religious others. The difference might be expressed in the notion that religion at home is assumed to be both tamed and free in a way not yet achieved by religion in other places or with the religion of certain internal "others." What we name here an inside/outside religious dynamic is, in other words, enabled by a productive and hierarchical ambiguity about what counts as "religion" at home and abroad, one that helps to maintain the gulf many Americans experience between themselves and others. This ambiguity, ironically perhaps, contributes to the stability of the practices of U.S. exceptionalism across different domestic constituencies, left, right, and center.

This volume explores the at-home and abroad politics of American religious exceptionalism. Seeing religion through the prism of a shifting and unstable inside/outside paradigm, the essays explore what Cooper Harriss calls the double-cross of religion in the United States as well as the symbiotic relationship between U.S. domestic and foreign policy with regard to religion and religious governance. Bringing domestic and foreign aspects of the politics of American religion into a single field of vision, the essays seek an understanding of the religious and political phenomenology of the disestablishment of religion that underlies U.S. history.

Disestablishment is arguably the defining feature of the U.S. internal legal regime with respect to religion. It differs significantly from other church/state arrangements in Europe and elsewhere. It is also poorly understood.[1] When projected abroad, it casts a distinctive shadow across the landscape. We suggest that disestablishment enhances the capacity of protestant Christianity to operate in American history both as a religion and not as a religion—that is, its capacity to not be a religion in disestablished mode but to be a religion in free exercise mode, to use the rubrics of the First Amendment to the U.S. Constitution, which enables certain political and religious possibilities. This Janus-faced capacity is crucial to understanding the politics of American religion at home and abroad. Integrating U.S. domestic and international history at the intersection of religion and politics, as this volume does, enriches our understanding of the complex roles played by Christianity as the prototype of religion in both venues.

U.S. foreign policy and diplomatic history typically segregate the study of religion from debates over the projection of U.S. power and the question of American empire. We contend that American history needs to be retold from a perspective that foregrounds the "at home and abroad" dynamic. It is impossible to tell this story without linking U.S. domestic and foreign religious and political history. The present volume, as well as a second volume, *Theologies of American Exceptionalism*, published by Indiana University Press, emerged from a series of interdisciplinary workshops that fostered sustained conversations on these issues between 2016 and 2019.[2]

FRAMING THE PROJECT: AT HOME AND ABROAD

In the United States the self-evident desirability and inevitability of legal protection for religion and religious freedom underwrites politics and policy at home and abroad, even while these two projects turn out, on close examination, to be quite different. U.S. foreign policy has most often pursued a policy of explicit "conversion" both abroad and in its internal colonization of indigenous and enslaved populations, while domestic policy with respect to white Americans has characterized itself as noninterference. While the United States has not consistently espoused a policy of explicitly promoting religious conversion abroad, if by that one means an overt government attempt to make people into Christians (although that has been done that from time to time), the United States has consistently intervened to convert others to a particular way of being religious. That is, it has attempted to change religious attitudes in both direct and indirect ways. Efforts to promote and institutionalize the protection of private property, capitalism, individualism, democratization, the rule of law, and other staples of the modern legal and political order all rest on reorderings of local ways of life, law, and governance, which imply new religious self-understandings and affiliations. One version of this effort is on display in Jolyon Thomas's chapter in this volume, which retells the religious politics of the U.S. occupation of Japan. In the U.S. domestic sphere, meanwhile, a rhetoric of nonintervention has not, of course, been an actual practice of nonintervention. There, too, there has been an effort to shape religious subjectivity through cultural and temporal imaginaries of American exceptionalism, as shown eloquently by Courtney Bender in her chapter on flight—even while other jurisdictions, closer to the ground perhaps, continue to be present and imagined, as Gregory Johnson shows in the Hawaiian case and Pamela Klassen notes in her concluding essay. It is the details of the ways in which formal and informal management of religion works in each context and their structural entanglement that interest us and can be seen in their variety in the rest of the chapters.

U.S.-sponsored advocacy for religion and religious freedom abroad is more than a question of inclusion or exclusion—or of compliance or noncompliance with what is often assumed to be a stable and singular international norm or legal standard.[3] The multiple discourses concerning religion and religious freedom cannot be resolved that easily. The United States is not simply a place of and for religion and religious freedom. The United States is a place, as Courtney Bender elsewhere expresses it, where religion itself is understood to have been perfected.[4]

This perspective helps to bring some curious aspects of U.S. foreign religion policy more clearly into view. Take, for example, one provision of the International Religious Freedom Act (1998): Congress required the State Department to prepare an annual global assessment of the state of religious freedom, country by country. The most recent such report (2019)—as with all of the previous reports—omits, without explanation and contrary to the requirement of the act, only one country, the United States itself. While one might dismiss this omission as either simply a matter of practical politics or even as an act of jingoistic hubris, a second look suggests that this omission is not meant to convey only that religious freedom has already been achieved in the United States; more importantly, it conveys the notion that different rules apply to the United States because religion in the United States is itself understood to be different.[5] Religion in the United States is understood to be by its nature more free.[6] Law is also differently understood, as Sullivan shows in her contribution to this volume. Notwithstanding a considerably more complex legal history, as shown in Nancy Buenger's essay on home rule, the rule of law, a law founded in Magna Carta, is understood today to be more perfectly realized in the United States than elsewhere. The Bill of Rights of the U.S. Constitution is, in most cases, understood not to constrain the executive branch in its conduct of foreign affairs and international legal instruments governing these issues are not routinely applied in the United States, as they are elsewhere, because they have not been made part of U.S. law.

The United States operates by its own set of rules with respect to religion, as with other matters. The particular religious voluntarism of the domestic American space—what is sometimes termed the free market in religion—is not the religion the United States is exporting—or that it has ever exported. The religion that is exported—and that the United States has sought to impose on various subjugated domestic populations (internal others, one might say) including at various moments Roman Catholics, Mormons, Native Americans, enslaved African Americans and American Muslims—is not one that is free in any absolute sense but one that serves the various interests of the state. In the first chapter in this volume, "A Home Made Abroad," historian Evan Haefeli explains how formal disestablishment in the United States, rather than being the result of deliberate colonial policy in Britain and elsewhere or as a result of the teaching of enlightened philosophers, emerged haphazardly, as a matter of practical politics and local compromise, in light of the chaotic religious politics in the metropole. The value of the inside/outside lens is dramatized by Haefeli's retelling of U.S. colonial and early republican history with the proto–United States positioned as merely a distant "abroad of another home." Haefeli's retelling also serves as an illuminating backdrop to other chapters in the volume including Greg Johnson's discussion of enactments of indigenous jurisdiction among contemporary Native Hawaiians and David Maldonado Rivera's analysis of property disputes involving the Catholic Church in early twentieth century Puerto Rico under the new American regime of disestablishment. These legal decisions, as Maldonado Rivera shows, re-created the juridical personality of the Church in Puerto Rico while affirming the continuity between the concordats between Spain and the Vatican and American corporate and religious law. Yet resistance by all of these various others is also always present, showing up the double-cross insisted upon by Muhammad Ali in his conversion as he performs his own exceptionalism.

Moving to contemporary politics, the inside/outside paradigm implies a new perspective on U.S. public conversations today about "un-American" religion. The view that religion comes in two kinds—coercive, violent, sexist religion, on the one hand, and voluntary, tolerant, and inclusive religion, on the other—has a very specific modern history that can be traced to various points at which political polemics against specific forms of religion drew these boundaries.[7] Domestically in the United States, constitutional religion—that is, disestablished religion—is understood to be a distinctively new form of religion in human history, one that relies on persuasion and a free market in religious ideas rather than on mandated and inherited membership.[8] Virtually all Americans understand this kind of religion to be the best. The fact that U.S. religion and policy toward religion is, and has often been, founded in a religion that is also inherited, intolerant, and violent is not allowed to displace the confidence most Americans have in what they take to be their superior form of religion.

At the same time, turning to foreign relations, American exceptionalism is not unsettled by the fact that what Americans would call "established"—and therefore undesirable—religion in other places can be seen to produce some goods that Americans profess to admire, including a concern for public welfare and the benefits of group membership. American foreign policy mobilizes this sense of exceptionalism when the U.S. government finds what it takes to be social and political pathologies in other societies that are then attributed to the wrong kind of religion, enabling interventions in religious and political institutions abroad that would not be tolerated at home.[9]

As Sarah Imhoff shows in her illuminating discussion of the gendered aspects of home and homemaking read through the life and times of Jessie Sampter, an American poet and visionary who lived most of her life abroad, the terms "at home" and "abroad" are not taken here in the usual sense as gesturing spatially to that which occurs only inside or beyond U.S. territorial boundaries. Rather, they are generative metaphors that describe the structure of the American religious imagination. What and who counts as home and abroad, and how and by whom are such distinctions drawn? How do these taxonomies relate to other axes of discrimination such as domestic/foreign, legal/illegal, inside/outside, religion/politics, freedom/tyranny, and self/other?

Melani McAlister's discussion of transnational evangelical networks connecting the United States and South Africa shows that political and theological debates centered around the beginning of chapter 13 of Paul's Letter to the Romans in the Christian New Testament ("Let everyone be subject to the governing authorities, for there is no authority except that which God has established") scrambled nearly all of these binaries in debates over apartheid in the 1980s. Noah Salomon charts the creation of a Muslim "minority" in the new South Sudan following the division of a unitary Sudanese state identified with Islam into putatively Muslim and non-Muslim polities, examining how its members came to constitute new national and political identities when the ground shifted beneath them. Extrapolating from the Sudanese case, Salomon concludes that the instability of the categories of home and abroad are not unique to citizens of a country undergoing partition but rather are shared by many figures in our fractured present: from the migrant to the mercenary, from the advocate of global governance to the purveyor of global finance. Finally, in their critique of the cultural appropriation argument in relation to yoga, Sunila Kale and Christian Novetske argue that yoga as we know it today was the result of a strident resistance to colonialism even as it was also shaped by colonial violence and prejudice. Each of these chapters illustrates the payoff of foregrounding specific conceptions of, and shifting relations between, "home" and "abroad," "religion" and "politics," and "inside" and "outside."

Beginning with our early research into the subject matter of this volume, we identified four historical moments, discussed in the next section, that illustrate for us the striking contrast between the United States as a global legal and political actor when it comes to religion and religious freedom and to evolving notions of religion and religious freedom at home. At each of these moments—the founding of Liberia, the U.S. mission to the Philippines, the Cold War, and the so-called war on terror, the United States was and continued to be actively engaged in exporting Christianity and its partner, civilization, while some of the same officials responsible for U.S. evangelizing abroad were and continued to be busy legally disestablishing religion at home. Other scholars have explored the complex histories of these ventures.[10] Of interest to us is how these moments reveal how the inside/outside dynamic has structured the politics of religion in the United States in the past and today, at home and abroad. How does the history of what counts as religion for the United States connect to its capacity to have differing religion policies with respect to different populations?

Noticing the foreign/domestic disjuncture is not simply a matter of revealing the inevitable hypocrisy of power politics. The capacity of the United States to have different religion policies at home and abroad is, we suggest, intimately connected to the discursive capacity of the dominant form of religion in the United States, protestant Christianity, to enable certain political and religious possibilities.[11] The subtle and complex disjuncture results from the ways in which Christianity is both visible and invisible and understands itself to be so, theologically speaking.[12] It is culturally invisible both because of secularization and because its ways have been the ways of the majority. The religiousness of the language it speaks has been largely naturalized. Its visibility only comes in the context of crystallizing moments of conflict with the secular, particularly the communist secular, or with "other" minority religions, whether, Catholic, Jewish, Muslim, Mormon, or Indigenous. The invisible ways of protestant Christianity—for example, with respect to the regulation of sexuality—are allowed to dominate, domesticating and disciplining other traditions through "neutral" laws, while Christian exceptionalism is invoked explicitly only within intra-Christian disputes or what are seen to be the irruption of un-American religious forms.[13] This Christian capacity for shape-shifting is not only characteristic of American ways of religion. It is intimately connected to the whole project of modernity. But it takes a particular form in the United States because of disestablishment.

It is now common to observe that religion, used to denote various cultural formations around the world, only emerged in the modern period. Both in response to the "discovery" of other religions in the course of European imperial expansion and colonialism, and in the context of intra-Christian disputes, protestant Christianity, in a singular achievement, came to be positioned, paradoxically, as not a religion because it was not implicated in material pagan practices, as Catholicism and non-Christian ways of life were, on the one hand, and as the most perfect and enlightened and modern form of religion, on the other.[14] This is a complex story, connected to supersessionist claims in relation to Judaism, a story that emerges in different guises in the early modern, enlightenment, and Cold War contexts.[15] The claim that Christianity is not a religion, having its roots in early Christian polemics against Judaism and famously argued for both by Karl Barth and Dietrich Bonhoeffer, among other theologians, both distinguishes and naturalizes Christianity. Helge Årsheim's essay in this volume provides a Norwegian perspective on what he calls the normalizing effect of modern Protestantism.

This book offers a portrait of the particular form that this theology has taken as it has informed and continues to shape American politics, even while its instability—even tragedy, as Matthew Scherer insists—is constantly being revealed. Being American is being religious when seen against godless secularism. But being Christian is not being religious when seen against other religions.

Being Christian, in the strongest form of this claim, is embracing the truth, a truth made perfect by the American political and economic order. American Christianity is also not religious because it often passes for secular, as Janet Jakobsen and Ann Pellegrini have so trenchantly explored in their book on U.S. domestic regulation of sexuality, *Love the Sin*.[16]

FOUR HISTORICAL MOMENTS

A brief rehearsal of four historical moments illustrates the significance of the inside/outside metaphor to understanding the history and politics of American religion. Each of these moments shows the different ways in which specific conceptions of, and shifting relations between, "home" and "abroad" and "religion" and "politics" have enabled a distinctively American national project whose implications cannot be accurately described if we continue to privilege divides between domestic and foreign while holding religion constant.

Early Republican America: Evangelization Abroad, Disestablishment at Home

In 1816, during the presidency of James Madison, Robert Finley founded the Society for the Colonization of Free People of Color of America, commonly known as the American Colonization Society (1816–1964). The expressed purposes of this society were to resettle American slaves in Liberia rather than to free them, to evangelize West Africa, and to open new markets for American products. Founding members included Henry Clay and John Randolph. The society's activities were founded on the assumption that Black and white Americans could not live together and that the former had no place in the American project. By 1821 the society had secured federal funding and purchased land for the new Black colony of Liberia in West Africa.[17]

Other American missionary efforts, such as the establishment in New England in 1810 of the American Board of Commissioners for Foreign Missions, were also founded during this period. The first missionaries from this board were sent to Hawaii in 1819.[18] American missionaries including Pliny Fisk, Levi Parsons, and Jonas King also traveled to Palestine, Ottoman Turkey, Egypt, and Syria.[19]

The U.S. government supported these missionary efforts to convert the "heathen" at home and abroad. Indeed, by the early nineteenth century there was a growing consensus among humanitarian reformers that survival of indigenous communities depended on "civilization and Christianization." This meant education in "white ways of life," adoption of single-family farms, and acceptance of protestant religious tenets.[20]

While the U.S. government was engaged in such missionizing, the newly founded U.S. states over the first third of the nineteenth century were also busy disestablishing Christianity through the slow elimination of various privileges for churches and for Christianity more generally.[21] Among other American statesmen, James Madison was a supporter of both projects. Madison was both president of the American Colonization Society for a period and considered among the most radical of those who would separate government from Christianity at home.[22]

Early American evangelization at home and abroad was, from the beginning, a part of the complex series of events that led to the naturalization of American Protestantism as the religion of America.[23]

Imperial America: Civilizing Heathens and Natives, at Home and Abroad

Moving to the late nineteenth and early twentieth centuries, the second moment again discloses American efforts to civilize non-Christians abroad in various overseas missions and engaging in a similar mission on the margins of the domestic scene vis-à-vis Mormon and Native American others while also further disestablishing religion for the majority. These efforts reflect internal as well as external imperialism, explicitly combining the spread of the gospel with the spread of American values, religion, religious freedom, and liberal property rights.[24]

During the Spanish–American War and the U.S. annexation of the Philippines (1899, independence 1946), the U.S. administration of the Philippines as an "insular area" involved a similar pattern of collaboration between the federal government and protestant missionaries to "civilize" the Filipinos.[25] In April of 1901 the Evangelical Union of the Philippines was established in Manila to coordinate activities among the protestant denominations, mainly by dividing territory. As President William McKinley expressed it in a speech to Methodist missionaries,

> When next I realized that the Philippines had dropped into our laps, I confess I did not know what to do with them. I sought counsel from all sides—Democrats as well as Republicans—but got little help. I thought first we would take only Manila; then Luzon; then other islands, perhaps, also. I walked the floor of the White House night after night until midnight; and I am not ashamed to tell you, gentlemen, that I went down on my knees and prayed to Almighty God for light and guidance more than one night. And one night late it came to me this way—I don't know how it was, but it came: (1) That we could not give them back to Spain—that would be cowardly and dishonorable; (2) that we could not turn them over to France or Germany—our commercial rivals in the Orient—that would be bad business and discreditable; (3) that we could not leave them to themselves—they were unfit for self-government—and they would soon have anarchy and misrule over there worse than Spain's was; and (4) that there was nothing left for us to do but to take them all, and to educate the Filipinos, and uplift and civilize and Christianize them, and by God's grace do the very best we could by them, as our fellow men for whom Christ also died. And then I went to bed and went to sleep and slept soundly.[26]

Senator Knute Nelson of Minnesota, who supported the expansionists during the debate in Washington on the ratification of the Treaty of Paris, is supposed to have said that "Providence has given the United States the duty of extending Christian civilization. We come as ministering angels, not despots."[27] Nelson is best known for promoting the Nelson Act of 1899 to consolidate the Ojibwe/Chippewa in Minnesota on a western reservation and to require the breakup of communal land by allotting it to individual households, selling off the remainder to any buyer.[28] The American colonial experiment in Puerto Rico also dates to this period, as discussed by Maldonado Rivera in this volume. Trade controversies surrounding the standing of Puerto Rico vis-à-vis the United States led to the invention of a new constitutional category, "unincorporated territories," in the oft-cited Insular Cases.[29]

Meanwhile at "home," among other secularizing efforts, litigation over Bible reading in the public schools, known as the "Bible wars," acknowledged religious diversity and the inadequacy of the nondenominational neutrality of the protestant settlement in the face of such diversity.[30] The result was the gradual elimination of the practice in state after state. The most well-known of these cases was in Cincinnati, the landmark decision by the Ohio Supreme Court in *Board of Education of Cincinnati v. Minor*.[31] In finding the Bible reading unlawful, Judge Alphonso Taft famously wrote, "True Christianity asks no aid from the sword of civil authority. It began without the sword, and wherever it has taken the sword it has perished by the sword. To depend on civil authority for its enforcement is to acknowledge its own weakness, which it can never afford to do. It is able to fight its own battles. Its weapons are moral and spiritual, and not carnal." Thus, again we see the gradual broadening out of the consensus religious culture, often with a genuine sensitivity for religious difference even while projects of active Christian civilization continued apace—abroad. A comparison of the language used by Justice Taft and that of President McKinley is telling.

Cold War America: Religious Offensives Abroad, Invention of Separationism at Home

U.S. foreign policy during the late 1940s and 1950s again included dedicated efforts of Christian evangelism and religious interventionism. "[Gen. Douglas] MacArthur's greatest disappointment may have been his failure to convert the ... Japanese to Christianity"; it was "his conviction that 'true democracy can exist only on a spiritual foundation,' and will 'endure when it rests firmly on the Christian conception of the individual and society.'"[32]

During the Cold War, often in partnership with the Vatican as well as with other Church representatives, the CIA fought communism and communist sympathizers abroad by promoting religious freedom and global spiritual health.[33] In the early 1950s the United States worked to counter communist sympathies abroad through a series of religious alliances in Southeast Asia. The United States sent a Buddhist advisor to Cambodia and cultivated a religious alliance with a Thai police general that founded the Society for the Promotion of Buddhism. In 1956 the U.S. Operations Coordinating Board, which reported to the National Security Council, formed the Committee on Buddhism to coordinate what was described as a "religious offensive."[34]

Meanwhile, at home in this period the Supreme Court's new incorporation doctrine led to the application of the First Amendment to the states for the first time, federalizing religious freedom jurisprudence. The Court's first establishment clause decisions, including *Everson v. Board of Education*, articulated a strong separationist position, insisting that no government favor or funding was ever to be given to any religious organization.[35] The separationist position relied on a careful secularizing of activities of the state, including making invisible the religious aspects of the celebration of Christmas.[36]

War on Terror America: New Establishments at Home and Abroad

Our fourth moment brings us into the present and to contemporary U.S. efforts to combat violent extremism by promoting religious freedom abroad in the so-called war on terror, the International Religious Freedom Act, and related initiatives. The religious freedom exported today by the United States is modeled on Cold War efforts to combat secularism and communism by promoting global spiritual health. The difference is that, rather than would-be communists, it is primarily Muslims who are subject to spiritual reform.

A leading advocate for U.S. religious freedom promotion, Thomas Farr of Georgetown University, recalls early Cold War efforts nostalgically: "However doctrinally diluted or exclusivist it was, the protestant-derived civil religion of the 1940s and 1950s provided America the context with which to understand and resist the mortal threat of communism. In other words, our shared religious principles helped us to understand who we were—and who the enemy was—back in the days of the Cold War. Do we still have the principles—and the wisdom—to know either?"[37] In response to pressure from Farr and other advocates, the U.S. State Department office established by the International Religious Freedom Act, alongside the United States Commission on International Religious Freedom and, later, the Office of Religion and Global Affairs at the State Department, among other agencies, were enlisted to promote religious freedom and religious engagement, with an eye on transforming religious leaders and groups into democratic civil society actors and empowering them to ensure that their rivals are in no position to threaten the United States or U.S.-allied interests. To this end, the United States became increasingly involved in the early 2000s in initiatives around the world to cultivate foreign religious subjects who are moderate and free and to modify other states' domestic laws so that religion is overseen in such a way that "extremism" is kept at bay. According to Nina Shea, one of the leaders of this charge, "since 9/11, the link between our own security and freedom, between our national interests and our ideals, has never been clearer. Winning the War on Terror turns on the battle of ideas and at its heart is the principle of religious freedom."[38] Religious freedom, American style, translates into support for religions that conform to an American understanding of what it means to be free. Those that conform are "free of the need for regulation," but others are less "free" and demand intervention.[39]

Meanwhile, at home, following the 1990 *Smith* decision (the so-called peyote case), American religious actors have been demanding, and to some extent receiving, self-governing autonomy from government regulation.[40] The Court's decision in *Hosanna-Tabor v. EEOC*, for example, appears to recognize churches as having a regulation-free zone of activity, exempt from the constraining demands of civil rights and employment discrimination legislation—exempt, one might say, from the demands of the First Amendment religion clauses.[41]

Many of the same American religious actors that have successfully demanded self-governing autonomy at home are also involved in the projection of particular forms of U.S. religious governance abroad.

STRUCTURE OF THE VOLUME

The essays in this volume explore the inside/outside dynamic of American religion in a series of specific contexts illustrating the productive ambiguity of the "at home and abroad" metaphor in practice.

The essays of the first section, "Making Religion American" (Haefeli, Maldonado Rivera, Buenger, and Bender) thicken the longitudinal story, giving specificity to the various mechanisms by which the inside/outside dynamic has been created over time. A second set of essays, "Making Ourselves" (Imhoff, Harriss, Johnson, and Scherer) focuses on internal religious others creatively inventing themselves as both religious and American. A third set, "Inside/Outside" (Sullivan, Thomas, Kale and Novetzke, and Hurd) examines the particular discursive and social mechanisms through which the borders between ourselves and others are negotiated and contested. A final section, "Abroad," (McAlister, Årsheim, and Salomon), considers the productivity of the inside/outside metaphor for the study of the religious and theological politics of the nation-state beyond the United States. The volume concludes with an afterword by Pamela E. Klassen.

Public conversations and policy debates about religion and politics in U.S. domestic and foreign affairs are rife with assumptions about religion. By interrogating these assumptions through careful historical and ethnographic research, it is our hope that this volume will help to articulate new framings of the structuring role of religion in the American project.

NOTES

1. See Winnifred Fallers Sullivan, *Prison Religion: Faith-Based Reform and the Constitution* (Princeton, N.J.: Princeton University Press, 2009); and Winnifred

Fallers Sullivan, *Church State Corporation: Construing Religion in U.S. Law* (Chicago: University of Chicago Press, 2020).
2. With the generous support of the Henry R. Luce Initiative on Religion in International Affairs, the project also supported the development of the Teaching Law and Religion Case Study Archive, an open access digital repository featuring cases from around the world and providing legal documents, analyses, and other resources for teaching religion and law (see https://sites.northwestern.edu/lawreligion/), a postdoctoral fellowship, and a series of summer graduate student fellowships for research related to project themes.
3. Winnifred Fallers Sullivan, Elizabeth Shakman Hurd, Saba Mahmood, and Peter G. Danchin, eds., *Politics of Religious Freedom* (Chicago: University of Chicago Press, 2015).
4. Courtney Bender, "The Power of Pluralist Thinking," in *Politics of Religious Freedom*, ed. Winnifred Fallers Sullivan, Elizabeth Shakman Hurd, Saba Mahmood, and Peter G. Danchin, 66–77 (Chicago: University of Chicago Press, 2015). While our previous work, and that of others, has touched on this question suggestively, for example, in Elizabeth Shakman Hurd's chapter on the politics of U.S. religious engagement in *Beyond Religious Freedom: The New Global Politics of Religion* (Princeton, N.J.: Princeton University Press, 2015), this volume presents the findings of collaborative efforts to study the inside/outside dynamics of U.S. history more systematically.
5. Winnifred Fallers Sullivan, "Exporting Religious Freedom," *Commonweal*, February 26, 1999, reprinted in *CSSR Bulletin* 28, no. 2 (April 1999), and *Context* 31, no. 11 (1999).
6. Sidney Mead made this point forcefully in *The Lively Experiment: The Shaping of Christianity in America* (Eugene, Ore.: Wipf & Stock, 1963).
7. Mahmood Mamdani, *Good Muslim, Bad Muslim: America, the Cold War, and the Roots of Terror* (New York: Doubleday, 2005).
8. Mead, *The Lively Experiment*.
9. Hurd, *Beyond Religious Freedom*.
10. See Sylvester A. Johnson, *African American Religions, 1500–2000: Colonialism, Democracy, and Freedom* (Cambridge: Cambridge University Press, 2015); Paul A. Kramer, *The Blood of Government: Race, Empire, the United States, and the Philippines* (Durham: University of North Carolina Press, 2006); and Emily Conroy-Krutz, *Christian Imperialism: Converting the World in the Early American Republic* (Ithaca, N.Y.: Cornell University Press, 2015).
11. Tracy Fessenden, *Culture and Redemption: Religion, the Secular, and American Literature* (Princeton, N.J.: Princeton University Press, 2007); and David Sehat, *The Myth of American Religious Freedom* (Oxford: Oxford University Press, 2010).
12. Gil Anidjar, *Blood: A Critique of Christianity* (New York: Columbia University Press, 2014).
13. Janet Jakobsen and Ann Pellegrini, *Love the Sin: Sexual Regulation and the Limits of Religious Tolerance* (New York: New York University Press, 2014).
14. On European imperial expansion and colonialism, see David Chidester, *Savage Systems: Colonialism and Comparative Religion in Southern Africa* (Charlottesville:

University of Virginia Press, 1996); and Tomoko Masuzawa, *The Invention of World Religions: Or, How European Universalism was Preserved in the Language of Pluralism* (Chicago: University of Chicago Press, 2005). On intra-Christian disputes, see John Locke, *A Letter Concerning Toleration* (Huddersfield, U.K.: Printed by J. Brook, 1796).

15. Robert Yelle, *The Language of Disenchantment: Protestant Literalism and Colonial Discourse in British India* (Oxford: Oxford University Press, 2013).
16. Jakobsen and Pellegrini, *Love the Sin.*
17. Samantha Seeley, "Beyond the American Colonization Society," *History Compass* 14, no. 3 (March 2016): 93–104.
18. Conroy-Krutz, *Christian Imperialism.*
19. Christine Leigh Heyrman, *American Apostles: When Evangelicals Entered the World of Islam* (New York: Hill & Wang, 2015); and Ussama Makdisi, *Artillery of Heaven: American Missionaries and the Failed Conversion of the Middle East* (Ithaca, N.Y.: Cornell University Press, 2007).
20. Eve Darian-Smith, *Religion, Race, Rights: Landmarks in the History of Modern Anglo-American Law* (Oxford: Hart, 2010).
21. Steven K. Green, *Inventing a Christian America: The Myth of a Religious Founding* (Oxford: Oxford University Press, 2015); Thomas J. Curry, *The First Freedoms: Church and State in America to the Passage of the First Amendment* (Oxford: Oxford University Press, 1986); and Merrill D. Peterson and Robert C. Vaughan, *The Virginia Statute for Religious Freedom: Its Evolution and Consequences in American History* (Cambridge: Cambridge University Press, 1988).
22. James Madison, "Memorial and Remonstrance Against Religious Assessments," in *The Writings of James Madison: Comprising His Public Papers and His Private Correspondence, Including Numerous Letters and Documents Now for the First Time Printed,* ed. James Madison and Gaillard Hunt (New York: G. P. Putnam's Sons, 1900).
23. Mead, *The Lively Experiment*; Jon Butler, *Awash in a Sea of Faith: Christianizing the American People* (Cambridge, Mass.: Harvard University Press, 1990); and Nathan O. Hatch, *The Democratization of American Christianity* (New Haven, Conn.: Yale University Press, 1989). See also Katharine Gerbner, *Christian Slavery: Conversion and Race in the Protestant Atlantic World* (Philadelphia: University of Pennsylvania Press, 2018).
24. Darian-Smith, *Religion, Race, Rights.*
25. Susan K. Harris, *God's Arbiters: Americans and the Philippines, 1998–1902* (Oxford: Oxford University Press, 2013); and Kramer, *Blood of Government.*
26. James Rusling, "Interview with President William McKinley," *Christian Advocate*, January 22, 1903, 17. Reprinted in Daniel Schirmer and Stephen Rosskamm Shalom, eds., *The Philippines Reader* (Boston: South End Press, 1987), 22–23.
27. "January 1899: Senate Debate over Ratification of Treaty of Paris," in *Crucible of the Empire: The Spanish-American War*, PBS (1999), https://www.pbs.org/crucible/tl17.html.
28. Darian-Smith, *Religion, Race, Rights.*
29. Sam Erman, *Almost Citizens: Puerto Rico, the U.S. Constitution, and Empire* (Cambridge: Cambridge University Press, 2018); Bartholomew H. Sparrow, *The Insular*

Cases and the Emergence of American Empire (Lawrence: University Press of Kansas, 2006); Gerald L. Neuman, *Reconsidering the Insular Cases: The Past and Future of the American Empire* (Cambridge, Mass.: Human Rights Program, Harvard Law School, 2015); and Christina Duffy Burnett and Burke Marshall, eds. *Foreign in a Domestic Sense: Puerto Rico, American Expansion, and the Constitution* (Durham, N.C.: Duke University Press, 2001).

30. John T. McGreevy, *Catholicism and American Freedom: A History* (New York: Norton, 2004); and Steven K. Green, *The Second Disestablishment: Church and State in Nineteenth-Century America* (Oxford: Oxford University Press, 2010).
31. *Board of Education of Cincinnati v Minor*, 23 Ohio 211 (1872).
32. "Occupation of Japan and the New Constitution," PBS, *American Experience*, n.d., https://www.pbs.org/wgbh/americanexperience/features/macarthur-occupation-japan-and-constitution/. See also Jolyon Baraka Thomas, *Faking Liberties: Religious Freedom in American-Occupied Japan* (Chicago: University of Chicago Press, 2019).
33. Michael Graziano, "William Donovan, the Office of Strategic Services, and Catholic Intelligence Sources During World War II," *U.S. Catholic Historian* 33, no. 4 (Fall 2015): 79–103.
34. Jonathan P. Herzog, *The Spiritual-Industrial Complex: America's Religious Battle Against Communism in the Early Cold War* (Oxford: Oxford University Press, 2011); and Eugene Ford, *Cold War Monks: Buddhism and America's Secret Strategy in Southeast Asia* (New Haven: Yale University Press, 2017).
35. *Everson v. Board of Education*, 330 U.S. 1 (1947).
36. *Lynch v Donnelly*, 465 U.S. 668 (1984). For a description of the complex intertwining of religious and economic motives in the invention of the American Christmas, see Leigh Schmidt, *Consumer Rites: The Buying and Selling of American Holidays* (Princeton, N.J.: Princeton University Press, 1987).
37. Thomas Farr, "Cold War Religion," Review of William Inboden III, *Religion and American Foreign Policy, 1945–1960: The Soul of Containment* (Cambridge: Cambridge University Press, 2008), in *First Things*, June 2009, https://www.firstthings.com/article/2009/06/cold-war-religion.
38. Nina Shea, U.S. Congress, House. Prepared Statement of Ms. Nina Shea, Director, Center for Religious Freedom, Freedom House, "In Defense of Human Dignity: The International Religious Freedom Report," Hearing before the Subcommittee on Africa, Global Human Rights and International Operations of the Committee on International Relations, 109th Cong., 1st Session, November 15, 2005.
39. Hurd, *Beyond Religious Freedom*.
40. *Employment Division, Department of Human Resources of Oregon v. Smith*, 494 U.S. 872 (1990).
41. *Hosanna-Tabor v. EEOC*, 565 U.S. 171 (2012).

PART I
Making Religion American

I

A Home, Made Abroad

American Religion from Colonies Through the Civil War

EVAN HAEFELI

American religion operates rather differently before and after the Civil War of the mid-nineteenth century, but we have yet to figure out how to critically connect the two phases. Work on the modern era makes only cursory reference to early American religious history, and then often to exceptional times and places like colonial New England. The modernists cannot be blamed, though, for scholarship on early American religion suffers from a reflexive exceptionalism that tends to read back present-day themes of diversity, pragmatism, and adaptation onto the past, naturalizing them as the inevitable outcome of early American history. It likewise tends to marginalize the countervailing forces insisting on religious unity and conformity to European religious norms. Who could do anything else but admit religious freedom, given the geographic expanse and demographic diversity of the country? In fact, there was nothing logical or inevitable about the modern American condition of pluralism and religious freedom. Rather than the inevitable fruit of colonizing a new land, it was the unexpected product of a dramatic series of political revolutions that radically reshaped the ecclesiastical landscape several times over between Europeans' first encounter with North America and the end of the American Civil War. Those contingent events need to be integrated into a broader interpretive framework for early American religion before we map out the big picture of American religious history or draw comparisons and contrasts with the religious histories of other times and places. Above all, we need to recognize many discontinuities alongside the persistent patterns in American ecclesiastical arrangements.

Developing an ecclesiastical model of early American religious history is tricky because it is never the history of a particular church, or even set of churches. For example, it has never been an exclusively protestant story, although it was a protestant hegemony. Instead, almost from the very beginning, it has involved different churches and religions fitting into a broader system that was never completely defined or controlled by a single institution. There was no equivalent to the Supreme Court's current role as the ultimate arbiter of modern American religious life. Britain's Monarch-in-Parliament performed a similar role before American independence, but not always, and even then it stumbled over jurisdictional limits. However, disestablishment is not right either, for religious establishments played a crucial role in most of the colonies until the American Revolution, and in some of the New England states for decades thereafter. Nevertheless, certain broad trends and patterns organized early American religious life if we emphasize issues of ecclesiology—church government, structure, and politics. This ecclesiastical perspective clarifies the relationships between these many different religious entities, while scholarship on personal belief or theology often approaches them in isolation from one another. We have good studies of individuals, particular churches, ideas, and social experience and practice. The challenge is to unite these many bits and pieces into a larger, inclusive, and comprehensive story.

From the beginning, America was the "abroad" of another home. Until 1783, the home was primarily England, but Scotland and Ireland figured in important ways as well, especially in the middle colonies of New York, New Jersey, Pennsylvania, and Delaware. In the second half of the seventeenth century, conquest and immigration from Europe added Dutch, Swedes, and French Huguenots to the mix. Beginning at the end of the seventeenth century a trickle of Germans (protestant, Catholic, and Jewish) grew to become the largest non-English-speaking group of European immigrants by the Civil War. Native American nations, initially existing outside of this British-dominated home, were either incorporated into it, like the Wampanoag of southern New England, or resisted it by moving steadily westward, like the Lenape of the Delaware River valley. Africans, originally almost nonexistent, steadily entered into the picture from the mid-seventeenth century until in the eighteenth century and became the largest group of new arrivals, almost all of them non-Christians. The economy of the British Empire, including its North American colonies, depended on the Atlantic slave trade and the products grown by slave labor from New England to the Caribbean. Meanwhile, on the southern and western fringes of the future United States, the Spanish and French Empires planted enduring Roman Catholic communities.

There was thus a diversity of influences within what became the United States, but the British inheritance is the most crucial. It comprised the bulk of the population and it established the framework on which future religious arrangements were constructed. This hegemonic original "home" of American religion was an unstable foundation, however, because it was internally divided from the beginning of colonization. That fact set the religious history of the United States on a very different trajectory from nations descended from the other European empires, who had largely resolved their internal religious differences before embarking on overseas colonization. The Church of England, by contrast, had failed to become the accepted religion of all of the monarchy's subjects even before the first permanent colonies were created. Consequently, a fundamental habit of confessional competition was imparted to Anglo-America in its infancy. The thirteen American colonies had few traits in common and no religious unity outside their common connection to Britain and its empire. The American Revolution was not a national war of liberation—the coming of age of an indigenous "home" incorporated into the empire—but rather an act of secession, cutting out a random piece of that much larger home. The United States thus began as a fragment of a global and religiously diverse empire that stretched from Canada to India, a parochial exile from an increasingly cosmopolitan feast. This internally divided character made the Constitution's chary attitude toward a national religious establishment inevitable. The United States of America was by all accounts a very religious place, but it was not a church.

The British imperial inheritance was crucial. It separated America from the religious fate of other empires. In the Spanish and French Empires, for example, which covered much more American territory than the British Empire, expansion did not lead to religious pluralism. It was British, not American, factors that divided British America into several religious cores. Ranged in unequal competition and linked to wider, international currents, they could be individually quite homogenous—like most of Virginia and New England. However, in the aggregate they represented a steady growth of religious diversity, primarily because the character of American ecclesiastical affairs changed radically several times over between the early seventeenth and the mid-nineteenth centuries. The religious landscape of 1620 was significantly different from that of 1680, as that of 1760 was from that of 1820 and 1860. In between were major breaks and changes in direction, all tied to broader political transformations. Had matters gone in a different direction at any one of these moments, America's religious diversity could have been limited—or augmented.

In addition to the British imperial connection, three main factors distinguish early American religious history from its modern cousin: expansion, immigration, and the lack of a single ecclesiastical authority. Ecclesiastical authority was not absent, but one has to look for it in several different places. The period before 1640 is somewhat of an exception to this rule—but even then, religious difference and dissension made their way into the colonies, both with and without the ultimate approval of the monarch, the nominal head of England's religious world. While none of these elements was decisive in creating religious diversity, they all fed into it. Expansion without a consistent ecclesiastical authority combined with immigration from various ethnoreligious groups extended pluralism, first up and down the East Coast and then into the interior. It was not planned or deliberate. Few individuals were truly at ease with religious diversity even after the Revolution enshrined it as national policy. In the colonial period, various efforts were made to tame it. In the early nineteenth century, restorationist religious movements like the Millerites and Mormons were explicit reactions against it. Missionary and evangelical efforts were also important for reducing religious pluralism. Methodism became a formidable force because it figured out how to maintain church discipline over a widely scattered membership. However, it was never alone. Since both the missionaries and the religious reactionaries originated in various, often competing, religious homes, the result of their efforts was as likely to undermine religious cohesion as restore it.

These cohabiting contradictions can be traced back to England's sixteenth-century Reformation. Unlike the Scots, who achieved a remarkable religious unity by the time Scottish King James Stewart became English King James I Stuart in 1603, the English had failed to impose a uniform Church order. Ireland, where the vast bulk of the population remained overwhelmingly Roman Catholic even as their established Church became protestant, was just the most extreme example of this failure. The process of reform had been contested at both the upper and lower levels of society, and the several changes in official religion between Henry VIII in the 1530s and Elizabeth I in the 1560s gave English and Irish Protestantism an unsteady foundation. When the first permanent American colonies were established, struggles over the form and content of the Church of England were splitting English Christianity into several competing groups. Outside of the official Church were small groups of Roman Catholics, Protestant Separatists, and Baptists. Those who conformed to the established religion made up a clear majority. However, they were divided into a variety of positions between Puritans demanding a more purely Reformed Protestant Church, conformists who accepted the Church as it was, and avant-garde conformists who were nudging the Church towards a middle position between Reformed Protestantism and Roman Catholicism. The struggles between these groups contributed greatly to the English Civil War of the 1640s. That conflict upended the established religious order, producing a revolution that dismantled the monarchy and its Church. The looser religious order that replaced it in the 1650s was predicated on protestant hegemony but not attached to a specific denomination. Protestant liberty of conscience prevailed, although its bounds and implementation varied from place to place. While Episcopalianism was proscribed and neither Roman Catholics nor non-Christians were supposed to enjoy its benefits, all found some protection under its shelter.[1]

The turmoil at the political and religious center allowed the colonies to direct their own religious affairs just as they began to take root. They responded by developing a series of different ecclesiastical arrangements, from Congregational Massachusetts to conformist Virginia. Rhode Island embraced a protestant disestablishment. In Maryland, a Roman Catholic minority presided over a protestant majority under the guise of religious liberty for all Christians. By the time the Church of England was restored in its modern, Anglican form in 1662, religious pluralism was too entrenched in colonial America for the Church of England to reclaim all the colonies. Nevertheless, Anglicans continued to aspire to religious hegemony up until the American Revolution. They had their victories, but they were mostly local. The Church of England became the single most important of the several competing colonial churches, but it was never always the most important church everywhere.[2]

Another key factor in making pluralism the norm is the contradictory role the ecclesiastical and political center of the British Empire played in colonization. The monarch was the head of the Church but also head of three kingdoms not all of whose subjects conformed to that Church. All the colonies established before 1640 were commanded to conform to the Church of England, but King Charles I knowingly granted Maryland to a Roman Catholic proprietor, and a powerful group of Puritans were able to gain control of New England. The revolutionary government of the 1640s and 1650s undermined local efforts to impose religious unity, giving Rhode Island a charter to protect it from being absorbed into the religious and political system of Massachusetts and breaking up Virginia's establishment. The English government also defended the rights of Lord Baltimore against Maryland's protestants, who repeatedly did all in their power to suppress Roman Catholicism in the colony. With the Restoration in 1660, the monarchy not only reinforced this support for the exceptional enclaves of Rhode

Island and Maryland, it then granted a series of colonies to proprietors who favored religious liberty over the established the Church of England: Carolina, New York, New Jersey, and Pennsylvania (which included Delaware until 1776). This was not a consistent or constant colonial policy, however. Elsewhere, most notably Jamaica, the monarchy proved willing to impose the Church establishment.[3]

This haphazard religious policy of expansion, lacking a coherent vision or plan and as likely to favor privileged religious minorities as the established Church, ended with yet another political revolution: the so-called Glorious Revolution of 1688. Protestant hegemony was secured by Parliament's so-called Toleration Act of 1689, which ensured a degree of formal recognition for protestant dissent from the episcopal Church of England but excluded Roman Catholics and non-Trinitarians. Under its star, the modern, liberal framework of tolerance associated with John Locke was launched. His famous "Letter concerning Toleration," published in 1689, became a common reference point for colonial Americans as well as Britons to describe the mixed religious inheritance their Stuart monarchs had bequeathed to them.

After 1688 Roman Catholics lost whatever privileges they had gained. Few concessions were made to religious minorities as the Church of England became the established Church everywhere from Maryland to Georgia (which began as a protestant colony without a Church establishment but eventually conformed, like the other southern colonies). While it varied from place to place, the trend toward establishment and against pluralism was clear. The Church of England benefited from the wave of evangelical fervor and institutional development that created the Society for the Propagation of the Gospel in Foreign Parts and by the Society for the Propagation of Christian Knowledge. Both established around 1700, these societies spread Anglican ministers and religious works around the colonies. With their help, the Church even made inroads into New England. It made converts from Connecticut to Maine, especially in the coastal towns and port cities. In the mid-eighteenth century, a number of those converts spearheaded a movement to establish a bishop in America, which was institutionally essential for consolidating Anglican power in America. The resulting episcopacy controversy reached its peak on the eve of the American Revolution. Without that great political upheaval, colonial America could conceivably have been brought under a single ecclesiastical authority notwithstanding its religious diversity, much as in England.[4]

Colonial American pluralism was thus never a static thing, even in the comparatively stable years between 1688 and 1774, because the "home" abroad kept disrupting the "home" in America. Even that ostensibly quintessential

American event, the Great Awakening, owed much to the Empire. Its pivotal figure was an English Anglican of Calvinist disposition, George Whitefield, who hit the colonies just as they were preparing for war against the Catholic empires of Spain and France. Frustrated by years of peace, entente, and Anglican expansion, the awakening, which only happened in the northern colonies, became a colonial statement of patriotic adherence to a militant and expansionist, yet multidenominational, protestant empire. Its divisive force was soon institutionalized in two new institutions of higher learning. Evangelicals established Princeton University. Those alienated by their "enthusiasm" supported Kings College (later Columbia University).

Although Anglo-America emerged from the Great Awakening more religiously divided than ever, the hitherto faltering process of incorporating its African and Native American population into the Christian community took an important step forward. Missionary work among Indigenous Americans was a fundamental justification for the colonization of America: saving souls for the glory of God was always cited as an ambition on par with personal enrichment and strengthening the realm. Yet, when compared to the Roman Catholic empires, very little effort was invested in missionary work. In large part, that failure derived from a lack of resources and personnel. English ministers were generally attached to a parish or specific congregation. There were no orders of regular priests dedicated to evangelizing beyond the bounds of British society. Efforts had been made in the seventeenth century, but conflicts destroyed the missionary college in Virginia and the Jesuits' mission in Maryland and devasted New England's "Praying Towns." In the early eighteenth century, ministers funded by the Society for the Propagation of the Gospel made modest gains among the Mohawks on New York's northern frontier. However, after the Great Awakening, Moravians made converts among the Lenape and others in Pennsylvania while New England Congregationalists established missions on their northern and western frontiers.

Overall, neither the British colonies nor the early American republic had much room for Indigenous Christians. Missions faced a host of obstacles, from militant Indigenous resistance to settler hostility rooted in a perennial greed for Indigenous land, a pattern that continued until the end of the era of Indian Wars in 1890. Among the so-called Five Civilized Tribes of the Southeast, the U.S. government enforced its policy of Indian Removal just as New England missionaries were beginning to enjoy success. In Indiana, Christianized Native Americans belonging to a successful French Catholic mission were also driven west of the Mississippi in the 1830s. The contrast with Roman Catholic territories like New Mexico or New France, where Indigenous mission communities established in the seventeenth century still thrive, even on the outskirts of major cities, is instructive.⁵

Anglo-American missionaries demanded a cultural, economic, and political as well as religious conversion. Indigenous men and women were expected to adopt Anglo-American clothing, hairstyles, domestic architecture, labor patterns, and foodways. Being Christian was sometimes more a way of life than a set of beliefs. The extreme case was the Quaker mission to the Senecas launched at the end of the eighteenth century, which devoted great efforts to teaching modern American modes of farming and domestic economy but said virtually nothing about Quaker religious beliefs. Conversion was also inseparable from colonization. Changing Indigenous religion was part of claiming Indigenous lands and turning Indigenous people into a useful underclass. Christian Native Americans were expected to be not just friends but also military allies: New England's Indigenous protestants lost many men in the imperial wars against the French. Christian or not, indigenous allies fought alongside Anglo-American forces all the way up through Col. George Custer's notorious defeat at the Little Bighorn. Of course, indigenous converts did their best to turn missionary zeal to their own advantage, but simply preserving their communities in the midst of dangerous and disastrous circumstances was a challenge.⁶

Similar issues apply to the Christianization of people of African descent. Their enslavement was initially justified by the fact that they were not Christian (indeed, popular attitudes developed insisting they *could not* become Christian since, being more beast than human, they probably lacked a soul). The Church of England pioneered the efforts to reconcile slavery with protestant Christianity. Historian Katharine Gerbner speaks of a transition from "Protestant Supremacy," when colonists justified slavery in these terms, to "Christian Slavery," when slaveholders accepted that slaves could become Christian yet still remain slaves. The transition to pro-slavery religion can be seen in the sense of racial difference developed over the eighteenth century as colonists began to distinguish themselves from their non-European neighbors by calling themselves "white" instead of Christian as they originally had done. With Christianity no longer a Euro-American prerogative, racist ideas and logic stepped in to justify the continuing exploitation and oppression of both Native and African Americans. The American Revolution accelerated the Christianization of non-European Americans, especially African Americans, few of whom had been Christian before then.⁷

In 1783, on hearing news of the peace with Britain that secured the independence of the United States, the residents of Northampton, Massachusetts, joyously toasted: "May the protestant religion prevail & flourish through all nations."[8] However, the Protestant cause had no leadership. The federal government of the new United States presided over a steady process of disestablishment. Its refusal to meddle in the religious affairs of individual states gave local authorities more power over religious life than in any period before or since. While the U.S. Constitution did away with religious tests for public service and forbade the federal government from establishing a religion at the national level, this by no means discouraged Anglo-Americans' religious ambitions. Protestantism retained its national hegemony through a system of loosely united local and state establishments (formal or informal) combined with increasingly powerful protestant institutions, both ecumenical (like the American Bible Society) and not (like the General Conference of the Methodist Church).[9]

Protestant pluralism, rather than any single church, emerged as the informally official religion of America after a drawn-out series of struggles waged on a state-by-state basis. The mid-Atlantic had never been strong on religious establishment, but Virginia set the most important precedent for both the new nation and the West when it disestablished religion in January 1786. The rest of the southern states, where the Church of England had been the established Church, more or less followed Virginia's example. This stance became national policy in July 1787, when the Northwest Ordinance prevented the federal government from determining the specific religious adherence of new states while simultaneously affirming the importance of religion to westward expansion. Western states accordingly rejected religious establishment while encouraging the founding of churches. Only New England (Massachusetts, Connecticut, and New Hampshire) retained a formal religious establishment. However, even there, after 1833, disestablishment prevailed.[10]

Protestantism is not a church. It is a compromise, one reached only after the failure of various efforts to achieve religious uniformity. Still, the one thing it most decidedly is not is Roman Catholicism: that element had made anti-Catholicism a cornerstone of American religious life from the time the first colonies were established. Indeed, a strong current of anti-Catholicism can be found in most early American religion and politics. At the very least, Roman Catholicism has represented the intolerant other against which American assumptions of liberty of conscience have been constructed since the seventeenth century. The twentieth-century American theologian Reinhold Niebuhr admired what he saw as the spiritual modesty of Oliver Cromwell, the acceptance that one could "be mistaken," that informed his support for liberty of conscience. However, Niebuhr also shared Cromwell's fundamental anti-Catholicism, arguing that the "intolerance to which the church is forced by its presuppositions is really dangerous to both civil peace and civil liberty."[11]

Anti-Catholicism figures in all three of the key dimensions of early American religious history. It was a fundamental justification and ambition driving expansion. Since Spain had colonized the Americas first, early English colonization was defined in part against Spanish (and then French) Catholic hegemony. John Winthrop, in his 1629 list of justifications for "the Intended Plantation in New England," said it would be "a service to the Church of great consequence to carry the Gospell into those p[ar]ts. Of the world, to help on the cominge in of fulnesse of the Gentiles and to rayse a Bulworke against the kingdome of Antichrist, w[hi]ch. the Jesuites labour to rear up in those parts."[12] By the nineteenth century, American visions of expansion had become more aggressive. In the 1840s one congressman called for the American flag to wave "over every foot of soil from Tierra del Fuego to the North Pole." Meanwhile, Andrew Jackson defined Manifest Destiny (a product of the 1840s), as "extending the area of freedom," an expression with deep anti-Catholic roots.[13]

Expansion, political liberty, and anti-Catholicism were closely interwoven in American history. Yet anti-Catholicism was more than just a force for unity against a religious and political other, whether at home or abroad. It also contributed substantially to the breakdown of ecclesiastical authority within the Anglo-American world. The powerful thread of religious and political instability that anti-Catholicism wove through Anglo-American history is often described by scholars as anti-popery, a concept developed by historians of early modern England to explain why English protestant fears of Catholicism were so often directed at otherwise upstanding protestants, whether the archbishop of Canterbury or even the king himself. Protestant institutions, like the Church of England, were subject to accusations of behaving in ways that imitated the head of the Roman Catholic Church. Popes, in this ideological frame, were tyrannical figures, ruling in arbitrary ways that exploited corrupt human nature to sustain a system that was religiously as well as politically oppressive: hence colonial Americans' association of slavery with Roman Catholicism. Anti-popery was a necessary cornerstone of protestant identity. It justified their break from the Christian Church that had once held Western Europe together in a shared communion. As such, anti-popery was also an ideology of liberty—the freedoms associated with Protestantism (intellectual, political, religious, economic, and ecclesiastical) were understood to be the fruit of rejecting popery in its many guises.[14]

Unfortunately, it was not easy to avoid popery. Anti-popery distinguished itself from the racial prejudices that also underpinned British Americans sense of entitlement to the land and labor of others in that being popish was not just something that other people were: it was something that anyone, including stalwart protestants, could become. As with protestant conversion experiences, there was always a potential for backsliding and corruption, requiring one to be ever vigilant. However, when, where, and how the line was drawn varied. Protestants had disagreed over where popery stopped and started since the English civil war of the 1640s. Kevin Philips, in a rare effort to think comparatively across English Civil War, the American Revolution, and the American Civil War, noticed these conflicts were fundamentally linked by "fears of Catholics, Catholic plots, and alleged tyrannies, which verged on paranoia."[15] That "paranoia" reflected tensions within protestant culture that sharpened the nativist anti-Catholic response to the thousands of Irish, German, and other Roman Catholics immigrants of the mid-nineteenth century. Nevertheless, the Roman Catholic church grew along with these immigrants until, by the time the Civil War petered out, it had become the single largest church in the United States. Protestants were still a majority, but they were broken up into ever more units, inadvertently confirming Roman Catholic criticisms of the fissiparous nature of Protestantism.[16]

Significantly, the United States had broken away from the British Empire just as it was making a dramatic turn toward toleration of Roman Catholics and non-Christian religions. In 1774 Parliament's Quebec Act had offered loyal French Canadians the right to retain and publicly practice their religion. Similar attitudes figured in India, where the East India Company (as in Quebec) governed without the elected assemblies that were characteristic of the thirteen colonies. In the 1780s East Indian officials began taking ostentatiously tolerant stances toward the strange "religions" (like Hinduism and Islam) of their new subjects as they expanded British control over ever more territory. They even began to study Indian religions with scholarly earnest. The hope, of course, was to better understand how to govern those non-Christians.[17]

An empire that could be so openly tolerant of non-protestants was not one that early Americans could love, as the emotional reactions to the Quebec Act indicated. From Virginia, George Washington lamented, "those from whom we have a right to seek protection are endeavouring by every piece of Art and despotism to fix the Shackles of Slavery upon us." He feared the "Invasion of our Rights and Priviledges by the Mother Country" would "make us as tame and abject slaves, as the blacks we rule over with such arbitrary sway."[18] In Connecticut, the Reverend Ebenezer Baldwin argued that the Quebec Act exposed Parliament's "fix'd plan for inslaving the colonies, or bringing them under arbitrary government." Reminding his audience of the seventeenth century history of England and the colonies, Baldwin argued that once America lost its "civil liberty" an "ecclesiastical tyranny ... will like a mighty torrent overspread our land." Invoking well-worn images of popish military occupation, he depicted British soldiers ready "to execute every arbitrary mandate of their despotic masters.... Robberies, rapes, murders, etc. will be but the wanton sport of such wretches without restraint let loose upon us." Those who dared resist would be killed by "their murdering hands," or "taken captive" and dragged "to the place of execution."[19]

This fear and hostility to "tyranny" was one of the fruits of British protestant imperial culture. With the empire gone, it fed resistance to centralized religious authority in the early republic. Colonial habits of combining religious and political demands, such as the English Test Acts that had restricted political rights to members of a particular church, were steadily challenged and eventually overthrown, contributing even further to the decentralization of American religious culture. Quakers fought a decades-long campaign to refuse to observe days of thanksgiving proclaimed by the government. It began as a campaign against the state of Pennsylvania in 1774 but became a national struggle in the 1790s. Against their neighbors' pressure to conform, the Quakers successfully insisted that there was no religious obligation to observe these state-proclaimed holidays because they were political, not religious, events. And so the idea that one could separate "Church" from "State" slowly worked its way into American culture.[20]

Up until the twentieth century, these struggles took place at the level of state, not federal, government. Supreme Court decisions reinforced the inclination of federal officials not to meddle in the ecclesiastical affairs of individual states. 1835's *Baron v. Baltimore* determined that the Bill of Rights did not apply to individual states. 1845's *Permoli v. New Orleans* declared that the free exercise of religion clause did not apply to the acts of state and local governments. With the brief exception of an intervention during the Civil War to allow northern Methodists to gain control of Southern Methodist churches in formerly Confederate territory, religious issues remained essentially a matter for the individual states to determine. The passage of the Fourteenth Amendment in 1868 gave the federal government the power to enforce constitutional amendments on individual states, but even then it was not until the 1940s that federal courts began applying the religious implications of the First Amendment to individual states.[21]

These decisions meant, among other things, that the federal government would not step in to protect the rights of religious minorities against discrimination or persecution by local authorities. The Mormons, who had been attacked, dispossessed, and driven out of Missouri, were an extreme case. Their leader, Joseph Smith, took their case to President Martin van Buren and Congress. They referred Smith back to the courts of Missouri for justice, insisting on the primacy of states' rights over religious affairs. Joseph Smith responded by trying to have the Mormon town of Nauvoo, Illinois, designated a federal territory. It failed, and Mormons decided they could only be safe if they moved further west, beyond the United States.[22]

In New Orleans, the key struggle was not between different religions but rather an intradenominational dispute over power, authority, and money between lay wardens and the Roman Catholic bishop. *Permoli v. New Orleans* pitted Father Bernard Permoli, a priest loyal to the bishop, against the Creole Catholic elite. Ever since the United States acquired Louisiana as a territory, it had favored the authority of the local laity over that of the Roman Catholic hierarchy. Father Permoli challenged this alliance by performing an open-casket funeral in defiance of a recently passed law that had banned such traditional Catholic funerals ostensibly on health grounds. It was an ethnic as much as ecclesiastical dispute. The bishops and many of their priests came from Europe and had strongly counterrevolutionary and ultramontane views. The Creole Catholics were supporters of the French Revolution and American democracy. They benefited from American support in this and other struggles with their bishop, with the Maryland Roman Catholic Roger B. Taney presiding as chief justice of the Supreme Court from 1836 until his death in 1864. However, immigration eventually shifted the local dynamic in favor of the Church hierarchy. By the 1850s Irish Catholics amounted to over half the city's Catholic community. They neither spoke French nor sympathized with the Creoles. As parishes proliferated, so did the power of the bishop. Thus, despite the support of the U.S. government, the Creoles lost control of their church. Federal noninterference gave them a brief victory but did nothing to stop the steady transformation of local religious politics.[23]

The New Orleans story brings together the roles of expansion and immigration in shaping early America's peculiar religious establishment. Expansion brought in new territories that, like Louisiana, were formerly parts of Catholic New France, New Spain, Louisiana, or Mexico, raising questions about how these Catholics could be incorporated into American democracy. Catholic migrants, especially from Ireland and Germany, added to the challenge of maintaining protestant hegemony after 1830. Internal immigration allowed Protestantism to expand west even as it lost its grip on the eastern cities. New Englanders moved west to upstate New York and Ohio. Southerners moved west to Kentucky and Tennessee; north into Ohio, Indiana, and Illinois; and south and west into Florida, Alabama, Mississippi, Texas, and Louisiana. These moves carried distinct religious cultures and ecclesiastical expectations that set the terms for religious life in the new territories. Foreign immigrants added to and transformed those arrangements, but they did not create them.

Missionary organizations sprouted up in the eastern states to cope with the challenge of incorporating new peoples and lands into the expanding nation. They were pioneered by Ezra Stiles, Congregational minister and president of Yale, who anticipated that the "United States will embosom all the religious sects and denominations in Christendom" but would be dominated by protestants.[24] His successor as president of Yale, Timothy Dwight, enlisted eager Yale graduates to extend American Protestantism to the expanding western frontier and overseas to Asia and the Middle East. Since their religious ambitions were not limited to the borders of the United States, the fit between the aims of their religious organizations and the ambitions of the United States polity was imperfect. The missionaries had a habit of reaching further than the state while also never representing more than a fraction of its inhabitants. Up through the Civil War, for example, New Englanders were overrepresented in missionary organizations, to the point where those organizations could plausibly be interpreted as a tool for New Englanders to maintain the prestige and influence of their region within a nation whose rapid expansion westward was quickly leaving them behind.[25]

The missionary organizations were seconded by a range of volunteer societies founded by northeastern elites of different protestant affiliations. To ensure that the expanding frontier remained within the protestant fold, they sent out a massive stream of religious tracts, cheap copies of the Bible, and missionaries as well as funding Sunday schools across the United States. This new religious-political climate favored religions that were good at organizing and missionizing: mostly Methodists (who thrived where Anglicanism had been strong) and Baptists, and Presbyterians to a lesser extent (Presbyterian is also what Congregationalists tended to become once they stepped out of the hallowed confines of the New England establishment). These organizations reinforced the expansion of American Protestantism by ensuring it also took root among the people of African, Indigenous, and Asian origin who were being colonized in North America and beyond. However, they increasingly had to contend with proliferating Roman Catholic religious orders performing much the same function in much the same field of operation.[26]

As the dust of the America Civil War settled, Americans continued to regard the world through anti-popish eyes, as this essay from the influential *Harper's Weekly* illustrates. Whatever American religion was, it was not the idolatry of Spain or the Chinese. Yet one of the great ironies of American religious history

FIGURE 1.1 "Idol worship," *Harper's Weekly*, engraving, April 21, 1866. "Idol Worship in Spain" is compared to "Idol Worship in Cochin China." In Spain, the archbishop of Toledo, assisted by a priest carrying the image of the Virgin "as though he were bearing a doll," arrives in Madrid to bring "the image" to the Queen "in her hour of trouble." Below, in Saigon, a large crowd watches the "Annual Procession of the Dragon," performed by the Chinese community. European sailors from the ships anchored in the harbor are among the spectators.

Courtesy HarpWeek.

is that the conditions of religious liberty created by its firmly anti-popish revolutionaries also, in the end, opened the country up to Roman Catholicism and, later, the very un-protestant religions of much of the rest of the world. The anti-popish disposition had created such a thoroughly decentralized set of ecclesiastical arrangements that both Catholics and non-Christians could carve out a fairly secure position within the United States, notwithstanding the occasionally violent prejudice they faced. These democratic conditions were not, as many scholars claim, a religious free market. On the contrary, the churches with the strongest institutions and clearest lines of authority did best: Methodists and Roman Catholics. Neither had strong roots in colonial America. Both depended heavily on European organizations and immigration, which continued to be a major religious influence well into the nineteenth century (even the Mormons drew significantly on British converts). Insofar as there was a religious market, anti-popery functioned as its hidden hand, simultaneously strengthening protestant hegemony and diluting it by holding open the door of religious liberty that could not be shut without violating the founding values of independent America's post-imperial ecclesiastical system.[27]

NOTES

1. Evan Haefeli, *Accidental Pluralism: America and the Religious Politics of English Expansion, 1497–1662* (Chicago: University of Chicago Press, 2021).
2. Evan Haefeli, "Toleration and Empire: The Origins of American Religious Diversity," in *British North America in the Seventeenth and Eighteenth Centuries*, ed. Stephen Foster, 103–35, Oxford History of the British Empire series (Oxford: Oxford University Press, 2013).
3. Haefeli, *Accidental Pluralism*; Evan Haefeli, "How Special Was Rhode Island? The Global Context of the 1663 Charter," in *The Lively Experiment: Religious Toleration in America from Roger Williams to the Present*, ed. Chris Beneke and Chris Grenda, 21–36 (Lanham, Md.: Rowman and Littlefield, 2015); Evan Haefeli, "Pennsylvania's Religious Freedom in Comparative Colonial Context," in *The Worlds of William Penn*, ed. Andrew Murphy and John Smolenski, 333–54 (New Brunswick: Rutgers University Press, 2019); and Evan Haefeli, "Delaware: Religious Borderland," in *Disestablishment and Religious Dissent: Church–State Relations in the New American States, 1776–1833*, eds. Carl H. Esbeck and Jonathan Den Hartog, 37–54 (Columbia: University of Missouri Press, 2019).
4. Peter Walker, "The Bishop Controversy, the Imperial Crisis, and Religious Radicalism in New England, 1763–1774," *New England Quarterly* 90, no. 3 (2017): 306–43.
5. Richard W. Cogley, *John Eliot's Mission to the Indians before King Philip's War* (Cambridge, Mass.: Harvard University Press, 1999); Laura M. Stevens, *The Poor*

Indians: British Missionaries, Native Americans, and Colonial Sensibility (Philadelphia: University of Pennsylvania Press, 2004); and Rachel M. Wheeler, *To Live upon Hope: Mohicans and Missionaries in the Eighteenth-Century Northeast* (Ithaca, N.Y.: Cornell University Press, 2008).

6. Among other works, see David Silverman, *Faith and Boundaries: Colonists, Christianity, and Community Among the Wampanoag Indians of Martha's Vineyard, 1600–1871* (Cambridge: Cambridge University Press, 2007); and Jennifer Graber, *The Gods of Indian Country: Religion and the Struggle for the American West* (New York: Oxford University Press, 2018).

7. Travis Glasson, *Mastering Christianity: Missionary Anglicanism in the Atlantic World* (New York: Oxford University Press, 2012); and Katharine Gerbner, *Christian Slavery: Conversion and Race in the Protestant Atlantic World* (Philadelphia: University of Pennsylvania Press, 2018).

8. *Maryland Gazette*, June 12, 1783, cited in William C. Stinchcombe, *The American Revolution and the French Alliance* (Syracuse, N.Y.: Syracuse University Press, 1969), 103.

9. William R. Hutchinson, *Religious Pluralism in America: The Contentious History of a Founding Ideal* (New Haven, Conn.: Yale University Press, 2003).

10. Carl H. Esbeck and Jonathan Den Hartog, eds. *Disestablishment and Religious Dissent: Church-State Relations in the New American States, 1776–1833* (Columbia: University of Missouri Press, 2019).

11. Quoted in Daniel F. Rice, "Niebuhr's Critique of Religion in America," in *Reinhold Niebuhr Revisited: Engagements with an American Original*, ed. Daniel Rice (Grand Rapids, Mich.: Eerdmans, 2009), 328 and 328n46.

12. Peter C. Mancall, *Envisioning America: English Plans for the Colonization of North America, 1580–1640* (Boston: Bedford/St. Martin's, 1995), 134.

13. Sam W. Haynes, "Manifest Destiny and the American Southwest," in *A Companion to the Era of Andrew Jackson*, ed. Sean Patrick Adams (Malden, Mass.: Wiley-Blackwell, 2013), 549, 551.

14. Evan Haefeli, ed. *Against Popery: Britain, Empire, and Anti-Catholicism* (Charlottesville: University of Virginia Press, 2020).

15. Kevin Phillips, *The Cousins' Wars: Religion, Politics, & the Triumph of Anglo-America* (New York: Basic Books, 1999), 615–17.

16. Maura Jane Farrelly, *Anti-Catholicism in America, 1620–1860* (Cambridge: Cambridge University Press, 2017).

17. Jakob de Roover and S. N. Balagangadhara, "Liberty, Tyranny, and the Will of God: The Principle of Religious Toleration in Early Modern Europe and Colonial India," *History of Political Thought* 30 no. 1 (2009): 111–39; and Penelope Carson, *The East India Company and Religion, 1698–1858* (Woodbridge, Suffolk, U.K.: Boydell, 2012), chap. 2.

18. George Washington, *George Washington: A Collection*, ed. by W. B. Allen (Indianapolis: Liberty Fund, 1988), 31, 39.

19. Ebenezer Baldwin, "An Appendix, Stating the heavy Grievances the Colonies labour under," in Samuel Sherwood, *A Sermon, containing Scriptural Instructions to civil rulers . . . Also, an appendix stating the heave grievances the colonies labour*

under . . . By Rev. Ebenezer Baldwin (New Haven, Conn.: T. and S. Green, 1774), 67, 72, 74. See also, Paul Langston, "'Tyrant and Oppressor!' Colonial Press Reaction to the Quebec Act," *Historical Journal of Massachusetts* 34, no. 1 (2006): 1–17; Thomas Kidd, *God of Liberty: A Religious History of the American Revolution* (New York: Basic Books, 2010), 66–73; and Vernon P. Creviston, "'No King Unless It Be a Constitutional King': Rethinking the Place of the Quebec Act in the Coming of the American Revolution," *Historian* 73 no. 3 (2011): 463–79.

20. Tara Thompson Strauch, "Open for Business: Philadelphia Quakers, Thanksgiving, and the Limits of Revolutionary Religious Freedom," *Church History* 85, no. 1 (2016): 133–39; and Jennifer Dorsey, "Conscription, Charity, and Citizenship in the Early Republic: The Shaker Campaign for Alternative Service," *Church History* 85, no. 1 (2016): 140–49.

21. Luke E. Harlow, "The Long Life of Proslavery Religion," in *The World the Civil War Made*, ed. Gregory P. Downs and Kate Masur, 132–58 (Chapel Hill: University of North Carolina Press, 2015); and David Sehat, *The Myth of American Religious Freedom* (New York: Oxford University Press, 2011).

22. Spencer McBride, "When Joseph Smith Met Martin Van Buren: Mormonism and the Politics of Religious Liberty in Nineteenth-Century America," *Church History* 85, no. 1 (2016): 150–58; and Spencer McBride, "Was the Constitution the Problem? The Politics of Religious Intolerance in Nineteenth-Century America," presented at the Symposium on Religious Pluralism and Democracy, Utah Valley University, March 30, 2018.

23. Michael W. McConnell, "Schism, Plague, and Late Rites in the French Quarter: The Strange Story Behind the Supreme Court's First Free Exercise Case," Stanford Public Law Working Paper No. 1675213. https://ssrn.com/abstract=1675213.

24. Ezra Stiles, *The United States Elevated to Glory and Honor: A Sermon* (New Haven, Conn., 1783), 52–54.

25. Sam Haselby, *The Origins of American Religious Nationalism* (New York: Oxford University Press, 2015); Emily Conroy-Krutz, *Christian Imperialism: Converting the World in the Early American Republic* (Ithaca, N.Y.: Cornell University Press, 2015); and Usama Makdisi, *Artillery of Heaven: American Missionaries and the Failed Conversion of the Middle East* (Ithaca, N.Y.: Cornell University Press, 2008).

26. Haselby, *American Religious Nationalism*.

27. Catherine O'Donnell, "John Carroll and the Origins of an American Catholic Church, 1783–1815," *William and Mary Quarterly* 68, no. 1 (2011): 101–26.

2

"A Perfect, Irrevocable Gift"

Recognizing the Proprietary Church in Puerto Rico 1898–1908

DAVID MALDONADO RIVERA

A chart with three columns, respectively labeled "Autonomic Regime," "Current Regime," and "Comparison," published in a local newspaper marked the ninth anniversary of the end of the Spanish–American War and informed readers about the political and legal climate of Puerto Rico in late July of 1907. The thirty-four points of comparison tersely parsed across the chart emphasized the gradual changes under the new state of affairs. The relationship between church and state was an example of the radical transformation that took place under the new regime. The chart described the situation under the Autonomic Charter of 1897 thus: "Freedom of Conscience. The Roman Catholic Apostolic religion is the religion of the state. The state is bound to maintain worship and its ministers. No other public ceremonies or manifestations shall be permitted except those of the Religion of the State (Art. 11 of the Constitution of 1876, at the present time in force in Spain). In the Spanish Penal Code, there used to be a chapter concerning offenses against Catholic worship and its ministers. The Council of Trent was a law of the Kingdom of Spain. Likewise, were the concordats celebrated with the Pope."[1] The Foraker Act (Organic Act of 1900), which set the first civilian government under the American occupation of Puerto Rico, codified a new, disestablished reality:[2] "There is no state religion. All worship has the same consideration before the law. There is no budget for worship and clergy [*culto y clero*]." The comparison was succinct, but it betrayed a sense of relief related to this new freedom, "Any sort of commentary is superfluous. We used to pay for the sustenance of worship and clergy under the Spanish regime. Today each religion is sustained by its followers."[3] This iteration of disestablishment entangled conscience, money, and property, while hinting at the corporate realities surrounding them. How the state and the church would recognize each other (and their respective properties) within this desired context of separation was still a matter of dispute.

This essay focuses on the period between 1898 and 1908, when the property disputes between the Catholic Church and the government of Puerto Rico served as a tutelary workshop to settle, borrowing from Brenna Bhandar's recent study, the colonial lives of property.[4] The resolution of these disputes re-created the juridical personality of the Catholic Church in Puerto Rico while it streamlined the concordats between Spain and the Vatican into American corporate law. Furthermore, the rulings in these cases framed the legal limits of municipal autonomy in Puerto Rico while clarifying the jurisdiction of the supreme court of that territory. This period post 1898 summons what Anthony Stevens-Arroyo notes as the obvious specter that has haunted scholarship devoted to the island's religious developments in this context: the idea of "Americanization."[5] This term has operated as an unwieldy shorthand for different trends and movements: an emic political agenda of empire, modernity, colonialism, dependency, welfare, liberalism, capitalism, separation of church and state, gendered racialization, population control, neoliberalism, protestantization, among others. The expansive and exceptionalist nature of what "Americanization" can be is part of the problem with which I am concerned, but like Stevens-Arroyo and others, I focus on the effects of the entanglements of these processes and forces involved, even if the assemblage of these elements may no longer be called "Americanization." The church property disputes at the dawn of the twentieth century in Puerto Rico illustrate how the translation of legal arrangements from different colonial regimes coded and privileged a particular legal option as the new status quo under disestablishment. The recognition of corporation sole for the Catholic Church in the Caribbean territory forms part of the trajectories of transition in the history of the legal incorporation of church property in the United States. While recent scholarship characterizes America's first disestablishment (1776–1865) as a period during which individuals were empowered vis-à-vis the institutional control of various religious bodies, the proprietary church emerging across various legal contexts in the United States and Puerto Rico in the colonial context of 1898 represents an example of an important shift in the state's recognition of corporate prerogatives across colonial regimes and their various governing apparatuses.[6]

POSSESSION, RECOGNITION, AND CORPORATE MODES OF EXISTENCE IN 1898

The extension of the American frontier into the Caribbean and the contours of America's first disestablishment entangle in the legal varieties of the corporate form post 1898. The parallel metaphors of incorporation at the core of this context are the proprietary capacity of the state to hold possessions that are not a part of it and the capacity for the state to administer a religious society's legal existence and form of self-management.

In the case of Puerto Rico, the Foraker Act of 1900 provided the island with a civilian government but left questions regarding the extension of the U.S. Constitution into the new territory. *Downes v. Bidwell*, one of the so-called Insular Cases, revealed that the levies on import duties for a shipment of oranges emerging from Puerto Rico under the Foraker Act did not conflict with Article I, Section 8, of the U.S. Constitution, which states that "all duties, imposts, and excises shall be uniform throughout the United States." The decision of the concurrent justices of the Supreme Court of the United States recognized that Puerto Rico was a "territory appurtenant and belonging to the United States, but not a part of the United States."[7] Puerto Rico, however, was not a foreign country, but it "was foreign to the United States in a domestic sense," a perplexing ontological argument for what constituted an unincorporated territory.[8] This approach bestowed a sense of continuity to the constitution; there was no need for an amendment to address the new territories of the union.

The doctrine of territorial incorporation—and unincorporation—that the Supreme Court created in the Insular Cases represented one trajectory in the innovative developments in corporate thought at the dawn of the twentieth century. As Brook Thomas has suggested, "This movement in corporate law from the view that corporations are contractually bound by the terms of their charter to one in which they have an independent existence with a 'personality' that is greater than the sum of the contracting individuals is similar to the movement in the notion of the nation as strictly bound by the terms of its 'charter'—the Constitution—which creates a compact of individual states, to one in which the nation is a corporate body with certain powers inherent in its very existence."[9] The United States as a proprietary entity could possess territories as other countries could, while it also had to recognize, adjust, and adapt to other corporate bodies in its territories. The property disputes of the Catholic Church in Puerto Rico in the early years of the twentieth century show another fold of these corporate trends.

America's "first disestablishment" weighed heavily in the legal imagination of American administrators, Puerto Rican government officials, and Catholic clergy at the conclusion of the Spanish–American War. As Sarah Barringer Gordon has characterized it, American disestablishment up to the antebellum period operated under some key principles: the identification of religious life as an arena of individual empowerment and the limitations on wealth and power of religious institutions. Although for the participants of the disputes in Puerto Rico these principles reflected the realities of the separation of church and state, one can argue that the effects of individual empowerment and institutional limitation set the confines of the state's vision, recognition, and management of religious societies.[10] This was, in other words, a system of "deep government involvement in religious institutions, rather than a strict separation or respectful support."[11] The private law of religion and the legal incorporation of religious societies (as aggregate, trusteeship, corporation sole, and other variations) rendered devoid of divine sanction yet full of state presence the realm of land grants, donations, titles, deeds, mortgages, and bank accounts. The climate of the Great Awakenings, disputes over slavery, doctrinal controversies, and religious innovation fostered the growth of religious societies along with the processes of lawmaking and litigation related to their properties.

This expression of lay empowerment was a matter of contention among Catholics in various jurisdictions of the United States during the nineteenth century. The trustee system (and similar legal forms) viewed Catholic lay associations as powerful enough to win in the courts claims to property and even the removal of clergy in various states.[12] The legal resistance to these trends took the Catholic hierarchy decades to carve. The First Provincial Council of Baltimore in 1829 ruled against lay organizations claiming the titles of church property. Catholic hierarchs in the United States and Rome were willing to foster lay inclusion in the trustee system inasmuch as the bishop (or priest, in the case of a parish) held control over them. As a more palatable option for the Catholic hierarchy, specific corporation sole statutes gained some track in the period spanning from 1832 to 1904.[13] Under their purview, the holders of the episcopal office and their successors would hold titles to property in the jurisdictions in question. The legal laboratory to extend the viability of corporation sole arrangements for the Catholic Church extended to the new unincorporated territories of the United States.

THE CHURCH PROPERTY DISPUTES IN PUERTO RICO 1898–1908

By the end of the Spanish–American War, Cuba, Puerto Rico, and the Philippines had experienced Catholicism as the established religion of Spain and its colonies under the *patronato real* (royal patronage). In the case of Puerto Rico, dozens of reports surveying the natural resources, customs, population, governmental structures, and potentials of the Caribbean territory painted the realities of Puerto Rican Catholicism as overextended yet fragile. The expenditures related to priestly salaries, building upkeep, and related matters amounted to little over $200,000. The clergy, barely reaching the hundreds, could barely engage a population of close to one million people. The island's topography and the spread of its population gave the impression of a two-tiered Catholicism, official and popular, whose former attachment to the state was in need to recast the legal demarcations of its new existence.[14]

The possibilities of what this new arrangement between church and state could be was a matter of debate and speculation that predated the American occupation of the island. Years before the short-lived Autonomic Charter and the Foraker Act, Puerto Rican intellectuals and political leaders envisioned the boundaries and possibilities of the process of reimagining establishment and disestablishment. Public intellectual and later official historian of Puerto Rico Salvador Brau defended a constitutional arrangement where, "if the religion of the state is the Catholic religion, that of the municipality could be as varied as many as there are the individuals that compose it: this is what the Constitution [of 1876] declares."[15] For others, freedom of conscience and no established religion identified a portion of the desired goals of Puerto Rican autonomy in relation to Spain.[16]

The American occupation appeared to its local supporters and detractors as a definitive break in the centenary traditions of clericalism that the *patronato real* and the concordats between Spain and the Vatican had extended globally. For Francisca Suárez, a freemason and Spiritist, this break signaled the extension of America's perceived social equality and economic dynamism into the Caribbean, "Praise to that nation that has known how to impede the disturbances of the priestly class, destroying its egotism and placing it in equal footing [with the rest of society]. Blessed be for the prosperity of its states!"[17] For others, there was less optimism regarding what had arrived to the island. Juan Perpiñá y Pibernat, the vicar capitular of the Diocese of Puerto Rico, lamented the end of Spanish sovereignty in the island territory and feared the coming economic challenges that this would pose for the Catholic Church there. Perpiñá envisioned a soft, almost imperceptible disestablishment that could still match Catholic doctrine: "Among Catholic principles, moreover, we cannot admit the doctrine of separation of church and state in the sense that the state shall not contribute to the material good of the church and the church to the moral and spiritual good of the state. Both powers perfect and complete each other. Furthermore, we can ensure that in general, the nations in which this separation is declared do not dismiss the resources that they should apportion for the purpose to look after [*atender*] the morality and religiosity of the people."[18] The military government of the island quickly shut down the vicar's proposal. In the fall of 1898, the Catholic Church in Puerto Rico received the last disbursement of funds devoted to its operation, while the status of church property remained in a legal limbo.

Henry K. Carroll, a commissioner for the United States to Puerto Rico, shares an expansive overview of the early perception of the church property problem and the various legal alternatives pondered to settle it. Carroll visited nineteen municipalities and interviewed various members of the clergy, mayors, and government officials. According to the Spanish code in force in the island, ecclesiastical property was not publicly registered; there were no titles to claim the dozens of chapels, shrines, parochial houses, and churches across Puerto Rico. The discussion between Carroll and Perpiñá focused on this perplexing scenario:

> DR. CARROLL. I understand from Father Sherman that the property is not held by the church, but is vested in the municipality, and that there is no way by which it can be confirmed to the church.
> How then is the title to church and parochial houses held—by trustees or otherwise?
> FATHER PERPIÑÁ. The church has no title in the sense of documents; it has always been an understood thing that these properties belong to the church.
> DR. CARROLL. Was not the property bought of some one?
> FR. PERPIÑÁ. Most of the lands held by the church were gifts, and the people who gave them did not bother about giving written titles. Most of the churches in the island were built on ground granted by the government. The government would say to a church, on the establishment of a new town,

"We will give you such and such a plot of ground in the middle of the town and you build a church."

DR. CARROLL. Would not such a proposition, or decree, on the part of the governor be evidenced by some writing?

FR. PERPIÑÁ. Much of this property has been held by the church for several hundred years, and a paper lasts a hundred years and is then dust. Moreover, everything in the way of gifts to the church has been done in good faith without documentation.

DR. CARROLL. Then is not the title to some of the church property still in the original donors as a matter of record?

FR. PERPIÑÁ. I do not know anything more about the question than this: A pious man would say, "Here is a piece of land; I make you a present of it; build a church." There may still exist some documents, but who knows where to find them?[19]

The ways of piety baffled Carroll's expectations. There were no trustees to engage, and various government officials emerged as claimants of the properties in question. Under these circumstances, Carroll proposed that the state could honor the churches' occupancy and give them the option to buy any properties from the municipalities that counted with the proper documentation. The state could also return the ecclesiastical property to the Catholic Church, unless the municipalities could produce title documents. During the first months of the occupation of Puerto Rico, various municipalities produced documents that ranged from old deeds to recent public registration under the current regime. It was the beginning of a new era of legal contention between church and state. An instance of legal tutelage would emerge across the greater United States.[20]

The early stages of the church property disputes in Puerto Rico (between 1899 and 1904) are characterized by the accumulation of municipal litigation against the Church's claims and the interruption of various out-of-court settlements between the Vatican and Washington. The Church's claims throughout this period focused on Article VIII of the Treaty of Paris (1898), through which Spain agreed to cede Puerto Rico to the United States. The article accepted the concordats between Spain and the Holy See (1851 and 1859) after different periods of *desamortización* (the seizure of property from the church and religious orders in Spain). More importantly, this article recognized what would amount to the legal incorporation of the Catholic Church in a new political regime.[21]

The municipality of Ponce was not the only one to challenge the Church's claims, but its legal strategies spread across the island.[22] First, the municipality obtained record of the grants and gifts dating back to 1827 that were used to build one of the churches in dispute. Second, the municipality challenged the juridical personality of the Catholic Church.[23] At the time this proved to be a novel—if shortsighted in hindsight—strategy inasmuch as the parallel legal disputes in Cuba and the Philippines had not focused on this issue, and, in the case of latter, the decision of *Barlin v. Ramírez* provided the precedent to confirm a transtemporal juridical personality to the Catholic Church in the post-1898 context.[24]

After a series of negotiation setbacks, the legislative assembly of the unincorporated territory passed a law that conferred jurisdiction to its supreme court to rule on this thorny matter on March 10, 1904. Representing the Catholic Church, Bishop James H. Blenk, the first American bishop of the Diocese of Puerto Rico, filed the suit that included the Ponce case and other pending ecclesiastical property cases in 1906. In the case of *La Iglesia Católica Apostólica y Romana en Puerto Rico v. Municipio de Ponce*, the three Puerto Rican (Catholic) members of the supreme court led a 3–2 decision that ruled in favor of the Church in all the cases under the court's jurisdiction. The split perplexed jurists and politicians across the mainland including President Roosevelt.[25]

One of the dissenting judges, Justice James H. McLeary, focused on the multiple ambiguities bypassed by the majority decision. First, it was not clear who was the complainant in the suit, either the church as an incorporated entity or the bishop. Second, the relationship between the religious orders and the church was not clear enough to the court to ensure if they could own property independently from each other. Moreover, even if the concordats of 1851 and 1859 between Spain and the Holy See were binding under the Treaty of Paris, the statute of limitations would have expired well before 1898, since the properties in question were seized in 1838. Finally, the colonial government of Puerto Rico made annual appropriations to fund the upkeep of various ecclesiastical properties and the salaries of the clergy, which favored the claims of the island's municipalities. McLeary appeared exasperated by the absence of any records: "There is no title of any kind shown, emanating from the sovereignty of the soil or from the Insular Authorities from the time of Ponce de Leon down to the American occupation or anyone else."[26] The municipality of Ponce's appeal to this ruling and the failure to settle the issue by means of a commission—an approach that advanced some results in Cuba and the Philippines—took this case to the Supreme Court of the United States.

Chief Justice Melville Fuller led a unanimous ruling on June 1, 1908. This decision is a bewildering survey of European Christian history and Spanish law. Starting with Emperor Constantine, passing through the Visigoths, *Las*

Siete Partidas of King Alfonso, the Laws of the Indies, and the concordats of the nineteenth century, one thing persisted: the juridical personality of the Church and its claims to property. Fuller, moreover, interpreted the true intent of Article VIII of the Treaty of Paris thus: "This clause is manifestly intended to guard the property of the church against interference with, or spoliation by, the new master, either directly or through his local governmental agents. There can be no question that the ecclesiastical body referred to, so far as Porto Rico was concerned, could only be, the Roman Catholic Church in that island, for no other ecclesiastical body there existed."[27] As part of the subsequent settlement, the Church received more than seventy properties and $120,000 as compensation for some properties in the San Juan area that remained under control of the U.S. government. In the opinion of Bartholomew H. Sparrow, this was an example of a "multiculturalist defense" protecting the unique culture of Puerto Rico under Spain.[28]

This ruling placed the Diocese of Puerto Rico along the parameters of the Plenary Councils of both Baltimore (1884) and Latin America (1900), which favored arrangements closer to corporation sole as an alternative to avoid the disputes around trusteeism of the early nineteenth century. This decision also streamlined what appeared to contemporaries like Carl Zollmann as a problematic foreign element into the domestic forms of church corporations present in the United States in the early twentieth century: "the Roman Catholic Church, is a Spanish product, thrust upon us by the treaty of Paris and ill-suited to our conditions."[29] The foreignness in question, however, was within the bounds of recognition in an imperial moment. The American excursion into the Caribbean and the Pacific was one framed by the rule of law;[30] moreover, it marked the proprietary church as the recognizable entity to emerge in a context of a broader proprietary alignment across the island. Property became a key node to navigate an evolving Puerto Rican secular as the Catholic Church in other American jurisdictions slowly ingrained corporation sole into its structures of governance.[31]

The proprietary church was also a state-disciplining resource. For various sectors in the island, *Ponce* meant a tutelary moment of clarification regarding what a regime of disestablishment may meet or fail to meet regarding broader political expectations. *El defensor cristiano*, a Methodist periodical published in the island, lamented that *Ponce* had all the trappings of a preordained outcome fixed by the pope and "Uncle Sam's wealth and power."[32] *La correspondencia*, a newspaper championing the cause of Puerto Rican self-government, cheered the rightful defeat of local politicians who did not know how to abandon their petty grievances with the past regime and chose the Church as their target.[33]

AFTERMATHS OF *PONCE*: VISIBILITY, CONTENTION, CHURCH REORGANIZATION

Ponce became the key ruling to frame the new administrative shapes of the Catholic Church vis-à-vis its religious and civic competitors across the island. The resolution of the church property cases inaugurated an era of adaptation in ecclesiastical administration that included the establishment of diocesan funds, the acquisition of new property, and investments in the sugar cane industry. During this period, the Diocese of Puerto Rico counted with an important ally in the Catholic Extension Society. Under the direction of Fr. Francis Clement Kelley, the Catholic Extension Society would disburse funds for the building of schools, the restoration of old temples, and the building of new ones. Bishops Blenk and Jones also coordinated the cultivation of lay associations, the arrival of various religious orders, and the publication of various periodicals across the island. These top-down initiatives did not take place in isolation from other Catholic sectors in the island. For instance, the Hermanos Cheos, a self-organized network of lay preachers—including men and women—active shortly after the American occupation, set at its task to evangelize, offer transportation to fellow Christians, and donate property to the Church hierarchy in San Juan (whose attitude toward the group oscillated between suspicion and accommodation).[34]

The presences of Catholicism in disestablished Puerto Rico were now part of a textured imagination and performance of Christian diversity and competition. As Anne M. Martínez has shown, the inroads of protestant groups into Puerto Rico were an essential element in the characterization of Puerto Rico as a Catholic borderland that conflated risk and progress, a territory religiously up for grabs that needed the affect and generosity of American Catholics to survive the arrival of Protestantism to the Caribbean territory.[35] In this respect, both the local Catholic and protestant press often supplemented and mirrored each other's accounts: growth—whether Catholic or protestant—was relational, the result of the interaction of competing forms of Christianity under an ongoing disestablishment regime. For instance, while *The Catholic World* celebrated how "the new regime ... has awakened all classes of people to the necessity of knowing their religion better, that they may be able to defend it with greater effectiveness. It has generated a healthy spirit of offence and of defence," *El testigo evángelico*, a publication of the United Brethren, boasted superior rates of church attendance among protestants in comparison to Catholics in just a decade of evangelizing labor and in spite of what it perceived as governmental favoritism toward Rome.³⁶ *Ponce* and its results highlighted the new realms of religious contention and its "benefits" across the Caribbean territory.

Ponce confirmed the standing of the juridical personality and the capacity of the Catholic Church to own property in Puerto Rico. This decision also set a line of continuity between the nineteenth-century concordats between Spain and the Holy See into American jurisprudence. The legal recognition of the Catholic Church in Puerto Rico made manifest one of the various modes of being and exceptions that this ecclesiastical body could claim in American law at the dawn of the twentieth century. This adaptation appears to have surprised audiences both domestic and foreign. Decades after the ruling, Fred Coudert, a member of the firm that was involved in various of the Insular Cases and who also served as counsel of the Catholic Church during the property disputes, reminisced on the exemplary nature of *Ponce*: "By decision of the Supreme Court we avoided all the civil dissension that came from conflicts between church and state in Latin countries. That's never passed into history, and so far as I know, no one except a few lawyers has ever paid attention to that decision . . . but it illustrates the value of our Constitutional system."³⁷ Coudert's fancy showcases how the political and legal tutelage in which the *Ponce* decision took place was a key component of the regimes of disestablishment featured in early twentieth-century American imperial imagination.

NOTES

1. José Tous Soto, "Estudio comparativo entre el régimen autonómico español y la ley Foraker," *El Aguila*, July 25, 1907, 9–10.
2. For a brief account of the changes and continuities of the Autonomic Charter and the Organic Act (Foraker Act) see José Trías Monge, *Puerto Rico: The Trials of the Oldest Colony in the World* (New Haven, Conn.: Yale University Press, 1997).
3. Tous Soto, "Estudio comparativo." Unless otherwise noted, all translations are the author's.
4. Brenna Bhandar, *The Colonial Lives of Property* (Durham, N.C.: Duke University Press, 2018).
5. Anthony M. Stevens-Arroyo, "Taking Religion Seriously: New Perspectives on Religion in Puerto Rico," *Centro Journal* 18, no. 11 (2006): 214–23. On the political valences of "Americanization" during the first decades of the twentieth century in Puerto Rico, see Cesar Ayala and Rafael Bernabe, *Puerto Rico in the American*

Century: A History Since 1898 (Chapel Hill: University of North Carolina Press, 2007), 70–88; and Julian Go, *American Empire and the Politics of Meaning: Elite Political Cultures in the Philippines and Puerto Rico during U.S. Colonialism* (Durham, N.C.: Duke University Press, 2008).

6. Sarah Barringer Gordon, "The First Disestablishment: Limits on Church Power and Property Before the Civil War," *University of Pennsylvania Law Review* 162, no. 2 (2014): 307–72; Steven K. Green, *The Second Disestablishment: Church and State in Nineteenth-Century America* (Oxford: Oxford University Press, 2010); and Patrick W. Carey, *People, Priests, and Prelates: Ecclesiastical Democracy and the Tensions of Trusteeism* (Notre Dame, Ind.: University of Notre Dame Press, 1987).
7. *Downes v. Bidwell*, 182 U.S. 244 (1901), at 287.
8. *Downes v. Bidwell*, at 341.
9. Brook Thomas, "A Constitution Led by the Flag: The Insular Cases and the Metaphor of Incorporation," in *Foreign in a Domestic Sense: Puerto Rico, American Expansion, and the Constitution*, ed. Christina Duffy and Burke Marshall (Durham, N.C.: Duke University Press, 2001), 84.
10. Gordon, "The First Disestablishment," 307–72.
11. Gordon, "The First Disestablishment," 311.
12. Patrick J. Dignan, *A History of the Legal Incorporation of Catholic Church Property in the United States (1784–1932)* (New York: P. J. Kennedy and Sons, 1937), 141–244; and Carey, *People, Priests and Prelates*, 233–78.
13. Vincenç Feliú, "Corporate 'Soul': Legal Incorporation of Catholic Ecclesiastical Property in the United States: A Historical Perspective," *Ohio Northern University Law Review* 40 (2013): 445–46.
14. Thomas Sherman, "A Month in Porto Rico," *Messenger of the Sacred Heart of Jesus* 33 (January–December, 1898): 1074–81; and Anne M. Martínez, *Catholic Borderlands: Mapping Catholicism onto American Empire, 1905–1935* (Lincoln: University of Nebraska Press, 2014), 71–79.
15. Salvador Brau, *Ecos de batalla* (Puerto Rico: Imprenta y Librería de Jose Gonzalez Font, 1886), 226.
16. Silvia Alvaraz Curbelo, *Un país del porvenir* (San Juan, P.R.: Ediciones Callejón, 2001).
17. Francisca Suárez, *Refutación al Vicario Capitular* (Mayagüez, P.R.: Tipografía Comercial, 1899), 12–13.
18. *Boletín Eclesiástico de Puerto Rico* 28, no. 16 (September 1898): 169.
19. Henry K. Carroll, *Report on the Island of Porto Rico* (Washington, D.C.: Government Printing Office, 1899), 654.
20. On the history of Puerto Rican anticlericalism, see José Manuel García Leduc, *¡La pesada carga! Iglesia, clero y sociedad en Puerto Rico (Siglo XIX)* (San Juan, P.R.: Ediciones Puerto, 2009); and Samuel Silva Gotay, *Soldado católico en guerra de religión* (San Juan, P.R.: Publicaciones Gaviota, 2012).
21. The relevant passages of Article VIII read thus:

> And it is hereby declared that the relinquishment or cession, as the case may be, to which the preceding paragraph refers, cannot in any respects impair the property

of rights which law belong to the peaceful procession of property of all kinds, of provinces, municipalities, public or private establishments, ecclesiastical or civil bodies, or any other associations, having legal capacity to acquire and possess property in the aforesaid whatsoever nationality such individuals may be.

The aforesaid relinquishment of cession, as the case may be, includes all documents exclusively referring to the sovereignty relinquished or ceded that may exist in the archives of the Peninsula. Where any document in such archives only in part relates to said sovereignty, a copy of such part will be furnished whenever it shall be requested. Like rules shall be reciprocally observed in favor of Spain in respects of documents in the archives of the islands above referred to.

In the aforesaid relinquishment or cession, as the case may be, are also included such rights as the Crown of Spain and its authorities possess in respect of the official archives and records, executive as well as judicial, in the islands above referred to, which relate to said islands or the rights and property of their inhabitants. Such archives and records shall be carefully preserved, and private persons shall without distinction have the right to require, in accordance with law, authenticated copies of the contracts, wills, and other instruments forming part of notarial protocols or files, or which may be contained in executive or judicial archives, be the latter in Spain or in the islands aforesaid.

Elihu Root, *The Military and Colonial Policy of the United States. Addresses and Reports by Elihu Root*, ed. Robert Bacon and James Brown Scott (Cambridge, Mass.: Harvard University Press, 1916), xxi.

22. Carroll, *Report on the Island of Porto Rico*, 688.
23. Elisa Julián de Nieves, *The Catholic Church in Colonial Puerto Rico* (Río Piedras: Editorial Edil), 28–35.
24. David A. Lockmiller, "The Settlement of the Church Property Question in Cuba," *Hispanic American Historical Review* 17, no. 4 (1937): 488–98; Winfred Lee Thompson, *The Introduction of American Law in the Philippines and Puerto Rico 1898–1905* (Fayetteville: University of Arkansas Press, 1989), 206–17; and *Barlin v. Ramirez* (1907): "It is suggested by the appellant that the Roman Catholic Church has no legal personality in the Philippine Islands. This suggestion, made with reference to an institution which antedates by almost a thousand years any other personality in Europe, and which existed 'when Grecian eloquence still flourished in Antioch, and when idols were still worshiped in the temple of Mecca,' does not require serious consideration."
25. Louis Sulzbacher to Archbishop James H. Blenk, January 19, 1907, Archbishop Blenk, Puerto Rico II (a), Archives, Archdiocese of New Orleans, Louisiana; and Theodore Roosevelt to Elihu Root, undated, Archbishop Blenk, Puerto Rico I (c), Archives, Archdiocese of New Orleans, Louisiana.
26. *Decision of the Supreme Court of Porto Rico and Dissenting Opinion in the case of The Roman Catholic Church of Porto Rico vs. The People of Porto Rico* (Washington, D.C.: Government Printing Press, 1909), 34.
27. *Municipality of Ponce v. Roman Catholic Apostolic Church in Puerto Rico, 210 U.S. 296* (1908).

28. Bartholomew H. Sparrow, *The Insular Cases and the Emergence of American Empire* (Lawrence: University Press of Kansas, 2006), 163.
29. Carl Zollman, *American Civil Church Law* (New York: Columbia University, 1917), 48.
30. Benjamin Allen Coates, *The Legalist Empire: International Law and American Foreign Relations in the Early Twentieth Century* (New York: Oxford University Press, 2016); and Efren Rivera Ramos, *The Legal Construction of Identity: The Judicial and Social Legacy of American Colonialism in Puerto Rico* (Washington, D.C.: American Psychological Association, 2001), 71–120.
31. Dignan, *Catholic Church Property*, 207–36; Frank T. Reuter, *Catholic Influence on American Colonial Policies 1898–1904* (Austin: University of Texas Press, 1967); and Tisa Wenger, *Religious Freedom: The Contested History of an American Ideal* (Chapel Hill: University of North Carolina Press, 2017), 34–46.
32. Quoted in Julián de Nieves, *The Catholic Church*, 60.
33. "La Mariposa," *La Correspondencia*, July 1, 1908.
34. Gerardo Alberto Hernández Aponte, *La iglesia católica en Puerto Rico ante la invasión de Estados Unidos de América* (San Juan, P.R.: UPR DEGI, 2013), 347–63.
35. Martínez, *Catholic Borderlands*.
36. Rev. A. Alonso-Alonso, "Religious Progress in Porto Rico," *Catholic World* 76 (1903): 449–50; *El testigo evangélico* VI, March 1, 1910; see also Michael Saenz, "Economic Aspects of Church Development in Puerto Rico" (Ph.D. diss, University of Michigan, 1961), 72–85.
37. Quoted in Virginia Kays Veenswijk, *Coudert Brothers: A Legacy in Law* (New York: Truman Tally Books/Dutton, 1994), 150.

3
Home Rule

*Equitable Justice in Progressive Chicago
and the Philippines*

NANCY BUENGER

In June 1900 U.S. Judge William Howard Taft arrived in the Philippines, a spoil of the Spanish American War, to establish "the largest measure of home rule." His first directive was to organize municipalities in which the natives might manage their local affairs "to the fullest extent of which they are capable."[1] Comparative studies of Spanish and Anglo-American law were the order of the day, which Taft touted as one of the most useful benefits of territorial expansion. In collaboration with Filipino jurist Cayetano Arellano, Taft and his Philippine Commission revamped the insular judiciary, specifying juryless criminal proceedings "analogous to those in a court of equity."[2] Both Spanish and Anglo-American courts have historically relied on equity, a Roman canonical heritage, to administer domestic and colonial dependents. Equitable courts can set aside the law's letter and craft discretionary remedies according to the dictates of conscience and alternative legal traditions. The juryless insular courts sparked heated national debate and fear that the constitutional rights of all U.S. citizens were imperiled.[3]

In June 1900 the Chicago Civic Federation launched a home rule campaign for municipal self-governance under the direction of Cook County judge Murray Tuley. Revered as chief justice and dean of chancellors, Tuley presided over the circuit court chancery, a distinctive equity jurisdiction that persists to the present day. Chancellor Tuley initially opposed municipal home rule, arguing that Chicago, like the Philippines, was not yet capable of self-government; there were times when the state must check evil tendencies in its municipal child. But

FIGURE 3.1 Plans for Manila (top) and Chicago (bottom), Daniel H. Burnham and Edward H. Bennett, *Plan of Chicago*, 1909.

D. H. Burnham and Pierce Anderson, "Plans for the development of Manila" and Jules Guérin, "Chicago. View, looking west, of the proposed civic center plaza and buildings" in Daniel H. Burnham and Edward H. Bennett, *Plan of Chicago*, ed. Charles Moore (Chicago: Commercial Club, 1909), plates 31, 132.

the Civic Federation persuaded the chancellor to direct enabling legislation for a new city charter and planning for a new municipal court that adopted juryless criminal proceedings analogous to those in a court of equity. The Chicago Municipal Court was championed as "the pioneer modern" archetype for U.S. judicial reform.[4] In consultation with Taft, Chicago jurists developed plans for model juryless courts that were adopted nationwide.

The national outcry over juryless U.S. insular courts stands in striking contrast to the accolades for Chicago's juryless municipal court. Both the insular critiques and paeans to Chicago modernism masked a long-standing reliance on equity to administer dependents and other quasi-sovereign populations at home and abroad. Equity's obscurity is in keeping with what William Novak has described as the strangely self-denying and extraordinary power of the American state.[5] A constitutionally vested judicial power, equity is virtually undocumented as a U.S. state and territorial court in scholarly studies.[6] According to Morton Horwitz, equity was contrary to the rule of law and succumbed to antebellum state codes that marked the "final and complete emasculation of Equity as an independent source of legal standards" and "the end of a separate, equitable system of substantive justice." Yet by 1938 equity procedure predominated in federal civil courts and, soon thereafter, state courts nationwide. Equity's midcentury resurrection has been described as a revolutionary development driven by American civil codes and English judicature acts.[7] But equity's persistence—and, indeed, thriving criminal authority—in early twentieth-century U.S. cities and colonies requires further explanation. Hidden contours of an elusive American state and rising global hegemon lie therein.

This essay looks beyond the law's letter to consider equity's metropolitan implications in Progressive Era Chicago and the Philippines. I do so through the lens of home rule, or the governance of dependents and other quasi-sovereign populations lacking full legal capacity. A richly ambiguous international agenda, home rule is commonly conflated with local and limited democratic governance in the United States. In Progressive Chicago and the Philippines, home rule drew deeply on the extraordinary power and expansive administrative capacity of equity, a court specializing in the guardianship of those who "have not discretion enough to manage their own concerns."[8] Home rulers invoked the authority of the medieval metropolis as they expanded equity's criminal jurisdiction, copied its administrative machinery, and exercised the prerogative to set aside the law's letter. Voyaging back and forth across the Pacific and comparing notes on the mainland, they enhanced the parental power of the American state.

First, an explanation of equity. Often associated with fairness or finance, equity is also a Roman canonical heritage, a juryless administrative court, and a discretionary prerogative. Saint Thomas Aquinas described equity as the virtue of setting aside the law's letter to expediently secure substantive justice and the common good. It was a particular virtue to set aside the law's letter on behalf of widows and orphans lacking the protection of a *paterfamilias*, who the Church was to succor above all as the essence of doing justice. The spiritual courts might claim jurisdiction over such *miserabile personae*, citing a failure in temporal justice, and administer their needs according to the dictates of conscience, the human faculty for discerning God's will. Medieval metropolitans (bishops and archbishops) administered the legal affairs of the *miserabiles* in chancery, the governmental machinery of the papacy and emerging European states. Over time, their ranks included others lacking full legal capacity: wards, servants, slaves, poor and ignorant country folk, scholars, the clergy, prostitutes, cities, and New World Indians. Anglo-American courts that evolved from chancery—synonymously known as courts of equity—inherited this power of guardianship by virtue of the doctrine of *parens patriae*: that all orphans, dependent children, and others unable to care for themselves are within the special protection, and under the control, of the state.[9]

Chicago and the Philippines retained nineteenth-century courts with distinctive elements of medieval chanceries, which were replicated in their Progressive offspring. These included juryless "nontrial" proceedings, administrative bureaucracies, and the prerogative to set aside the law's letter. Nontrial proceedings were a series of discontinuous and often closed hearings designed to inform state officials. A jury was the defining feature of a common-law trial, an open court hearing to inform twelve laymen. A common-law judge was "a mere moderator" in a trial bound by rigid procedural rules, which could only remedy *past* harms.[10] A judge in equity appointed an administrative bureaucracy to investigate suits under his direction, established his own procedural rules, and compelled *future* behavior. His discretionary decrees could provide extraordinary remedies (exceptional judicial relief when other methods were unavailable or unacceptable) and might reference case precedent; alternative legal traditions such as Indigenous, ecclesiastical, or foreign law; or equity maxims (guides to conscience passed down through the centuries).

The prerogative to set aside the law's letter was infused with equity's Christian heritage. Equity, Chancellor Tuley explained, was a "higher" legal authority, imbued with the spirit of "the meek and lowly Jesus," which could ignore, disregard, or even oppose the law.[11] The spiritual authority to transcend the law, observes Vicente Rafael, is an imperial legacy that haunts the Philippines. The imperial sovereign recognizes nothing, after God, that is greater than himself. Rather than limiting the sovereign's power, God figures as an infinite force that enables him to transcend human law. The sovereign thus operates both inside and outside of the law, or, as Carl Schmitt opined, "Sovereign is he who decides on the exception."[12] President William McKinley's 1900 instructions to the Taft Commission similarly claimed transcendent authority: God had set the Philippines "under the sovereignty and protection of the people of the United States."[13]

Taft acquired the reins to a Spanish colonial judiciary whose sophistication, power, and reach far exceeded that of its Cook County cousin, particularly in criminal affairs. Manila's *real audiencia chancillería*—modeled on Iberian chanceries—was the imperial machinery of the Spanish Philippines.[14] Chicago's equity jurisdictions, allegedly limited to *private* or civil suits, were defined by England's court of chancery, which lost its criminal jurisdiction during the seventeenth century. Although the English chancellor eventually regained a nominal criminal jurisdiction, it was seldom invoked.[15] Nineteenth-century American jurists were far less reluctant to invoke equity's extraordinary remedies for the prevention of *public* or criminal concerns, particularly when morals, alcohol, or labor was involved. Federal judges in Chicago expanded equity's criminal jurisdiction in 1877 to suppress industrial servants' boycotts and strikes, a project in which Taft later figured.[16]

Scholars have established the separate importance of Chicago and the Philippines for Progressive state building, emphasizing judicial innovation. Jury-less U.S. insular courts in the Philippines—the nation's largest, most diverse, and strategically important insular dependency—are attributed to creative constitutionalism, missing the interstitial space informed by equity. Taft's central role in the reconstruction of both insular and mainland courts has not yet been recognized. Path-breaking studies of juvenile and municipal courts in the so-called Metropolis of the West—the fastest-growing U.S. city—are essential for an understanding of equitable justice in the Progressive Era, particularly for women's key role. But the courts are characterized as novel tribunals that overturned American understandings of the rule of law; equity is only referenced in passing. Equity's turn-of-the-century religious implications and common legal heritage in Spanish and Anglo-American courts have been overlooked altogether.[17]

I track Progressive metropolitans who simultaneously revamped insular and municipal courts under the banner of home rule, drawing on Spanish and Anglo-American precedent. Championing equity's higher Christian authority, they expanded its criminal jurisdiction over dependent populations, particularly those of foreign and Black parentage. Copying chancery's machinery, they adopted inquisitorial nontrial proceedings in administrative judiciaries. Exercising the equitable prerogative to look beyond the law's letter, they experimented with alternative legal remedies. Prominent among them were quasi-sovereign actors intimately acquainted with equity's capacity for home rule, including women and Filipino jurists. Philippine Commissioner and Governor Taft—later U.S. secretary of war, president, and chief justice—was equity's foremost proponent and a pivotal player in the Progressive reconstruction of U.S. courts.

Reconnecting insular and municipal home rule reveals equity as a powerful metropolitan engine rather than an emasculated legal standard. Equitable experimentation in Chicago and the Philippines was a comparative, overlapping, and mutually influential project underwritten by a common demographic: large alien populations deemed lacking in discretion, the mark of the sovereign.[18] Equitable criminal courts enhanced state discretionary power and infrastructural reach among *miserabiles* around the corner and around the world. Ultimately, equity emerges as a cornerstone—rather than a revolutionary overturning—of American understandings of the rule of law. Embodying the Christian, imperial, and constitutional authority to decide on the exception, equity powered American state expansion at home and abroad.

HOME RULE

"What, now, do we mean by the term home rule?" queried Frank Goodnow—the "father" of American administration—as he considered 1900 Chicago governance.[19] The disciplinary order of the home has been a perennial model for statecraft. As the *Monthly Religious Magazine* observed, a parent must make his will felt to establish home rule, but the subtle irresistible power of a loving mother was more effective than inflexible rules. To establish home rule, Goodnow similarly argued, Chicago must reject rigid constitutional and legislative restraints imposed by the "rule of law," recapturing the discretionary authority of the medieval metropolis over "purely local" concerns.[20] Equity embodied medieval metropolitan authority over the most intimate of local concerns: the home. In Chicago, domestic affairs were administered by the nation's largest complex of distinctive equity jurisdictions. And women's intimate knowledge of "home conditions," observed Chicago attorney Mary Bartelme, "with all domestic relations and the unfolding of the child's character," perfectly prepared them for equitable court administration.[21] Chicago women spearheaded an unprecedented expansion of equity's criminal jurisdiction to include delinquent children, enhancing the court's utility as a model for parental governance.

Equity's jurisdiction over married women, unrecognized by the common law, is well documented in scholarly studies; its power of guardianship over others afflicted with civil disabilities is not. The court was uniquely suited for recognizing the "peculiar character" of human property, free Blacks, Indians, and extraterritorial aliens.[22] Illinois's equity jurisdiction was born in the 1787 Northwest Territory—where the court was explicitly prohibited—when judges cited the impossibility of "protecting the persons and securing the property" of French natives, which included valuable slaves in an allegedly slave-free territory. Throughout the nineteenth century and into the twentieth, equitable American probate, surrogate, and orphans courts were widely vested with the guardianship of household dependents: wives, minors, wards, apprentices, servants, and the elusive category of persons declared *non compotes mentis*: the feebleminded, insane, inebriates, spendthrifts, and religionists suffering from undue influence.[23] Model code states such as New York and California, which attempted to fuse common law and equity beginning in 1848, continued to recognize equity as a distinctive jurisdiction for guardianship purposes. As a late nineteenth-century New York equity treatise observed, the jurisprudence of any country would be extremely defective if it lacked a tribunal with sufficient jurisdiction to protect "those who are laboring under natural or civil disabilities."[24]

In Chicago's decentralized, overlapping, and redundant 1900 judicial system—described as an empire in itself—distinctive equity jurisdictions were vested in county, state, and federal courts. State jurisdictions were broadly defined as "according to the general usage and practice of courts of equity," which was interpreted by the Illinois Supreme Court in *Mahar v. O'Hara* to imply the same jurisdiction "which the court of chancery in England has" unless limited by express implication.[25] Jurisdictional boundaries were never absolute, and ultimately depended on the chancellor's prerogative, but typically included familial, spiritual, and financial affairs historically entrusted to ecclesiastics, including marriage, guardianship, inheritance, trusts, and churches.[26] Chancery had general jurisdiction over domestic affairs delegated to specialized courts, such as probate. Federal equity jurisdictions were meager compared to their state counterparts.[27]

Chancellor Tuley wielded considerable authority as chief justice of Cook County's circuit court—the largest cog in the state judicial machinery—for two decades; his decisions were followed across the nation and abroad.[28] He controlled the court docket and held veto power over the judicial appointment of chancellors, considered the highest honor on the Cook County bench. Tuley assumed countywide responsibility for assigning judges to the criminal and appellate courts, calling in out-of-town jurists to assist with heavy caseloads. He temporarily initiated juryless Cook County common-law proceedings when backlogged cases greatly exceeded court capacity. The Illinois General Assembly approved the experiment, which provided for the waiving of jury rights, summary proceedings, and the elimination of appeals until the state increased the number of judges.[29]

Tuley and his fellow Cook County chancellors presided over complex administrative bureaucracies that included chancery masters, assistant masters, notaries, stenographers, accountants, and auctioneers. Appointed by the chancellors, they held office at their pleasure and charged litigants fees for their services. Following a preliminary meeting with case counsel, a chancery master determined which issues would be admitted to court, heard oral testimony, ordered the production of textual evidence, detailed financial accounts, prepared a final report with a recommended decision (which was rarely reversed), and continued oversight of certain cases post decree. All official communication between chancellor and master had to be in writing. Fees were carefully tabulated for each word written and every report read or filed, order or oath administered, and hour in hearings. The press of Chicago court business often necessitated a single master to oversee three or more simultaneous hearings in adjoining rooms. A master could investigate cases beyond the confines of the courthouse in a place he designated, such as a home or saloon or even in another state or country. Masters also conducted weekly auctions, selling bankrupts' properties and decedents' assets by court decree. Authorized to administer oaths, they could earn additional pre-election income by naturalizing immigrants in the solid Chicago tradition of turning out the vote.[30]

Progressive jurists cherished equity's Christian heritage, and the boundary between the court's temporal and spiritual authority was obscure. An authoritative equity treatise argued that conscience had evolved as a civil standard in Anglo-American courts, governed by an orderly system of principles, rules, and doctrines. Equity rested on the truths of moral law—a code of divine origin—but the chancellor was no longer "governed by his own interpretation of the divine morality."[31] According to Tuley, the morality of a court of equity was "not the morality of the world" but "higher, broader, and purer than that which prevails among men." No moral code had ever exceeded the equity maxims that guided the chancellor's conscience, excepting "the teachings of the man who spoke as never man spoke before."[32] The administration of equity depended on the moral purity and conscience of the chancellor, he claimed, who must leave personality, prejudices, and human frailties behind him as he ascended the bench.[33]

Chicago litigants petitioned chancery for discretionary legal remedies in summary hearings underwritten by moral requisites and powered by injunction. In contrast with common-law courts, in which litigants could claim certain rights, equity was "a matter of grace," available at the option of the court.[34] Petitioners were expected to enter chancery with "clean hands," a moral assessment. If anyone seeking relief had himself violated equity or good faith "by sharp practice, over-reaching, unfair concealment of facts, by taking undue advantage of his position or by other unconscientious means," Chancellor Tuley admonished, "the doors of the court will be closed against him."[35] If scandalous or impertinent allegations arose during a hearing, the court could expunge them from the record and award a financial remedy to the aggrieved party. Chancellors could compel future behavior by injunction (cease this) or specific performance (do that) and order ongoing case oversight; violation could result in imprisonment for criminal contempt. They also established their own procedural rules.[36]

Tuley recognized a broad array of alternative legal traditions that lay beyond the law's letter. Equity applied some rules analogous to the common law, Tuley explained, but not the common law itself, which he disparaged as only suitable for a semi-barbarous people and totally inadequate for advanced civilizations. In a suit involving a bequest to purchase masses for the repose of souls in purgatory, Tuley ruled that Catholic doctrine trumped Illinois's statutory adoption of the English common law, which held such gifts superstitious and void. Equity could borrow freely from the codes or laws "of any nation, written or unwritten," he argued. A large part of equity jurisprudence lay completely outside, or in direct opposition to the law, which was "substantially nullified" by equity. Rather than follow the law, the law followed equity, which disregarded all forms that interfered with "exact justice between man and man."[37]

Married women and children were the largest categories of *miserabiles* consigned to equity's jurisdiction. Chancery heard suits involving married women's separate property, marital disputes, desertion, nonsupport, separation, and divorce. Women faced far-reaching decisions in probate courts concerning their children and property following the loss of a spouse through death, marital breakup, or his commitment for bankruptcy or drunkenness. Restrictions on a married woman's right to her earnings or property could prevent her from serving as legal guardian to her children, and remarriage might terminate her natural guardian rights. Illinois legal guardians were required to give bond, with good security, for a sum *double* the amount of a minor's real and personal estate. If a husband died intestate, the most that a widow could expect from jointly owned property, real and personal, would be a share *equal* to that of her children.[38]

Probate officials had a vested interest in close regulation of familial affairs, a fee-based service that could consume the better part of small estates. Even if the deceased left nothing but debts, family members might be charged to void their liability in a court hearing requiring an attorney, court fees, and posting of legal notice in newspapers, on city bridges, and with justices of the peace. Ongoing court supervision followed the appointment of an Illinois guardian, who could not expend a ward's money without first obtaining a probate court order. Widows regularly petitioned probate for permission to purchase everyday necessities with their children's inheritances, such as food, rent, clothing, or childcare. Legal expenses for one court filing approving an $8.85 shopping spree totaled $10. Undoubtedly many guardians did not bother to file court reports, but family members or concerned neighbors could and did compel court accountings, and guardians who failed to comply faced prison sentences for criminal contempt.[39]

The *Chicago Legal News* cautioned readers of the perils of incapacity, which could subject both persons and property to state supervision and control. Equitable courts determined the legal incapacity of habitual drunkards; spendthrifts; and feebleminded, insane, and distracted persons, appointing conservators to manage their affairs or committing them to the poorhouse. If people were not careful how they conducted themselves, the *Chicago Legal News* warned, neighbors or family members might testify that their minds were impaired. Elizabeth Packard's husband committed her to an Illinois insane asylum for her heterodox religious beliefs in 1860. Following her release she settled in Chicago as a woman's rights activist and successfully lobbied for an 1867 Illinois law requiring jury trials for insanity commitments. But equitable courts were not bound by a jury's decision, which could be disregarded in a final decree.[40]

Equity was a powerful model for women, particularly Chicago's female attorneys, the largest such cohort in the world between the 1880s and 1920s. Women lauded equity as "the savior of woman" for its recognition of their legal existence.[41] Several Chicagoans were members of the Equity Club, the first national professional organization for women at law. Equity appealed to devout first-generation women lawyers, such as an Equity Club member who pledged to acknowledge "No object but country. No umpire but conscience. No guide but Christ."[42] Women attorneys commonly specialized in probate, which involved behind-the-scenes investigations rather than courtroom litigation. Attorney Myra Bradwell, editor/publisher of the *Chicago Legal News*, assisted renowned Chicago probate judge James Bradwell, her husband. Her protégé Mary Bartelme served as a Cook County public guardian and juvenile court judge.[43] Women lawyers published "law made easy" guides emphasizing equitable remedies, gave popular lectures, and assumed positions at the helm of key local, national, and international organizations, including the Woman's Christian Temperance Union, the first mass organization of American women. Equity Club member Ada Bittenbender was the legal advisor to Chicago-based national Woman's Christian Temperance Union president, Frances Willard, who led a national "home protection" campaign to expand woman suffrage.[44]

The Woman's Christian Temperance Union and other temperance activists relied on equity's capacity to enjoin nuisances to protect the home from the tyranny of drink, an expansion of the court's criminal jurisdiction. From an early date, American jurists had invoked equity to enjoin and abate moral nuisances. In an 1857 case involving a brothel, a Maryland court observed that "it would be strange, indeed" if equity did not exercise its power to suppress moral hazards, a function "amenable to its penalties from the earliest times."[45] Chicago judges significantly expanded equity's abatement of nuisances in the suppression of the late-nineteenth-century labor movement. But labor injunctions were limited to the protection of property, while morals and alcohol suits invoked equity for the protection of the common good, a more expansive jurisdiction. Chicago attorney Samuel Packard—son of women's rights activist Elizabeth Packard—was a lead counsel in the 1887 U.S. Supreme Court temperance case *Mugler v. Kansas*, which affirmed equity's capacity to abate potential harms to the "health, morals, or safety" of the community.[46]

Chicago women asserted a discretionary jurisdiction over impoverished and delinquent children in the 1890s, citing the failure of local justice of the peace courts. The nucleus for this extraordinary legal initiative was Jane Addams's Hull House in one of the city's poorest and most ethnographically diverse neighborhoods; over 75 percent of the children served were of "foreign" or Black parentage.[47] The settlement workers were no strangers to equity. Julia Lathrop, who coordinated the juvenile initiative, was a legal aide who investigated state institutions for dependent populations. Jane Addams helped Tuley promote an equitable labor arbitration tribunal that he had established as a state alternative to federal prosecution. More men like Tuley were needed, Addams wrote, who would admit the inadequacy of written law and help establish new courts embodying the conscience of the community.[48]

Beginning in 1895 Lathrop and members of the Chicago Woman's Club lobbied for state recognition "of the delinquent child as a ward in chancery" and a juvenile probation system. Probation, or the suspension of a criminal sentence prior to imprisonment, evolved as an informal practice in American courts and was not statutorily recognized for Illinois juveniles until 1899. Courts often linked the origins of the practice to benefit of clergy—the protective jurisdiction available to ecclesiastical *miserabiles*—which was recognized as a power inherent in common-law courts. A chancery master historically investigated and specified the terms of a suspended criminal sentence in noncapital cases, a role later assigned to probation officers. In Chicago, Hull House residents served as volunteer probation officers while the practice remained in legal limbo. Appearing in criminal court at the trials of juvenile offenders, they investigated their home backgrounds and advised the judge how best to address their welfare; some children were dismissed into their custody. The women also lobbied for separate hearings for delinquents in Cook County's circuit court chancery, which were offered on an informal basis from 1894. The 1899 Illinois Juvenile Court Act gave a legal basis to the Hull House experiment and incorporated the practices developed there; similar courts were quickly established across the United States and around the world.[49]

Chicago Juvenile Court founders asserted its chancery jurisdiction as they expanded equity's public or criminal domain; they also labored to distinguish between juvenile and criminal courts. Addams described how equity underwrote the court's developing theory and practice, which Lathrop discussed with court officials over coffee at Hull House. The recognition of a child as a ward in chancery was not new, Lathrop observed, and chancery business had always been "intimately involved in the most delicate and complicated questions of social life." What was new, according to Addams, was "the conception that a child that broke the law was to be dealt with by the state as a wise parent would deal with a wayward child."[50] Presiding Judge Julian Mack championed chancery's power to save a child from "the brand of criminality" while acknowledging objections that his court was "nevertheless a criminal proceeding."[51] Unlike criminal courts that punished children for past wrongs, he argued, juvenile courts were designed to save children from future "downward careers." If possible, juvenile courts should be "vested with full and complete chancery and criminal jurisdiction."[52] A British visitor observed that England's juvenile court act, which built on common-law criminal procedure, "makes no such radical alteration in juvenile court procedure as obtains in the Chicago chancery juvenile court."[53] Under chancery procedure, "*it is not necessary to wait until a neglected child commits an offence* before taking needful action in his interests." The court revealed "the state *in loco parentis*."[54]

The juvenile court initiative was closely interwoven with the Civic Federation's home rule campaign, which coalesced at Chicago's 1893 World's Columbian Exposition. The "White City" stoked dreams that the metropolis might resume the "commanding position" it had enjoyed in medieval Europe. Prominent among the dream-stokers were exposition planner Daniel Burnham and British home rule enthusiast William Stead. For Stead, home rule was the key to "sane" imperial expansion and an exercise in millennial state building, a vision he articulated in *If Christ Came to Chicago!* (1894). Stead called for a mendicant order of men and women to fan out over Chicago, reminding residents of God's higher law by protecting the fatherless and destitute. Then Christ would establish a Civic Church in City Hall, modeled on the Catholic Church in its prime. This centrally administered "confessional" would hear complaints, give council, and assist in removing spiritual and moral evils. A female police force—inspired by Jane Addams—would keep watch and ward over the welfare of children, remodeling the city "on the ideal of the family."[55] Concluding with the Civic Federation's incorporation papers, Stead's book inspired municipal reform initiatives across the United States and Britain.[56]

INSULAR COURTS

Courts loomed large in the governance of the Philippines. A U.S. Hall of Justice commanded the insular skyline in Daniel Burnham's 1905 Plan of Manila, commissioned by Taft. Described as "majestic, venerable, and sacred ... representing sentimentally and practically the highest function of civilized society," the hall was intended to compel an attitude of respect.[57] Although U.S. officials envisioned an Anglo-American Hall of Justice, they realized a more sophisticated model for metropolitan governance in Manila's Spanish *real audiencia chancillería*. The care of Spanish colonial dependents had been entrusted to the *audiencia*, observed historian Bernard Moses, a Taft commissioner. The court embodied the legal basis of Spain's colonial authority, issued as a papal grant, which was contingent on the benevolent protection and Christianization of the natives. The Taft Commission established municipal governance over "local affairs" by stripping recent Spanish reforms limiting the *audiencia*'s power, reconstructing a centralized administrative judiciary that had sustained imperial rule for three centuries.[58]

Taft's 1900 Philippine Commission initially planned to sweep away Spanish colonial institutions, modify Spanish laws, and build a new government from the ground up. But U.S. officials came to recognize the Spanish imperial judicial system as "more completely unified and systematized than that of any other nation," according to Moses.[59] English and Dutch models were inappropriate for natives who had converted to Christianity and acquired "a certain infusion of European blood" and aspirations.[60] The Spanish legal order had advantageously shaped "the popular mind," adapting Filipinos to European culture and preparing "a rude people" for a higher stage of civilization.[61] According to Manila judge Charles Lobingier, Americans were amazed by the comprehensiveness of Spanish legal codes, unlike "the lawless science of our law."[62] The thirteenth-century Castilian Siete Partidas was "by far the most valuable legal monument" since the Justinian code, and the 1899 Código Civil was superior even to the French Code Napoleon.[63] There was never any serious proposal to undo these great Spanish works, he noted, quoting from the Partidas: "A despot uproots the tree; a wise monarch prunes its branches."[64] "One of the far-reaching consequences" of the U.S. occupation was a realization that Americans had as much to gain from Spanish law as the Filipinos from U.S. jurisprudence.[65]

The problem with Spanish law, Taft emphasized, was one of procedure rather than substance. The Spanish code of civil procedure caused substantial delays in the administration of justice, he complained, particularly by appeal. Litigants could challenge the competency of judicial officers before the *audiencia*, keeping a case in court for years. But Taft had no quibble with juryless Spanish procedure. Beginning in 1900 Taft lobbied U.S. Supreme Court justice John Harlan to deny jury trial rights in the archipelago, deemed fundamental for insular governance. The Supreme Court affirmed that the administration of justice according to Anglo-Saxon principles might "for a time be impossible" among alien races differing in their religion, customs, laws, and modes of thought.[66] Equitably recognizing alternative legal traditions—including native Hawaiian and Spanish precedent—the Court held that grand and petit jury trial rights were inapplicable in unincorporated territories, which were held as U.S. dependencies.[67]

Taft inherited a Spanish judicial leviathan informed by Castilian and Roman canonical precedent. Although courts of chancery have been described as an English innovation, Manila's 1583 *real audiencia chancillería* was explicitly modeled on chanceries at Granada and Valladolid, Castile's oldest and most important court. A bishop historically presided over the *chancillería* at Valladolid, serving in the double capacity of royal official and ecclesiastical prince, and exercising the prerogative to set aside the law's letter. The Castilian chancellor served as the mediator between the king and his people, the Siete Partidas explained. All questions to be decided in writing came within his purview, including petitions from minors, widows, the old, diseased, poor or any others consigned to "wretchedness or misery."[68] The Castilian chancellor was the only royal official vested with the power to cancel a law. "If he finds a law which ought not to have been drawn up he must tear it, or deface it with his pen, which is called in Latin *cancellare*, and from this word the term chancery is derived."⁶⁹

Spanish colonial *audiencias* had far greater power and more extensive functions than their Iberian counterparts, observed Progressive historian Charles Cunningham. By law, a governor-general presided over Manila's *audiencia* until the 1860s, exercising judicial, executive, and legislative powers. The court appointed and supervised judicial officials, oversaw certain ecclesiastical affairs, penned laws, collected tithes, and assumed the powers of absent governors-general and military captains-general. A specialized tribunal recognized indigenous rites, customs, and practices. Indian plaintiffs testified before an inquisitorial bureaucracy, including a salaried *protector de indios*, scribes, interpreters, and advisors who prepared a final decision for the court. To ensure that legal technicalities did not obscure the truth, indigenous hearings were conducted with summary rather than full legal process. Judges were expected to issue prompt decisions, reducing or eliminating fees.⁷⁰ The procedural delays that raised Taft's ire reflect the engagement of Philippine plaintiffs with the *audiencia*, where they sought both judicial and administrative relief, challenging the competency of judicial officers.

Taft enjoyed what home rulers on the mainland could only dream of: the comprehensive powers of a Spanish governor-general. Philippine administrator David Barrows emphasized the office's importance in the *American Historical Review* as a "disturbing but great and magnetic" necessity for controlling tropical peoples. Americans were loath to delegate centralized administrative control to a single executive, he acknowledged, but "the abiding influence" of Spanish Philippine governors-general had happily prevented diffusion of such control.⁷¹ Although Americans disparaged the Spanish failure to separate governmental functions, Taft was vested with broad executive, legislative, and judicial powers. Officially designated civil governor, Taft revived the Spanish title governor-general for his successors to place the office on "a parity of dignity with that of other colonial empires of first importance."⁷²

Drawing on Spanish precedent, Taft reestablished gubernatorial control over Manila's *audiencia* with guidance from Filipino jurist Cayetano Arellano. The Spanish crown had stripped the governors-general of this power in 1861 to separate governmental functions, transferring judicial oversight to an administrative agency. The U.S. military appointed Arellano to reorganize and preside over the *audiencia* in 1899 as chief justice. The Taft Commission worked closely with Arellano to refine the judiciary, publishing his detailed history of Spanish Philippine courts and continuing his appointment as chief justice over what became known as the Supreme Court of the Philippines. Civil Governor Taft reestablished the gubernatorial power to appoint, transfer, and remove insular judicial officials, an authority that had been vested in the U.S. Philippine Commission. In another bow to Spanish tradition, Taft retained a bureau of justice to coordinate insular judicial business. The bureau administered subordinate court officials and published detailed judicial statistical reports, a long-established Spanish practice. Monthly caseload reports induced judges to quickly clear their dockets; those who did not went unpaid.[73]

The Taft Commission established judicial procedures that drew heavily on Spanish precedent, including juryless criminal proceedings "analogous to those in a court of equity."[74] The Spanish code of criminal procedure was retained together with an amending 1900 military order that imported some U.S. due process protections. A penal code drafted by the commission was rejected by U.S. jurists, who argued that it was unwise to abandon a code developed by "the best legal minds in Spain" over three or four centuries for one written "in as many months."[75] The commission did create a successful 1901 code of civil procedure in consultation with Spanish and Filipino attorneys, and members of the American Bar Association (ABA). California's code of civil procedure was cited as the "true legal precedent" for the Philippine civil code, but the impact of the California code was open to question, even in its home state.[76] In nontrial civil proceedings, insular litigants could apply for two assessors to advise a judge on questions of fact, but, as in equity, the court could disregard the decision. The civil code vested the Philippine Supreme Court with the power to establish uniform procedural rules for the entire insular judiciary.[77] Taft and the ABA would spend decades lobbying on the mainland to establish the U.S. Supreme Court's authority to create uniform federal procedural rules.

U.S. jurists experimented with Spanish law as well as procedure. To begin with, the insular administration failed to supply jurists with American legal reference materials. Chicagoan Paul Linebarger, a first instance judge for Batangas, shipped his personal law library overseas when he learned of the omission. Other jurists likely relied on the legal knowledge of the Filipino judges they had replaced, as did Judge James Blount, whose predecessor served as his clerk. To practice law in the Philippines, he noted, it was necessary to become familiar with "the whole body of the Spanish law."[78] And U.S. jurists did not remain long in the archipelago, an insular official complained, resigning just as they mastered the new legal order.[79]

Equitable courts could readily accommodate Spanish provisions for governing households, which far exceeded those of U.S. domestic relations law. In the *Illinois Law Review*, Philippine Supreme Court justice George Malcolm affirmed that Spanish laws pertaining to family relations, religion, or sentimental feelings were generally not superseded. The 1889 Código Civil elaborated legitimate and illegitimate birth, relations between adopters and the adopted, familial consent for marriage, rights and obligations between husband and wife, parental power, and the selection of guardians by court-appointed family councils. Spanish law zealously guarded the rights of minors and orphans, and provisions for wives and widows were "infinitely more liberal" than in U.S. state law, according to a first instance judge who regularly published on the mainland.[80] A Filipino jurist observed that Americans had acquired their adoption laws from earlier Spanish colonial borrowings on the mainland.[81]

Filipinos experimented with equitable Anglo-American judicial remedies. Although the Taft Commission abolished Spanish provisions for challenging the competency of judicial officers, natives initiated multiple suits challenging Lobingier and other U.S. judges under the extraordinary remedies of mandamus (compelling performance of a judicial act) and prohibition (commanding an inferior court to cease a prosecution). Others petitioned for gubernatorial pardons and paroles, a Spanish tradition retained by the Americans. Although the governors were never officially vested with this authority, it was "liberally used" by Taft and his successors.[82]

Lobingier and Taft proudly pointed to the Filipino embrace of habeas corpus, an equitable remedy. But in a case that did not win favor with U.S. officials, the Mangyans of Mindoro Province petitioned the Philippine Supreme Court to protest their confinement to a reservation, citing constitutional religious freedom protections. Reservations for non-Christian Mangyans were underwritten by a 1902 Philippine Commission act providing for local Mindoro governance. Provincial governance, the act affirmed, should facilitate the "knowledge and experience necessary for successful local popular government." Toward this end, supervision and control of the uncivilized Mangyans could include relocation to bring them under municipal governance. Provincial officials ordered the Mangyans' confinement for their own protection as well as that of the valuable public forests in which they roamed.[83]

The Philippine Supreme Court cited Spanish precedent, the authority of self-governing municipalities, and equitable principles to deny the Mangyans' petition. Sixteenth-century Spanish precedent had established that *indios* could be concentrated into towns and reservations for instruction in the sacred Catholic faith so that they might live in a civilized manner. An 1881 decree affirmed that it was a "duty to conscience" to help backward races grasp the moral and material advantages of living in towns under the protection of the law. The designation "non-Christian" was not religious in intent; rather, it was a geographical reference to those living apart from settled communities. Invoking a guardian's responsibility to his ward, the court did not want to interfere with the decision of local Filipino authorities. If proactive measures were not taken, the Mangyans would commit crimes and make depredations or be subjected to involuntary servitude. Theoretically, all men were created equal, but practically, the axiom was not precisely correct. Public policy must be flexible; distinctions must be made according to the dictates of sound reason and a true sense of justice.[84]

Insular lawmakers disseminated knowledge of their judicial experimentation on the U.S. mainland. Lobingier published prolifically on the blending of Spanish and Anglo-American legal systems, including articles in popular journals, and facilitated an English translation of the Siete Partidas. Streams of legal ideas flowing from Europe and America were converging in cosmopolitan Manila, according to the jurist. The discovery of the unappreciated Spaniard was "one of the far-reaching consequences" of the recent war: Americans had as much to gain from Spanish law as the Filipinos from U.S. jurisprudence.[85] Lobingier also corresponded with Chicagoan John Wigmore, dean of Northwestern University School of Law, supplying him with studies of Philippine customary and Chinese family law.[86]

Wigmore was a critical conduit for Manila's legal streams. A former professor at Tokyo's Keio University, he had a special interest in comparative law. Wigmore corresponded with native and U.S. Philippine jurists, encouraged them to publish in journals he edited, and arranged for Filipinos to study law at Northwestern. Attorney General Ignacio Villamor prepared analyses of Philippine crime for his *Illinois Law Journal* and the *Journal of the American Institute of Crime and Criminology*. Wigmore praised Villamor's statistics as far superior to anything published in the United States and a model for American courts. Correspondent George Malcolm, a Philippine Supreme Court justice and University of the Philippines law school dean, documented the ongoing relevance of Spanish, Mohammedan, Roman canon, and Malay customary law in U.S. insular court decisions. Malcolm chastised Wigmore for omitting references to Philippine decisions in his definitive 1904 treatise on evidence; a second edition included decisions for the Philippines, Puerto Rico, Alaska, and the United States Court for China.[87]

MUNICIPAL COURTS

Daniel Burnham turned to his *Plan of Chicago* after completing his 1905 Manila blueprint. City Hall was Chicago's focal point, where Christ was to establish his civic church under a massive dome modeled on Saint Peter's papal basilica. Burnham chaffed at the cumbersome democratic processes that threatened to impede his Chicago plan, unlike its Manila counterpart, which enjoyed the U.S. insular administration's compelling authority. To overcome "rigid constitutional constraints," Burnham argued, a new city charter should endow Chicago with broad powers of local self-government. The Civic Federation's charter bid failed but the 1906 municipal court of Chicago secured far-reaching home rule powers. Three stories of juryless municipal courtrooms dominated Chicago's new city hall, a twin of the Cook County courthouse rather than the papal basilica, with specialized jurisdictions for domestic dependents.[88] The municipal court became the poster child in a national campaign to expand equity's jurisdiction.

Chicago's municipal court took shape amid comparative analyses of city and colonial governance in popular and professional forums nationwide. Discretionary governance was a theme in paired sessions on colonial and municipal administration at the 1904 Louisiana Purchase Exposition in St. Louis, where President Theodore Roosevelt and Secretary of War Taft promoted U.S. expansion with a forty-seven-acre Philippine reservation. Political scientist Paul Reinsch argued that divergence from standards was essential for colonial administration and the governance of racially multiform societies. Jane Addams attributed urban failings to repressive legislation and attempts to govern "multitudes of immigrants" by one set pattern "whether it fits or not."[89] At the exposition's Universal Congress of Lawyers and Jurists, Chicago lawmakers joined with native U.S. insular judges—including Cayetano Arellano—to consider the history and efficacy of various systems of jurisprudence. University of Chicago Law School professor Ernst Freund described the law's evolution as a gradual, covert process that was difficult to trace. Equity and legal fictions, Freund noted, often accomplished silent revolutions.[90]

The University of Chicago encouraged comparative studies within its professionalizing schools of law, political science, and anthropology. Freund—a Goodnow student—shaped the law school's intellectual development, introducing courses on international and administrative law. He also drafted municipal home rule legislation in affiliation with the Civic Federation and Charles Merriam, another Goodnow student and the university's first political science professor. The university appointed a colonial commissioner to the Far East, who completed a comparative study of European and U.S. dependencies, including "institutions of local self-government." The appointment was intended to promote Chicago's advantages for training Asian colonial advisors; a number of Filipino and Chinese students completed graduate studies there. Philippine administrator David Barrows, who studied with Goodnow, Freund, and Chicago anthropologist Frederick Starr, returned to the university in 1902 to plan the Bureau of Non-Christian Tribes and secure workers for its ethnological research.[91]

Comparative sessions on colonial and local administration were featured at the first annual meeting of the American Political Science Association at the University of Chicago in 1904, over which Goodnow presided. Participants struggled to reconcile the decentralization of Spanish colonial rule with the centralization of U.S. insular and municipal administration. Philippine commissioner Bernard Moses championed the Spanish colonial legal order while Leo Rowe—a municipal activist and Puerto Rican insular code commissioner—argued that its deep impress stymied local self-governance. A commentator resolved the divergence: once a state had attained complete political responsibility, citizens need not fear the consolidation of power.[92]

Secretary of War Taft promoted equity in recently acquired U.S. protectorates and mainland courts. He established juryless criminal courts in the Panama Canal Zone that could try U.S. citizens as "the power to do this has been upheld by the Supreme Court in the Philippines."[93] Taft's provisional U.S. government in reoccupied Cuba, where he served briefly as governor, was established on the "novel" legal premise of a trustee administering "the business of his ward."[94] In a 1905 Yale commencement address, Taft argued that jury trials were a "fetish... worshipped without reason" that had outlived their usefulness on the mainland.[95] Criticizing the caveat emptor spirit of the common law, he praised the equity and morality of Spanish civil law. There was "more of paternalism in the civil law—more care for the subject by the government" and greater protection from crime.[96] All American criminal and civil courts should adopt equity procedure "derived from the canon law and ecclesiastical courts," eliminating juries, replacing courtroom testimony with written depositions, and abolishing the right of criminal appeal, leaving only the court's power to pardon.[97] Taft's attack on trial by jury, the *Boston Globe* announced, vindicated fears that colonial rule would subvert constitutional safeguards on the mainland. Although Americans might be indifferent to the denial of due process rights in the Philippines, they would resent any attempt to impair this fundamental liberty on the mainland.[98]

Yet, within six months, Chicago voters approved a municipal court bill that provided for the waiver of "inviolate" state constitutional criminal and civil jury trial rights. Virtually all municipal court cases were heard without a jury, which had to be demanded quickly in writing and paid for in advance at a cost of six dollars; weekly working-class wages were typically five to fifteen dollars.

Chancellor Tuley and two chancery attorneys designed the municipal court to serve the urban poor, replacing justice of the peace courts—a centuries-old English tradition—abolished by the bill.[99] The Civic Federation invoked *miserabiles* to justify the replacement: justice of the peace courts were "a lamentable failure of justice," responsible for the suffering of the "unfortunate portion of the community, the class above all others requiring such protection."[100] The justices hurried through cases, committed blunders, and failed to discriminate "between trivial offenders and confirmed criminals."[101] Tuley's original municipal court plan had included criminal jury trials at state expense, but state legislators unexpectedly waived juries for criminal as well as civil trials. The chancellor voiced regret that he had given time to the cause before he died in late 1905, a month after Chicago's electorate approved the measure.[102]

In addition to juryless proceedings, the municipal court incorporated chancery's administrative structure and discretionary prerogative. A chief justice presided over twenty-eight associate judges and an inquisitorial bureaucracy of bailiffs, clerks, and assistants who investigated cases beyond the courthouse; Cook County chancery masters could supplement their ranks. Tuley's circuit court judicial machinery informed municipal court administration: the chief justice supervised court business, controlled the docket, assigned judges to city branch or county courts as needed, and appointed assistants who held office at his pleasure. Judges were vested with the discretionary authority to establish their own procedural rules "as they may deem necessary or expedient for the proper administration of justice," subject to supreme court review. Chancery jurisdiction was ostensibly limited to equity suits transferred by a Cook County judge, but the municipal court was vested with the power "to prevent commission of crimes," expanding equity's public jurisdiction.[103]

The court's first bench—all but one a Republican—took their 1906 inaugural oaths in a colonial Illinois courthouse, recently exhibited at the Louisiana Purchase Exposition, that had facilitated French, English, and American rule. Chief Justice Harry Olson announced that the municipal court's first object would be equal justice for "poor and ignorant litigants."[104] The city charter bill was defeated the following year by an alliance that included the Democratic Party, the Chicago Federation of Labor, and ethnic organizations under the aegis of the United Societies for Local Self-Government, which espoused an alternative vision of home rule.[105]

Chief Justice Olson associated the municipal court with Taft's judicial vision. In a 1908 letter to Taft, Olson wrote "your recent utterances concerning the need of reforms in the administration of justice lead me to think that you might be interested in the organization of the Municipal Court of Chicago. It is a unique development in the history of American jurisprudence, and we believe was based on many of the ideas to which you have given voice."[106] Taft elaborated his agenda for equitable reform during his 1908 Republican presidential campaign, which convened in Chicago. Cheap and speedy justice was necessary, he declared, to prevent popular protest over inequalities in wealth, emphasizing his concern for the poor man. "We cannot, of course, dispense with the jury system" but every means by which litigants "may be induced voluntarily to avoid the expense, delay, and burden of jury trials ought to be encouraged."[107] Courts should adopt simplified equity procedure and determine their own rules. The Philippine practice of statistical caseload reports could compel judges to quickly clear their dockets. Taft also urged limits on appeals, recalling Spanish procedures that had kept Philippine plaintiffs "stamping in the vestibule of justice until time had made justice impossible."[108] Although some argued that the poor should be allowed appeals to the highest tribunal, in truth, "there is nothing which is so detrimental to the interests of the poor man."[109]

Olson championed the municipal court in scholarly and popular forums. His article "The Proper Organization and Procedure of a Municipal Court" began with Taft's call for the elimination of undue delay. The municipal judges, Olson noted, had adopted Taft's procedural reforms. A *World's Work* article featured the story of a thief arrested at eleven o'clock, tried without a jury, and jailed by noon the same day. Olson was described as the manager of a unique corporate body with "singular and great powers" serviced by nearly 250 bailiffs, clerks, and their assistants. The court was "master of its own rules of practice" and had eliminated superfluous procedural details. Jury trials comprised less than 2 percent of court business, and successful appeals were limited to less than a tenth of 1 percent. To encourage the efficient administration of justice, judges submitted audited monthly caseload reports, which were compiled in annual statistical reports. Abbreviated court records were filed in card catalog drawers. The municipal court, the article concluded, "has made justice cheap, speedy, and final."[110]

Olson's public relations campaign coincided with state reductions of the municipal court's jurisdiction. The transfer of Cook County cases—the only official source of equity suits—was ruled unconstitutional in 1907. The municipal jurisdiction over any crime punishable by both a fine and imprisonment was whittled away in 1908; jurisdiction over petit and grand larceny was eliminated by 1910. Larceny of any amount—even a fifteen dollar petit larceny—was constitutionally defined as an "infamous crime" and required a grand jury indictment as those convicted lost the right to vote, hold public office, or serve as a juror. The municipal court did conduct preliminary investigations for all felonies committed in Chicago but was required to bind them over to the Cook County criminal court for a grand jury indictment and trial. The court's procedural rules were revised by the state supreme court, which held that rules prescribed by the legislature for similar circuit court proceedings were binding.[111]

The municipal justices relied on probation to enhance their narrowing authority. Despite probation's limited statutory basis for adult offenders, it had been practiced irregularly for decades in Chicago and beyond. In 1884 Chancellor Tuley observed that he differed "with all, or nearly all of the judges" on the Cook County bench and beyond who exercised the prerogative to suspend criminal sentences when they believed circumstances merited intervention.[112] In 1917 it was revealed that federal judges nationwide had been equitably suspending criminal sentences since the 1860s—based on claims of benefit of clergy—leading to a presidential proclamation pardoning five thousand persons, one of the largest wholesale acts of clemency in the United States.[113]

Municipal Court judge McKenzie Cleland, a devout Moody Bible Institute trustee and a former Civic Federation attorney, made extensive use of probation to augment a religious mission to the poor before it was statutorily approved. The Moody Bible Institute, at the vanguard of the emerging fundamentalist movement, trained "gap-men" to stand between the laity and the ministry, committed to living and declaring the word of God. Cleland played a prominent role in a massive religious revival that coincided with the municipal court's opening, presiding at a lawyers' night service together with seventeen other judges. Continuing the revival in his courtroom as a "new gospel in criminology," Cleland invited ministers and temperance advocates to share his bench, and Sunday school students to observe the proceedings. Imposing a criminal sentence on offenders—who typically lacked legal representation—Cleland then vacated his judgment, ordering them to stay sober, support their families, and report to evening "family receptions" under threat of a heavy fine or imprisonment. When an Illinois Supreme Court justice questioned the legality of Cleland's public and pervasive use of probation—involving 1,200 defendants in a single year—he was relegated to a civil jurisdiction.[114]

The municipal bench turned to statutory initiatives following the Cleland controversy, blending judicial, executive, and legislative powers. The justices penned a successful law to legalize probation that bore a marked resemblance to Cleland's practices. They also invaded equity's domestic jurisdiction, criminalizing men who failed to adequately support their families. Olson drafted unsuccessful state bills in 1909, 1913, and 1914 to abolish the requirement for grand jury indictments in all criminal prosecutions other than treason or murder. He drafted a bill to raise the jury fee in 1914, explaining to a fellow jurist that it was necessary to keep this fee high "to discourage demands for jury trial."[115] The court was much more capable of judging the credibility of a witness than a jury, he explained, and "the few cases tried by a jury accounts for the capacity and vast volume of business in our court."[116]

The protection of domestic dependents proved the most potent device for expanding the municipal court's jurisdiction. Turning the tables on traditional probate courts, women assumed primary responsibility for investigating men in a 1911 Court of Domestic Relations, dedicated to adjudicating wrongs against women and children. Jane Addams and Hull House activists organized as the Juvenile Protective Agency convinced Chief Justice Olson to create the tribunal by deploying his discretionary power to establish branch courts. Specialized jurisdictions for prostitutes and young adult males followed. Olson described the domestic tribunals as a unified system for investigating families. "The father and mother appear in the Court of Domestic Relations; the boy in the Boys' Court and the girl in the Morals Court. Often one family is represented in all three courts . . . in the city hall." Those of Black or foreign parentage were far more likely to be prosecuted in the domestic courts than their white native-born neighbors.[117]

Women managed the day-to-day business of Chicago's domestic courts, building on the model of a chancery master. Serving as salaried court personnel and voluntary "protective officers," they fanned out over the metropolis to inspect working-class homes and communities. Taking the inquisitorial process to a new level, they referred litigants for medical and psychological examinations in a municipal psychopathic laboratory, established by a Juvenile Protective Agency activist. When a suspected feebleminded person was charged with a felony, a municipal judge could file a continuance to keep the case in his jurisdiction rather than turning it over to Cook County. Allegations of mental deficiency maintained a high defendant volume in the domestic courts. Approximately a thousand new inmates were committed each year to state institutions for the insane or feebleminded to prevent future crime, even absent a conviction. The domestic courts also administered support payments to wives and children lacking the protection of a *paterfamilias*, expanding probate's traditional role regulating familial affairs.[118]

Chief Justice Olson and Northwestern dean John Wigmore were key directors and financial sponsors of the Chicago-based American Judicature Society, which generated publicity to "fire up" jurists, legislators, and the American public in support of procedural reforms advocated by President Taft and the

ABA. Taft argued that the best hope for revamping American courts was "to empower the Supreme Court to do it through the medium of the rules of the court, as in equity" and urged Congress to act on 1910 ABA-drafted judicial reform legislation.[119] Popular education was considered key to the ABA campaign to "free" the people from "legislative domination" and common-law procedure. Between Taft's 1912 White House departure and 1921 Supreme Court arrival, he spearheaded annual ABA congressional initiatives to vest courts with the power to determine their own procedural rules. Such a reform, he argued, was "vindicated by the example of the Municipal Court of Chicago."[120] Taft served on the advisory council of the American Judicature Society, which reviewed model acts for municipal and state courts. Some forty cities revamped their court systems according to the Chicago plan.[121]

Congress vested the Supreme Court with extensive administrative powers following Taft's 1921 appointment as chief justice, approving a 1922 bill that Taft shaped and pressed on the Senate Judiciary Committee. Reprising his role as head of Manila's *audiencia*, Taft assumed executive control of the entire federal judiciary, transforming the role of chief justice. Recreating his Philippine Bureau of Justice, a judicial council was established to administer lower court officials, collect judicial statistics, and consider further reforms. The chief justice presided over the council—known as the Conference of Senior Circuit Judges—and could assign or transfer federal judges nationwide to facilitate the administration of justice. Federal judges protested the loss of their authority, leveling charges of "a dictatorial power over the courts unrecognized in our jurisprudence." Taft continuously lobbied Congress to enhance the Court's authority as chief justice, acknowledging that his legislative role was a violation of separation of powers precedent.[122] Nevertheless, his quest to establish uniform procedural rules "as in equity" proved elusive. Congress withheld this power until 1938, four years after Taft's death.

A Chicago treatise explicating the 1938 Federal Rules of Civil Procedure noted the rules would be familiar to many bar members, being substantially those urged by Taft and the ABA for over twenty years. Chicagoan Edgar Tolman, a former federal chancery master, prepared a final draft of the rules for the Supreme Court. Jury trial rights were preserved in cases historically tried at common law, but only if demanded quickly and in writing. Stephen Subrin has noted that the underlying philosophy of the rules and the procedural choices they embodied were almost universally drawn from equity rather than the common law. Approximately half of the states adopted almost identical rules; the remainder bears their impress.[123]

CONCLUSIONS

"The administration of colonial possessions has in due time affected the legislation, the morals, the tendencies and the character of every nation owning them," observed U.S. colonial advisor and Chicago home rule activist Henry Morris in December 1906 as the municipal court opened for business.[124] Could the United States, "lately undertaking similar enterprises, however disguised in name, claim to be exempt from the rule?"[125] Insular litigation would spur interest in alien legal precedent, he surmised, as the East became the new West. U.S. jurisprudence would acquire "a stronger tinge of Spanish law" and courts would "draw their doctrines from the broader principles of fundamental equity which partake of an international character."[126] The "control of dependencies" was working innumerable changes in the national fabric that called for careful study. Far from detrimental, such changes would "inevitably impress us with a more liberal conception of our duties as a nation."[127]

Morris captured the nesting of metropolitan state building at home and abroad. Progressive home rulers drew deeply on equity's fundamental principles, administrative structure, and prerogative power as they simultaneously revamped insular and municipal governance. Equity's metropolitan authority—Christian, imperial, and constitutional—facilitated an expansion of its criminal jurisdiction, enhancing the discretionary power and infrastructural reach of state officials. The court's machinery provided a time-tested model for the administration of semi-sovereign populations and a capacious bureaucracy in which women and Filipinos gained state purchase. The prerogative to experiment with alternative Spanish and Anglo-American legal remedies contributed to equity's gradual and covert transformation of the national fabric, which has extended across two centuries.

Equity's elusiveness is a measure, in part, of its present-day ubiquity. Equitable remedies are now ordinary rather than extraordinary in vast areas of American law, and discretion pervades the U.S. justice system. Jury trial rights remain enshrined in state and federal constitutions, but their applicability is a complex equation, and trials themselves are vanishing. Less than 3 percent of criminal and civil cases proceed to jury trial. Most criminal cases are settled by discretionary plea bargaining; in the remainder, constitutional jury trial rights are applicable in "serious" offenses with potential sentences exceeding six months. In civil cases, federal jury trial rights are limited to suits that would have been tried at common law in 1791; state provisions are variable. Progressive efforts to "voluntarily induce" litigants to forego jury trial should also be considered in the context of the huge jurisdiction committed to burgeoning administrative agencies, which explicitly adopted equity procedure.[128] We no longer recognize equity because we cannot differentiate it from the everyday business of American governance.

Equity's obscurity is also a function of its troubling implications in a nation ideologically committed to a rule of law that privileges the law's letter. U.S. legal historians often remind me that equity is a "bad court." The accolades to equity presented here are those of historical actors, not my own, and the court's positive or negative impact on the U.S. justice system is beyond the scope of this essay. Equity is a constitutionally vested cornerstone of American governance that has provided a mechanism for maintaining a system of differential legal rights. It has also been a powerful device for addressing legal disparities. Following on the heels of the 1938 Federal Rules of Civil Procedure, courts invoked equity as they decreed the recognition of indigenous claims, the desegregation of public schools, and the protection of civil rights.[129] Equitable courts have historically empowered those in its bureaucratic ranks—including women and colonial subjects—as well as the chancellor on its bench. Human empowerment is the ultimate expression of local self-governance. Equity's paradoxical potential, its troubling and beneficial consequences for human liberty, is finally that of human nature.

NOTES

1. Senate, "Report of 1st Philippine Commission (Schurman)," 3885-1 S. Doc. 138, sess. 56-1 (1900), 4; House, "Public Laws Passed by Philippine Commission," 4278 H. Doc. 2/10, sess. 57-1 (1901), 6.
2. House, "Report of Philippine Commission," 4276 H. Doc. 2/8, sess. 57-1 (1901), 89; William H. Taft, "The Administration of Criminal Law," *Yale Law Journal* 15 (1905): 1.
3. House, "Jury Rights Denied in Philippine Island and Hawaii—Slavery in Both Territories," appendix to Cong. Rec. 35/8, sess. 57-1 (1902), 35.
4. "Home Rule Is Attacked," *Chicago Tribune* (hereafter, *CT*), March 19, 1899, A6; "Move for Town Consolidation," *CT*, June 2, 1900, 9; Murray F. Tuley, *McKinley and the Philippines: Imperialism* (Chicago: Iroquois Club, 1900); and Roscoe Pound, "The Organization of Courts," *Journal of the American Judicature Society* 11 (1927): 80.
5. U.S. state and territorial chanceries as well as equitable probate, surrogate, and orphans' courts held jurisdiction over domestic relations. Tapping Reeve, *The Law of Baron and Femme; of Parent and Child; of Guardian and Ward; of Master and Servant; and of the Powers of Courts of Chancery* (New Haven, Conn.: Oliver Steele,

1816); and Walter C. Tiffany, *Handbook on the Law of Persons and Domestic Relations* (St. Paul, Minn.: West, 1896). Extraterritorial equity included consular and international "mixed" tribunals and the U.S. Court for China. "An Act to Carry into Effect Provisions of the Treaties Between the United States, China, Japan, Siam, Persia, and other Countries," 12 Stat. 72 (1860); Tahirih V. Lee, "The United States Court for China: A Triumph of Local Law," *Buffalo Law Review* 52 (2004): 923–1075; and William J. Novak, "Police Power and the Hidden Transformation of the American State," in *Police and the Liberal State*, ed. Markus D. Dubber and Mariana Valverde (Stanford, Calif.: Stanford University Press, 2008), 55.

6. U.S. Constitution, Article III, Section 2. The historical literature on English equity is voluminous, but its U.S. counterpart is decidedly less well known. There are general studies of equity jurisprudence, e.g., Peter Charles Hoffer, *The Law's Conscience: Equitable Constitutionalism in America* (Chapel Hill: University of North Carolina Press, 1990); and Amalia D. Kessler, *Inventing American Exceptionalism: The Origins of American Adversarial Legal Culture, 1800–1877* (New Haven, Conn.: Yale University Press, 2017); equity in American colonies and territories, e.g., Stanley N. Katz, "The Politics of Law in Colonial America: Controversies over Chancery Courts and Equity Law in the Eighteenth Century," in *Law in American History*, ed. Donald Fleming and Bernard Bailyn, 257–84 (Boston: Little, Brown, 1971); and William Wirt Blume, "Chancery Practice on the American Frontier: A Study of the Records of the Supreme Court of Michigan Territory, 1805–1836," *Michigan Law Review* 59 (1960): 49–96; nineteenth-century code reforms that merged law and equity, e.g., Morton J. Horwitz, *The Transformation of American Law 1780–1860* (Cambridge, Mass.: Harvard University Press, 1977); equity and labor disputes, e.g., William E. Forbath, *Law and the Shaping of the American Labor Movement* (Cambridge, Mass.: Harvard University Press, 1991); and the equitable underpinnings of twentieth-century civil procedure, e.g., Stephen N. Subrin, "How Equity Conquered Common Law: The Federal Rules of Civil Procedure in Historical Perspective," *University of Pennsylvania Law Review* 135 (1987): 909–1002; and Douglas Laycock, "The Triumph of Equity," *Law and Contemporary Problems* 56 (1993): 53–82. Only Delaware's chancery appears to have been documented as a distinctive U.S. state jurisdiction: William T. Summer Quillen, "Constitutional Equity and the Innovative Tradition," *Law and Contemporary Problems* 56 (1993): 29–52.

7. Horwitz, *The Transformation of American Law 1780–1860*, 265; and Morton J. Horwitz, *The Transformation of American Law 1870–1960* (New York: Oxford University Press, 1992), 17; Subrin, "How Equity Conquered," 910–13, 922; Laycock, "Triumph of Equity," 53; and John H. Langbein, Renée Lettow Lerner, and Bruce P. Smith, *History of the Common Law: The Development of Anglo-American Legal Institutions* (New York: Aspen, 2009), 390.

8. David J. Barron, "Reclaiming Home Rule," *Harvard Law Review* 116 (2003): 2261; William Blackstone, *Commentaries on the Laws of England*, 2 vols. (Chicago: Callaghan, 1884), 1:303.

9. Equity has deep Greco-Roman and Judeo-Christian roots; most scholars agree that Roman canonical precedent informs Anglo-American courts of chancery.

Kessler, *Inventing American Exceptionalism*, 24. See also Timothy S. Haskett, "The Medieval English Court of Chancery," *Law and History Review* 14 (1996): 245–313. Aquinas references *epieikeia*, which he explicitly equates with equity: "Epieikeia—we call it equity." Thomas Aquinas, *Summa theologiae*, II-II, q. 120, a. 1, in vol. 41, ed. Thomas Gilby (Cambridge: Blackfriars, 1972); R. H. Helmholz, *The Spirit of Classical Canon Law* (Athens: University of Georgia Press, 1996), 120, 129; Maria Drakopoulou, "Law and the Sacred: Equity, Conscience and the Art of Judgment as Ius Aequi et Boni," *Law/Text/Culture* 5 (2000): 350; Reginald L. Poole, *Lectures on the History of the Papal Chancery Down to the Time of Innocent III* (Cambridge: Cambridge University Press, 1915), 2; Joseph R. Strayer, *On the Medieval Origins of the Modern State* (Princeton, N.J.: Princeton University Press, 1970), 34; Woodrow Borah, *Justice by Insurance: The General Indian Court of Colonial Mexico and the Legal Aides of the Half-Real* (Berkeley: University of California Press, 1983), 11; and George B. Curtis, "The Checkered Career of *Parens Patriae*: The State as Parent or Tyrant?" *DePaul Law Review* 25 (1976): 895–915.

10. Charles H. Cunningham, *The Audiencia in the Spanish Colonies as Illustrated by the Audiencia of Manila (1583–1800)* (Berkeley: University of California Press, 1919). The linkage between trial and jury was so tight that there was no such thing as a nonjury trial at common law until the later nineteenth century. John H. Langbein, "The Disappearance of Civil Trial in the United States," *Yale Law Journal* 122 (2012): 527. Chancery could order a jury to try "feigned issues" but was not bound by its decision. Sabin D. Puterbaugh, *Puterbaugh's Chancery Pleading and Practice* (Chicago: Callaghan, 1888), 238–41; and William H. Taft, "Recent Criticism of the Federal Judiciary," *Annual Report of the American Bar Association* 18 (1895): 248.

11. Murray F. Tuley, "Equity Maxims," *Chicago Legal News* (hereafter, *CLN*) 35 (1903): 437–38, citing John Norton Pomeroy, *A Treatise on Equity Jurisprudence, as Administered in the United States of America*, 3 vols. (San Francisco: A. L. Bancroft, 1881), 1:468.

12. Carl Schmitt, *Political Theology*, tr. George Schwab (Chicago: University of Chicago Press, 1985), 5; see also Vicente L. Rafael, "The Afterlife of Empire: Sovereignty and Revolution in the Philippines," in *Colonial Crucible: Empire in the Making of the Modern American State*, ed. Alfred W. McCoy and Francisco A. Scarano (Madison: University of Wisconsin Press, 2009), 342.

13. House, 4278 H. Doc. 2/10, 10.

14. The nineteenth-century court was renamed *audiencia territorial*. Corazon L. Paras, Oscar L. Paras Jr. and Ma. Corazon P. Villanueva, *The Chief Justices of the Supreme Court of the Philippines. An Update* (Queson City, Philippines: Giraffe Books, 2008), 13; and Cunningham, *Audiencia in the Spanish Colonies*. See also Borah, *Justice by Insurance*; and Brian P. Owensby, *Empire of Law and Indian Justice in Colonial Mexico* (Stanford, Calif.: Stanford University Press, 2008).

15. Edward Judson Hill, *Chancery Jurisdiction and Practice* (Chicago: E. B. Myers, 1873), 5. The chancellor exercised a criminal jurisdiction in chancery and as a member of the King's Council in the Court of Star Chamber until 1645. George Spence, *The Equitable Jurisdiction of the Court of Chancery*, 2 vols. (Philadelphia: Lea and

Blanchard, 1846–1850), 1:349–50; and Edwin S. Mack, "The Revival of Criminal Equity," *Harvard Law Review* 16 (1903): 390–403.

16. I am indebted to Bill Novak for his invaluable research on equity's early public domain: William J. Novak, "Enjoining Immorality: Considerations of Justice and Public Policy," unpublished manuscript in author's possession, 1985, 14. Joseph Story was an early facilitator of equity's criminal revival in *Commentaries on Equity Jurisprudence: as Administered in England and America*, 2 vols. (Boston: Hillard, Gray, 1836), 1:261, 273. See also *Hamilton v. Whitridge* 11 Md. 1128 (1857). For Chicago and the labor movement, see *Secor v. Toledo*, 21 F. Cas. 968 (1877); Taft, "Recent Criticism," 237–74; and Forbath, *Law and the Shaping of the American Labor Movement*.

17. Christina Duffy Burnett and Burke Marshall, eds. *Foreign in a Domestic Sense: Puerto Rico, American Expansion, and the Constitution* (Durham, N.C.: Duke University Press, 2001); Bartholomew H. Sparrow, *The Insular Cases and the Emergence of American Empire* (Lawrence: University Press Kansas, 2006); Peter G. Fish, "William Howard Taft and Charles Evans Hughes: Conservative Politicians as Chief Judicial Reformers," *Supreme Court Review* (1975): 123–45; Robert C. Post, "Judicial Management: The Achievements of Chief Justice William Howard Taft," *OAH Magazine of History* 13 (1998): 24–29; Michael Willrich, *City of Courts: Socializing Justice in Progressive Era Chicago* (Cambridge: Cambridge University Press, 2003); and David S. Tanenhaus, *Juvenile Justice in the Making* (Oxford: Oxford University Press, 2004).

18. In 1900 Chicago, 80 percent of residents were born abroad or children of immigrants. Walter Nugent, "Demography," *Electronic Encyclopedia of Chicago*, Chicago Historical Society, 2005, http://www.encyclopedia.chicagohistory.org/pages/962.html. For Philippine diversity, see Jacob G. Schurman, "The Philippines," *Yale Law Journal* 9 (1900): 216.

19. Frank J. Goodnow, "Municipal Home Rule," *Political Science Quarterly* 21 (1906): 82. On Goodnow as the "father" of the American administration, see Michael Tolley, "Goodnow, Frank Johnson," *American National Biography Online*, Oxford University Press, 2000, https://doi.org/10.1093/anb/9780198606697.article.1400233.

20. Frank J. Goodnow, "Municipal Home Rule," *Political Science Quarterly* 21 (1906): 77–90; and Frank J. Goodnow, "Municipal Home Rule," *Political Science Quarterly* 10 (1895): 1–21. See also "Home Influences," *Monthly Religious Magazine* 27 (1862): 341 and "Home Rule," *OED Online*, Oxford University Press, 2011, www.oed.com/view/Entry/87930.

21. Mary Bartelme, "The Opportunity for Women in Court Administration," *Annals of the American Academy of Political and Social Science* 52 (1914): 189. New York City's 1900 judiciary was likely larger than Chicago's, but state codes limited equity's development as a distinctive jurisdiction.

22. Equity took jurisdiction over married women's property, contracts, marital disputes, divorce, and nonsupport. Marylynn Salmon, *Women and the Law of Property in Early America* (Chapel Hill: University of North Carolina Press, 1986), 11–14; and Tiffany, *Handbook on the Law of Persons*, 6, 40, 85, 100–107. Equity jurisdictions were ubiquitous in southern slave states: Charles M. Hepburn, *The Historical Development of Code Pleading in America and England* (Cincinnati: W. H. Anderson, 1897), 15, 151; Henry H. Ingersoll, "Confusion of Law and Equity,"

Yale Law Journal 21 (1911): 58–71. See also *Keeton v. Spradling*, 13 Mo. 321 (1850); *Peter v. King*, 13 Mo. 143 (1850); *Bennett v. Butterworth*, 52 U.S. 669 (1851); *Hunt v. White*, 24 Tex. 643 (1860); and *Sanders v. Devereux*, 25 Tex. 1 (1860). Slaves and free blacks regularly petitioned equitable courts, initiating approximately 18 percent of a sample of over fourteen thousand petitions filed in southern county courts prior to the Civil War. Equity had jurisdiction over manumission by will and Southern free blacks, who were required to secure a white guardian: Loren Schweninger, ed., *The Southern Debate over Slavery*, 2 vols. (Urbana: University of Illinois Press, 2008), 2:2–4, 6, 30; *Seekright v. Carrington*, 1 Va. 45 (1791); *Wade v. American Colonization Society*, 15 Miss. 663 (1846); *Cooper v. Blakey*, 10 Ga. 263 (1851); and *Campbell v. Campbell*, 13 Ark. 513 (1853). Native American equity suits: *Laguna v. Acoma*, 1 N.M. 220 (1857); *Victor de la O v. Acoma*, 1 N.M. 226 (1857); and *Sloan v. United States*, 95 F. 193 (1899). Extraterritorial equity: "Provisions of the Treaties," 12 Stat. 72, 72–79; "An Act Creating a United States Court for China," 34 Stat. 814 (1906); and Teemu Ruskola, "Colonialism Without Colonies: On the Extraterritorial Jurisprudence of the U.S. Court for China," *Law & Contemporary Problems* 71 (2008): 219.

23. The 1787 Northwest Ordinance proclaimed that trial by jury would "forever remain unalterable"; judges were "clothed with a common-law jurisdiction... restrictive of any powers in equity." Arthur St. Clair, *The St. Clair Papers*, ed. William Henry Smith, 2 vols (Cincinnati: Robert Clarke, 1882), 2:69–76. Nevertheless, equity powers were quickly secured in 1788 probate courts, 1795 orphan courts, and an 1805 chancery. Theodore Calvin Pease, ed., *The Laws of the Northwest Territory 1788–1800* (Springfield: Illinois State Historical Library, 1925), 9, 181; and Frances S. Philbrick, ed., *The Laws of Indiana Territory 1801–1809* (Springfield: Illinois State Historical Library, 1930), xvi, clxvi–clxvii, ccxxxvii, 108, 137, 307. If these courts proved inadequate, higher equity jurisdictions could be petitioned for relief. Reeve, *Law of Baron and Femme*, 317; Charles C. Bonney, "The Powers of Non-Resident Guardians, and Incidentally the Authority of the Probate Court," *CLN* 1 (1868), 102; and Tiffany, *Handbook on the Law of Persons*, 300–303. For undue religious influence, see *Stevenson v. Dowie*, 3 Ill. C.C. 135 (1901).

24. John Willard, *A Treatise on Equity Jurisprudence* (New York: Banks, 1875), 805. The extent to which common law and equity were fused remains open to question. Gunther A. Weiss, "The Enchantment of Codification in the Common-Law World," *Yale Journal of International Law* 25 (2000): 505. In New York, Willard noted that "the continuance of equity as a distinct branch of jurisprudence... [has] been repeatedly recognized by the courts," in *A Treatise on Equity Jurisprudence*, 10. See also John Norton Pomeroy, *The "Civil Code" in California* (New York: Bar Association, 1885), 6, 57, 62. Territorial legislatures were denied the power to abolish equity jurisdictions in *Dunphy v. Kleinsmith*, 78 U.S. 610 (1871) and *Stevens v. Baker*, 1 Wash. Terr. 315 (1871).

25. "An Act to Regulate the Practice in Courts of Chancery," *Revised Statutes of the State of Illinois* (hereafter, *Revised Statutes*), ed. Harvey B. Hurd (Chicago: Chicago Legal News, 1904), §22.1, p. 225; and *Mahar v. O'Hara*, 9 Ill. 424 (1847). Illinois State Bar Association, "Report of Special Committee on Masters in Chancery," *CLN* 47 (1915): 579.

26. In 1900 Chicago, equity jurisdictions were vested in state circuit and superior court chanceries, state probate courts, a county court, a special state arbitration forum, and federal district and circuit courts. For the English court, see Spence, *Equitable Jurisdiction*; for ecclesiastical precedents, Harold J. Berman, *Law and Revolution [I]: The Formation of the Western Legal Tradition* (Cambridge, Mass.: Harvard University Press, 1983), 225–26.
27. Bonney, "Powers of Non-Resident Guardians," 102. From 1877 to 1900, when the Cook County bench more than doubled to twenty-eight judges, only two federal judges handled the business of Chicago's U.S. circuit and district courts, which included crowded common-law, equity, admiralty, and appellate dockets in a three-state district. As one judge had poor health and bad eyesight, almost the entire business of the federal courts devolved on a single judge for ten of those years. John M. Palmer, *The Bench and Bar of Illinois* (Chicago: Lewis, 1899), 248.
28. Tuley was elected to the Cook County Circuit Court in 1879; he served as chief justice from 1885 to 1905. Palmer *Bar and Bench*, 256–58; "A New Chief Justice," *CT* November 30, 1885, 7; and Jane Addams, *The Excellent Becomes the Permanent* (New York: Macmillan, 1932), 73–80. For the impact of his decisions, see the volume 1 preface in *Illinois Circuit Court Reports*, ed. Francis E. Matthews and Hal Crumpton Bangs, 3 vols. (Chicago: T. H. Flood, 1907–1909).
29. Chancellorships were honorary; by law, no judge held authority over another. Tuley assigned circuit and superior court judges to criminal, appellate, chancery, and common law courts. "Will Be Chancellor," *CT* October 6, 1893, 1; "To Thwart Judge Tuthill," *CT* October 8, 1893, 5; "In a Justice Shop," *CT* March 18, 1894, 36; "Busy Day for the Judges," *CT* July 6, 1903, 7; and "Judge Tuley Memorial Services," *CLN* 38 (1906):177–9.
30. John Greene Henderson, *Chancery Practice with Especial Reference to the Office and Duties of Masters in Chancery* (Chicago: T. H. Flood, 1904), 556–62; Illinois State Bar Association, "Masters in Chancery," 579–82, 584–86; *Buda v. Columbian*, 1 Ill. C.C. 398 (1903); Henderson, *Chancery Practice*, 242–47; Hill, *Chancery Jurisdiction*, 230; *Glover v. Couch*, master's report in Circuit Court of Cook County case 43233 (1884). "Of Judicial and Execution Sales," *Chicago Bench and Bar* 3 (1873): 97–120; "The Naturalization of a Russian," *CT* November 17, 1888, 3; and "Caught in the Act," *CT*, October 30, 1894, 1.
31. Pomeroy, *Treatise on Equity*, 1:48, see also 1:45–47, 53–57.
32. Tuley, "Equity Maxims," 438.
33. Tuley, "Equity Maxims," 436–38.
34. Hill, *Chancery Jurisdiction*, 3.
35. Tuley, "Equity Maxims," 430.
36. Puterbaugh, *Chancery Pleading*, 53, 62. Labor strikes commonly involved criminal contempt for violating injunctions. Mack, "Criminal Equity"; Forbath, *Law and the Shaping of the American Labor Movement*; and "Courts of Chancery," *Revised Statutes* (1904), §22.2.
37. Tuley, "Equity Maxims," 427, 436–48; and *Kehoe v Kehoe*, 1 Ill. C.C. 164 (1883).
38. "Law Made by Man, For Man," *CLN* 1 (1869): 220; "Habitual Drunkards," *CLN* 1 (1869): 246; Mary Ann Mason, *From Father's Property to Children's Rights* (New

York: Columbia University Press, 1994), 64–68; and Bonney, "Powers of Non-Resident Guardians," 102.

39. County Court of Cook County cases: *Estate of Harriet Spoffard*, 4-7043 (1888–1912); *Estate of Charles Weiman*, 4-180 (1872); and *Estate of Matthew Wells*, 2-180 (1872). Probate Court of Cook County cases: *Lester Thorn*, 5-7070 (1900); *Daniel O'Day*, 5-7070 (1900); *Anton Barthelmes*, 4-7070 (1900–1903); *Emily Gnadt*, 9-7042 (1900–1913); and *Hilda Lichthardt*, 2-7070 (1898–1911). See also "The Norton-Clark Case" *CT* October 30, 1866, 4; and "The Clark-Norton Case," *CT* December 2, 1866, 4.

40. "Habitual Drunkards," *CLN*, 246; Mary Bartelme, "Spendthrift Trusts," *Albany Law Journal* 50 (1894): 10; Elizabeth P. W. Packard, *The Prisoners' Hidden Life, or Insane Asylums Unveiled* (Chicago: printed by the author, 1868); Hendrik Hartog, "Mrs. Packard on Dependency," *Yale Journal of Law & the Humanities* 1 (1988): 79–103; and Puterbaugh, *Chancery Pleading*, 238.

41. Virginia G. Drachman, *Women Lawyers and the Origins of Professional Identity in America: The Letters of the Equity Club, 1887–1890* (Ann Arbor: University of Michigan Press, 1993), 15.

42. Lettie Lavilla Burlingame, *Lettie Lavilla Burlingame: Her Life Pages, Stories, Poems and Essays* (Joliet, Ill.: J. E. Williams, 1895), 315.

43. Drachman, *Women Lawyers*, 259; and James B. Bradwell, "Women Lawyers of Illinois," *CLN* 32 (1900), 341.

44. Lelia Josephine Robinson, *The Law of Husband and Wife* (Boston: Lee and Shepard, 1889); Mary A. Greene, *The Woman's Manual of Law* (New York: Silver, Burdett, 1902); "Day Law Class for Women," *CLN* 39 (1906), 91; Drachman, *Women Lawyers*, 153, 170, 211, 229, 235, 241, 249, 251-254, 259; Rima Lunin Schultz and Adele Hast, ed., *Women Building Chicago 1790–1990* (Bloomington: Indiana University Press, 2001), 537, 560, 922; and Frances E. Willard, *Home Protection Manual* (New York: Independent, 1879).

45. *Hamilton v. Whitridge*.

46. *Mugler v. Kansas*, 123 U.S. 623 (1887). For equity's criminal jurisdiction in the abatement of nuisances see Mack, "Criminal Equity," 390–403; Henry Schofield, "Equity Jurisdiction to Abate and Enjoin Illegal Saloons as Public Nuisances," *Illinois Law Review* 8 (1913): 19–41; Novak, "Enjoining Immorality." For morals and labor, see *Hamilton v. Whitridge*; *Secor v. Toledo*; Forbath, *Law and the Shaping of the American Labor Movement*; Samuel W. Packard, correspondence concerning *Mugler v. Kansas*, 123 U.S. 623 (1887), Walter Eugene Packard Papers, ctn.12, Bancroft Library, University of California, Berkeley; and Samuel W. Packard, introduction to *The Great Prohibition Decision* (New York: Funk & Wagnalls, 1888).

47. For justice of the peace courts, see Willrich, *City of Courts*, 3–28. For Jane Addams and Hull House, see Jane Addams, *My Friend Julia Lathrop* (1935; repr. Urbana: University of Illinois Press, 2004), x–xiii, 83; Sophonisba P. Breckinridge and Edith Abbott, *The Delinquent Child and the Home* (New York: Charities Publication Committee, 1912), 1–4, 55–57; and Elizabeth J. Clapp, *Mothers of All Children: Women Reformers and the Rise of Juvenile Courts in Progressive Era America* (University Park: Pennsylvania State University Press, 1998).

48. The chancellor's groundbreaking 1887 "Tuley Law" provided for voluntary summary adjudication of "any matter in controversy" by a judge. Addams, *Excellent Becomes the Permanent*, 73–80; "An Act to Enable Parties to Avoid Delay in the Administration of Justice," *Revised Statutes* (1904), §100.1; and Andrew Wender Cohen, *The Racketeer's Progress: Chicago and the Struggle for the Modern American Economy, 1900–1940* (Cambridge: Cambridge University Press, 2004), 150–151. Addams served with Tuley on labor arbitration tribunals created under the act: "Arbitration Bill in Disfavor," *CT* February 28, 1891, 3; "Judge Tuley on the Wrong Side," *CT* September 4, 1894, 6; and "Tailors End Their War," *CT* February 1, 1903, 7.
49. Breckinridge and Abbott, *Delinquent Child*, 4; Tanenhaus, *Juvenile Justice*, 4–13; Clapp, *Mothers of All*, 35–45, 64–67; and Addams, *Excellent Becomes the Permanent*, xxi, 83. For probation's evolution see Joseph Chitty, *A Practical Treatise on the Criminal Law*, 4 vols. (London: A. J. Valpy, 1816), 1:667–694; *People ex rel. Forsyth v. Monroe County*, 141 N.Y. 288 (1894); *People ex rel. Boenert v. Barrett* 202 Ill. 287 (1903); Frank W. Grinnell, "The Common Law History of Probation: An Illustration of the 'Equitable Growth' of Criminal Law," *Journal of Criminal Law and Criminology* 32 (1941): 15–34; and Tanenhaus, *Juvenile Justice*, viii, 11, 17.
50. Addams, My Friend Julia Lathrop, 96.
51. Julian W. Mack, appendix to Breckinridge and Abbott, *Delinquent Child*, 189.
52. Julian W. Mack, "The Juvenile Court," *Harvard Law Review* 23 (1909): 118, 120.
53. Cecil Leeson, *The Probation System* (London: P. S. King, 1914), 14.
54. Leeson, *Probation System*, 12; italics original. *In loco parentis* denotes in the place or position of a parent. See also Timothy D. Hurley, ed., *Origin of the Illinois Juvenile Court Law* (Chicago: Visitation and Aid Society, 1907); and *In re Gault* 387 U.S. 1 (1967), holding that the Fourteenth Amendment's Due Process Clause applies to juvenile as well as adult defendants.
55. William T. Stead, *If Christ Came to Chicago!* (Chicago: Laird & Lee, 1894), 422.
56. Frederic C. Howe, *The City: The Hope of Democracy* (New York: Charles Scribner's, 1914), 300; William T. Stead, "The Civic Church," in *The World's Parliament of Religions*, ed. John Henry Barrows, 2 vols. (Chicago: Parliament, 1893), 2:1209–15; Joseph O. Baylen, "A Victorian's 'Crusade' in Chicago, 1893–1894," *Journal of American History* 51 (1964): 418–34; and Joseph O. Baylen, "Stead, William Thomas," *Oxford Dictionary of National Biography*, Oxford University Press, 2010, https://doi.org/10.1093/ref:odnb/36258.
57. House, "Report of the Philippine Commission," 4951 H. Doc. 2, sess. 59-1 (1905), 632.
58. House, "Report of the Philippine Commission"; Thomas S. Hines, "The Imperial Façade: Daniel H. Burnham and American Architectural Planning in the Philippines," *Pacific Historical Review* 41 (1972): 35; Bernard Moses, *The Establishment of Spanish Rule in America* (New York: G. P. Putnam, 1898), 17, 69; House, 4278 H. Doc. 2/10, 6; Anna Leah Fidelis T. Castañeda, "Spanish Structure, American Theory: The Legal Foundations of a Tropical New Deal in the Philippine Islands, 1898–1935," in *Colonial Crucible: Empire in the Making of the Modern American*

59. Bernard Moses, "Colonial Policy with Reference to the Philippines," *Proceedings of the American Political Science Association* (hereafter, *APSA*) 1 (1904): 90. See also Lebbeus R. Wilfley, "The New Philippine Judiciary," *Ohio Law Bulletin* 49 (1904): 407.
60. Moses, "Colonial Policy," 100.
61. Moses, "Colonial Policy," 94–95.
62. Charles Sumner Lobingier, "A Spanish Object-Lesson in Code-Making," *Yale Law Journal* 16 (1907): 416.
63. Charles Sumner Lobingier, "Blending Legal Systems in the Philippines," *American Review of Reviews* 32 (1905): 336.
64. Charles Sumner Lobingier, "Las Siete Partidas and its Predecessors," *California Law Review* 1 (1913): 495. See also Charles Sumner Lobingier, "Civil Law Rights Through Common-Law Remedies," *Juridical Review* 20 (1908): 98.
65. Lobingier, "A Spanish Object-Lesson," 416.
66. *Downes v. Bidwell*, 182 U.S. 244 (1901). House, 4276 H. Doc. 2/8, 75–6; William H. Taft to John Harlan, September 22, 1900, December 27, 1900, and January 7, 1901, in William H. Taft, *William H. Taft Papers* (Washington, D.C.: Library of Congress, 1969), microfilm reels 30, 463–64.
67. *Hawaii v. Makichi*, 190 U.S. 197 (1903); *Dorr v. United States*, 195 U.S. 138 (1904); and *Rassmussen v. United States*, 197 U.S. 516 (1905).
68. Samuel Parsons Scott, trans., *Las Siete Partidas*, 5 vols. (Chicago: Commerce Clearing House, 1931), 3:18:41. See also Cunningham, *Audiencia*, 19; Richard L. Kagan, *Lawsuits and Litigants in Castile 1500–1700* (Chapel Hill: University of North Carolina Press, 1981), 165–209; and Antonio Angel Ruiz Rodríguez, *La Real Chancillería de Granada en el Siglo XVI* (Granada: Diputación Provincial de Granada, 1987).
69. Scott, *Las Siete Partidas*, 2:9:4.
70. Cunningham, *Audiencia*, 22–25, 48–53. See also Owensby, *Empire of Law*; Borah, *Justice by Insurance*; and Tamar Herzog, *Upholding Justice: Society, State, and the Penal System in Quito (1650–1750)* (Ann Arbor: University of Michigan Press, 2004).
71. David P. Barrows, "The Governor-General of the Philippines Under Spain and the United States," *American Historical Review* 21 (1916): 289, 301.
72. Barrows, "The Governor-General of the Philippines," 306; see also Castañeda, "Spanish Structure, American Theory," 365–74.
73. Senate, "Reports of Taft Philippine Commission, 1900," 4040 S. Doc. 112, sess. 56-2 (1901), 225–41; House, "Report of Major-General Commanding Army," 3902 H. Doc. 2, sess. 56-1 (1899), 145–6; Barrows, "Governor-General," 16, 303; House, 4278 H. Doc. 2/10, 289; Wilfley, "New Philippine Judiciary," 410; House, "Report of Philippine Commission," 5113 H. Doc. 2, sess. 59-2 (1906), 8, 43–50; William H. Taft, "The Delays of the Law," *Yale Law Journal* 18 (1908): 33.
74. House, 4276 H. Doc. 2/8, 89.

75. James H. Blount, "Some Legal Aspects of the Philippines," *American Lawyer* 14 (1906): 496. W. F. Norris, "The Criminal Code of the Philippines," *Green Bag* 15 (1903): 433–35; House, 4079 H. Doc. 2, 17–20.
76. Lobingier, "Civil Law Rights," 99. John Pomeroy describes the California code as replete with uncertainties and inconsistencies, relying on principles omitted from the code and left untouched by codification; courts proceeded on the assumption that settled rules of law and equity were not changed but reenacted "in all their force and with all their effect" in *Treatise on Equity* and in *The "Civil Code" in California*, 6, 57, 62. Taft agreed with Pomeroy's assessment, citing California as an example of codification attempts that had "utterly failed." William H. Taft, "The Attacks on the Courts and Legal Procedure," *Kentucky Law Journal* 5 (1916): 5.
77. House, 4276 H. Doc. 2/8, 86 and House, 4278 H. Doc. 2/10, 425.
78. Blount, "Some Legal Aspects," 495. Paul Linebarger to Clarence Edwards, June 19, 1901, Records of the U.S. Bureau of Insular Affairs, RG 350, Entry 5, file 2513-27, National Archives and Records Administration, College Park, Md.; James H. Blount, "The Founding of Civil Government of the Philippines," *Green Bag* 20 (1908): 363.
79. Wilfley, "New Philippine Judiciary," 411.
80. Norris, "Criminal Code of the Philippines," 435. George A. Malcolm, "Philippine Law," part 1, *Illinois Law Review* 11 (1916): 333; and Clifford Stevens Walton, trans., *The Civil Law in Spain and Spanish-America* (Washington, D.C.: W. H. Lowdermilk, 1900). First Instance Judge W. F. Norris published eleven articles in *Green Bag* and *American Law Review* between 1901 and 1918.
81. Serafin P. Hilado, "A Comparative Study of the Adoption Law under the Spanish Civil Code and the Code of Civil Procedure," *Philippine Law Journal* 4 (1918): 313.
82. *Gonzaga v. Norris*, 1 Phil. 529 (1902); *Salinas v. Norris*, 2 Phil. 194 (1903); *Aznar v. Norris*, 3 Phil. 636 (1904); *Castaño v. Lobingier*, 9 Phil. 310 (1906); *Chan-Suangco v. Lobingier*, 23 Phil. 71 (1912); and Barrows, "The Governor-General," 308.
83. Lobingier, "Civil Law Rights," 102; and *Rubi v. Provincial Board of Mindoro*, 36 Phil. 660 (1919).
84. *Rubi v. Provincial Board of Mindoro*.
85. Lobingier, "Spanish Object-Lesson," 416. Insular jurists who frequently published on the mainland included Attorney General Lebbeus Wilfley (*North American Review, Ohio Law Bulletin, Yale Law Journal*); Judge James Blount (*American Lawyer, Green Bag, North American Review*); and Judge W. F. Norris (*American Law Review, Green Bag, Yale Law Journal*). Lobingier also wrote the introduction to Scott, *Siete Partidas*, and published studies of equity, international, and extraterritorial law; for a partial bibliography, see Far Eastern American Bar Association, *Twenty Years in the Judiciary* (Shanghai: Oriental Press, 1922); Lobingier, "Civil Law Rights," 97.
86. Lobingier, "Judicial Superintendent in China," *Illinois Law Review* 12 (1918): 403–8; and Lobingier correspondence in John H. Wigmore Papers, June 1913 through March 1931, box 88, folder 3, Northwestern University Archives, Evanston, Illinois.

87. Donna Grear Parker and Edward M. Wise, "Wigmore, John Henry," *American National Biography Online*, Oxford University Press, 2000, https://doi.org/10.1093/anb/9780198606697.article.1100915; George R. Harvey, "The Administration of Justice in the Philippine Islands," *Illinois Law Review* 9 (1914): 73–97; Ignacio Villamor, "Propensity to Crime," *Journal of the American Institute of Criminal Law & Criminology* 6 (1916): 729–45; John H. Wigmore to Ignacio Villamor, June 16, 1925, folder 23, box 121, Wigmore Papers; John H. Wigmore, "A Model Report on Crime from an Attorney-General's Office," *Journal of the American Institute of Criminal Law & Criminology* 4 (1913): 479–80; Malcolm, "Philippine Law," parts 1 and 2, *Illinois Law Review* 11 (1916): 331–50; 11 (1917): 387–401; George Malcolm to Wigmore, September 30, 1916, and Wigmore to Malcolm, December 18, 1928, box 90, folder 5, Wigmore Papers; and John Henry Wigmore, *A Treatise on the Anglo-American System of Evidence in Trials at Common Law*, 5 vols. (Boston: Little, Brown, 1923).
88. Daniel H. Burnham and Edward H. Bennett, *Plan of Chicago*, ed. Charles Moore (Chicago: Commercial Club, 1909), 115–16, 128, 155; Hines, "Imperial Façade," 51; "Woman's Court Now a Certainty," *CT* December 2, 1910, 14; "Part of the Worker in Building Chicago's New City Hall," *CT* January 1, 1911, E1; and Willrich, *City of Courts*, 132.
89. Howard J. Rogers, ed., *Congress of Arts and Science, Universal Exposition, St. Louis, 1904*, vol. 7, *Economics, Politics, Jurisprudence, Social Science* (Boston: Houghton, Mifflin, 1906), 436, 444.
90. Paul A. Kramer, *The Blood of Government: Race, Empire, the United States, & the Philippines* (Chapel Hill: University of North Carolina Press, 2006), 237; Howard J. Rogers, ed., *Congress of Arts and Science, Universal Exposition, St. Louis, 1904*, vol. 7, *Economics, Politics, Jurisprudence, Social Science* (Boston: Houghton, Mifflin, 1906), 408, 619; and V. Mott Porter, ed., *Official Report of the Universal Congress of Lawyers and Jurists* (St. Louis: Executive Committee, 1905).
91. Courtney Johnson, "Understanding the American Empire: Colonialism, Latin Americanism, and Professional Social Science, 1898–1920," in *Colonial Crucible: Empire in the Making of the Modern American State*, ed. Alfred W. McCoy and Francisco A. Scarano, 175–90 (Madison: University of Wisconsin Press, 2009); Paul D. Carrington, "Freund, Ernst," *American National Biography Online*, Oxford University Press, 2000, https://doi.org/10.1093/anb/9780198606697.article.1100314; Ernst Freund, "Some Legal Aspects of the Chicago Charter Act of 1907," *Illinois Law Review* 2 (1908): 427; Willrich, *City of Courts*, 33; Alleyne Ireland, *The Far Eastern Tropics: Studies in the Administration of Tropical Dependencies* (Westminster: Archibald Constable, 1905), v; "Will Tell of University of Chicago in the Far East," *CT* March 8, 1902, 7; "Oriental Alumni Meet," *University of Chicago Magazine* 11 (1918): 320; Far Eastern Bar, *Twenty Years in the Judiciary*, 46; M. C. Powell, ed., "Mr. Hu I-ku (Wenfu Yiko Hu)," *Who's Who in China* (Shanghai: China Weekly Review, 1925), 369; and David P. Barrows to Frederick Starr, January 15, 1902, box 1, David P. Barrows Papers, Bancroft Library, University of California.
92. Axel R. Schäfer, *American Progressives and German Social Reform, 1875–1920* (Stuttgart: Steiner, 2000), 95; and "Papers and Discussions," *APSA* 1 (1904): 88, 109, 143, 151, 177.

93. Senate, "Hearings Relating to Panama Canal," 5099 S. Doc. 401, sess. 59-2 (1906), 2521.
94. Ralph Eldin Minger, "William H. Taft and the United States Intervention in Cuba in 1906," *Hispanic American Historical Review* 41 (1961): 87.
95. Taft, "Administration of Criminal Law," 4.
96. Taft, "Administration of Criminal Law," 2.
97. Taft, "Administration of Criminal Law," 6.
98. Taft, "Administration of Criminal Law," 1–17; "Mr. Taft's Reaction," *Boston Daily Globe*, July 1, 1905, 6; and "A Grave Blunder," *Boston Daily Globe*, July 17, 1905, 6.
99. Illinois Constitution, Article II, Section 5; and Willrich, *City of Courts*, 122. For working-class wages, see Hull House, *Hull-House Maps and Papers* (New York: Thomas Y. Crowell, 1895), 20. Attorneys John P. Wilson and John S. Miller worked with Tuley on the original Municipal Court bill. Willrich attributes the court's design to Hiram Gilbert, who penned the legislative bill. Gilbert wrote "Messrs. Wilson, Tuley and Miller were, of course, relied upon to and did determine the main feature of the original draft of the Act," while he assisted "in putting into proper form the provisions which they might decide upon as proper to regulate the organization, jurisdiction and practices of the new court." Hiram T. Gilbert, "New Municipal Court System," *CLN* 38 (1906): 296. A Wilson memoir credits Tuley, Wilson, and Miller with the court's design and does not mention Gilbert. In later years, Gilbert claimed a larger role in the court's design. Willrich, *City of Courts*, 3–28, 36–37; Hiram T. Gilbert, *New Municipal Court System, Address Delivered Before the Union League Club of Chicago* (Chicago: unknown, 1906), 17; and Hiram T. Gilbert, *The Municipal Court of Chicago* (Chicago: printed by the author, 1928), 19; and John P. Wilson Jr., "John P. Wilson, 1844–1922," n.d., University of Chicago D'Angelo Law Library.
100. Wallace Heckman, *The Extent of Necessary Constitutional Amendment* (Chicago: Barnard & Miller, 1901), 9.
101. Chicago New Charter Movement, *Why the Pending Constitutional Amendment Should be Adopted* (Chicago: New Charter Campaign Committee, 1904), 7.
102. Gilbert, *Municipal Court of Chicago*, 27–28, 482; and "The Law Providing for a Municipal Court in Chicago," *CLN* 38 (1906): 401.
103. "An Act in Relation to a Municipal Court in the City of Chicago," *Revised Statutes* (1908), §37.271, 282–83, 293, 313b, 318.
104. "Installation of Municipal Court Judges," *CLN* 39 (1906): 138.
105. "Parks Lead All in Useful Beauty," *CT* November 30, 1910, A16; and Willrich, *City of Courts*, 43–45.
106. Harry Olson to Taft, August 4, 1908, in Taft, *Taft Papers*, reel 90.
107. Taft, "Delays of the Law," 38.
108. Taft, "Delays of the Law," 31.
109. Taft, "Delays of the Law," 33; see also Taft, "Inequalities in the Administration of Justice," *Green Bag* 20 (1908): 441–48.
110. Harry Olson, "The Proper Organization and Procedure of a Municipal Court," *APSA* 7 (1910): 78–96; and William Bayard Hale, "A Court that Does Its Job," *World's Work* 19 (1910): 12695–703.

111. Gilbert, *Municipal Court of Chicago*, x, 38, 249–50, 272–76; *Miller v. People*, 230 Ill. 65 (1907); *People v. Dada*, 141 Ill. App. 557 (1908); *People v. Glowacki*, 236 Ill. 612 (1908); *People v. Russell*, 245 Ill. 268 (1910); *People ex rel. Melton v. Whitman*, 243 Ill. 471 (1910); and Olson, "Proper Organization," 83.
112. *People v. Carroll*, 2 Ill. C.C. 170 (1884). Willrich, *City of Courts*, 89; Leeson, *Probation System*, 4–6.
113. Grinnell, "Common Law History," 15–34.
114. "Resolve to Continue the Fight," *CT* June18, 1893, 2; "M'Kenzie Cleland, Former Judge, Dead at Home," *CT* February 14, 1924, 7; A. P. Fitt, "Annual Meeting of the Moody Bible Institute," September 10, 1907, Secretary's Minutes and Charter By Laws, Moody Bible Institute Archives, Chicago; "Revivals Grow in Fervor," *CT* January 9, 1907, 4; "Torrey Talks to Lawyers," *CT* November 7, 1907, 3; "3,000 Converted in Eight Weeks," *CT* November 30, 1907, 7; "Husbands to be Paroled," *CT* January 31, 1907, 1; "Judge Paroles 50; Wives are Happy," *CT* February 2, 1907, 1; "Men on Parole as Model Husbands," *CT* Februrary 16, 1907, 3; "Censures 'Pull' as Aid to Crime," *CT* June 24, 1907, 7; McKenzie Cleland, "The New Gospel in Criminology" *McClure's* 31 (1908): 358–62; and Willrich, *City of Courts*, 66.
115. Olson to George Wentworth Carr, February 19, 1913, box 1, folder 7, Harry Olson Papers, Northwestern University Archives, Evanston, Illinois. See also Willrich, *City of Courts*, 89–95, 148–49, 185; "Agree on New Court Bill," *CT* March 27, 1909, 13; "Rehearing Asked by Olson," *CT* April 23, 1910, 5; "Dunne Will Veto City Court Bill," *CT* June 25, 1913, 2; and "Explains New City Court Act," *CT* March 20, 1914, 14.
116. Olson to George Wentworth Carr, February 19, 1913.
117. Harry Olson, "The Municipal Court of Chicago—Its Organization and Administration," *Central Law Journal* 92 (1921), 88. See also Willrich, *City of Courts*, 120, 133, 174, 208, 228.
118. Willrich, *City of Courts*, 149–71; and Olson, "Municipal Court," 86–88.
119. "Taft's Message Urges Reforms," *CT* December 7, 1910, A15. Michal R. Belknap, *To Improve the Administration of Justice* (Chicago: American Judicature Society, 1992), 15–17, 22, 35–36, 58–59; House, "Hearing on Bill H.R. 14552 to Regulate Judicial Procedure," HRG-1910-HJH-0007, sess. 61-2 (1910).
120. Taft, "Attacks on the Courts," 17. Thomas W. Shelton, "Progress of the Proposal to Substitute Rules of Court for Common Law Practice," *Annals of the American Academy of Political and Social Science* 73 (1917): 178, 182–83; American Bar Association, "Report of the Committee on Uniform Judicial Procedure," *American Bar Association Journal* (hereafter, *ABAJ*) 1–6 (1915–1920); Willrich, *City of Courts*, 285–86.
121. Belknap, *To Improve the Administration of Justice*, 35, 58; Michael Willrich, "The Case for Courts: Law and Political Development in the Progressive Era," in *The Democratic Experiment: New Directions in American Political History*, ed. Meg Jacobs, William J. Novak and Julian E. Zelizer (Princeton, N.J.: Princeton University Press, 2003), 200.
122. "An Act For . . . an Annual Conference of Certain Judges," 42 Stat. 837 (1922); William H. Taft, "Possible and Needed Reforms in Administration of Justice in Federal

123. Courts," *ABAJ* 8 (1922): 601–7; Post, "Judicial Management," 28; Henry D. Clayton, "Popularizing Administration of Justice," *ABAJ* 8 (1922): 45; and Shelton, "Proposal to Substitute Rules," 10.
123. Palmer D. Edmunds, ed., *Federal Rules of Civil Procedure*, 2 vols. (Chicago: Callaghan, 1938), 1:iv, 9; "Tolman Named Special Master in Insull Cases," *CT* June 2, 1933, 20; *Federal Rules of Civil Procedure*, 308 U.S. 645 (1938); James Alger Fee, "The Proposed New Rules for Uniform Procedure in the Federal District Courts," *Oregon Law Review* 16 (1937): 108, 115; and Subrin, "How Equity Conquered," 910–12, 922.
124. Henry C. Morris, "Some Effects of Outlying Dependencies upon the People of the United States," *APSA* 3 (1906): 194, 207.
125. Morris, "Some Effects of Outlying Dependencies," 194.
126. Morris, "Some Effects of Outlying Dependencies," 207.
127. Morris, "Some Effects of Outlying Dependencies," 207. See also Henry C. Morris, *The History of Colonization from the Earliest Times to the Present Day*, 2 vols. (New York: Macmillan, 1900); Henry C. Morris, "A New Phase of Municipal Regulation," *World To-day* 19 (1910): 760–68; and "Fate of Charter to Be Seen Today," *CT* May 11, 1909, 1. Morris, a U.S. consul and international lawyer, was extensively cited in Bureau of Statistics, *Colonial Administration 1800–1900*, 2 vols. (Washington, D.C. : Government Printing Office, 1903). See also Henry C. Morris, Theodore Marburg, and W. W. Willoughby, "Discussion," *APSA* 1 (1904): 139–43.
128. Laycock, "Triumph of Equity," 54, 57, 66–67; Subrin, "How Equity Conquered," 924; Marc Galanter, "The Vanishing Trial: An Examination of Trials and Related Matters in Federal and State Courts," *Journal of Empirical Legal Studies* 1 (2004): 461–63, 495–96, 506–13; Langbein, "Disappearance of Civil Trial," 524, 562–63; T. Ward Frampton, "The Uneven Bulwark: How (and Why) Criminal Jury Trial Rates Vary by State," *California Law Review* 100 (2012): 198–200; and Senate, "Administrative Procedure in Government Agencies," 10562 S. Doc. 8, sess. 77-1 (1941), 24, 61, 70.
129. *Seminole Nation v. United States*, 316 U.S. 286 (1942); *Brown v. Board of Education*, 349 U.S. 294 (1955); *Civil Rights Act*, 78 Stat. 241 (1964); and Voting Rights Act, 79 Stat. 437 (1965).

4
America Is Hard to See

COURTNEY BENDER

If we agree with this collection's guiding that the "practices of American exceptionalism" are rooted in the ambiguous yet durable distinctions of home and abroad, then we might consider how these distinctions of place are imagined and observed, and how religion is constituted within these visions. There are admittedly many threads in the tangle of American exceptionalism's political imaginary, religious and otherwise. In this essay I offer several examples that allow us to consider how religion works to shape the future-tense orientation of America's exceptionalist claims. In these examples, America's "exceptional" qualities and the exceptional place of American religion within it are consistently visible on the horizon, but never yet present. (This episteme of future-tense exceptionalism thus has religious qualities of its own.) Such a future-tense orientation within American exceptionalism is regularly assumed rather than defended: it is not found primarily in declarations or explicit argument but rather is present in norms of experiencing and seeing an American landscape and an American future that provide the grounding for its more explicit claims. By calling attention to the qualities of this orientation, I show how the recurrent claim that America is hard to see (that is, too complicated to map, too vast to fully comprehend, and above all too incipient or not yet arriving in its own history) depends upon and shapes a range of familiar claims about American religion and religiosity. In considering the religious aspects of this future-tense orientation, we gain a different look at the qualities and outlooks of American exceptionalism and perhaps a better understanding of its uncanny durability.

Throughout the twentieth century, American writers and essayists, popular writers and speechwriters worked a spatial-temporal seam of American exceptionalism that became visible from the air and that marked a durable understanding of the nation's expanding temporal and physical horizons. Throughout the nineteenth and twentieth centuries, America's nature was contrasted with Europe's civilization, an America frontier's tabula rasa to the European continent's "ancient lands." Becoming American meant inhabiting a space where one could "breathe free," where the nation's harbor threshold appears indistinct and ethereally "air bridged," and where freedom means liberty of movement and purchase but also, more certainly, a freedom to flourish, "unencumbered"—and to soar as more free, complete, versions of themselves. Or, so all Americans learn from Emma Lazarus's sonnet *The New Colossus*, written in 1883 and enshrined in the base of the Statue of Liberty in 1903: "From her beacon-hand / Glows world-wide welcome; her mild eyes command / The air-bridged harbor that twin cities frame. / 'Keep, ancient lands, your storied pomp!' cries she / With silent lips. 'Give me your tired, your poor, / Your huddled masses yearning to breathe free . . .'"[1]

The robust critique of American exceptionalism as a cultural mode of being American and as a political theology has raised to our attention a number of contradictions within its claims. Celebrations of American exceptionalism and visions of the nation's special role in history are built upon, and tend to perpetuate, a story that occludes histories of expansion, dispossession, and violence that undercut American exceptionalism's claims to its special relationship in creating democratic freedoms. The violence that was (and is) necessary to reproduce the North American continent as an open and empty space ready for a fresh human start free from tyranny or tradition is infrequently admitted and, as such, appears as an aberration to correct rather than as a defining component in the creation of a vision of America.

Yet while critiques of exceptionalism clearly expose its limits, it also seems that one of the functional capacities of the episteme of American exceptionalism is its capacity to acknowledge and in fact to incorporate a range of criticisms (particularly but not limited to criticisms that American exceptionalism's claims for universality are only partial), with little apparent weakening of its own claims. Religion and religious pluralities play a valuable role in supporting this chronotope, so it seems that thinking through the ways that religion and religions are embedded in these chronotopes helps us to better understand the durability of American exceptionalism. With this in mind, my interest is not to reiterate familiar frames of critique but, rather, to consider how some epistemic or chronotopic aspects of American exceptionalism work to see and envision its better future self, the better future—and expansive—nation.

My approach concentrates on the ways that spatial and temporal sensibilities (narratives, practices, imaginations) organize and shape American exceptionalism. Mikhail Bakhtin's concept of the chronotope is helpful here, as his analyses of literary genres turn attention to the ways that distinct genres develop or draw upon a distinctive set of relations between time and space. Taken together, these chronotopes (space-time-narrative relations) become "thickened" in literature and speech. A chronotope might be understood as the socially agreed upon background or context wherein action and plot takes place and where actors, agents, and even emotions are set as recognizable and regular parts of the landscape. Not only do space and time take on different forms in particular social-cultural and historical milieu, but the world itself—its actors, its sense of the possible, its moods and emotions—are differently inhabited as well. The sense of what is possible and acceptable to a reader, Bakhtin argues, is much different in Greek epic than it is in a modern novel. In any particular genre characters may be more or less complexly rendered; time more or less flexible, linear, or fungible; distances more or less extensive or visible.[2] In extending Bakhtin's chronotopic notion to American exceptionalism, I am paying attention to the kind of space and time coordinates that are embedded in and support ideas of America: which social settings and scales, which periods and places come into view? What kinds of American religions (or American citizens) are rendered as more or less central to this narrative? What kinds of experiences are thus supported to make this seem real? In the examples I concentrate on in this essay, we see how exceptionalism of America is oriented toward an American future that is always just over the edge of the current time. The promise and reality of America is just out of reach, even as it is visible as coming into being in a visible landscape. It is "hard to see."[3]

While America is hard to see, it seems to me that this particular chronotope of American exceptionalism comes into better focus when we look at the ways that religion figures within it, in two distinct respects. On the one hand, this chronotope takes in stride that in the hard-to-see America, religious freedoms enable a vast plurality of religions—that is, a growing religious multiplicity always exceeds the capacity of a census taker, pollster, or surveyor to fully map or describe.[4] Within this chronotope, the expansiveness of religious plurality both seen and unseen is a signal and sign of American exceptionalism; the incapacity of anyone to actually "see" this diversity as a whole provides a vision of the American religious landscape as inchoate as well, unmappable and also unfinishable, always changing. Indeed, changing definitions of religion (expanding concepts of religion) or the shift in religious identity from "religion" to "spirituality" provides ever renewing evidence of American exceptionalism.[5] And this suggests further a second sense of religion within this chronotope, which is less interested in religious pluralism or in "revealed religions" than in cultivating its own religious claims and experiences for exceptionalism itself. This second sense of religion resonates within discussions and descriptions of American civil religion or "invisible religion" or the "American sublime." While these forms of religion are no less socially felt and experienced, they nonetheless are typically marked or indicated by an apophatic gesture, meaning that they identify themselves by what they are not. Thus, civil religion is "not" actual, real religion, or it is "not" Christianity; the technological sublime is similarly "not" religious, all the while remaining tethered to those terms through those negative claims. American exceptionalism's "not religious" claims similarly develop within and support an idea that America is hard to see—that the real America remains visible from prophetic orientations and experiences that allow at least some Americans to participate in a mystical way in seeing that future promise and hope for its realization.

NO BOUNDARIES

Toward the end of World War II, American Airlines contracted with Rand McNally to manufacture an air globe. The air globe found its way to American high schools through the reach of the airline's nonprofit Air Age Education Research program and was also widely advertised in national news magazines. The air globe was a novel creation distinguished by its features—or, rather, by its utter lack of them. Small dots and city names representing airports were the only things that marked the globe's light-blue surface: large swaths of unpopulated land made equivalent as an empty and featureless ocean.

It announced a new "human geography in the air age"—a new way to plot distance and connection and to see and experience the world. "Mountains, oceans, arctics, deserts, jungles and other surface barriers, which long have kept people apart, have disappeared.... The innumerable boundary and dividing lines found upon maps of the earth's surface also are omitted, because air, itself, is indivisible."[6] The globe represented what jet-age Americans would see on their ascent and what they would experience below: the world that they were entering was limitless. Human life no longer needed to be organized by topography. The distinguishing boundaries that had kept people apart and that had reinforced human differences could now be seen for what they were—or, for that matter,

FIGURE 4.1 "Air Globe" advertisement for American Airlines.

"All Mother Earth's Children Live on the Same Street," American Airlines, Inc., 1946. John W. Hartman Center for Sales, Advertising & Marketing History, Digital Collections, Ad*Access. Downloaded 24 August 2020. https://idn.duke.edu/ark:/87924/r4d795v97.

for what they were not. As historian Joseph Corn put it, the air globe symbolized "in tangible form the new world which Americans believed the airplane was about to create, a world of peace where national boundaries and topographical features were no longer pertinent."[7] Or, as the advertisement copy read, "All Mother Earth's Children Live on the Same Street."

The United States nonetheless remained central to this vision of the future, at least within this American Airlines ad copy. The United States was represented on it in pointillist form, with each airport marking a dot that made the country visible. If all children in the world would soon live on the "same street," it nonetheless remained certain that it was the United States and its airlines and airplanes that would be central actors in future neighborly and peaceful endeavors.[8] But the air globe's barely visible America, for all of its novelty, was in many respects the up-to-date version of a durable story of the America coming into being.

Nearly sixty years before American high schoolers encountered the American Airlines air globe, Coloradan William Gilpin presented a similar vision of a global American future that fused new ideas about technology and enduring notions of the American horizon to craft a story of the promise of an ever-expanding American global future. Gilpin's 1890 treatise *The Cosmopolitan Railway* offered readers a vision of an expanding peaceful world order that would soon take shape through a worldwide and singular railroad network stretching across the Bering Strait, Asia, and Europe to South America and to Africa. This cosmopolitan consciousness that such a network would make possible was nonetheless rooted both materially and ideologically in America: Gilpin mapped Denver as the future national capital and eventually the center node in the cosmopole. Gilpin's view of an outwardly expanding America depended, however, on a vision of the world's civilizations also entering the United States and being transformed in its open landscape. The world's nations, cultures, and religions would flow in to "open" land untouched by history and would be able—would, in fact, be compelled—to change, shape, and mix. This new human culture developed in America would eventually be carried back outward by that same cosmopolitan railway. This was already what he saw taking shape in Colorado: immigrants were already fusing "together into one race ... whose individualities are obliterated in a single generation." America itself was the same and was showing what "mixing" could do. Soon "the rest of the world" would follow suit.[9] Gilpin was hardly the first or the last to see cosmopolitanism in part not whole: "Our North America will gradually accumulate a population equaling that of the rest of the world combined," he wrote "a people one and indivisible, identical in manners, language, customs and impulses; preserving the same civilization, the same religion; imbued with the same opinions, and having the same political liberties."[10] America will come into existence in the near future as it draws in more of the other and translates more of itself into a cosmopolitan human. Gilpin's treatise is built on the proposition that what exists in America "today" is not the real America that is coming into this full potential. We might further observe that both the cosmopolitan railroad and the air globe represent "America" as a substantial yet porous object. Its boundaries are clear yet also open. They both thus reflect the strange translations that took place after the "closure" of the American frontier, which marked for Americans the introduction of other openings within the imaginative and actual landscape as well as a softening rather than a solidification of international boundaries.[11]

The unvarnished nineteenth-century optimism of a project such as Gilpin's was difficult to sustain. By the 1920s few could still imagine that the "open" spaces of the American West or transportation advances would lead to a single American culture. In a time when it seemed highly unlikely that "racial or national" differences would be tempered or become unimportant in American political life, American religious pluralities and religious cooperation emerged as a more important sign of American cultural cooperation. In the 1923 book *The Frontier Spirit in American Christianity*, University of Chicago professor Peter G. Mode argued that "fragments" of racial and national identities remained impediments to assimilation to American ideals and that religious cooperation among denominations was a much more fertile ground for nation building. Mode took as his example life in the American "frontier." In its "almost inexhaustible resources of our plains and mountain areas," American Christians had needed to learn to work together and put aside their theological differences. Necessities of living took priority, and "sectarian sensitiveness had to give way to interdenominational comity and cooperation," he wrote.[12]

As Mode's title makes more than amply clear, his vision for assimilation to American values through religion was explicitly about protestant cooperation, and it was this form of religion that he understood would become "American religion." Much as Gilpin's vision of the cosmopolitan railway was riven with exclusions of non-European inhabitants of America—Native Americans, Blacks, and Asians—Mode's vision of this America's pluralist cooperative future is marked by numerous exclusions, including Catholics and Mormons. But just as importantly, we should note that these exclusions not only exclude people but also enable the frontier vision to continue—that is, to identify American "open spaces" where "new" and unique American cooperative culture develops. In both Mode's and Gilpin's writings, it is not the people but the frontier and the technologies that expand that frontier that become the central actor in Americanness. The land as they conceive of it—or as they envision it—is the active agent shaping peaceful religious coexistence.[13] A free landscape, rough and open, large enough to accommodate all—wild enough that it cannot be contained or charted—demands cooperation and creates a new culture for all who venture there.

Mode's book presages Sidney Mead's well-known explorations of frontier religion. Mead begins his 1963 *Lively Experiment* with an extended discussion of Americans' "space, time, and religion" wherein he extends the claim that the American frontier has transformed American religion or, rather, made a particular kind of religion that is American. Mead's essay argues that the experience of westward movement transformed pioneers' thinking about religion, cutting them free of the temporal and traditional ideas about religiosity that they had experienced in the past, and reoriented religion around particular experiences of space. As he describes at length, the vastness of the American landscape, the struggles that it presented to pioneers (through its size and its wildness) shaped new kinds of responses to the world and new forms of religion. Some who went west found it a soaring experience and "dwelt in the golden promise of the untried space of the west," while others were overwhelmed and "lost in the limitless spaces, overwhelmed and terrorized by brute nature given voice and arms by wild animals and savage Indians" articulated alternative religious responses. Despite these variations, it was the sheer scope of America and the effects of moving "through space so vast" that had formed American religion. "Space came to take precedence over time, in the formation of their most cherished ideals."[14]

The space that takes precedence over time is an American frontier and, beyond that, the globe itself that America gathers into it. As did Mode and Gilpin did before him, Mead's America is an unreal, unmarked place, without specificity or history or culture, onto which the growth of "American" culture then becomes possible. Images of this America required the effective erasure of specific landscapes and actual people who shaped and named them, a theme that is recurrent and visible in all three texts. On the invisible and extensive spaces imagined in these scholarly and political texts, an "early" promise of ethnic and racial "amalgamations" into a single American unity becomes less tenable, but, rather than dissipating, it is transformed. By the twentieth century, religious pluralities and cooperations (meaning most specifically, protestant pluralities) become the focus of the unfolding promise of American exceptionalism. An imagination of religious pluralism becomes rooted in the future-tense chronotope of American exceptionalism, its expansiveness and "freedom" making it both highly visible and equally hard to see.

ON THE THRESHOLD

By the beginning decades of the twentieth century, the position from the deck of an ocean liner docking in New York Harbor had become the signal position of entry to the United States, the evident threshold through which a visitor or a newcomer—or a returning expatriate—would first confront America. The view of the city's skyscraper skyline and the Statue of Liberty is inscribed in volumes of memoirs, novels, and journalistic essays as the moment of arrival to the "new world" (and is no less frequently invoked today in nostalgic and historical representations of coming to America). The city skyline was itself striking—the full-on urban sensorium invoked in the smells, sights, and sounds crowded in the harbor and in Manhattan and Brooklyn piers. Perhaps not surprisingly, then, those who wrote of this scene of coming to America often abstract it, paying less attention to what the acute observer Henry James observed as the burgeoning skyscrapers' "empty-eyed" affronts to any refined aesthetic and spiritual sensibility than to the "air bridged" harbor's sky and clouds.[15] The essayist Paul Rosenfeld describes a turn of perspective, a shift in the sensations that travelers from Europe to the American shores now felt. Now they felt themselves rising up rather than falling as they reached New York. This sensation announced the beginning furthermore of a genuine American culture that had shed its dependence on European traditions and weaknesses. Or as he puts it, "not so long ago"

> [it] seemed the [ocean] liners did not come across the Atlantic on a single plane. Somewhere, in the course of their voyage from the European coasts, they left one plane and descended to another. True, they were steam-packets plying in a huge oceanic ferryboat business.... Nevertheless, a mysterious translation took place before they reached their American terminus. If indeed they did plow over the regular surface of the globe, they also came out of delicious unknown qualities of light, and out of wafts of air lighter and fierier than any aplay this side the water. In coming, they had descended as one descends from a heaven-near plateau under blue skylands into a dank and shadowy vale.[16]

Rosenfeld ignores the brackish, smelly water at Manhattan's piers and instead looks up into the sky. It is the skyline and the air over America itself that carries travelers and newcomers into the new world. "America" is represented less by the street scenes and people than by the lightness of the ocean-borne air: those alighting on the shore might even feel that they have never left that formative and powerful oceanic realm. Or, as he writes, the "steamers no longer descend from one plane to another." "A kind of strong, hearty daylight has come upon the port.... To-day, it brings a wash of strength and power over us." Rosenfeld take his reader's eye from the activity of the port to the skyscrapers overlooking the water, to the sun setting on the New Jersey hills, and to the "almost beauty" of the sky. Whatever the cause of this psychic and spiritual shift, he and his reader stood on the harbor anew, looking up, sensing in the city a "fundamental oneness we have with the place and the people in it.... We know it here, our relationship with this place.... The buildings cannot deprive us of it. For they and we have suddenly commenced growing together." The "ineffability" of the Atlantic crossing supplanted by the ineffability of "America." "Day after day in gray and desperate weather even, one can see its mystic aspiration above the skyscrapers of New York."[17] The proverbial tide has shifted, the winds have turned.

For those who have missed the meaning of his metaphors, Rosenfeld helpfully states: "We have been sponging on Europe for direction instead of developing our own, and Europe has been handing out nice little packages of spiritual direction to us. But then Europe fell into disorder and lost her way, and we were thrown back on ourselves to find inside ourselves sustaining faith.... The new world has been reached at last."[18]

Rosenfeld was an eager American modernist, focused on promoting the careers and the ideas of the artists and writers in his expansive circles.[19] Neither he nor any in his group would name the "sustaining faith" that he spoke of, even as he—and his group—would gesture to an American spirit. But by midcentury testimony such as his would be recognizable as a genre of civil religion or "invisible religion" or perhaps even related to the American technological sublime, each a term developed to evoke the ways that Americans sacralize their belief in the nation and their experience of confronting the boundless possibilities of the better America evoked by this natural and built topography or in shared social rituals. The topographical imagination is most clearly developed in works such as David Nye's *American Technological Sublime*, which provides language to explain the experiences to which Rosenfeld attests. Nye's American "technological sublime" is—like Rosenfeld's—contrasted to a "European" sublime and marked as distinct from elitist quests for "Romantic rapture." The American sublime, he says, is not in search of irrational experience but rather is driven to "seek the awakening of sensibilities to an inner power"—that is, to the inner power of an America that cannot be seen directly but can be experienced through the technological developments of Americans and of the national landscape that supports it. Thus, in visiting the Hoover Dam, "human beings [could] temporarily disregard divisions among elements of the community." A sublime experience shows that the American and the human are indeed one and the same. The experiences propel individuals beyond any particular cultural or social frames or, as he says it, "taps into fundamental hopes and fears. It is not a social residue, created by economic and political forces, though both can inflect its meaning. Rather, it is an essentially religious feeling, aroused by the confrontation with impressive objects."[20] Nye calls the technological sublime a human—religious—experience that is beyond culture. It touches something "fundamental." Anyone can experience this, and it is through this experience that Americans (or humans) shuck off their "divisions among elements of the community." It is "religious," and at the same time an experience of becoming America.

The resonating links between Nye's (and also Perry Miller's) claims for the humanness of an American technological sublime, its value to show or experience unity in a noncultural, nonhistorical way, and those of Gilpin, Rosenfeld, Mead, and Mode are striking. What Nye's and others' claims to the "technological sublime" (or, as I will note, to "civil religion") offers in extension is an expression of such feelings as "not religious." Yet such expressions are also unquestionably fused with histories of American Protestantism and have privileged particular conceptions of religious experience, both the fulcrum of human connection to the divine and in its latter articulations as the wellspring of all religions worldwide. Translated into secular modes, the sublimity of American landscapes, both built and "natural," continue to resonate with these pasts, as numerous scholars have observed. Yet equally important to our understanding of these expressions are the claims that are made for them *as* religious or, rather, as "near" or "quasi" religious. In some cases those who attest to the sublime are not working to distance their projects from religion but rather to make a claim for a deeper and more real religion—one that at the same time is difficult to assert directly, as doing so either leads to charges of embracing a national religion or to interpretations that would reduce their felt universality to particularisms. What remains visible on the horizon are analogical gestures and apophatic utterances, all of which do their own work of reestablishing an orientation toward it or an expectation for its fulfillment. It is this sensibility that motivates and courses through stories of American exceptionalism.[21]

Nye is among the many authors of American civil religion who have carried forward the chronotopic projection of America as mystical, writing and testifying to a form of collective mysticism while simultaneously deeming it "not religious." By retaining the designation of "religion," the various groups that are understood to flourish and expand in number in America (while simultaneously continuing to develop cooperation and "comity" among them), the American "sublime"—the religiousness of civil religion—becomes available as a post-religious project or orientation or experience. Distinguished from the specificities of "religion," civil religion and national sublime offer ways to summon the sacred nation without (it appears) summoning religion. Yet "seeing" America and her future from the air, or crossing the nation's mystical threshold into unencumbered air, also draws us close to seeing these projects as religious.

THE TRI-FAITH CHAPEL PLAZA

Between 1966 and 1988 the Jewish International Synagogue, Protestant Christ for the World Chapel, and Catholic Our Lady of the Skies Chapel stood side by side at John F. Kennedy Airport's Tri-Faith Chapel Plaza. While airport chapels are now common both in the United States and around the globe, the plaza was a unique architectural project at its dedication in December 1966 and attracted considerable attention. Hundreds of New Yorkers were invited to take part in the dedication, most making the journey to the airport on the traffic-clogged highways that snaked through Queens and then walking through parking lots, around a broad reflecting pool, and into the International Synagogue. Each of the chapels jutted dozens of feet out over the long, shallow pool (called the "Lagoon") that reflected the skies above.[22]

Among the few attendees who flew to the dedication event was Vice President Hubert Humphrey, the guest of honor and main speaker of the day. Following a brief invocation and introductory remarks from the plaza's board president, Humphrey read from prepared remarks that borrowed liberally from the Tri-Faith Chapel Plaza's promotional materials, describing the plaza as of a piece with the story of religious cooperation across sectarian lines, yet another iteration of an important if familiar story of American pluralism and unity among diversity. "There are so many phrases in American History that underscore this unity from diversity that one is sometimes hard put to choose or select." As he spoke, he reminded his listeners that the plaza might be a new form of cooperation, but it did not include a new idea for a nation where "faith shines equal." The Tri-Faith Chapel Plaza, he asserted, was a symbol of America that would instruct newcomers and visitors. "Let the Tri-Faith Chapel Plaza...stand as a symbol and a pledge to those who come here from other nations—a symbol of the essential unity of our great religions, and a pledge of their united determination to make this a better nation and a better world."²³

Where Humphrey's remarks invoked the arc of a common narrative of American religious pluralism wherein diverse religious groups work together in common cause, a closer look at the plaza's origins tell a somewhat different story. In 1951 airport employees established a Catholic guild at the airport, asked for a place to say mass, and soon after raised money to build a modest chapel on the airport grounds. Our Lady of the Skies Chapel opened in 1954 and was served by local priests; its daily masses were well attended, mostly by Catholic airport and airline employees. The airport was expanding, however, and the Catholic chapel was marked for demolition in the Port Authority's 1959 master plans for its "Terminal City." In identifying a site for a new Catholic chapel, the Port Authority also invited the New York Board of Rabbis and the Protestant Council of New York to sponsor chapels of their own. Indeed, the plaza did not develop out of an organic tri-faith effort or collaboration among religious groups but was rather a top-down concept that was led by the Port Authority itself. Or, as one former chaplain would reminisce, the Port Authority "not only encouraged but actually induced the Catholic, Protestant, and Jewish Sponsors of the Chapels to invest their interest, efforts and funds in planning and building the three houses of worship."²⁴

That the Protestant and Jewish groups were not advocating on their own behalf to build chapels is clear from internal records of both the New York Board of Rabbis and the Protestant Council of New York. The Protestant Council discussed the Port Authority's invitation at its executive meeting in 1959. While there was great interest in building the chapel, the committee did not arrive at a clear idea about how they would use the chapel or who might visit it. They noted that while Catholics had a tradition of "industrial chapels" that served workers and performed mass and confession, Protestants were not used to the practice of attending services at work, nor was there a felt need. The Protestants observed that an airport chaplain would be important in the event of an airplane crash or on a more regular basis to assist travelers in distress. With this sketchy concept for the chapel's use, they nonetheless went ahead and in the intervening four years would come to expect for the chapel a similar kind of program as would take shape at the Protestant Center in the 1964 New York World's Fair. Indeed, the chaplain at the World's Fair was tapped to continue his role at the airport chapel, and the silent film that had been the centerpiece of the center's exhibit was shown daily in the airport chapel.²⁵ Of the three groups, only the New York Board of Rabbis appeared to work the airport's role as an international hub explicitly into its understanding of the chapel's activities. The chapel at an airport was also new for the board, but the project was soon to be overseen by Israel Mowshowitz, an Orthodox rabbi who was active in international Jewish relief efforts and who envisioned the Jewish chapel as a space to anchor Jewish identity and practice at the onset or end of travel and to help Jewish travelers experience and see their participation in a global Jewish community.[26] Mowshowitz also used his worldwide connections to establish a small museum of Jewish ritual objects donated by worldwide Jewish communities. In the years to come, the chapel would be a gathering place for prayer and meeting for travelers to and from Israel.

The Chapel Plaza took shape at the behest of the secular Port Authority, and each group developed its plans for its chapel, and what would happen within it, without consultation or discussion with the other groups. Indeed, it appears that when the three groups looked to the others' efforts, they were as much concerned about competition as they were about collaboration. Some of the Catholic priests active at the Catholic chapel at Kennedy expressed grave concerns about the development of a Protestant chapel. Catholic religious presence in the airport expanded throughout the 1950s in response in part to the desire to attend to the thousands of Puerto Rican residents who were moving to the mainland. New York's international airport had been the landing place for thousands of these internal migrants and had prompted priests to consider how to greet their co-religionists and begin their integration into the city. As plans for the Tri-Faith Plaza were initially announced in 1959, priests on the ground implored the Brooklyn bishop to increase the numbers of priests and sisters on hand at the airport. "It would be well for us to be organized for this work before the Protestant Church [sic] is completed," one wrote. "A review of their architectural plans shows that the front of the Protestant Chapel will provide for many offices which I am sure will be used for the interviewing of new arrivals."[27]

The bishop's office responded with reassurances, saying that it was highly unlikely that Protestants were poaching Catholic Puerto Ricans for their own churches. Yet such concern about Protestant architectural presence at the airport was likely not entirely misplaced. Drawings and site maps made by the architect Edgar Tafel show that the Port Authority had initially designated a different site for the chapels on the airport grounds and put the chapels in three unequally spaced lots, with the Protestants offered the largest one. When this site was rejected, the new site offered three equally sized spots along a broad reflecting pool. With this shift, the Port Authority also demanded new plans from all three architects that conformed to shared design criteria. This determined that each chapel would be equal in height and volume, would have similar shape (a large central worship area flanked by two single-story "wings"), and would employ similar building materials on their exteriors. Not all were happy about the changes. Tafel, the architect for the Protestant chapel who had drawn plans for a larger and more distinctive building before the site was shifted, engaged in a lengthy battle with the Port Authority to use his original plans, resulting in a two-year delay in its construction.[28] In the meantime the architects for both the Jewish and Catholic chapels developed striking designs for their respective chapels. The International Synagogue fashioned its terminal-facing wall as a forty-foot tall Decalogue, advertising Jewish presence at the airport in a highly visible and unmistakable way. The Catholic guild at the airport raised the funds to build a stunning and award-winning building covered on three sides with abstract stained-glass panels. The interior light in the chapel was so unusual and beautiful that in the two decades it stood it would become a popular site for weddings.

The differences in the chapels' uses and self-understandings would remain outside the casual visitor's sight. There were, not incidentally, few casual visitors to the chapels. The Port Authority had all but ensured that only the most intentional and intrepid travelers would visit the plaza. The plaza was surrounded by interminably congested access roads and giant parking lots. Architectural critics complained even at their opening that the chapels were "symbols unrelated to their use."[29] Yet it was precisely their symbolic presentation that *became* their use, and it was precisely the distance from which the chapels were most regularly observed or seen in which this "use" became most apparent. Looking down at the Chapel Plaza made visible the national story of "unity amid diversity" and "shared purpose." This vision, manufactured by the Port Authority and situated as a uniquely harmonious set of architectural forms within Kennedy's jumbled "terminal city," represented a modernist future of American religion.[30]

A promotional booklet distributed at the dedication made an even larger claim, calling the Tri-Faith Plaza the twentieth century's answer to the Statue of Liberty. Where the iconic statue had greeted generations of seafaring travelers arriving in New York's harbor to welcome the "poor, tired, and hungry," that port now stood nearly twelve miles from the airport. Air travelers might get a glimpse of her from the sky, but her distance from Kennedy made room for a new, up-to-date, and modern beacon of American liberty. This was the plaza's role, and one that the chapels could likewise supply. It was perhaps particularly the Cold War–era "refugee and immigrant" who would find particular comfort, if not in the chapels' modernist embrace then in the very sight of the three religions side by side, the very sign of religious liberty.[31]

This broader vision seemed very much on Vice President Humphrey's mind. He strayed from the prepared version of his speech at several moments to reflect on how the plaza made an inchoate vision of an American spirit concrete. Where his written speech focused on the theme of equality amid diversity, Humphrey could not help but comment that the various religious groups visible in the plaza were supported by a wider spirit that entailed "commitment not only to the material richness of life, [but also] the oneness of our nation and also of our spiritual commitment and our sense of brotherhood." In these flights of rhetoric Humphrey seemed quite close to leaving the three great religions behind. There was an even bigger, more spiritual, more unified country. This spiritualized country had become visible on his flight into Kennedy, as he looked down at the plaza's unity and at the horizon of the continent that extended out beyond. It was at the airport where, "amidst the coming and going of men and women from the corners of this wondrous world of ours and, too, all corners of the [nation]," the international traveler learned that "all men are brothers not just in the word but in the spirit, and they are all equal, equal in the sight of God."

Humphrey did not need an air globe. He did not need to imagine the creation of a cosmopolitan railway. On his flight in to Kennedy Airport that morning, he had inhabited the god's-eye view and had glimpsed once more the nation's sacred potential—a potential for which the tri-faith "symbol" stood in a land of expanding freedom, possibility, and spiritual unity across the nation.

"AMERICA IS HARD TO SEE"

"America is hard to see." Robert Frost's lines condense the thought that "America" always exceeds perception, measurement, and comprehension.[32] Its boundaries are inchoate or expanding, and its interior is similarly unsurveyable. We are accustomed to hearing the claim that it is impossible to describe or explain America and the full meaningful multiplicity of its cultures, politics, religions, and potentialities. We continue particularly in our darkest hours to see in this unchartable vastness a possibility for, and the seeds of, a better future (no matter what we think that future might be). The nation's multitudinous diversity (it is "more plural" or "more regional" or "more complicated" or "more . . . etc. etc.") is signaled in both the signs of religious diversity and the testimonies of mystical encounters with its spiritual expanse. We can add the further observation that in this epistemic project America not only "receives" all of the world religions but also shapes and brings forth all the future religions yet to be imagined and realized.

Of course, we know that the air-bridged harbor and the open frontier have never been quite so present in the world as these visions articulate. Nearly fifty years ago Charles Long penned a critical essay about the epistemic limits of civil religion and the historiographies of American religion that put the frontier at their center. The essay, subtitled "Visible People and Invisible Religion," did not ask for more inclusivity within the spiritualized episteme of a free and open America. Rather, Long argued for the dismantling of its imagination altogether. As he wrote, the "episteme as a pre-methodological concept allowed for an organizing principle of coherence and gave a normative center for the organization of data, it simultaneously operated as a center, a presence, making impossible the permutation or transformation of the other data." As a consequence, "the 'mighty saga of the outward acts' of American religion ... meant that all the *other* peoples and cultures had to remain *in their places*—places allotted to them by this centered reality of the European tradition of immigrants."[33] We have for a long time known that celebrations of religious pluralism and religious freedom have contributed to, if not depended upon, activities that also designate other religions, peoples, and civilizations as not yet equipped to take part. And we know that these narratives and meanings endure. Despite scholarly efforts to reorient a story of American history, the narrative of exceptionalism continues to transform and expand further into the air. How, then, might we think differently about this imaginary, to trace or identify its particular durability?

I have turned to a chronotopic approach in this essay in order to think through this question. As I have suggested throughout, efforts to "map" the landscape, to "survey" and to otherwise "observe" America in its entirety have offered ongoing opportunities for Americans to attest to the impossibility of seeing America—and to connect this apparent impossibility to a story of the American future, where a better nation is (or must be) taking shape under our noses but not yet visible to us. The impossibility of seeing America is often expressed as a matter of wonder. It incites an experience of a promise that one day the many parts that we see will give way to that new and unified world. Americans are encouraged to feel and experience this future promise in numerous places—including the view from a plane window, from an ocean liner's deck, and in our poetry, literature, and arts. But exceptionalism does not end there. We should also think further about how languages of pluralism, multiplicity, or visibility also participate within this articulation of a future or present (if invisible) hope of the promise of American exceptionalism. We might begin by observing that this chronotope of American exceptionalism is not upended by demands to make American life more thoroughly and completely visible in its varieties and complexities. It is not challenged by demands for greater diversity or recognition of difference. It is instead strengthened by them.

This form of American exceptionalism is at its core religious. From the chapel and the mountaintop, from the jet window or the poem, its open-aired sublime renews a messianic aspiration for the nation. It activates a hope that no matter what, the real America is still coming into being, just beyond the visible horizon.

This is a religious sentiment that keeps us oriented to a particular kind of future and that demands of us a particular orientation toward our present. Giving up this particular attunement certainly does not require giving up on the future. On the contrary, it only requires giving up on the broken narratives and perspectives that have proven they lead nowhere. Or, more precisely, that lead only to more of the same.

NOTES

1. Emma Lazarus, "The New Colossus," in *Emma Lazarus: Selected Poems and Other Writings* (Peterborough, Ont.: Broadview Press, 2002), 233.
2. Mikhail Bakhtin, "Forms of Time and of the Chronotope in the Novel," in *The Dialogic Imagination: Four Essays* (Austin: University of Texas, 1981). See also Mariana Valverde, *Chronotopes of Law: Jurisdiction, Scale, and Governance* (New York: Routledge, 2015). Amitav Ghosh analogously softens the boundary between literary and social chronotopes in querying how the modern novel's chronotope and its emphasis on prosaic everyday life creates a challenge for modern readers to accept the verities of narratives that include cataclysmic events that seem to be out of this world—the proverbial acts of God. In Ghosh's view, this is part of a piece with a modern derangement that looks away from (much less has a way of accounting for) ongoing, unstoppable environmental disaster. Amitav Ghosh, *The Great Derangement* (Chicago: University of Chicago Press, 2018).
3. Daniel Immerwahr, *How to Hide an Empire: A Short History of the Greater United States* (New York: Random House, 2019).
4. The "problem" of counting and surveying religion in America has its own curious history and becomes a matter of faith, in some respect. The U.S. Census has not asked for religious identity (as a private matter) since the late nineteenth century; interest in reviving census questions post–World War II was blocked by various religious groups. Religion has thus been "counted" by surveys and polls; part of this history and the cultural and sociological imagination surrounding this can be found in Robert Wuthnow, *Inventing American Religion: Polls, Surveys, and the Tenuous Quest for the Nation's Faith* (New York: Oxford University Press, 2015).
5. See Evan Haefeli, this volume; also Carrie Tirado Bramen, *The Uses of Variety: Modern Americanism and the Quest for National Distinctiveness* (Cambridge, Mass.: Harvard University Press, 2009); Courtney Bender and Pamela Klassen, eds., *After Pluralism: Reimagining Religious Engagement* (New York: Columbia University Press, 2010); and Courtney Bender, "Pluralism and Secularism," in *Religion on The Edge: De-Centering and Re-Centering the Sociology Of Religion*, ed. Courtney Bender, Wendy Cadge, Peggy Levitt, and David Smilde, 137–58 (New York: Oxford, 2011). The chronotopic aspects of this exceptionalism frame religious pluralism as an unfulfilled promise and, as it is unfinished, any particular project of religious pluralism or interfaith is understood and accepted as pointing toward a

future when it would be realized. In practice, this may mean that future-tense interfaith imaginaries have the capacity to incorporate and thereby apparently neutralize a genealogical criticism of pluralism as extending from a secular-liberal-protestant discourse.

6. "All Mother Earth's Children Live on the Same Street," American Airlines, Inc., 1946. John W. Hartman Center for Sales, Advertising & Marketing History, Digital Collections, Ad*Access. Downloaded August 24, 2020. https://idn.duke.edu/ark:/87924/r4d795v97.

7. Joseph Corn, *Winged Gospel: America's Romance with Aviation* (Baltimore: Johns Hopkins University Press, 2002), 130. The air globe's indivisible imaginary overlooked the significant number of conventions and international laws that carved up the sky into bounded and identified airspace regions and that determined impassable borders and various kinds of technologically and internationally mediated jurisdictions.

8. We can compare the space–time imaginaries of American efforts as a peacemaking emissary with many other examples in this volume—for example, Helge Årsheim's observations that, while "the origins of the idea of Norway as a peacemaker in international affairs" are complex, they are often posed as result of "centuries of subjugation at the hands of Denmark and Sweden."

9. William Gilpin, *The Cosmopolitan Railway: Compacting and Fusing Together all the World's Continents* (San Francisco: History Company, 1890). Gilpin's treatise is one of hundreds of late-nineteenth-century American utopian books. Books in this popular genre fused science fiction and moral treatise, often offering up in addition articulated imaginations of the future of America and its role in the world. See Susan Matarese, *American Foreign Policy and the Utopian Imagination* (Boston: University of Massachusetts, 2001).

10. Gilpin, quoted in Richard Slotkin, *The Fatal Environment: The Myth of the Frontier in the Age of Industrialization 1800–1890* (Tulsa: University of Oklahoma Press, 1985), 221. Slotkin observes that Gilpin's cosmopolitanism did not extend to Native Americans or Black Americans: "although Gilpin cited the 'unity' of the Indian races as proof of the unifying tendency of the American continent, he had no brief for preserving Indian title or cultural existence . . . They were legitimate targets of wars of extermination—those wars that Gilpin asserted were the peculiar geomorphically induced destiny of Europe and Asia." Slotkin, *Fatal Environment*, 222. These evident omissions (and the violence that they underwrite) are crucial to the narrative. Yet I wish to pause to consider in this essay how arguments to "bring in" those groups violently excluded from these projects do little to destabilize the idea that Gilpin and Rand McNally and many others take in stride—namely, that the "freedoms" and "openness" of America exist and that, at some point in the future, all of the diversity of the world will be embraced by this promise.

11. Frederick Turner, *The Frontier in American History* (New York: Henry Holt, 1921); and John B. Boles, "Turner, the Frontier, and the Study of Religion in America," *Journal of the Early Republic* 13, no. 2 (1993): 205–16.

12. Peter G. Mode, *The Frontier Spirit of American Christianity* (New York: Macmillan, 1923), 12, 13.

13. Mode, *The Frontier Spirit of American Christianity*.
14. Sidney E. Mead, *The Lively Experiment* (New York: Harper and Row, 1963), 12. The landscape does not work the same way on all people. Mead observes that not all travelers appear equipped for the transformation into a spatially oriented frontier. All those stuck in time (that is, history) included Catholics, Native Americans, and "Orientals." See also John Corrigan, *Emptiness: Feeling Christian in America* (New York: Oxford University Press, 2015).
15. Henry James, *American Scene* (1907; repr. New York: Penguin Classics, 1994).
16. Paul Rosenfeld, "Epilogue: Port of New York," in *Port of New York: Essays on Fourteen American Modernists* (New York: Harcourt Brace, 1924), 283.
17. Rosenfeld, "Epilogue: Port of New York," 292. By the 1920s the skyscraper was bundled into other projects of an American vision of a future of strength taking shape through worldwide connectivity. Courtney Bender, "No Horizon: Some Considerations on the Standpoint of the Secular," paper prepared for the workshop Anthropology Within and Without the Secular Condition, CUNY Graduate School, New York, September 2017; and Adrienne Brown, *The Black Skyscraper: Architecture and the Perception of Race* (Baltimore: Johns Hopkins University Press, 2018).
18. Rosenfeld, "Epilogue: Port of New York," 295.
19. On Rosenfeld's circle (that of Alfred Stieglitz), see Wanda Corn, *The Great American Thing: Modern Art and National Identity, 1915–1935* (Berkeley: University of California Press, 1999).
20. David Nye, *American Technological Sublime* (Boston: MIT Press, 1996) xiii–ix. Nye's history extends the frame of "technological sublime," coined by Perry Miller in *The Life of the Mind in America* (New York: Harcourt, Brace & World, 1965). The technological sublime, as a popular description of industry, science, technology—and also their blurring and reimagination or linking to the landscape's natural wonders—fused together Americans' sense of their own place in human history and progress.
21. For two different and extended treatments of American landscapes, secularism and religion, see Nicholas Howe, *Landscapes of the Secular: Law, Religion, and American Sacred Space* (Chicago: University of Chicago Press, 2016); and Kerry Mitchell, *Spirituality and the State: Managing Nature and Experience in America's National Parks* (New York: New York University Press, 2016). We might include in a list of apophatic speakers Robert N. Bellah, "Civil Religion in America," *Daedalus* (1967): 1–21; various contributions in Russel Richey, ed., *American Civil Religion* (New York: Harper and Row, 1974); and Philip Gorski, *American Covenant: A History of Civil Religion from the Puritans to the Present* (Princeton, N.J.: Princeton University Press, 2017).
22. Wendy Cadge, "The Evolution of American Airport Chapels: Local Negotiations in Religiously Pluralistic Contexts," *Religion and American Culture* 28, no. 1 (2018): 135–65.
23. The dedication ceremony was a fundraiser. The prepared speech by Humphrey and a transcript of the full event are available online through the Minnesota State Historical Society portal, or directly at this link http://www2.mnhs.org/library/findaids/00442/pdfa/00442-02083.pdf (accessed 15 March 2020).

24. Correspondence, Monsignor Thomas J. Flanagan to Robert J. Aaronson, June 28, 1985, RG Public Information Office, Topic Files, File Unit: Our Lady of the Skies Chapel—Kennedy Airport, Roman Catholic Diocese of Brooklyn, Diocesan Archives, Brooklyn, New York.
25. Minutes and correspondence regarding John F. Kennedy airport chapel, William Adams Brown Ecumenical Archives, Council of Churches of the City of New York, Department of Church Planning and Research, Series 3A, Box 33, Folder 5, Burke Library at Union Theological Seminary, Columbia University in the City of New York.
26. "Agreement of Lease," New York Board of Rabbis Records, I-506, box 6, folder 13, American Jewish Historical Society, New York, New York, and Boston, Massachusetts.
27. Correspondence (Very Rev.) Monsignor Frances X. Fitz Gibbon to Very Rev. Msgr. John J. Heneghan, March 26, 1959, RG Public Information Office, Topic Files, File Unit: Our Lady of the Skies Chapel—Kennedy Airport, Roman Catholic Diocese of Brooklyn, Diocesan Archives.
28. Drawings, Protestant Chapel, 1962, Box 57, Roll 102, Edgar Tafel architectural records and papers, 1919–2005, Department of Drawings & Archives, Avery Architectural and Fine Arts Library, Columbia University.
29. "Controversy over Airport Chapels," n.d., RG Public Information Office, Topic Files, File Unit: Our Lady of the Skies Chapel—Kennedy Airport, Roman Catholic Diocese of Brooklyn, Diocesan Archives.
30. The theme of "unity" in the chapels was more evident from the air, as the three buildings had been designed in architectural coordination, unlike the rest of the airport. As Nicholas Bloom writes, the Port Authority designed the airport as a "terminal city" and allowed each U.S. airline carrier to design and build its own terminal—the resulting architectural noncoordination of the terminals and the array of other buildings for freight, cargo, and hangars and access made the airport visually un-unified, with the exception of the three chapels. Nicholas Bloom, *The Metropolitan Airport: JFK International and Modern New York* (Philadelphia: University of Pennsylvania Press, 2015).
31. "Faith Shines Equal," Tri-Faith Chapel Plaza promotional booklet, n.d. [1966], RG Public Information Office, Topic Files, File Unit: Our Lady of the Skies Chapel—Kennedy Airport. Roman Catholic Diocese of Brooklyn, Diocesan Archives.
32. Robert Frost, "And All We Call American," in *The Poetry of Robert Frost: The Collected Poems, Complete and Unabridged* ed. Edward Connery Latham, 416–17 (New York: Henry Holt and Company, 1979).
33. Charles Long, "Civil Rights—Civil Religion: Visible People and Invisible Religion," in *American Civil Religion*, ed. Russel Richey and Donald G. Jones (New York: Harper and Row, 1974), 219–20.

PART II
Making Ourselves

5

Homemaking in Palestine

Jessie Sampter, Religion, and Relation

SARAH IMHOFF

Jessie Sampter, a thirty-six-year-old single American Jew, packed her bags and moved to Palestine in 1919, when much of it was still a "malarial swamp," in the words of her friend and fellow Zionist Lotta Levensohn.[1] Just weeks before she left, she wrote to her sister, Elvie: "I write in the full consciousness that my not returning to America is among likelihoods, either because I may not outlive the year of probation, or because at the end of that year I shall have found in Palestine that spiritual fulfillment, that 'at-homeness.'"[2] Sampter felt elements of home in the United States, the land of her birth and citizenship, but with her embrace of Zionism, she also searched for something more.

Her move to Palestine, where she would live the rest of her life, was both political and religious. "I believe with the prophets that humanity is one as God is one. Our life both in our own land and elsewhere has brought this home to us, as we have always mingled with many peoples, and probably always shall," she wrote the year before she sailed. But she also acutely felt the need for "the reestablishment of a Jewish homeland in Palestine."[3] In addition to the political need for safety and self-determination of the Jewish people, Sampter was driven by the need for "spiritual fulfillment," a home of theologically infused geography. Biblical landscapes and histories made Palestine the place for this home. She wrote these words—and many other Zionist essays and poems—from the United States before she had ever visited the faraway land. Yet they represented the complex feelings about home that she would have for the rest of her life.

As fascinating as Sampter's story is, telling it raises the question: Why think about the categories "at home" and "abroad" through the life and thought of a single person? Why explore these categories through a microscope, as it were?

A QUESTION OF SCALE

Since the time of Galileo, scientists have warned us about the limitations of our intuitions about scale. Could there be an elephant-sized insect? A human as tall as a redwood? A skyscraper a mile high? The answer is no, in essence: simply scaled up, all of these would collapse under their own weight. We cannot use what we know about these organisms and structures to extrapolate linearly. A human who was proportioned just like you but twice as tall as you would, in fact, weigh an awful lot more than twice what you do. (Eight times what you do, to be precise.) Making these kinds of quantitative observations and calculations is straightforward once we understand the math underpinning them, although the results may not be intuitive.

Mathematical observations about scale can also point us to another kind of difference—not only a quantitative difference, but also a qualitative one, which is neither straightforward nor possible to extrapolate. A colony of bees, for example, does not have just the biology of one bee scaled up by fifty thousand. The colony is a new and different structure. So if we want to understand bees, bee culture, and bee concepts, we need to study both levels: the individual bee and the bee colony. In *Scale*, physicist Geoffrey West writes: "a typical complex system is composed of myriad individual constituents or agents that once aggregated take on collective characteristics that are usually not manifested in, nor could easily be predicted from, the properties of the individual components themselves."[4] Bee colonies are complex systems. So are human governments and religious bodies.

These scientific warnings about the reality of non-scalability also have anthropological and political analogs. Scaling up or down with respect to human society is not a merely matter of size. Different levels entail different structures and relationships. A nation may be an aggregate of humans, but it is not merely that. And it is surely not just one giant human. Likewise, a person is not just a very tiny nation. So, I suggest, we can best understand the conceptual categories of home and abroad by looking at a variety of "sizes" of social and political groups because what we can learn from each of these sizes is not always easy to predict or extrapolate from others. Looking at a complex system, such as a nation or a nongovernmental organization, can tell us only some of what we want to know about families or an individual person. Our observations about one point on the scale of human society cannot reliably help us predict the processes and experiences at another level.

Yet humans are a central part of what makes up a nation. So humans are both like and unlike a nation. If we want to study home and abroad, concepts that operate at both individual and national levels, then we will need to look at both. The "right" scale for studying religion and politics at home and abroad, then, is necessarily a number of different scales, from the individual person to the social group to the nation.

The Religion at Home and Abroad project entails close studies at a variety of locations: the international networks of U.S. Baptists and other evangelicals thinking about apartheid in South Africa, the religious norms of Norway in both domestic and international senses, and the relationship of religion and education in Japan, but also the 1899 hurricane in Puerto Rico and a handful of days from a play about Muhammad Ali's life. In one way, like Cooper Harriss's essay on Ali in this volume, this essay represents the extreme end of the spectrum of social groups: the case of a single person. But Jessie Sampter's life and thought also show that the small-scale, single-person approach intersects with the larger-scale ones. It is not isolated, and as much as we may try to concentrate on an individual, her life continually forces us to incorporate other people, institutions, and larger-scale ideas.

Jessie Sampter also interests me as a locus of studying "at home" and "abroad" because of what she was not. She was not a political leader. No one would mistake a study of her as a representative example for a study of American public policy as a whole, or even as a representative example for a study of institutional Zionism writ large. Unlike the assumptions possible in the case of the study of, say, Helge Årsheim's chapter in this volume on the church and the Norwegian normal, Sampter's life and thought cannot reasonably be taken as a microcosm of some larger and more complex social or political group.

So what do we see when we look at Sampter's life that we might not see in studies of other "sizes"? Two things in particular have caught my attention, and I think both are worth attending to: affect and relationships. Although Sampter often felt lonely, her life and thought were profoundly relational. Her personal relationships deeply informed her writing, coming through in intellectual work, her Zionist propaganda, her letters to her sister and friends, and even some of her professional life and work. Both relationships and affect also influenced what counted as home and what seemed foreign, and in this sense studying Sampter illuminates the at-home and the abroad at the level of the individual person.

Sampter also draws our attention to a theme that recurs across many of the "sizes" of these studies: she developed a sense of what religion is and should be in the United States and brought that version with her as she crossed boundaries, relocated, and even engaged in homemaking elsewhere—Palestine, in her case. At first glance, Jessie Sampter's religious thought exemplifies American religion "at home." But her life seems to tell another story. In her own words, she left New York to find "at-homeness" in Palestine when contracting malaria was par for the course, when women could not vote, and where her preferred toilet paper was nowhere to be found. She went to participate in the experiment in Jewish nationalism, but she also knew that the land was politically in flux, still transitioning into British imperial hands during her first years there. What's more, unlike other American Zionists of her time, Sampter gave up her U.S. citizenship.[5] Yet even while she exchanged one home for another, her conception of religion stayed relatively steady.

This chapter considers religion both at home and abroad through the life of a single person. Perhaps predictably, Sampter's life suggests that the two blurred and shifted—in some ways the United States was home, in other ways Palestine was home, and in yet other ways neither was ever quite home. In Sampter's life, "abroad" does not fully capture home's opposite: not-home was not only a geographical and political concept, but it was also a religious and historical concept characterized by distance from ideals more than distance from a site. Even where they were geographically or socially fraught, the concepts of home and its opposite were meaningful in Sampter's writings. There, home appears as an unrealized ideal, whose contours were shaped by Sampter's experiences of home and not-home in both the United States and Palestine.

THE UNITED STATES AS HOME

I find Sampter's life and thought to be a particularly helpful way to think through American assumptions about religion "at home" because they embody a dichotomy: on the one hand she seems to run against the grain of American religious norms, and yet in other ways she was quintessentially American. She was inside, then chose to be outside, and yet even after she relinquished her U.S. citizenship, she still exemplified a model of combination and incorporation typical of American religion.

Jessie Sampter was born to an upper-middle-class, New York, Ethical Culture family with Jewish background. Jessie only understood herself to be Jewish after her eight-year-old playmates called her a Jew and she ran to her parents in confusion. She recounted the emotionally charged moment several times in her essays and autobiographical writing in a way that hints at her lifelong interest in religious belonging and at-homeness. In her early life she was a quintessential product of U.S. religious norms: she grew up in a household that emphasized the individual, conscience-based, ethical essence of religion. Sampter crafted her own religious worldview through choosing insights from a wide variety of religious texts, from the Hebrew Bible and New Testament to the Vedas, Christian Science literature, Theosophy, and the transcendentalists, and eventually the theosophically influenced thought of Jiddu Krishnamurti. But as she grew to embrace Judaism and Zionism, she came to see herself as heir to a peoplehood-based tradition that was far less concerned with individual belief than corporate belonging. She joined a kibbutz and advocated the radical reorganization of social and economic life in favor of the collective rather than the nuclear family. Nevertheless, a fascinating tension between the individual and the collective remained in her own understanding of religion.

Religion "at home," "in America," in the protestant way Winnifred Sullivan and Elizabeth Shakman Hurd describe in this volume, tends to take the individual as the essential unit of religion. This protestant mode assumes that religion is based on belief or faith, both of which are understood as interior to the individual. This is not a transhistorical characterization, but, following Evan Haefeli, we can see it as part of a "modern American condition of pluralism and religious freedom [that] ... was the unexpected product of a dramatic series of political revolutions that radically reshaped the ecclesiastical landscape of possibilities several times over between Europeans' first encounter with North America and the end of the American Civil War." This belief model increasingly describes the way Americans have seen religion in the twentieth and early twenty-first centuries. For instance, we can see this in the language of recent U.S. Supreme Court decisions, which have routinely referred to "faiths" and have located the validity of a religion at the level of a single person's belief rather than institutional interpretations. Even in the 2015 case concerning Hobby Lobby, which is a corporation and not a person, both majority and dissenting opinions focused on the sincerity of "belief." Belief. Faith. These seem to be the location of real religion, and these are located within the individual person. Even when a business is under consideration, the real locus of religion seems to be in the interior of the persons who run that business.

I am not claiming that this individual-focused protestant model of religion is actually the best way to understand religion in the United States, but rather that it was the primary way most U.S. Americans *did* see religion—Sampter included. So "American religion" is short for "the predominant ways U.S. Americans thought about religion" rather than a scholarly view that claims this is the best way to understand how Americans actually did religion. As Winnifred Sullivan's essay in this volume demonstrates so clearly, seemingly abstract categories such as religion and law are not only the purview of scholars; people use these categories when they make sense of the world around them. Even when scholars might disagree with those people about, say, what religion really is, these people's ideas are not merely mistaken or fantasies. In Sullivan's chapter, the litigant and the church see their conflict process as law even though many scholars do not recognize it as "real" law. It matters that the actors see it as law, and they have a robust understanding of what that means. Here I recognize that Sampter's ideas about religion may not map seamlessly onto scholarly ones, but that does not diminish the power for her ideas to structure her own life and world. To talk about American religion is also not to claim uniqueness; people all over the globe drew on multiple religious traditions when creating their own worldviews, but disestablishment allowed some US Americans to identify this move with the state in ways that differed from many other nations.

In addition, this model in which religion "really" resides in the individual and her own faith or belief works far better for some religious communities—and religious individuals—than for others. To take a salient example here, for many traditional Jewish communities, Jewishness is not founded primarily in faith or belief. Jewishness exists and is reinforced by communal belonging and by religious practices. In this way, Judaism doesn't fit the dominant American model.

But for some of the Jews around Jessie Sampter, a model of religion with the individual, and individual belief, at its center did resonate. For example, many late nineteenth- and early twentieth-century Reform rabbis simply loved the philosopher Immanuel Kant, whose thought emphasized the individual and her will as the center of religious life. Many of these rabbis, such as Kaufmann Kohler and Hyman Gerson Enelow, articulated a Judaism that centered on the individual person's intellectual apprehension of God and the Bible—not the Talmud and its nonlinear and perhaps even nonrational modes of expression. Ethical Culture, founded by former Reform rabbi Felix Adler, emphasized the importance of a rational ethical system, which each individual should come to herself, rather than ingesting dogma from a community.

Jessie Sampter lived her early years immersed in this worldview. Her first book, *The Great Adventurer* (1909), used a hybrid prose-poetry style to theorize each individual person as an adventurer. In it, religion appears as a set of beliefs consonant with a person's individual experience, and this experience is a profoundly relational one: "I hear a voice, and I know my friend is near me. I behold a face, and I know it is the face of one I love.... I behold a green hill, and I believe that the upheaved rock is beneath it; I see the surface of a lake, and I believe there is a depth below. Such is my faith. I behold the surface and believe in the depth."[6] She dedicated the book to her dear friend and mentor

Josephine Lazarus, with whom she had spent many hours discussing writing and philosophy.

The following year she published *The Seekers*, a chronicle of a weekly seminar she had conducted with six teenagers. Their discussions focused on religious questions but pursued them through joint philosophical inquiry while eschewing dogma, devotion to particular religious texts, communally recognized authorities, and even God language. Sampter developed her ideas through the personal relationships with the teenagers: "This is a live book," she began. "It was lived first, and written only afterward.... It is a philosophic adventure, an experiment, written down by one but lived by seven."[7] Her intellectual investment in the participants is palpable; religious ideas were not merely ideas but ideas developed and tested through life experience and relationships. Although *The Seekers* was not a commercial success, the Harvard philosopher Josiah Royce wrote its praise-laden introduction, and it won her wider recognition in intellectual circles. G. Stanley Hall offered her a position at Clark University on its basis, even though she did not have a college degree. Her model of an interior, personal, belief-centered religion made her right at home in the United States.

THE UNITED STATES AS NOT-HOME

And yet in the United States Sampter often felt unmoored, religiously and politically—feelings that made themselves clearer when she encountered Zionism. In the early 1910s she had been attending a Unitarian Church, but when the Jewish poet Hyman Segal came and shared his poetry from *The Book of Pain-Struggle*, she felt "as if a door had been opened."[8] The book featured a single hero who inhabited a world (unsurprisingly) of pain and struggle, which he tried to comprehend. After finding an ancient parchment in the desert, the protagonist heard a voice say: "the land / Languisheth without its own people / And man without his ancient faith."[9] Segal's description of the spiritual and physical worlds as one of pain as well as of belonging and unity resonated deeply with Sampter. She credited Segal with her awakening as a Zionist and as a Jew.

Her Zionism began with a feeling of profound kinship with other Jews—a sense that, both religiously and politically, Jews were her people. She began attending synagogue with Hadassah leader Henrietta Szold and Szold's mother. "I have a people, a congregation. It is not in the church of the synagogue. It is in the streets, in the tenements, in the crowded 'Pale' of Russia and Poland, in the little agricultural settlements in Palestine.... It is my people, a chosen people.

God has called it, has chosen it for suffering and service. The God that is in me, is also in my people."[10] She lived for a time in a settlement house, where she was closer to immigrant Jews than to the acculturated Jewish life she had known, and became more religiously observant.

As she began to feel more connected to Jewish peoplehood and the possibility of a Jewish home, Sampter also began to feel less at home in American political space. World War I, and later American involvement in it, shook her sense of the United States as a space she could call hers. Sampter had often been proud to be an American because of democracy, but the war made her critical of both the government and her fellow citizens. The war demonstrated that there was something about Americanism that had become wrapped up in imperialism: "My pacifism threatened my Americanism, my Zionism, and yet not their intrinsic spirit, but the false ideal set up for a moment by a war-mad people."[11] She and fellow Zionist Henrietta Szold offered their resignations from official Zionist positions over their pacifism. When Louis Brandeis and other Zionist leaders insisted that they stay, these men claimed that pacifists could be good patriots too.

But her sense that there was something at odds between a Zionist vision of Jewish peoplehood and dominant American ideas about religion was not misplaced, and her sense of this combined with her own religious ideals would soon lead her to Palestine.

HOMEMAKING IN PALESTINE

Sampter arrived in Palestine and went quickly to the Hadassah hospital. Sick and exhausted from the trip and still living with the effects of childhood polio, she needed care. But the hospital also brought her community. Soon she met Leah Berlin, a Russian labor Zionist, who would become her housemate, dear friend, and partner in Zionist life. Berlin also became an acute observer of Sampter herself. Almost a year after Sampter's arrival, she had been feeling depressed and wrote to her sister, "Leah says I am not homesick but friendsick, and I suppose she is right."[12] Although Sampter missed her friends who were abroad, she developed new friendships too. In Palestine, as everywhere, relationships and affect intertwined with politics, religion, and ideology in the quest to make a home.

From her earliest days in Palestine, Sampter observed the religious dynamics around her. She wrote to her sister, Elvie, complaining about observant Jews who refused to help their neighbors with physical labor, Arabs who held outdated ideas, and both sides who fought over religious sites unnecessarily. "I want the Arabs to drop their outworn romantic nationalism as I have dropped mine. I want Jews to drop theirs," she wrote, still advocating for a rational religion consonant with one's own experiences.[13] Sullivan and Hurd write in this volume's introduction, "religion at home is assumed to be both tamed and free in a way not yet achieved by religion in other places or with the religion of certain internal 'others.'" Sampter, I think, would have agreed. But if she bought into this type of American exceptionalism, why would she go to Palestine?

Sampter's Zionism entailed intimate connection with a people, with a land, and with the divine. She described it in this way:

> It meant social salvation, for the Jews and through the Jews for mankind. The Jewish people has a social religious ideal, the socialist foundation but with a watch tower facing the stars; the divinity, the holiness of man because God is holy, the equality, the oneness of man because God is one.... For the scattered Jewish people they are only dreams, but in our own land, lived by a community, they will become a beacon to mankind, a Messiah to the world. The Jewish people is the Messianic people; it is the crucified; by its sufferings the world shall be saved, and its resurrection in its own land shall give life to mankind.[14]

Sampter's fascinating portrait of Zionism drew on Judaism and Christianity and her understanding of Hinduism, which exemplified the recombinatory spirit of her religious thought. And yet it also staked a particular claim for a particular people in a particular land. She saw these people as her people, and the land as rejuvenating the people. These rejuvenated people would in turn help to improve humanity as a whole.

From the time of her Zionist conversion, Sampter discussed Zionism and Judaism in fundamentally collective ways. In 1915 the American Zionist women's organization Hadassah published Sampter's *A Course on Zionism*. There she framed the Jewish problem in terms of chronic illness, which reflected her own disability from childhood polio: "We are a sick people. Our national will has been atrophied by age-long inertia. But here and there certain organs are coming back to life and action. We must exercise and strengthen them with work, and through their force and activity the whole body shall be revived."[15] Sampter saw all Jews as sharing a collective body. Even beyond a body politic (although Jews might become that too), Jews shared an interpersonal connection at an almost physical level. In fact, throughout her life, starting even before her Zionism, she also held that all humans were spiritually and materially connected.

Sampter's Zionism marked Palestine as the collective Jewish home in a theological sense, but she did not always see that reflected in political reality. To become the true home of the Jewish people, she and others would need to engage in homemaking. For Hadassah, this took more stereotypically gendered forms of medical care for mothers and children, hospitals, school lunches, and educational systems. Eradication of malaria constituted a priority, as did the Tipat Halav program, designed to reduce infant mortality by teaching mothers about hygiene and providing milk to mothers who could not nurse their babies.[16] Along these lines of "women's work," Sampter took a keen interest in education for Yemenite children and their education. But her homemaking also took the intellectual form of bringing her vision of religion to the society.

Not all Jews shared her way of understanding religion, and she was overtly critical of both Jews and Jewish life as she saw them in Palestine. After living in Jerusalem for a little more than a year, she wrote to her friend and mentor Mordecai Kaplan, "It is all much better and much worse than we could possibly have imagined."[17] Palestine did not offer religious communities that provided the "at-homeness" in the way she had hoped. After an unexpected snowfall in her first winter in Jerusalem, for example, she railed against the young religious men who refused to work because they were "too fine" and insisted on leaving the shoveling of roofs to others—to teachers and engineers and Yemenites who lived in the city.[18]

"I love my land. I shall live and die here, with this suffering people," she wrote. "But where is the vision? I see the past, pious, tragic, ineffectual. I see a present arrogant, disillusioned, uncertain. I see no future." Rather than giving up or declaring the movement failed, she declared, "we ourselves are the future; I am the future. There must be a way."[19] It was not a triumphant declaration; it was a desperate one. She saw no real options for a path toward realizing the idealized connection of land, history, and people—*home*—and yet she believed that one must still be possible.

And, as any astute observer would note, many people already lived in Palestine before Zionists began to immigrate in large numbers. According to the British government, the year after she arrived, Palestine had about 75,000 Jews, 75,000 Christians, and 560,000 Muslims.[20] Zionism could claim a national home for the Jewish people, but a significant part of that project would need to be homemaking. Unlike in the poetry of Hyman Segal, the land of Palestine did not "[languish] "without its own people." On the contrary, several peoples claimed it. Intellectually, Sampter claimed that Jewish homemaking would not require subjugation of others: "The 'holy land' means one land for one people—the national body for the national soul—and it precludes conquest and empire."[21] Yet she lived through violence in 1920 and 1929 that suggested otherwise. Jews would have to fight non-Jewish Arabs who lived in Palestine if they wanted to claim the land as a Jewish state.

Britain started issuing Palestinian passports in 1926, and Sampter applied for one as soon as she could.[22] During the 1929 Hebron massacre, in which sixty-seven Jews were killed, Sampter wrote:

> The American citizens in Jewish Palestine sent a cable to Washington asking the Government to protect against the criminal negligence of the local administration which, among other horrors, was responsible for the piecemeal butchery—to be precise—of eight American boys, defenseless students in the Academy at Hebron. Although I contributed a word or two to the cable, I was not able to sign it because I am no longer an American citizen but a Palestinian. Never have I been so glad of this change of citizenship. I have a right to the protection of my own government in my own country and I do not want to be tempted to ask for special privileges.[23]

Sampter saw homemaking as an activity that should rightly be undertaken by people permanently living in Palestine. They had the political and emotional experiences that Zionists abroad and others in Palestine (particularly the British) lacked.

In "Nationalism," an unpublished piece she later retitled "Arab," Sampter wrote about her hopes for the future of Palestine. We would now label Sampter a binationalist, a person who wanted a state for Jews and non-Jewish Arabs together. Although she wanted to upbuild the land as a Jew, she vehemently rejected the idea of a Jewish state: "I want no special government; only that which is good for us all. I surely want no such anachronistic idol as a Jewish state, a racial state!" Nationalism could poison societies. World War I had proven that for the pacifist Sampter, and Palestine should not follow down a similar path. The proper goals of Zionism were "to re-settle Palestine with Jews" and to work the land. And part of this resettlement was designed to help "make life for the Arabs and other inhabitants a richer, cleaner, more exciting experience."[24] Sampter insisted that a good Jewish Zionist was a good neighbor, although, as this passage suggests, her neighborliness sometimes had significant undertones of Orientalism.

In addition to her political theorizing, she engaged in more personal kinds of homemaking. When she and Leah Berlin moved in together, Sampter described their rooms in great detail, including a sketch of everything from clothes closets to cupboards to chairs. "We are so comfortable and cozy," she wrote, "and I think our sitting room is really beautiful. Everyone loves it, and it is a pleasure to entertain our friends with our new tea cups."[25] Sampter and Berlin continued to live together even after Berlin's mother and siblings arrived in Palestine. Sampter eventually moved out to have a house built in Rehovot for herself and Tamar, a Yemenite orphan she adopted. Throughout their time in the Rehovot house, Sampter sent her sister descriptions and diagrams of the house and the garden. Her reflections on these material aspects of homemaking highlight both the role of affect and the centrality of relationships.

Sampter also brought to life the Zionist adage of "making the desert bloom:" She eagerly awaited the Burpee seed catalog. She pruned her roses. She exchanged nasturtium seeds with her sister. She fell in love with orange groves. When she moved out of her house in Rehovot to go to Kibbutz Givat Brenner, she wrote: "I find it hard to leave the garden, the trees, but I realize that 6 years ago this was bare earth, and in three years I can have as lovely a one again, on what is now bare earth. That is the joy of creation."[26] The deal she made when she and Leah Berlin joined Givat Brenner included using her money to build a "rest home" for workers—one with vegetarian food and an avidly tended garden beside it.

Although Palestine was not a blank canvas, not a "land without a people," Sampter and other Zionists imbued it with meaning. They sought to change the

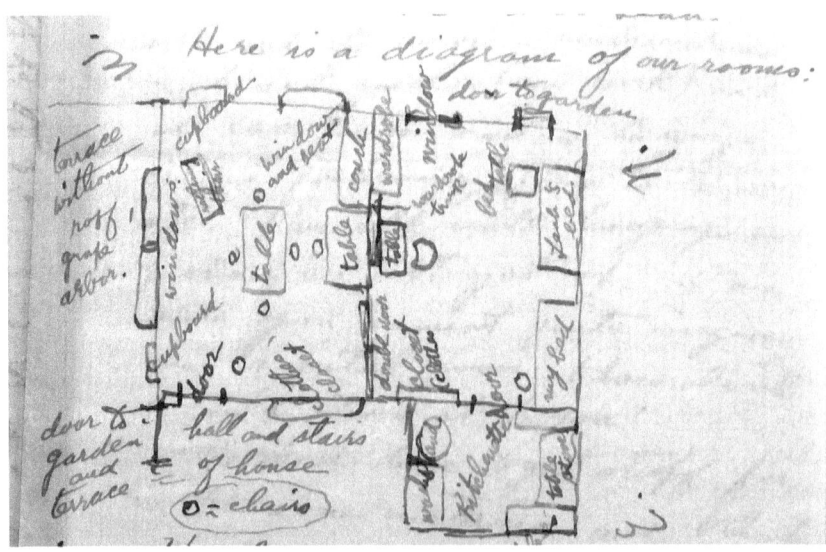

FIGURE 5.1 Sampter's sketch of the home she and Leah moved into in late 1920.

Courtesy of Central Zionist Archives.

space of the land into their own place (a process that was, of course, contested by others with their own affective attachments, politics, and meanings). This homemaking took place on familiar political levels, such as the 1917 Balfour Declaration, which declared Great Britain's support for "the establishment in Palestine of a national home for the Jewish people."[27] And as Sampter's story suggests, it also took place at the intimate level of the individual and her affective relationship to the land.

CONCLUSION: AMERICAN RELIGION ABROAD

Throughout her life Sampter retained her outlook on what religion should be. Even at her most religiously observant, she wasn't a recognizably Orthodox Jew. Nor was she ever a secularist Zionist. Although she strongly identified as Jewish, she remained nearly omnivorous when it came to religious thought. Even after she moved into collective kibbutz living—what most saw as the icon of the new Jewish life in Palestine—she spent a significant amount of her time translating the theosophically inclined thought of Jiddu Krishnamurthi into Hebrew.

Sampter's views of religious collectivity also did not mirror most of the American Zionist community. In its early years, American Zionism was more about American Jews supporting the idea of a safe haven for fellow Jews abroad than it was about a homeland for themselves. They had a homeland: the United States. Moving to Palestine, or even visiting, was unlikely and, for most, downright undesirable. Even Henrietta Szold, long-time president of Hadassah, deeply wanted to come back home to the United States to live her life but felt needed in Palestine. Jessie Sampter was one of the few who moved to Palestine, and one of even fewer who stayed. She understood herself to be spiritually—and even, it seems at times, materially—connected to other Jews.

In this way, just as Sampter was both religious insider and religious outsider in the United States and Palestine, she also made use of both insider and outsider ideas of what religion was. Sampter continued to think that the essential unit of religion is the individual. But she also thought that the enlightened individual will realize that the collective—peoplehood—is the ideal (and truthful) vision of spirituality and the world. Her decision to adopt Tamar, a Yemenite Jewish orphan, and move with Leah onto a kibbutz with communal finances and land was in concert with this vision of peoplehood as religion. Her Zionism did not fit easily into a model of religion centered on individual belief.

And yet, even as she took on Judaism and Zionism, Sampter retained many of her structural assumptions about what religion was and how it should work. True religion, even after Sampter became a Zionist, was something the individual person should come to, intellectually and experientially. Through reading, relationships, discussion, observation of the world, and experience, a person would realize that the world has a unity. Each person is one with other people and with the natural world. In this way Sampter's religious thought had elements of both the individual-as-essential-unit (a protestant American model) and peoplehood (one Judaism/Zionism model). We might say that Sampter took American religion with her when she went abroad.

NOTES

1. Lotta Levensohn, *Vision and Fulfillment* (New York: Greystone, 1950), 20.
2. Sampter to Elvie Wachenheim, July 16, 1919, A 219\3, Central Zionist Archives, Jerusalem (hereafter, CZA).
3. Jessie Sampter, "I Told You So," *Maccabaean* (March 1918).
4. Geoffrey West, *Scale: The Universal Laws of Growth, Innovation, Sustainability, and the Pace of Life in Organisms, Cities, Economies, and Companies* (New York: Penguin, 2017), 21.
5. The Justice Simon Agranat also gave up his citizenship in 1942, but in his case it was only with extreme reluctance, and his judgeship depended on it. Pnina Lahav, *Judgment in Jerusalem: Chief Justice Simon Agranat and the Zionist Century* (Berkeley: University of California Press, 1997), 63–65.
6. Jessie Sampter, *The Great Adventurer* (New York: R. Kerr Press, 1909), no pagination [section: "Into the Depths" I].
7. Jessie Sampter, *Seekers* (New York: Mitchell Kennerley, 1910), 1.
8. Joyce Antler, *The Journey Home: Jewish Women and the American Century* (New York: Free Press, 1997); and Bertha Badt-Strauss, *White Fire: The Life and Works of Jessie Sampter* (Arno Press, 1956), 32.
9. Hyman Segal, *The Book of Pain Struggle, Called: The Prophecy of Fulfillment* (New York: self-published, 1911), 71.
10. Jessie Sampter, "The Speaking Heart," 160–62, CZA A 219\11.
11. Sampter, "Speaking Heart," 244.
12. Jessie Sampter to Elvie Wachenheim, September 20, 1920. CZA A219\42.
13. Sampter, "Arab" CZA A219\10.
14. Sampter, "Speaking Heart," 162.
15. Sampter, *A Course on Zionism* (New York: Federation of American Zionists, 1915), 7.
16. Erica Simmons, "Playgrounds and Penny Lunches: American Social Welfare in the Yishuv," *American Jewish History* 92, no. 3 (September 2004): 263–97.
17. Jessie Sampter to Mordecai Kaplan, December 30, 1920, Mordecai Kaplan papers, SC-6102, American Jewish Archives, Cincinnati, Ohio.

18. Jessie Sampter, "Snowbound," 231, CZA A219\1.
19. Sampter, "Speaking Heart," 296.
20. Herbert Samuel, *An Interim Report on the Civil Administration of Palestine* (London: H.M. Stationery Office, 1921).
21. Jessie Sampter, "The Ideal of Peace in Jewish Thought and Life," 4 (1915), CZA A219\14.
22. Mutaz M. Qafisheh, *The International Law Foundations of Palestinian Nationality: A Legal Examination of Palestinian Nationality Under the British Rule*, vol. 7 (Leiden: Brill, 2008), 149.
23. Jessie Sampter, "Testimony," 1 (1929), CZA A219\1.
24. Sampter, "Arab," 1.
25. Jessie Sampter to Elvie Wachenheim, October 14, 1920, CZA A219\42.
26. Jessie Sampter to Elvie Wachenheim, July 6, 1933, CZA A219\31.
27. The text is available at the Jewish Virtual Library website, https://www.jewishvirtuallibrary.org/text-of-the-balfour-declaration.

6

On the Abroad of a Different Home

Muhammad Ali in Micro-Scope

M. COOPER HARRISS

HITTING THE SCALES

A significant challenge for any critic attempting to "make sense" of the boxer Muhammad Ali as a persona and public figure hinges on the question of which Ali one references. Beyond prima facie concerns such as his religious conversion or the attendant changing of his name from Cassius Clay to Muhammad Ali, the sheer length and ambivalence of Ali's public career, spanning nearly six decades, presents its own set of problems. Ali's relationship to U.S. exceptionalism, for instance, changes across the many decades of his career. He ranges from an Olympic-champion boxer, fighting for his country in the 1960 Rome Games, to what I call "the fighter who wouldn't fight," taking religiously derived exception to exceptionalist policies at home and abroad by refusing military induction in 1967. In the final decades of his life he became an all-around "exceptional" American, serving as an official and unofficial emissary for U.S. interests abroad in several African nations circa 1980 and a decade later in Iraq and taking up the mantle of American hero in public both in U.S. and global contexts. How do such reversals square with Ali's long-term popular reputation for political integrity and humanitarian action, rooted in public conceptions of his religious identity? How might this unstably ironic persona find synthesis as it moves through space and time at home and abroad, inflecting these specific moments with the longer legacies that they construct?

One solution might consider the dynamic simultaneity of Ali's exceptionalist identities taken over time, understanding his long career as something of an enclosed system, the variables of whose conversions chart a range of identity and political meaning that yields, over time, to what we might call an "exceptionalist double cross."[1] By taking exception in 1967 Ali eventually *becomes* "exceptional" in the 1980s and beyond, a conversion that in turn alters the meaning of this earlier exception taking (which itself resulted from Ali's 1964 conversion to Islam) and, indeed, the exceptionalism of his first fame as an Olympian. In this way all of his conversions must remain in tension. Ali is never singular, never *either/or*; he always signifies the *both/and*—a plenitude of meaning, the masked *and* the mask.

Such variability, however, does not only play out over the long haul. In many ways the example of Ali requires one to consider questions of scale, which I want to begin speaking about here as "scope"—a term that encompasses temporal spans and visual horizons, deliberately isolating discrete parts of a larger story through shifting frames of periodization. Such mutable frames reconceptualize historical moments as moving targets of accumulated meaningful activity. Consider this example: I recently completed an essay that focuses on three movies about Ali (*The Trials of Muhammad Ali*, *When We Were Kings*, and the feature film *Ali*).[2] In my research it quickly became clear that almost every film about the boxer (and this is not mere selection bias) focuses either directly on or most fully within a single decade span of Ali's life and career—that fecund period between 1964 and 1974.[3] In the former year (1964) he won the heavyweight championship from Sonny Liston and announced his conversion to the Nation of Islam (NOI) the next day. The latter year (1974) represents Ali's regaining of the heavyweight championship from a previously undefeated George Foreman in Kinshasa, Zaire (now the Democratic Republic of the Congo). Within the scope of this temporal frame, Ali films generally narrate an archetypal story of rise, fall, redemption/resurrection, and even an Eliadan sense of "return"— foundational myths whose structures drive the popular reception and digestion of "Muhammad Ali."

One major problem with this particular temporal frame resides in the implications it raises for understanding Ali as a Muslim. The "Rumble in the Jungle" in Zaire, where Ali retook the championship from Foreman (he had been stripped of the title in 1967 as a consequence of his refusal of military conscription), took place in late October 1974. Indeed, NOI leader Elijah Muhammad would die less than four months later and the power struggles for his succession were already well in motion. By ending the story—the didactic myth itself of Ali's career (and his "life," in the biopic)—at this moment in 1974, Ali remains a perpetual member of the NOI. He never joins Warith Deen Muhammad's tack to Sunni Islam via the establishment of the World Community of Al-Islam in the West (later the American Society of Muslims) in 1976; he never comes to reflect this organization's international vision; and he never comes to work with growing immigrant populations to develop new visions of American Islam at home as part of emerging global networks linked abroad.[4] Furthermore, as Ali grows into this exceptional persona from the mid-1970s on, this presumptive (though mistaken) NOI identity becomes domesticated, secularized as an expression of civil rights and religious freedom in the United States. By taking exception, Ali becomes exceptional; as exceptional, his Islam becomes managed and "good," distinct from the "bad" Islam derived from global contexts at home and abroad that culminate with the terror attacks of September 11, 2001.

In this way Ali's late style derives, at least in part, from the secularization of his earlier Islamic status to label him a "good Muslim" for his capacity to transform sincerely held belief in (perhaps unsavory to some) NOI theology into twin expressions of civil rights political theology and its extraordinary exercise of religious freedom. In this way Ali's later Islamic identities beyond the old NOI (Sunni, Sufi, transnational American, and so forth—and of course these also represent an extension of the NOI) become inconsequential to the received myth—a development of inordinate convenience in a post-9/11 world yet also an obfuscation of the broader legacies associated with Ali's status as signal American Muslim. A man named "Muhammad" may still qualify as "the Greatest" American in an age of rampant U.S. Islamophobia because he is, according to the context of 1964–1974, only Muslim *just so*. Such domestication, such secularization, limits a fuller understanding of Ali's persona and its specifically religious negotiations of U.S. and global contexts to which it necessarily responds.

Nevertheless, attention to scope (and its creative deployment) can help to redress the problem of Ali's domestication and secularization. One such approach would maintain the decade span while moving it around to different frames of reference within Ali's life and career. Rather than 1964–1974, what would it mean to consider 1974–1984, which includes his recapturing the title (as starting point, not culmination), the death of Elijah Muhammad and Ali's move to Sunni Islam, his duties as an emissary for the U.S. government around 1979–1980 concerning a boycott of the Moscow Olympics, his retirement, and his Parkinson's diagnosis? To take another example, how might 1991–2001 (from his negotiations with Saddam Hussein, through his Olympic appearance in 1996, and on to the aftermath of September 11, all performed through the guise of escalating disability) offer insight to a beloved figure named "Muhammad," whose signal act of resistance against U.S. colonial violence at home and abroad rendered him (putting a fine point on things) a mascot, a prop for benefit shows and all-star games, part of the pop cultural furniture?

FETCH SCOPE, MAKE SMALL

While these movable decades seem promising, for the purposes of this chapter I want to entertain a third option concerning a sense of scope—that of the extreme close-up. Rather than highlighting different decade spans, or the turning tides of Ali's convoluted long game, here we take a deep dive into the span of a very few days. Of course, it remains impossible to occlude longer trajectories of Ali's life and persona. We know the details and certainly cannot pretend that they never did or never shall occur. Nevertheless, if the decade span, like the long-term perspectival view, can remain powerful in its capacity to shape a myth that alters and even renders later "fact" irrelevant or unknown in a popular cultural imaginary, then the suspension of certain eventualities may also be assumed. How can we benefit from careful examination (indeed, the inhabitation) of events where everything remains in the balance and might still go differently, and how might what amounts to a phenomenological exercise in historical contingency contribute to clearer understanding of Ali's larger-scale persona that works around the more usual attempts to domesticate and secularize his religiousness?

In order to achieve this micro-scope (as it were), this chapter works through a series of close readings in Will Power's stage play *Fetch Clay, Make Man* (2011), a production of which I was fortunate to attend at the New York Theatre Workshop in October of 2013. The play covers a span of roughly two days in advance of Ali's second fight with Sonny Liston (a title defense that took place on May 25, 1965) in Lewiston, Maine—a venue selected because of low demand for the fight itself. Rumors of mob violence from Liston's people and strong fear of reprisal-seeking Malcolm X supporters, who were allegedly planning to shoot up the arena (in retribution against the NOI for Malcolm's assassination precisely three months before), tanked interest in the event. It is also important to remember, in a way that perhaps Martin Luther King Jr. provides one of the only sufficient corollaries, how thoroughly despised Ali was by large swaths of the general population in 1965—an almost unimaginable reality in this hagiographic age that this scalar adjustment permits us to see and, indeed, to dwell within. Ali chafes against NOI restrictions (embodied by the character of Brother Rashid—who is conflicted himself). He bickers with his wife, Sonji Roi ("Sonji Clay," as she is listed in the script)—a pistol of a young woman from South Side Chicago who cannot and will not play the role of "good" Muslim woman and wife that has become her lot. He contends with secret doubt and dread that his first win against Liston, which secured him the heavyweight title, was a fluke (as most believed—or even a fix, as many still believe), and that his reign as champion would soon come to an ignominious, humiliating, or even incapacitating end at Liston's powerful (and pissed-off) hands.

Enter Lincoln Perry, better known as "Stepin Fetchit"—"The laziest man in the world."[5] Perry turned his depiction of the shuffling, whiny-voiced ne'er do well—a characterization that drew on some of the more egregious racial myths and stereotypes of 1930s film and the vaudeville and minstrel entertainment traditions on which they were built. Ali ostensibly wants to meet the actor, to have Perry join his entourage—a prospect that of course horrifies the NOI brothers among the ranks of Ali's handlers. More covertly, Ali also wants to learn the secret of Jack Johnson's "Anchor Punch" from Perry (who knew Johnson): a devastating feat of speed and deception that marked Johnson's style as he became the first Black heavyweight boxing champion nearly sixty years before (and eventually paid a price for such audacity).[6] The action on stage culminates not at ringside but with Stepin Fetchit, barred from attendance by Brother Rashid, alone at Ali's compound where he watches the truncated fight (it lasted less than two minutes) on a portable television as the play's final curtain falls on Ali's victory.

Power's play emerged in response to two photographs that dramatize in their reception both the assumptions that surround the Ali persona and the necessity for scalar adjustments that can cast such assumptions in relief. The first photo he found in a large retrospective book on Ali's career:

> The book contained some wonderful photos of the champ, from early in his career all the way to present day. One of the pictures caught my eye—Ali on the eve of his rematch with Sonny Liston, he and his entourage looking defiantly at the camera, looking like they were set to insert Ali and his legacy into the books of history. The caption of the photo listed the names of the men who stood with Ali during that critical time, when he had recently won the championship, but was thought of as a fluke, sure to lose the rematch. He had also recently come out as a member of the controversial Nation of Islam, had befriended and then broken his friendship with Malcolm X, had boldly changed his name and renounced Christianity, and in only a couple of years would revolt against the massive entity that is the U.S. Government in refusing to enter the Vietnam War. Here was Ali; young and pretty, cold, cocky, and ready to take on and overcome whatever the world would throw at him. And here were the men who stood by him: his trainer, his bodyguards, his lovable sidekick Bundini Brown, and with them just over Ali's right shoulder was Stepin Fetchit. Stepin Fetchit? What?[7]

Power proceeds to describe his own Bay Area Black Nationalist upbringing in the 1970s, how an instructor at his school (a school named for Malcolm X), enraged by a clip from a Stepin Fetchit film he had shown to exemplify "those who loved the Man more than they loved themselves," screamed at his young charges: "You see this dude Stepin Fetchit? He is the ultimate sellout, brothers and sisters! He is a traitor to our race! NEVER be like him!" (9–10).

This episode reflects the way a collapsing temporal frame can undermine presumptions of myth and history that have themselves become naturalized. At first Power sees what he expects to see in the photograph. He sees the received archetype: Ali ascendant into inevitability, set to be "insert[ed]" into a Whiggish history, the culmination of an old, old story, the representative Black man. Yet the small detail, the jarring bit of insight, establishes Stepin Fetchit as some kind of matter out of place—here in this photograph, frozen in time. We witness the mystery of a stolen moment, the undoing of inevitability for a young man with impeccable family ties in the Student Nonviolent Coordinating Committee, the Black Panthers, and the NOI (10). He continues in this way:

> You can imagine my shock when, many years later ... I came across [another] photo of Muhammad Ali and Stepin Fetchit together. What's more the caption listed Stepin Fetchit as Ali's friend and "Secret Strategist." What? How could this be? Staring at the photo, it was as if things I had learned from the past were being broken apart, an unquestionable truth being questioned. If these two seemingly opposite iconic figures were partners, what did that say about race politics and the complexities of American culture? This photo set me on a quest to discover if not the truth, then at the very least a better understanding of these two complicated, enigmatic figures and the world in which they lived. (10–11)

Power experiences an uncanniness in these photographs that collapses his longer worldview into epistemological crisis. In the process the scope of his vision alters as well. At first he cannot see beyond the photo. Such uncanniness fractures—even violates—his own secularized (and secularizing) assumptions about Ali. "Muhammad Ali was Superman," he writes (10). How could Superman so betray his own ideals? Power's epistemological collapse necessitates the collapse in scope that characterizes the play he creates, the play through which he works out a phenomenology of this unthinkable interaction in careful detail. Stepin Fetchit disorients NOI management of Ali's Black body and persona as well as the naturalization of this management in which a young Will Power has been instructed.

Such uncanniness also accords with what I take to reside in the mandate of Evan Haefeli's wonderful phrase contained in his own contribution to this volume: "the 'abroad' of another home." At stake for Haefeli is the necessity to break out of the dreary inevitability that ordinarily characterizes studies of the Great Awakening (another putatively "religious" phenomenon whose excesses have been tamed by intellectual, ecclesial, and phenomenological management) by shifting, doubling—or, better yet, converting—the terms of "home" and "abroad." For his chapter, redirecting emphasis from colonial American contexts to transatlantic ones seeks to unsettle—to disorient—assumptions about the Great Awakening and the blind spots they constitute. Haefeli destabilizes figures, movements, and events that have effectively become their own phenomena and are rendered, thus, invisible. We feel at home in them, and so they must be undomesticated. They render the framework through which we perceive the world, and so they must be desecularized.

I want to claim something similar here about Muhammad Ali through scalar attention to his various Islamic and U.S. exceptionalist "conversions." Katharine Gerbner, whose *Christian Slavery* also serves as a source for Haefeli, provides a model for conversion in her study of Afro-Caribbean slavery as the negotiation of ongoing tensions between religious and racial identities that both cohere and diverge: African and Christian, Slave and Christian—these categories, deemed incommensurate through the seventeenth century, come to coexist by the eighteenth century in the figure of the Christian slave.[8] Furthermore, such tensions also convert slaveholders and other colonial authorities, who presume themselves to control the nomenclature, from Christian to White in a way that emphasizes the tenuous link between these two concepts and their broader political empowerment concerning categories of race and religion.[9] Conversion for enslaved Africans both relies upon *and* adjusts the terms of Christian identity by disrupting what had become naturalized—the incommensurability of Christian and African identities in colonial contexts. By focusing on particular contexts of conversion—on conversion in micro-scope, as it were—we may focus on negotiations of these seemingly incommensurate concepts not necessarily over the long term (not, for instance, as the transformation from one thing to another) but in their particulars. In this way details of the phenomenology of such conversion between home and abroad, race and religion, come into focus in a way that deliberate scalar consideration might then extend out to larger contexts.

This is precisely how *Fetch Clay, Make Man* functions as an imaginative retort, a particular speculation, that Will Power renders in response to the two photographs of Stepin Fetchit and Muhammad Ali that he describes. Through disruption, the uncanny presence of Stepin Fetchit allows Power actually to *see* the photo and thus to *see* Ali, who in turn offers a new perspective on Stepin Fetchit. Disoriented by the phenomenon of Ali's conversion on these terms (which negotiates both the heroism and betrayal, exception taking and exceptionalism, that Step's presence emphasizes), Power is forced to renegotiate his terms through the process of writing and the performance it generates. The invention of a kind of creative empathy becomes requisite for answering the question "Stepin Fetchit? What?" No longer at home with Ali in this photo, it casts him abroad (Power most specifically, but also Ali and Stepin Fetchit).

The following readings in *Fetch Clay, Make Man* track Power's efforts to reconstitute this abroad of a different home as it performs Ali's conversion within these terms and concepts in real time. In particular, it emphasizes the collapse of scope to a period of just a few days in order to consider how certain religious and racial boundaries and their assumptions of territory and jurisdiction function not as large-scale political dynamics but as interpersonal conflicts that demand Ali's (and Stepin Fetchit's—and thus Power's and our own) undomestication, an example of desecularization that speaks more broadly to the terms of American religion at home and abroad. Seeing these characters anew in microscope permits for adjustment and insight, then, at a larger scale.

Following on these active dimensions, I remain especially interested in the question of performance—its playful mutability—in order to invoke the category of "repertoire" as a way of understanding Ali as *persona* (an active, performative property moving through space and time) over and against the more fixed inevitability of archive (this with recourse to Diana Taylor's argument in *The Archive and the Repertoire*[10]). In the process, the categories of home and abroad (and their relationship to Muhammad Ali as an exemplary global American Muslim) themselves become converted, taking on new meaning for twenty-first-century contexts—especially as they push beyond the secularized editions of Ali that have come to manage the productive contradictions of his persona across space, time, and scalar frames.

BOUNDARY MAINTENANCE

Fetch Clay, Make Man has four primary characters played by four actors.[11] Each character negotiates at least two identities—the name by which he or she is known and another (perhaps secret, perhaps former or hidden name): Muhammad Ali, of course, was once Cassius Clay and now he is the "champ." Stepin

Fetchit goes by his stage name most prominently but is also Lincoln Perry, the actor (Ali will call him "Lincoln Perry" at a pivotal moment in the action). Sonji Roy (Sonji Clay in the play) only goes by the name Sonji and struggles through the demands that attend this denomination: her role as Ali's wife over and against her own past (and her present tastes). Finally, Brother Rashid, the put-upon bow-tied-and-bespectacled NOI Brother who has his limits, was once the evocatively named Canard, who Sonji appears to have known back in his pre-Nation, South Side neighborhood days in Chicago. In this way we may also recognize that, like the photograph that so flummoxed Power, within the scale of this drama every character bears a certain disjuncture with whom they may claim or appear to be at any given moment. They dwell in the abroads of a different home. Conversion for them is not a neat affair, a clean break, but something consistently negotiated and improvised—performed—within these old and new identities in the present tense.

For the sake of efficiency, I intend to drop Sonji and Brother Rashid from this discussion to focus on Ali and Stepin Fetchit. When Stepin Fetchit first enters, the boxer pretends to be angry at him: "Why would I, the greatest of all time, a champion to black people, want you [Rashid] to bring me this, this coon man, this Uncle Tom, this lazy, shiftless, man do you realize how much this chump has held our people back?... 'Cause now I'm enraged. That's right I'm enraged and outraged by the sight of this darky, is he not the white man's flunky?" Rashid answers a delighted affirmative: "That he is brother." Ali makes Step put up his "dukes" and "for once in your miserable wretched life, stand up and be a man!" (22).

It all proves a ruse, of course. Ali has invited Step to talk about Jack Johnson. Gradually, over the course of their conversation, Ali betrays a crisis of confidence. He never lapses into periods of explicit self-doubt, but the uneasiness of his assurance is evident. As he finishes one of his signature rhymes, he ends not with a flourish but a hedge:

> I'm gonna come so fast, like a piston
> Straight to the dome of Mr. Sonny Liston
>
> But wait Sonny's trained harder
> Well this is what they say
> He's gonna put a whoopin on you, just you wait Cassius Clay
>
> But I'm the true champ
> And Ali's my name

And even half my wits can't fit, into Sonny Liston's little brain

Because I am the boxer
With a mind that rhymes

I'm the prettiest and the fastest
I'm the Greatest of all times!

[*return to conversational voice*]: But the truth is, Sonny is training harder see. Last time he did underestimate me, and he won't do that again. This time he'll be prepared. (24)

Amid this uncertainty Ali asks Step how well he knew Jack Johnson. "We were friends, yeah," is the reply (24). Ali seeks some form of gnosis from his older guest, and at this juncture the viewer can't quite piece together what it might be—related perhaps to training, technique, or some other insight? Nevertheless, Ali's follow-up remark dramatizes uncertainty. It humanizes the defiant inevitability of the photo to which Power responds.

What emerges at last is that Ali seeks the secret to Johnson's Anchor Punch: "It was so fast, it could knock you out without the crowd even seeing it— whooooop!—just like that, and the other man was on the ground" (44). At its core the Anchor Punch would seem to represent a performative talisman, according some mode of protection, some competitive edge in the ensuing fight derived from Johnson's tragic bona fides. Ali becomes desperate just before he leaves for the bout. Having tangled with Sonji and Rashid, he berates Step for considering joining the NOI. "I been a drifter all my life," Stepin Fetchit claims, "and right here with yall, this is startin' to feel like home"—the home of another abroad. "Don't do this," Ali says, noting that Step is Christian and carries Rosary beads in his pocket: "in your heart you ain't no Muslim" (93). Note the double negative: Step may be Christian, but he also contains the contradiction; he "ain't no Muslim" as well.

Ali and Step proceed to tangle. Convinced that Ali will lose, perhaps not physically, immediately, but spiritually and politically over the long run, to be sure, Step tries to temper Ali's own expectations in the name of Jack Johnson. To Ali's claim to a kind of exclusivity, that he himself is not a "negro" but the "heavyweight champion," Step replies:

Yeah so was Jack Johnson. And he was the greatest, you ain't the greatest, he was. And still they broke him down until he was nothin,' you understand?

When Jack lost the belt, that young white boy hit 'im so hard, he knocked his gold teeth loose in his mouth, and Jack had to swallow his teeth to save face in front of all them white men. Now if Jack Johnson couldn't win, and I couldn't win, what the hell make you think you got any chance of being anything else but a fool? (102)

"It ain't gonn' do no good," Step concludes, referring to the Anchor Punch. Ali replies, "Let me be the judge a' that. Man give me this and maybe this time it'll be different" (103).

Maybe this time it will be different. Power conjures a moment of contingency—one that likely never happened, one whose performance on stage can never be replicated; thus, it represents a home in the abroad of this far country where it no longer proves inevitable that Ali will win. We know that he does, as Power knew with full certainty Ali did when he first saw the photo of Ali and Stepin Fetchit together. Nevertheless, the larger point depends on the contingency that playing this back through—not as historical narrative, not as a determined eventuality, but in the ritual phenomenon that "*maybe* this time it'll be different" highlights a full range of possibility. It questions Ali and makes him—the baddest Black Superman—beholden to a minstrel caricature as the carrier of the Anchor Punch's mythical Black authenticity. This revision of Ali's conversion, and any inevitability one may wish to retrieve, becomes the abroad (indeed, the many abroads) of this other home.

ALI AND THE REPERTOIRE OF IDENTITY

Significantly, Will Power beheld a range of possibilities when deciding how to represent Stepin Fetchit's bestowal of the Anchor Punch—this secret gnosis of authentic Blackness delivered by a minstrel performer—to Muhammad Ali. He could have the older man instruct Ali, demonstrate on Ali, or he even could have cut, dimmed, or obscured the scene and preserved an element of mystery (a version of the old umbrella trick). Power elects none of these options. Instead, as the stage direction puts it, "STEPIN FETCHIT *channels the energy of Jack Johnson*" (103). He—Lincoln Perry as Stepin Fetchit—performs a soliloquy *as* Jack Johnson:

Look at me, talkin' to my ole friend Stepin Fetchit. Fetch you better drink that drink man before I give you some of this—a deadly right, a lethal left and my secret, the Anchor Punch. Now Step, you don't wanna be on the other side of the Anchor Punch do ya?. . .

Alright now it's time for the kill. I go inside. What do I mean? I'm sayin' I go deep, pass the gut to my ass and back to my lungs. I pull from all them slaves they brought over, all the pain and beauty, and blood and magic and faith and rage that them slaves went through see. I anchor up to them, then I pull it through, all the way from my lungs like air to my fist, and here it comes, riding the wind of 50 million strong—who can dodge a punch like that? No man can withstand my Anchor Punch! (103–4)

The speech ends, the spell breaks, and Stepin Fetchit returns in Jack Johnson's place. But the performance has been rendered again as a contraction of scope—hundreds of years and scores of millions of people concentrated in this embodied feat of dramatic conversion. The work that the Anchor Punch enacts, "pull[ing]" from "pain and beauty," "blood and magic and faith" ranges not across outright contradiction but, rather, among conflations of ambiguous properties. The very performative mode here proves crucial for making sense of the contingency and the mutability of home and abroad that Step, a la Jack Johnson, enacts.

First, there are other performative modes of Stepin Fetchit (or of his repertoire at the very least) that Ali has assumed into his own *body* of work (as well as the work of his body). Consider minstrelsy, one tradition from which Step derives. Ali, too, knows his minstrelsy. The boxer's emergent persona in the 1960s (including and beyond the second Liston fight) drew especially on a subversive adaptation of minstrelsy—from the doggerel of its rhymes to the bug-eyed over-exaggeration of its performance style. The danger that he represents to white audiences through these performances, this persona, harnesses white anxieties that popularize minstrel depictions in the first place—offering Black feedback, we might call it. For Black audiences the audacity of this characterization transforms such feedback into clapback. Again, this persona will become managed by media as part of Ali's broader conversion, encompassing his long-term trajectory from exception-taker to exceptional American, but at the core of this depiction—and especially in this reduced scope offered by Power's play (contraries contained in a singular persona)—resides Ali's recursive weaponization of minstrelsy against secularizing stereotypes. His disorienting home wields the terms of such an abroad.

Still, it remains minstrelsy nonetheless, a crime for which Stepin Fetchit continues to suffer. In a staged press conference Power has Ali preen before the press. "What are you gonna do?" asks a reporter. "Well first I'm gonna dance."

Ali shuffles then poses cooperatively for the white reporters (though he maintains the boundary of his name—insisting that he be called "Ali," not "Clay"). Still he obliges them, cooperating when told "Now give us a mean stare, and open that mouth, bigger, bigger yes there it is" (65). "*Cameras flash wildly*" read the stage directions. Ali next tries to introduce Step, but the reporters show little interest. Finally, after Ali insists, they go straight for the parallel:

> REPORTER 1: Yeah, you gonna do the Stepin Fetchit champ and turn lazy when you fight?. . .
> REPORTER 2: [To Stepin Fetchit] How does it feel to be an Uncle Tom?
> REPORTER 3: How does it feel to be hated by your own people? (67)

Stepin Fetchit takes umbrage:

> You see me on the screen, but you don't understand what I was doin.' Now you go back, and look at them films, go look at 'em, go see how I made somethin' from nothin.' You wanna talk about Malcolm X? You wanna talk about Dr. King? I was the first negro militant [*The press laughs at the suggestion*] . . . I defied white supremacy!. . . I was the first of my race to receive a screen credit. In Hollywood we were seen but never heard, faces with no names. I fought hard to get us a name, and in doin' so proved that negroes were equal. And I made some sacrifices but . . . but let me say this right now. I'm more than Stepin Fetchit. My name is Lincoln, Lincoln Perry. And you wanna call me an Uncle Tom? (68–69)

Stepin Fetchit (one wants so very badly to call him Lincoln Perry here, although no one, not even name-sensitive Ali, does, and the multiplicity of names and identities proves overwhelming) finds success by one measure. Step longs for his contributions to be recognized in keeping with Ali's minstrel abroad of another home. He breaks through Hollywood racial codes yet does so in a way that reinforces harmful stereotypes, leading to an ignominious future. If Ali represents Power's compromised Superman, then Step too offers some kind of monstrous myth. Furthermore, the emerging disjuncture with names, these multiple identities, calls back to the instability of categories like home and abroad, and the conversion that holds them in tension. Through stylized minstrelsy, Step and Ali find their respective homes and abroads to exist on separate planes that become joined only in Ali's swift victory—via the Anchor Punch—as the curtain falls.

By collapsing the historical anxieties raised by disorienting photographic evidence to distilled and stylized action, all performed in a ritually demarcated space outside of ordinary time, Power turns away from history, from the archival authority of books and photographs, to some other, some preferable, some messier and less determinate source of authority with which to wrangle and perhaps to wring some kind of sense from this surprise encounter between Muhammad Ali and Stepin Fetchit. The photograph archives the two men's proximity, but it cannot perform such proximity's negation of a home and abroad outside of historical inevitability. Through this emphasis on performance, Power invokes a repertoire of home and abroad that reframes historical inevitability as performative and contingent, shot through with the negotiations that characterize conversion.

Diana Taylor's *The Archive and the Repertoire* invokes performance as a way to parse what I understand to be afoot in Power's reduced-scale contention with the Ali myth. Concerned as she is with the recovery of embodied modes of meaning-transmission that have been overwritten (and otherwise deemed irrelevant) by textual and material (and thus archival) cultures, Taylor focuses on the way "expressive culture" stakes political claims, transmits memory, and forges identities—despite the fact that "claims manifested through performance, whether the tying of robes that signify marriage or performed land claims, ceased to carry legal weight" in the face of written Word and words.[12] Taylor's tension, however, "does not lie between the written and spoken word, but between the *archive* of supposedly enduring materials (i.e., texts, documents, buildings, bones) and the comparatively ephemeral *repertoire* of embodied practice/knowledge (i.e., spoken language, dance, sports, ritual)."[13]

Efficiently put, the crisis raised by Power seeing the photograph of Muhammad Ali and Stepin Fetchit ruptures his archival knowledge. Ali's iconization ("Superman"), his secularization as "the greatest," a man engaged inevitably in proscribed excellence and racial viability, the fact that all of this knowledge may be found in a "big" book—all of this points to archival characterization. By turning to the stage ("acts usually thought of as ephemeral, nonreproducible knowledge"[14]), by limiting the general scope of his focus, Power runs back through these interactions (for which no archive exists).[15] He moves outside the archive and discovers the common repertoire that Ali and Step share and the historical contingencies of a moment in time that render eventual fact never a "done deal" but always in the process of conversion. The photos' uncanniness has exposed his location not at home but in the abroad of some different home— generated and sustained by the ongoing negotiation of these and other vagaries contained within Muhammad Ali's religious and exceptionalist conversions that Stepin Fetchit both brings into relief and amplifies.

CONCLUSION

I want to emphasize a couple of points as we head to curtain. Evan Haefeli's example of seeking "the 'abroad' of another home" raises important implications for critical engagement with a figure like Muhammad Ali, whose fame derives from myths and illusions of the familiar and thus conceals in the performance of his persona the very mechanisms of celebrity. He is converted, and so he acts accordingly (in multiple valences of this action—activity, actor, activist)—especially amid ongoing negotiations of race and religion that seem, on a cursory glance, to be settled political matters. Some deeper engagement with this persona depends on the capacity to become disoriented to, even alienated from such expectation. It demands, through the performative character of this persona, willingness to step outside of archival sources and to flirt with the repertoire (or even to take it home) when possible.

Ali proves uniquely fruitful for pursuing versions of such a mandate for a couple of reasons. First, we have really only begun to understand the multiplicities of home and abroad that constitute Ali as a global American religious figure in the postwar era. The long view affords one larger-scale attempt to negotiate this excess, a kind of exceptionalist double cross that emphasizes certain accumulations of identities through a lifetime of conversions (not just his conversion to Islam in 1964 but the wide range of racial and religious contradictions that complicate the arc of this more singular conversion: his racial treachery toward the likes of Ernie Terrell and Joe Frazier in the 1960s and 1970s, his endorsement of Ronald Reagan in 1984, and so many other instances[16]). Insofar as we may focus on Ali as a performer, this scalar interpretation also deals in repertoire. Emphasizing repertoire collapses the temporal frame. It adjusts the scope, even focusing on speculative (although thoroughly researched) sources like *Fetch Clay, Make Man*, illuminating how matters of scale and attentiveness to performance can help to calibrate performative disorientations through specific moments of conversion that reframe a sense of home and abroad when the go-to myths no longer suffice.

Second, *Ali is repertoire*. He boxes—in the ring, certainly, but even in his attempts to connect with people, he puts up his dukes, displays a fist, spars, circles, and so forth. When not physically boxing, he spars verbally, plays on words, signifies, and performs. Such contradictions both contribute to and demand conversion, the negotiation of seemingly incommensurate positions and postures. Ali is persona, and so out of his religious and exceptionalist conversions spring other ongoing conversions that enrich our understanding of this almost uncontainable figure. Disabled, for instance, by Parkinson's Syndrome in the last decades of his life, his affect flattened. He lost his ability to speak and the muscular physicality that contributed to his evocative repertoire as a Black man (which made him so attractive to the NOI as a Black Muslim). Still, Ali troubles these expectations, negotiates with them, through the uncanny "abroad" that they impose.

His lasting legacies in this way are not archival but the product of radical exteriority moving through space and time, responding, responded to, consistently adjusting, improvisatory. Ali is exteriority, a performative body—dangerously Black, queerly gorgeous ("pretty," he liked to say)—constantly negotiating the distance between his role as exceptional American and taker of exception to such exceptionalism that both changes him and is changed by him. In order to account for the long arc of his career, narrated through the conceptual conversion or racial and religious terms according to shifting modes of home and abroad, we must first learn to examine the terms of such conversion in micro-scope for the repertoire that can fracture the more stale assumptions about Ali's political pose.

NOTES

1. For the dramatic origins of the double cross, see Wendy Doniger, *The Woman Who Pretended to Be Who She Was: Myths of Self-Imitation* (New York: Oxford University Press, 2004). Significantly, the double cross itself derives etymologically from the history of boxing. In one sense it refers to the deceptive second punch with the same hand (rather than the more powerful shot that the other hand could produce). What this double punch, this double cross, lacks in power it makes up for in surprise. Furthermore, the *OED* traces the double cross back to an 1848 *Sporting Life* article that details suspicion of a double cross leading to the suspension of all betting on a given match. In this way the double cross refers to a fighter both accepting a bribe or a "fix" to take a fall and lose on purpose, *and* winning the bout, collecting that money as well. Many thanks to Christian Lee Novetzke for detailing both of these etymologies and pointing me to the *OED* reference.
2. Bill Siegel, dir., *The Trials of Muhammad Ali* (Kartemquin Films, 2013); Leon Gast, dir., *When We Were Kings* (Gramercy Pictures, 1996); and Michael Mann, dir., *Ali* (Sony Pictures, 2001). See M. Cooper Harriss, "The Cinematic Secularization of Muhammad Ali," in *Muslims in the Movies: A Global Anthology*, ed. Kristian

Petersen (Cambridge, Mass.: ILEX Foundation and Harvard University Press, 2021).

3. There are exceptions, yet their limitations often prove the rule. Consider, for instance, *Muhammad Ali: The Unauthorized Story* (2009), a fifty-two-minute made-for-television hagiography directed by Chip Taylor that rehashes events from Ali's entire life—a work most notable for its thorough unremarkability. Conversely, *Ali: The Mission* (2013), an ESPN 30 for 30 short film directed by Amani Martin (weighing in at thirteen minutes) is quite good, yet it is too short to warrant comparison with the heft or depth that characterizes these other films.

4. Ali, of course, became part of a Muslim International through the NOI quite soon after winning the championship in 1964—a point I do not wish to deny. See Melani McAlister, "One Black Allah: The Middle East in the Cultural Politics of African American Liberation, 1955–1970," *American Quarterly* 51, no. 3 (September 1999): 622–56. My emphasis here focuses on Ali's reception and the contours of the myth that continued reliance upon this temporal frame reinforces.

5. See Mel Watkins, *Stepin Fetchit: The Life and Times of Lincoln Perry* (New York: Vintage, 2005), 4.

6. See Theresa Runstedtler, *Jack Johnson, Rebel Sojourner: Boxing in the Shadow of the Global Color Line* (Berkeley: University of California Press, 2013).

7. Will Power, *Fetch Clay, Make Man: A Play* (New York: Overlook Duckworth, 2016), 9.

8. Katharine Gerbner, *Christian Slavery: Conversion and Race in the Protestant Atlantic World* (Philadelphia: University of Pennsylvania Press, 2018), 10.

9. Gerbner, *Christian Slavery*, 85.

10. Diana Taylor, *The Archive and the Repertoire: Performing Cultural Memory in the Americas* (Durham, N.C.: Duke University Press, 2003).

11. A small fifth role—that of studio owner William Fox, who appears in a series of flashbacks with Stepin Fetchit—also appears in the play but finds no discussion here.

12. Taylor, *The Archive and the Repertoire*, 18–19.

13. Taylor, *The Archive and the Repertoire*, 19. An important caveat here is that repertoire is not in fact *ephemeral*, only relatively so—indeed, in its own way it also functions archivally. The distinction resides in the authority accorded to performance as opposed to more material, inscripted modes of preserving knowledge and tradition. Therefore, the tack here to Taylor's "repertoire" seeks to invoke this same privilege for performance.

14. Taylor, *The Archive and the Repertoire*, 20.

15. I should note here the internal contradiction of my own inscription and dissemination of this essay to you—in the authoritative archival form of the academy, of course. And, also, I essentially write about and certainly cite the script—an object in tension with repertoire—although I have seen the play performed and do call up my memories of specific scenes when I discuss them (memory at the nexus of archive and repertoire presents another fascinating question). We might consider the script, the words I inscribe (and that Power has inscribed) as frames of reference for a repertoire that exists outside of such an archival orientation. It may well prove

impossible to break out of archival knowledge and authority (Taylor allows for this likelihood, and in many ways I would not want to), but I do hope that gestures here toward repertoire may illustrate its effectiveness and its evocativeness in this project of troubling the borders of home and abroad.

16. For a good starting point for deeper engagement with these moments in Ali's life, see Jonathan Eig, *Ali: A Life* (New York: Houghton Mifflin Harcourt, 2017), 279–84, 303–5, 357, and 503.

7

Domestic Bones, Foreign Land, and the Kingdom Come

Jurisdictions of Religion in Contemporary Hawaii

GREG JOHNSON

HUNTING FOR JURISDICTION

On a misty July morning of 2018, Mike and I were making our way down the verdant but rocky slopes of Mauna Kea looking for signs. He was sheep hunting and I was tagging along for the day. Curious about our endeavor, I asked some basic orienting questions, "What land jurisdiction is this gulch? How long does sheep season run?" "Hawaiian, brah, no worries," Mike responded in his typically clipped phrasing. Hawaiian what, I wondered. The land, the sheep, his hunting rights? Continuing in silence, we tracked a herd, eventually descending to the main access road. Once there, Mike whispered, "Car coming, get behind one *pohaku* [rock, boulder]; no need rangers on us." "*Oh* . . ." I thought. Whatever else "Hawaiian" meant back up the gulch, it seemed less certain here, perched as we were on the asphalt shoulder of state's primary capillary in the region.

Let me reframe the matter in more general terms. Consider two statements about the status of Native Hawaiian rights, one from the state of Hawaii, the other federal.

> 1. The State reaffirms and shall protect all rights, customarily and traditionally exercised for subsistence, cultural and religious purposes and possessed by ahupua'a tenants who are descendants of native Hawaiians who inhabited the

Hawaiian Islands prior to 1778, *subject to the right of the State to regulate such rights*. [emphasis added]

—Hawaii State Constitution, Article 12/7, 1978

2. SECTION 1. ACKNOWLEDGEMENT AND APOLOGY
The Congress—
(1) on the occasion of the 100th anniversary of the illegal overthrow of the Kingdom of Hawaii on January 17, 1893, acknowledges the historical significance of this event which resulted in the suppression of the inherent sovereignty of the Native Hawaiian people;
(2) recognizes and commends efforts of reconciliation initiated by the State of Hawaii and the United Church of Christ with Native Hawaiians;. . . .

SEC. 3 DISCLAIMER.
Nothing in this Joint Resolution is intended to serve as a settlement of any claims against the United States.

—Public Law 103-150, 103d Congress, November 23, 1993

As constitutional double-speak and waffling apologies suggest, Hawaii is a place of tremendous legal ambiguity of a sort that amplifies its insider/outsider status vis-à-vis the mainland and mainstream United States. Perhaps more than any other facet of the islands and their diverse people, Native Hawaiian traditional and customary practices and attempts to assert and protect them illustrate the betwixt and between nature of Hawaii. These practices include, for example, hunting, harvesting, and various forms of religious action. The latter are my focus here.

In what follows, I attend to how Hawaiians are navigating legal jurisdictions on a number of scales, ranging from county and state levels to federal and international domains. Throughout this way-finding process, to invoke a voyaging trope, their homing instincts have proven strong. So strong, in fact, that the primary jurisdiction they now appeal to is their "inherent sovereignty," as one activist put it. Just how this move to foreground and act upon such a vision will play out remains to be seen. But, for our purposes, the way Hawaiians articulate and perform what I call "auto-jurisdiction" is important for understanding how some indigenous peoples are asserting their religious practices and identities in the contemporary moment.[1] After contextualizing key concepts and issues, this chapter explicates two recent examples that illuminate different inflections of indigenous jurisdiction.[2] These examples represent tactical, concrete responses to jurisdictional struggles and have achieved some traction, as I describe, but their implications for broader sovereignty claims remain unclear. Of direct relevance for this volume, these cases suggest the outlines of an identity formation in the making, one in which the articulation of identities is decoupled, in some measure, from the channels and ruts of state shaped religion making.[3]

IWI AND 'ĀINA

Iwi (bones) and *'āina* (land) define Hawaiian religious life in conceptual and practical ways. This is largely as true now as it has been throughout the historical span of the tradition, even before settlement of the islands. Hawaiians are voyagers. Even so, they are profoundly rooted in place—by stories, names, and bones.[4] After launching across the Pacific in canoes with only family, plant sprouts, and perhaps a pig or two, they surely experienced intense joy upon sighting and landing on the most remote island chain in the world. Robust oral traditions suggest that this period catalyzed intense mythical thinking and associations, and for understandable reasons.

Cherished Polynesian myths were rooted anew, transplanting genealogies to the new *'āina*. Ancestors' memories were vigilantly kept alive precisely because their remains and the ancestral land had been left behind.[5] The *kuleana* (obligation) to bring stories of the ancestors to their new land was binding. Many Hawaiians today continue to feel and respond to this *kuleana*, which has intensified over centuries. Now *iwi* take on the metonymic role of mythic-historic anchors. As Hawaiians say, "ola nā iwi"—the bones live.[6] *Iwi* are material trigger points of traditional memories, practices, and the land ethic these convey. In addition, they are *kanu* (buried). They are planted in the same way as life-giving staples (taro, sweet potatoes) and are regarded as a necessary source of mana for plants to thrive. In this way, the *'āina* depends on the *iwi* to be productive. In much Hawaiian thinking, the *iwi* and *'āina* are mutually dependent and together form the literal and conceptual substratum of Hawaiian culture.

JURISDICTIONS OF RELIGION

At the moment, three potentially watershed legal matters about *iwi* and *'āina* in Hawaii are being contested. The first pertains to a large-scale burial dispute at

Kawaiaha'o Church in Honolulu that has triggered state and federal law; another involves ongoing protests asserting the sacred status of Mauna Kea in the face of telescope development; the third concerns federal recognition of Native Hawaiians on the model of American Indian tribes/nations.[7] Jurisdictional issues are front and center in each of these disputes and cut across debates about all of them. Of particular relevance for my analysis, the caretakers of the *iwi* and the *'āina*—historically united and cooperative—are divided on these issues at one level. The caretakers of the *iwi* usually articulate their standing and responsibilities by means of domestic law whereas the *kia'i* (protectors) on Mauna Kea often articulate their aspirations in terms of a restored Kingdom of Hawaii (i.e., a form of political sovereignty wholly external to the United States). However, even while the *iwi* and *'āina* protectors are sometimes at odds due to the framing force of law, they are increasingly moving to a shared articulation of indigenous jurisdiction. This trajectory—of Hawaiians speaking law claims in their own voices without mediation—is a homegrown provocation to rethink the history and present status of the United States' asserted sovereignty in Hawaii.

But why have Hawaiians been pulled in opposite jurisdictional directions up to now? Simply put, bones receive fairly strong protection under federal and state law in Hawaii whereas land does not. Hawaiians faced significant threats to burial grounds in the 1980s, rallied around these threats, prompted a proactive state legislative response as a result, and catalyzed living Hawaiian tradition in the process. The federal Native American Graves Protection and Repatriation Act was passed shortly thereafter (1990), with considerable input from Hawaiians. While imperfect by most any measure, this federal act and the state burial law are widely regarded as being effective, including by many Native Hawaiians, religious leaders among them.[8] However, as I describe below, international repatriation cases have recently decentered the place of law in favor of more autonomous modes of jurisdiction.

In stark contrast, land claims—whether sacred or not—have met little in the way of relief. Settler governments, especially those whose narratives are shaped and undergirded by cosmological assumptions and discourses of discovery and destiny, tend not to acknowledge indigenous claims to land and seldom concede that native religious sensibilities outweigh the government's "right to use its own land as it sees fit" (as infamously formulated in the *Lyng* [1988] decision, by which the Supreme Court effectively gutted the American Indian Religious Freedom Act [1978][9]). This general picture holds true in Hawaii. Therefore, when land protection activists like the Mauna Kea *kia'i* seek redress, they have little reason to have faith in the state of Hawaii or the United States. Instead, they find the future in the past. Claims to a restored Kingdom of Hawaii are on the lips of many of the land activists.

A comparative note is warranted here. Indigenous communities around the globe are quite literally defined by the ways they stand at odds with hegemonic jurisdictions; at the same time, they also often struggle internally over what jurisdictions maximize their potential to self-determine in lasting ways. How they articulate and pursue the protection of "religion" in these precarious positions is something that demands attention. What can be said in the wake of the protracted and highly mediatized struggle over the Dakota Access Pipeline, among other recent conflicts, is that indigenous jurisdiction is having real-world impacts, even when self-assured representatives of nation-state jurisdictions and their subsets choose to downplay this phenomenon.[10] The fact that criminalization of indigenous protest movements is on the upsurge speaks to the success of indigenous jurisdiction, for it is not protests per se or even specific violations of law (e.g., trespassing or obstruction) that have prompted such a response. Rather, it is the move to stand beyond law that is so provocative. Let us consider two examples, one short and the other longer.

CASE #1: HOMECOMING OF THE *IWI*

This sketch provides brief examples of one successful and one pending auto-jurisdictional claim in the heavily bureaucratic world of postcolonial repatriation politics. It is a story about tradition, authority, and their expression beyond the frames and limits of law.

The repatriation of three Native Hawaiian *poʻo* (skulls) and an *ʻālalo* (jaw) (collectively *iwi kūpuna*) took place in October of 2017. After an emotional ceremony at the Museum für Völkerkunde Dresden, we traveled back with them in our carry-on suitcases for immediate reburial, a story in its own right. I was with Halealoha Ayau, a longtime repatriation and reburial expert, and a number of his associates. From Ayau's perspective, what got the *iwi kūpuna* home in the end was simple human engagement and accountability. For twenty years, Ayau and the group he headed, Hui Mālama I Nā Kūpuna O Hawaiʻi Nei (hereafter, Hui Mālama), articulated its claims through law in numerous jurisdictions. The museum refused to budge and pointed to the fact that neither United States law nor UN declarations had legal force regarding German museums. German laws likewise yielded no traction. These avenues failing, Ayau emphasized his group's moral standing by means of a claim that had always been a core precept of Hui Mālama: they speak for and *as* the ancestors.¹¹

Framed thus, Ayau's claims cut through layers of obstructionism and jurisdictional dead zones to find an audience willing to listen, although not at first. Along the way he got to know people at the museum and cultivated relationships with them. He was particularly drawn to a younger generation of museum professionals who have come of age in an intellectual and moral climate wherein repatriation is regarded as a human right. These leaders were now in positions of power to influence Hui Mālama's pending repatriation request and, more broadly, to shape a new repatriation policy for the museum, with specific attention to returning all indigenous human remains. In the summer of 2017 the museum approved Hui Mālama's request.¹²

In short order, Ayau assembled a team of experts to travel with him, which is how I became involved. Others in the group included Kamanaʻopono Crabbe, then chief executive of the Office of Hawaiian Affairs, which funded much of the trip; Kaleikoa Kaʻeo, a professor of Hawaiian studies and a vocal sovereignty activist; Noelle Kahanu, a museum studies professor; and Kauila Kealiʻikanakaʻole, the team's ritual protocol leader.

But why a team of six, especially since the terms of the repatriation had been agreed to in advance? The answer has to do with Ayau's sense of strategy and foresight. In order to support Hui Mālama's self-referential authority claims, the group would need to convey legitimacy at numerous levels. A related piece had to do with a carefully brokered display of "authenticity" for the museum and its public and to cement the idea that the Hawaiians were giving more than they were taking, especially in the form of indigenous connections and authority. But, most of all, the team was assembled for the second half of the trip.

From Dresden we departed for Berlin to visit the Ethnologishes Museum in Dahlem. In the middle of reorganization, the museums in Berlin have been for some years grappling with the material remains of Germany's colonial past. As it so happens, the museum has a massive collection of Hawaiian objects, including numerous *kiʻi* (carved statues) that are both rare and clearly made for ritual purposes as well as some human remains.¹³ Ritual use—in the past and prospectively in the present—is a primary trigger for repatriation considerations under U.S. law and the UN Declaration on the Rights of Indigenous Peoples.¹⁴

Ayau had been stonewalled initially in his communications with the museum. The old guard was still in charge in Berlin, and the stakes of precedent were high, given the nature of the museum's holdings from Greece, Italy, and Egypt, for example. Ayau persisted. He realized the trip to Berlin would present a good opportunity to foster relationships and, if needed, to engage in cultural and human rights educating. Once at the museum, the team offered prayers, legal arguments, genealogies, and a mini lecture on contemporary museum ethics.

The curator who handled our meeting was clearly impressed with our team's preparation, but she was also careful to say she was not in charge. Further, she told us that a different entity handled requests for human remains and that this bureau, in a Kafkaesque manner, was notoriously hard to contact directly. Subsequently, and after months of trying, Ayau was undaunted.

In some respects this story is about the ways simple human diplomacy can be more effective than laws or other forms of pressure in situations where the politics of religious freedom and human rights are hampered by nation-state constructs, not to mention the gaps between them. It is also a story about indigenous auto-jurisdiction on the move, taking the authority of Hawaiian religion abroad. Ayau and his colleagues are hoping to create new frames of reference for international repatriation wherein precedents have weight and force in ways that outlast human relationships and that do not require each claimant group to rehearse and validate their claims to authority from scratch.

CASE #2: HALE O KUHIO

A humble protest and protection encampment sprung up on Hawaii Island in early 2018. A single room, brightly painted in red and yellow and with the Hae Hawaii (Kingdom of Hawaii flag, which was then colonized by the state of Hawaii) flying upside down as a symbol of distress, stood just *mauka* (uphill) from the intersection of Saddle Road and Mauna Kea Access Road (Figure 7.1). The encampment was aggressively dismantled by a state agency a little more than a year later, and its short life was subsequently overshadowed by the renewed and massive protests on Mauna Kea against the Thirty Meter Telescope (TMT) project in 2019–2020.[15] But for fifteen months it had stood as way station between the protests of 2015 and the more recent eruption, and in retrospect it was a prophecy in plywood form, literally holding space where the ongoing protest would lodge starting on July 15, 2019. Much has been written already about the 2019–2020 encampment. Its scale has been unprecedented in Hawaiian history in terms of numbers of participants; its range of facilities, including a medical tent and a grassroots university; and its grounding in thrice-daily ritual action.[16] But it was not born ex nihilo. It had an immediate precursor, which is part of why I want to draw our attention to the 2018 camp, Hale o Kuhio (House of Kuhio).

FIGURE 7.1 Hale o Kuhio and Mauna Kea.

Photo by Greg Johnson.

Beyond its historical role in prefiguring the 2019 protest, this modest camp is revealing for the purposes of this volume in several respects, including the ways it enacted resistance to American exceptionalism, especially in militarized and scientific manifestations; the manner in which the idioms of homeland and occupation stood in tension at the camp; the way the protestors assumed and performed indigenous jurisdiction; and, not least, the ways religion—ritual action, in particular—played an ever-present but understated role in maintaining solidarity and will in the camp. Further, in a comparative scope, religiously framed environmental concerns were very much at the heart of the protectors' agenda.

Let us begin the story in the early morning hours of Prince Kuhio Day, March 26, 2018. The protectors' action, they said, was to honor Kuhio's legacy of land-related advocacy for fellow Hawaiians.[17] Under the cover of darkness, the protectors trucked in a micro house to serve as their camp. Additionally, they announced the rollout of a "Kanaka Rangers" program whereby they were exerting jurisdiction and stewardship over that portion of the *mauna*. Doing so, they assumed the role of rangers not only as a means to challenge the authority of state rangers but precisely to usurp it. As Mykay, one of the *kiaʻi*, put it, "we are living our inherent sovereignty."[18]

Curious police from various jurisdictions soon arrived on the scene. The *kiaʻi* live-streamed many of these interactions. The police appeared bemused and uncertain as to what to do and clearly were unprepared to address the Kanaka Rangers' jurisdictional claims. The county police were satisfied that the rangers were not dangerous and decided to leave them to their self-assigned duties. The state police were grumpier and set up a surveillance on a nearby hill. Mykay quipped, "now they getting paid to watch us do their jobs!"[19]

On island at the time, I headed up to Hale o Kuhio to see for myself how matters were developing. Forty or so people were present that morning to establish the camp, but the organizers made a point of saying that they expected the camp to be occupied by a minimalist crew of several people for the time being—just enough to monitor traffic and field inquiries. Once phase 2 was ready, Lakea told me, more people would join the camp. Phase 2 was planned to involve semipermanent structures and educational facilities.[20] This second phase of the camp was subsequently manifested in the form of the 2019 camp at Puʻuhuluhulu, just down the road.[21]

The stated goal of the protestors in 2018 was to get Kanaka (Native Hawaiians) on the *ʻāina*. Their mantra was "the Kanaka need *ʻāina*, the *ʻāina* needs Kanaka." The first part of this elegant framing names the plain fact that too many Hawaiians are landless, which threatens to sever them from life- and culture-sustaining relationships to the earth itself. More specifically, the protestors were applying pressure to a state agency that is charged with administering land on their behalf, the Department of Hawaiian Home Lands.[22] One reason they chose their encampment location is because it is a highly visible tract within the department's jurisdiction. The message of the camp leaders to the press and the public was that the department has a long history of sluggish administrative behavior, which has led over decades to a situation wherein thousands of Hawaiians are on a waiting list for land awards. The campers were promoting a direct-action approach—settle on the land now, settle bureaucratic details later.

The second part of their refrain—"the *ʻāina* needs Kanaka"—is the necessary cultural complement to the people needing land. As noted above, in Hawaiian traditions, land and humans are genealogically related and stand in a relationship of mutual care. The land only thrives if shown *mālama ʻāina* (care for the land), a core Hawaiian religious tenet.[23] This idea and its practice are evidenced throughout Hawaiian history, if in a range of ways. Today this ethic and ethos is receiving renewed articulation through the Aloha ʻĀina (love the land) movement, which has many prongs but is unified through its core members' cultural and environmental commitments.[24]

At Hale o Kuhio, *mālama ʻāina* had two immediate and unavoidable resonances. The first pertains to militarization of the island. The encampment was perched at 6,000 feet above sea level on the lava bench between Mauna Loa (13,678 feet) and Mauna Kea (13,803 feet). Immediately *makai* (seaward) on the Kona side of camp is Pōhakuloa Training Area, a live-fire training site for the U.S. Army that occupies 108,863 acres and is the island's largest landholder. This use of the land is alarming to many Hawaiians, not least because, for them, the *ʻāina* is alive both in a general sense and in specific ways. Land is inseparable from its animating force, *wai* (water). Fresh water is among the highest of Hawaiian concerns, historically and in the present. Along with many other Hawaiians, the protestors pointed to Pōhakuloa as a site of mass desecration not only because of the immediate and blatant effects of bombing and live-fire training but also due to the effects of ammunition degradation on the massive aquifer beneath the base.

As part of their goal in founding the camp, the protestors were calling attention to this slow-motion debacle at Pōhakuloa. An April 3, 2018, state circuit court ruling heartened the campers. The court ruled that the state Department of Land and Natural Resources had been delinquent in conducting and publishing annual impact assessments, which is a violation of lease terms with the army. The state was ordered to rectify this shortcoming. In the words of Judge Gary Chang, the state was long overdue to uphold the value of "*mālama ʻāina*."[25] Formulating the matter thus—in the idiom and moral register of many Hawaiians—set a significant precedent and one that some Hawaiians have agitated for persistently over many years, going back to the bombing of Kahoʻolawe in the 1970s and 1980s.[26] To have their terms of care and redress articulated in law is a major victory in the eyes of many of the activists. For some, it is a step in the direction of fixing broken domestic law; for others, it is evidence of a cracking façade, an indication that the "fake state" is crumbling. I return to this theme below, but first we need to take stock of the second major *mālama ʻāina* agenda of the protestors, the Mauna Kea situation discussed earlier.

The camp was located at the entrance to the only vehicle access to Mauna Kea, the site of a multiyear struggle over Hawaiian traditional and customary rights in the context of proposed telescope development. In many respects, Hale o Kuhio strongly resembled the *kiaʻi* camp at Hale o Kūkiaʻimauna that was built in April of 2015 during mass protests against the TMT. The idea of the 2015 camp, which was constructed adjacent to the visitor center at nine thousand feet on the *mauna*, was to enact indigenous jurisdiction through occupation of land that the state deemed its own while simultaneously creating a checkpoint along the access road to surveil and block construction vehicle traffic. A successful tactic, Hale o Kūkiaʻimauna served as a staging point for one of the largest Hawaiian protests and collective religious actions in decades. Due to the protests launched there in the summer of 2015, the TMT project was on hold for four years while permit and lease issues were stalled in administrative proceedings and in the courts.[27]

As noted earlier, by 2019 TMT was front and center in the news again. The court cases had ended, and the building permit and lease issues were resolved in favor of the state and the telescope developers. Matters came to a head in the summer of 2019 when the state announced that it would escort construction equipment up the mountain, which in turn catalyzed the present protest movement. The *kiaʻi* at Hale o Kuhio had anticipated these events. Already in the spring of 2018 they had crafted plans to engage in culturally based direct action once again if necessary.

They set the tone for the future movement through grounding in daily ritual protocol (prayers, chants, modest offerings) anchored by an *ahu* (altar) constructed near the site in 2017. For example, a *kiʻi* of the god Kū stood at the front of the hale, ready to focus prayers and thoughts. Kū is a complex deity who oversees many domains, but one of his primary *kuleana* (responsibilities) is warfare.[28] Historically, Kū's domain was largely male. But in today's context women also stand in his name, as do numerous transgendered leaders of the movement. His name is called in moments of political resistance: Kūʻe—stand fast!

It is worth noting here, and what became very apparent in the 2019–2020 movement, that there is a generative tension at the heart of the religious dynamics that animate contemporary Hawaiian land-based activism. On the one hand, Kapu Aloha ("rule of love" or nonviolent direct action) is the stated imperative of activists and one that is hewed to in a consistent manner, even in tense confrontations with police. To be sure, there is a self-protective aspect of this ethic insofar as it keeps activists from actions that could lead to physical harm or arrest, just as it plays well to certain stereotypes in the media about the prevalence of the aloha spirit in Hawaii. On the other hand, Kū is ready to be activated in all of his ferocity. Calls to Kū have so far been metaphorical, as noted earlier. But I am not alone in worrying that the situation could change. The balance of Kapu Aloha and Kū is precarious at best, and the state and mainstream media outlets have been eager to consolidate a narrative around potentially violent future protests, although not in terms of Kū prevailing or any other acknowledgment of cultural forces at play. The story parlayed is one of thugs with nothing better to do.[29]

What this story of thugs and putatively anti-science protests fails to capture is a cultural-historic sensibility on the part of the *kiaʻi* that is jurisdictionally informed through and through. It also fails to name the reasons why activists have "nothing better to do," living as they do at the margins of an empire whose flows of capital seldom favor them. Finding meaning beyond the impositions of the state, these young Hawaiians insist that they are descendants of the Hawaiian Kingdom and its rightful heirs.[30] Their religious freedom on the *mauna*— indeed, even the freedom to be there—is not something for the state or the federal government to decide. In their eyes, they are "at home" even while their so-called home lands are a fiction of a foreign regime. They work through the systems of the settler government when and where it seems there is traction to be had, but few equivocate when it comes to stating the grounds of their authority in Hawaiian nationalist terms.

THE VOICE OF GOD AND THE BLIND STATE

The day after we returned from Germany on the repatriation trip described earlier, one of our team members, Kaleikoa Kaʻeo, who has also been a core figure among the Mauna Kea *kiaʻi*, was arrested for disrupting a state Department of Land and Natural Resources meeting concerning the proposed TMT permit. His disruption was in the form of prayers, chants, political commentary, and oratory in emphatically spoken Hawaiian—that, and not stopping when asked. In the course of his oratory, Kaʻeo invoked the powerful words of Queen Liliʻuokalani, saying, "the voice of the people is the voice of God."[31]

In January of 2018 Kaʻeo was arrested again, this time on his home island of Maui *during a hearing* about his involvement in protests against telescope development on Haleakalā. The arrest warrant was issued by the presiding judge, who charged Kaʻeo with failure to appear, despite the fact that Kaʻeo *was in the room and the judge was speaking directly to him*. What rendered Kaʻeo invisible was his chosen diction—he spoke in Hawaiian, which the judge refused to acknowledge, despite its status in the constitution as a state language.[32] Kaʻeo was not alone in his use of Hawaiian in legal settings. He stands as paradigmatic of a movement. Numerous twenty- to thirty-year-olds in Hawaii command the language and demand their constitutional right to use it.

The judge's hasty action prompted a swift and vocal response from the Native Hawaiian community and in the media. Subsequently, the judge dropped the charge and allowed Kaʻeo to testify in Hawaiian. More broadly, this episode prompted the state legislature to take up the issue, and now interpreters are provided in courts statewide. Here I want to call our attention to ways that assertions of indigenous jurisdiction—in the literal sense of speaking law—sometimes result in positive gains for communities in the face of asymmetrical legal frames, even while larger order aspirations, such as land protection, remain unfulfilled.

Another point to be made here concerns the tension and irony—if not paradox—found in the fact that state and federal funds have supported the successful immersion school movement in Hawaii. In a Polynesian way, language acquisition begets engagement with traditional sources, which in turns sparks curiosity about genealogy and place. Recognition of deep connections and family commitments to the land follow. This then becomes a profoundly political education once questions are posed by students feeling the dissonance of being alienated from the very land their language and stories would attach to them. Thus the threat of the fluency. Much like protest itself, the challenge to the state is not so much in the spoken word per se but in the ways those words know differently.

CONCLUSION: JURISDICTIONAL FUTURES?

It is premature, at least with reference to Hawaii, to say anything conclusive about the lasting impact and possible futures of auto-jurisdiction. As a mode of being and speaking, and in a global comparative frame, claims to self-jurisdiction are not available to all indigenous peoples, at least not without tremendous potential costs. But in a place like Hawaii, with putatively democratic mechanisms in place as a check on state violence, an acknowledged history of a stolen kingdom, and a very robust and youthful generation willing to exert claims and take chances, the future of indigenous jurisdiction is almost certain to be lively.

It is one thing to improvise tactics of inherent jurisdiction on the ground; it is quite another to launch and sustain a movement that seeks a thoroughgoing revolution and maximal sovereignty. It should be an urgent agendum for scholars of indigenous religions and law to track and understand moments and movements that evince bridgework from the former to the latter, and current trends suggest that we can reasonably expect more along these lines in coming years from communities across the globe. For the time being, my examples enable me to advance an initial claim that I hope has been made clear. Namely, the Hawaiians I have described are invoking their own jurisdiction in a manner that has the effect of rupturing "law's perpetuity," to cite Justin Richland's compelling formulation of jurisdiction's labor.³³ In other words, and regardless of apparent successes and failures vis-à-vis forces of the state, Hawaiians asserting autojurisdiction have tapped into the law's most intimate language about itself *as speakers of it*.

What remains to be seen, among other things, is the effectiveness of such movements for protecting religious practices and sacred places. It has become increasingly obvious in Hawaii that neither the state constitution nor federal frameworks are providing any substantial relief. Even more troubling are the manifest failures of due process in a number of recent disputes that are so egregious as to cause already marginalized Hawaiians to distance themselves yet further from a state not of their own making. To give but one example, in the TMT contested case hearing, which lasted six months and included forty-four days of testimony by Native Hawaiians, the hearing officer found virtually no new facts with regard to claims about the purportedly sacred status of Mauna Kea.³⁴

Hovering above the issues and examples I have explored is the unresolved question of federal recognition, which has created intense friction within the Hawaiian community. Because they have no federally recognized governing body, there is no direct means for Hawaiians to negotiate with the government, fend off challenges, or make and implement collective decisions, among other considerations. Seeing an opportunity in the acephalous status of Hawaiians vis-à-vis federal laws and oversight, some conservative groups have begun to attack Hawaiian programs and trusts, asserting that these are race-based and otherwise unconstitutional. In response, some Hawaiians and their allies have been working to secure the status of Hawaiians as a political body so as to "more effectively implement the special political and trust relationship" that Congress has established between Native Hawaiians and the United States.³⁵ This effort festered for more than a decade at the legislative level (e.g., the so-called Akaka Bill).³⁶

In 2014 the Obama administration's Department of the Interior took steps to implement an administrative remedy to this quagmire through a rule-making process and community meetings. Announced suddenly, the meetings became a major site of political drama. Most notable for our purposes, the jurisdictional frame and stage of the commission was coopted by audience members time and again. In these quintessentially performative meetings, presenters used their time to address one another, to speak back to and challenge dominant histories, to envision possible futures.

Throughout the process, two primary rhetorical stances were announced by those who testified at the meetings. By far the loudest, most vocal position was "a'ole!" This word, frequently shouted at the bewildered commission, simply means "No." In short, representatives of this position made the following argument: No, we don't want to be recognized. No, we aren't a tribe. No, you don't have jurisdiction here. Your proposed remedy is exactly the injury we've been trying to heal from ever since you stole our kingdom. The less dominant argument was "Ae": yes. This position is more prominent in written testimonies (of which more than five thousand were submitted) and is that of the Office of Hawaiian Affairs, the Kamehameha Schools, and other institutionalized Native Hawaiian organizations and trusts. It is also a position cautiously voiced by some long-time Hawaiian activists who emphasize the short- and mid-range importance of working with and through existing political structures, even while aspiring to decolonized futures. Over the course of the meetings, the rhetorical divide between the positions became notably reified and the issue is currently at an impasse.

How will jurisdictional paths into the future be navigated by Native Hawaiians? Major issues loom about community buy-in, actionability, and facing down the stark realities of military presence and the stubborn normativity of the tourist economy. But if ever the hold of the nation-state was felt to be loosening just as people on the ground are prepared to wrestle, my sense is we are at that moment.

Whatever happens next, we can be sure idioms and actions in the name of religion and tradition will be central and that these will be reconfigured in their unfolding. Such a context calls for skilled comparison with other times and places with an eye to how these discourses and events challenge our inherited categories and conceptual ruts.

In this spirit, I venture a final comparative point. Religion animates so much of indigenous life, but often in a low key. However, political and legal crises that threaten ideas of the good life and the ability to live it often push indigenous religious practices to the foreground and amplify their presence. In the process, this kind of performativity reshapes religion in lasting ways. One particular way this is happening in Hawaii today, as evinced by the examples we have considered, is in response to the fact that settler jurisdictions have failed to recognize Native Hawaiians' political status, which is articulated and enshrined in the state constitution.

Addressing this failure, some Hawaiians are looking to their religious traditions as the ground of their jurisdictional authority, as we have seen. This move seems apt insofar as it enacts a deep structural response to settler colonial claims to indigenous land anchored in the Doctrine of Discovery and related theological justifications. Thus, settlers and Native Hawaiians alike ultimately root their claims to place in religious narratives, however differently grounded these may be. This paradox demands our attention, especially in an age where jurisdictional borders are perceived to be so fragile that walls are needed to shore them up.

NOTES

A number of people helped me with this chapter in several respects. I would like to thank Michael McNally, Kari Robinson, Pamela Klassen, Halealoha Ayau, Ty Kāwika Tengan, Marie Alohalani Brown, Winnifred Sullivan, and members of the At Home and Abroad project for their engagement and suggestions.

1. Hawaiian rejections of non-indigenous jurisdictions can be read in the register of refusal, which has recently been theorized by Audra Simpson, among others. See Audra Simpson, *Mohawk Interruptus: Political Life Across the Borders of Settler States* (Durham, N.C.: Duke University Press, 2014). For a recent theorization of indigenous jurisdictions, see Shiri Pasternak, *Grounded Authority: The Algonquins of Barrier Lake Against the State* (Minneapolis: University of Minnesota Press, 2017).
2. Following Justin Richland's analysis of jurisdiction and his review of recent scholarship regarding the concept, I foreground the manner in which jurisdiction in the cases I describe is not only a matter of territoriality but also involves notions of social space and time and, crucially, metajurisdictional reflections upon the authority of authority. See Justin Richland, "Jurisdiction: Grounding Law in Language," *Annual Review of Anthropology* 42 (2013): 209–26. On the intriguing concept of "spiritual jurisdiction," see Pamela Klassen, *The Story of Radio Mind: A Missionary's Journey on Indigenous Land* (University of Chicago Press, 2018).
3. On religion making in the sense I intend here, see, among others, Markus Dressler and Arvind-Pal S. Mandair, eds., *Secularism and Religion-Making* (New York: Oxford University Press, 2011).
4. On Hawaiian traditions and religious sensibilities see, among others, Lilikalā Kameʻeleihiwa, *Native Land and Foreign Desires: Pehea Lā E Pono Ai?* (Honolulu: Bishop Museum Press, 1992); and Pualani Kanakaʻole Kanahele, *Ka Honua Ola: The Living Earth* (Honolulu: Kamehameha, 2011).
5. For a discussion of the role of ancestors in Hawaiian traditions, see, e.g., Steven Friesen, ed., *Ancestors in Post-Contact Religion: Roots, Ruptures and Modernity's Memory* (Cambridge, Mass.: Harvard University Press, 2001).
6. See, e.g., Edward Halealoha Ayau and Ty Kāwika Tengan, "Ka Huakaʻi O Nā ʻŌiwi: The Journey Home," in *The Dead and their Possessions: Repatriation in Principle, Policy and Practice*, ed. Cressida Fforde, Jane Hubert, and Paul Turnbull (London: Routledge, 2002), 171–89.
7. On Kawaiahaʻo Church, see Dana Nāone Hall, *Life of the Land: Articulations of a Native Writer* (Honolulu: ʻAi Pohaku Press, 2017). Regarding the Mauna Kea dispute, see Marie Alohalani Brown, "*Mauna Kea: Hoʻomana Hawaiʻi* and Protecting the Sacred," *Journal for the Study of Religion, Nature, and Culture* 10, no. 2 (2016): 150–69; and Noelani Goodyear-Kaʻōpua, "Protectors of the Future, Not Protestors

of the Past: Indigenous Pacific Activism on Mauna a Wākea," *South Atlantic Quarterly* 116, no. 1 (2017):184–94. On recognition politics in Hawaii, see J. Kēhaulani Kauanui, "Precarious Positions: Native Hawaiians and U.S. Federal Recognition," in *Recognition, Sovereignty Struggles, and Indigenous Rights: A Sourcebook*, ed. Amy E. Denouden and Jean M. O'Brien, 314–36 (Chapel Hill: University of North Carolina Press, 2013).

8. On the Native American Graves Protection and Repatriation Act, see, e.g., Kathleen Fine-Dare, *Grave Injustice: The American Indian Repatriation Movement* (Lincoln: University of Nebraska Press, 2002).

9. See Amy Bowers and Kristen Carpenter, "Challenging the Narrative of Conquest: The Story of *Lyng v. Northwest Indian Cemetery Protective Association*," in *Indian Law Stories*, ed. C. Goldberg, K. Washburn and P. Frickey, 489–533 (New York: Foundation Press, 2011).

10. Nick Estes, *Our History Is the Future: Standing Rock Versus the Dakota Access Pipeline and the Long Tradition of Indigenous Resistance* (New York: Verso, 2019).

11. Greg Johnson, "Courting Culture: Unexpected Relationships Between Religion and Law in Contemporary Hawai'i," in *After Secular Law*, ed. Winnifred Fallers Sullivan, Robert A. Yelle and Mateo Taussig-Rubbo, 282–301 (Palo Alto: Stanford University Press, 2011).

12. See, e.g., a newspaper account of the meeting and new policy: "Sachsen gibt Gebeine an Hawaii zurück," *Sächsische Zeitung*, Dienstag 24, October 2017, front page. See also, Victoria Stapley-Brown, "Dresden Museum of Ethnology Returns Ancestral Remains to Native Hawaiian Group," *Art Newspaper*, October 26, 2017, https://www.theartnewspaper.com/news/dresden-museum-of-ethnology-returns-ancestral-remains-to-native-hawaiian-group; and "Emotional Ceremony in Germany Brings Iwi Kupuna Home to Hawaii," KITV4 News, October 27, 2017, http://www.kitv.com/story/36706310/emotional-ceremony-in-germany-brings-iwi-kupuna-home-to-hawaii.

13. For an account of the collection, see Adrienne L. Kaeppler, Markus Schindlbeck, and Gisela E Speidel, eds., *Old Hawai'i: An Ethnography of Hawai'i in the 1880s* (Berlin: Ethnologisches Museum Berlin, 2008).

14. See the definition of "sacred object" in the Native American Graves Protection and Repatriation Act (1990), Public Law 101-601; 25 U.S.C. 3001 Sec. 2 (c). For related provisions of the UN Declaration on the Rights of Indigenous Peoples (A/RES/61/295, 2007), see Article 11 and Article 12, https://undocs.org/A/RES/61/295.

15. For the state's official press release describing destruction of Hale o Kuhio and several other structures, including ceremonial sites, see "Office of the Governor—News Release—State Issues Notice to Proceed for Thirty Meter Telescope Project," Press release, June 20, 2019, https://governor.hawaii.gov/newsroom/latest-news/office-of-the-governor-news-release-state-issues-notice-to-proceed-for-thirty-meter-telescope-project/.

16. For a range of scholarly perspectives on the 2019–2020 protest, see J. Kēhaulani Kauanui et al., *The Abusable Past: Mauna Kea*, a special online forum of *Radical*

History Review available at https://www.radicalhistoryreview.org/abusablepast/category/forums/mauna-kea/ (accessed April 2, 2020).

17. On Prince Kuhio's legacy, see J. Kēhaulani Kauanui, *Hawaiian Blood: Colonialism and the Politics of Sovereignty and Indigeneity* (Durham, N.C.: Duke University Press, 2008).

18. Personal communication, March 26, 2018. Due to the nature of the events described, I do not use interlocutors' full names in this section. For a news report on the Kanaka Rangers, see Brittany Lyte, "Kanaka Rangers: It's Time to Move Forward with Hawaiian Homesteads," *Civil Beat*, April 2, 2018, http://www.civilbeat.org/2018/04/kanaka-rangers-its-time-to-move-forward-with-hawaiian-homesteads/.

19. Personal communication, March 26, 2018.

20. Personal communication, March 26, 2018. For a multifaceted account of various contemporary forms of Hawaiian responses to status quo expectations, see Stephanie Nohelani Teves, *Defiant Indigeneity: The Politics of Hawaiian Performance* (Chapel Hill: University of North Carolina Press, 2018), which includes an account of Hawaiian rap, the preferred genre of the Kanaka Rangers, who released their own song, "Kanaka Come Home" (https://soundcloud.com/selftarget/homework-simpson-kanaka-come-home-ft-the-kanaka-rangers-1).

21. For information about the 2019–2020 camp, see https://www.puuhuluhulu.com (accessed April 24, 2020).

22. On the Hawaiian 'Homes Commission Act (1920), see Kauanui, *Hawaiian Blood*.

23. On *mālama ʻāina*, see Hall, *Life of the Land*.

24. For background on the Aloha ʻĀina movement and related movements, see Noelani Goodyear-Kaopua, Ikaika Hussey, and Erin Kahunawaikaʻala Wright, eds., *A Nation Rising: Hawaiian Movements for Life, Land, and Sovereignty* (Durham, N.C.: Duke University Press, 2014).

25. See "Pohakuloa Court Ruling: State Breached Trust in Lease to Army," *Big Island Video News*, April 3, 2018, http://www.bigislandvideonews.com/2018/04/03/pohakuloa-court-ruling-state-breached-trust-in-lease-to-army/.

26. On Kahoʻolawe, see Mansel Blackford, "Environmental Justice, Native Rights, Tourism, and Opposition to Military Control: The Case of Kahoʻolawe," *Journal of American History* 91, no. 2 (2004): 544–71.

27. For a complete record of the primary legal and administrative documents pertaining to the dispute, see the Mauna Kea Department of Land and Natural Resources Documents Library, http://dlnr.hawaii.gov/mk/documents-library/.

28. For a nuanced discussion of contemporary interpretations of Kū, see Ty Kāwika Tengan, *Native Men Remade: Gender and Nation in Contemporary Hawaiʻi* (Durham, N.C.: Duke University Press, 2008).

29. For example, see the following story pertaining to the 2015 Mauna Kea Protests: "State Proposes Limiting Access to Mauna Kea Summit in Wake of Protests," *Star Advertiser*, July 7, 2015, www.staradvertiser.com/news/breaking/20150707_State_proposes_limiting_access_to_Mauna_Kea_summit_in_wake_of_protests.html?id=312253371.

30. An example of literature published by members of the movement is David Keanu Sai's book, *Ua Mau Ke Ea—Sovereignty Endures: An Overview of the Political and Legal History of the Hawaiian Islands* (Honolulu: Puʻa Foundation, 2011).
31. "Huli Members Arrested After Halting BLNR Meeting (Oct. 27, 2017)," Big Island News, YouTube, October 27, 2017, https://www.youtube.com/watch?v=u4vMCRhUP5Q.
32. Timothy Hurley, "Maui Judge Issue Arrest Warrant Over Refusal to Speak English," *Star Advertiser*, January 24, 2018, https://www.staradvertiser.com/2018/01/24/breaking-news/maui-judge-issues-arrest-warrant-over-refusal-to-speak-english/.
33. Richland, "Jurisdiction," 219.
34. For the hearing officer's full findings of fact, see Board of Land and Natural Resources State of Hawaiʻi, "Proposed Findings of Fact, Conclusions of Law, and Decisions and Order," July 26, 2017, https://dlnr.hawaii.gov/mk/files/2017/07/783-Hearing-Officers-Proposal.pdf.
35. For the Advance Notice of Proposed Rulemaking, meeting transcripts, and other related documents, see U.S. Department of the Interior, Office of Native Hawaiian Relations, "Advanced Notice of Proposed Rulemaking," https://www.doi.gov/hawaiian/reorg (accessed April 28, 2020).
36. Native Hawaiian Government Reorganization Act of 2009, S1011/HR2314.

8

"Legacy"

MATTHEW SCHERER

Why is America "hard to see," in the words of Robert Frost, as Courtney Bender invokes to such great effect in her contribution to this volume?[1] While Bender's argument is inventive and quite persuasive in many respects, this essay takes a different tack to think about some aspects of America that are omitted from the perspectives she examines.[2] Where Bender focuses on an exceptionalism that emerges by turning its glance upward toward unbounded futures and freedoms, my concern is with the underside of the upward glance: Many of America's legacies stare us in the face, and American exceptionalism is often produced by looking away from American history. So we might also ask what America looks away from when it makes itself hard to see, how it can continue to do this, and what an alternative might look like. Looking up and looking away, my thought is, are one and the same gesture; perhaps two sides of a distinctly American way of being at home by being abroad. In the context of American exceptionalism, this means looking away from the presence of the past, particularly the legacies of slavery, genocide, appropriation, and white supremacy that Americans inherit with this past. Perhaps in every instance, the Americas that are "hard to see," are produced by collective refusals to see America. It is not a particularly novel suggestion that when America is hard to see, it is because Americans are looking away from what is right before them. Although the general dynamic is fairly obvious how the exceptionalist avoidance and disavowal of historical legacies nonetheless persists, why it is so hard to escape is not obvious at all.

America is a mixed-up place, and the problem of American exceptionalism is contested and complex. If not unavoidable, and if not necessarily uniquely American, exceptionalism has proven a persistent feature of America's legacy, evidenced most recently by the promises of placing "America First" and "Make[ing] America Great Again." Arguably, the notion of an exceptional American Greatness has existed in tension with the actual lived complexity and diversity of American experiences since the founding. According to the eminent historian of American political thought Joyce Appleby, "Necessity mothered this ideological invention because Americans in 1776 had to create the sense of nationhood that other countries inherited. The United States' nationhood—its juridical standing—preceded the formation of a national ideology, and this peculiar inversion of sentiment and status led to a quest for national identity."[3] Her point here is that an America national identity was at the outset an emergent formation, the *unum* it projected always fictive, and yet always regulating and sustaining the complex *pluribus* that not only forms its concrete historical and material basis but also demands its production. America in this view is not a bright historical exception transcending the rest of the world's mundane and particular traditions, yet the everyday lives of Americans, diverse as they have always been, have nonetheless unfolded within the compass of an exceptionalist fiction they could not but demand.[4]

Returning to Appleby's words, "it would be hard to exaggerate the dissonance between history recounted through the doings of the individual—the American Adam—" with the alternative histories "reconstructed with the modular units of group experience" through the archival research and demographic techniques of contemporary scholars.[5] Mighty is the work of sustaining our simple fictions—directing and fastening our gazes upward—in the face of our complex facts and legacies. Appleby, as a historian, does not suggest that we could or should simply replace the former image of a unified America with the unmediated reality of a million fragmented groups. The diversity of American experiences is accompanied at every point, *necessarily*, by simplifying narrative unity. American experiences are marked by the coexistence and co-implication of an actual diversity and a fictive unity.

At this still early moment in the twenty-first century, in comparison with the early republic that is Appleby's point of reference, it may be that the layered relations between a complex diversity and a simple, authorized, singular exceptionalist ideal are being profoundly reconfigured. Nonetheless, the connections between ideological representations and material conditions remain as dense as ever. Whereas in the history of the early republic, America is plausibly staged as geographically, geopolitically, and economically relatively remote and insignificant but morally and politically exemplary, at present a quite different accounting is in order. Put simply, today America remains a global exception with respect to wealth and power. American wealth and power dominate the postwar and post–Cold War moments through

1. A broad cultural trajectory (individualist, consumerist, antinomian, and entrepreneurial) expressed within but not reducible to the products of the American culture industry;
2. A distinct economic style and set of possibilities ("neoliberal" trending toward "libertarian," enforced and expressed in the "developing world" through World Bank and International Monetary Fund policies of state austerity, private marketization, global free trade; adopted more freely, but within increasing uniformity in the hyperdeveloped world); and
3. A political form (lately in ethnonationalist authoritarian style, heretofore in liberal and increasingly neoliberal constitutional democracies featuring limited government, circumscribed representation, and strong legal protections for economic liberties of property and contract).

While this picture could be more carefully qualified, the general thrust of an America that has played an outsized, leading role in remaking the world seems difficult to contest.

At the same time, America is surely not an exception in terms of the extent and quality of freedom enjoyed by its citizens; the moral uprightness of its conduct domestically or internationally; or the piety, secularity, or freedom of its religious practices. If Appleby's eighteenth-century *philosophes* could sketch America as a minor player in the global game of wealth and power but a major player in the moral and political histories of human freedom, contemporary theorists might roughly reverse that assessment. A renewed reckoning with American exceptionalism reveals a deeply compromised moral agent with extreme material influence. Arguably, the critical problem central to the American exception at the founding might once have been thought of as how to disseminate an idealized, exceptional American rectitude and freedom in the absence of American power. At present, the problem might be more appropriately staged as how to limit or redirect the effects of American wealth and power given the moral and political compromises of the American state.

These observations on American exceptionalism—as blunt and in need of closer specification and argument as they are—have a particular bearing on this volume's more narrowly and precisely delimited questions about the connections among American exceptionalism and religion.[6] Two issues bear emphasis.

First, the formations of "American exceptionalism" and "religion" are problematic concepts in similar ways. These are contested concepts, and scholars generally share a deep skepticism about the analytic purchase of each even while acknowledging their historical significance. Insofar as each concept is unstable, each maintains an internal tension between what it claims as proper to itself (the exceptional, the religious) and what it defines itself against (the ordinary, the nonreligious). These tensions are dynamic and incapable of resolution insofar as they are constitutive tensions and dynamic configurations (the exceptional and the religious emerged continuously by making, remaking, implementing, and guarding the boundaries between themselves and their others—for example, by ever directing their glances upward and away from what is before them but what they will not see as proper to them). These are examples of what I elsewhere call layered, crystalline structures; intellectually as well as practically such structures make for a difficult terrain to navigate.[7]

Second, there are numerous tragic dimensions to the predicament of American exceptionalism, which includes America religious exceptionalism. Whether or not this is a necessary condition, it is compounded by key aspects of American history. One aspect of this history, invoked above by way of reference to Joyce Appleby, is that the United States was peopled by European settlers in relatively recent and well-recorded history, requiring the invention of a new collective identity. However necessary, this fiction belied and sacrificed the actual diversity underlying it. Another, as universally known but nonetheless endlessly disavowed, aspect is that that United States was at this same time peopled by African slaves and depopulated of Indigenous peoples, requiring the invention of a collective identity that omits, erases, and looks away from these parts, another fiction that refuses to tell what has been.

Niccolò Machiavelli may have been grappling with one of these tragic modes—what Appleby notes, and what we may take as a generic function of a narrative, an ideal, a fictional unity standing in for an unruly multiplicity—when he observed, "In all human affairs we see, if we analyze things carefully, that you cannot get rid of one cause of trouble without introducing another.... So in all discussions about policy, we should decide which course of action has the fewest disadvantages and we should regard that policy as the best, for we will never find a policy that gives you no grounds for anxiety, that involves no cost."[8] This should not be read to urge action without reflection but instead to argue that, given a sufficient understanding of the human predicament, acting judiciously requires tarrying with anxiety.

Along with the apparent necessity of acting under conditions of uncertainty, there is a second tragic dimension, a certain kind of unknowingness that is arguably less generic and more specifically American. Following Stanley Cavell, one might find that dimension of tragedy thematized in Shakespeare (in *King Lear* and *Othello*, particularly): tragic unknowingness in those plays may begin with the absence of a certain piece of information, but it becomes a desire for a particular kind of knowledge that is impossible to have. In Cavell's telling, that demand changes as it grows from a benign or ethically indifferent lack of knowledge into a malign and ethically untenable failure to acknowledge the humanity of others. The protagonists' demand that *you prove that you love me*, as it were, is an ordinary human demand, but one that the nature of human relations does not allow us to resolve, and one that can become quite destructive when it runs out of hand. In Cavell's view, nationalisms can be wrapped up in an analogous desire or demand that citizens prove their love of country.[9]

Another wrinkle comes from asking if we can continue to take this lesson from Cavell and Shakespeare. How do we address the further tragic fact that in these tales of Lear and Othello, Shakespeare sacrifices Cordelia and Desdemona in service of their stories? He has Othello murder Desdemona with his own hands, and he arranges for Cordelia to be hanged before Lear's eyes as a consequence of his choices and as the culmination of Lear's suffering. Consider by way of contrast, Pat Barker's *The Silence of the Girls*, a retelling of the *Iliad* from Briseis's perspective, and Madeline Miller's *Circe*, a retelling of the *Odyssey* from Circe's perspective, as well as her *Song of Achilles*, a retelling of the *Iliad* from the perspective of Patroclus, imagined by her as Achilles's lover.[10] These contemporary works imagine voices and stories for some of the women, and some of the men, in the literary canon heretofore instrumentalized as plot devices, made into corpses, regarded as anything but fully human. As so often in the Homeric Epics, Lear's and Othello's stories turn on the murdered bodies of women, and, to an extent, Shakespeare and Cavell have made this hard to see. To an extent, Barker and Miller force us to see and reckon with this. My point is not that this should come as news, as a great discovery; rather, it is obvious that it is what stares us in the face. There are nonetheless mysteries here, such as how we can continue not to see it, what we are doing when we avert our glances, how and why our gaze wanders from what was always there (even already in Homer, and Shakespeare, and certainly in America).

Exploring the various aspects of humanity's tragic predicament in Homer, Shakespeare, and Machiavelli may be a familiar exercise, but are scholars as practiced at this with respect to our peculiar, modern concepts of religion? In this, "religion" carries legacies as complex and conflicted as "America." There is a relatively longstanding and widely held consensus in the field of religious studies that the concept of religion distorts the fields it is deployed to map.

More specifically, the politics of religious freedom is insufficient to its ostensible task of protecting religious lives and traditions; for the panoply of policies enacted to support religious freedom remake the individuals, communities, traditions, and problematic multidimensional fields of relation that they engage. Yet, on the other hand, a wide variety of legal, political, and sociological tendencies as well as a welter of relatively narrow interests are currently aligned to press religion to the forefront of scholars' and policymakers' concerns. Improving upon the conventional wisdom of secularist or separationist stances toward religion and its roles in public life, however, proves difficult. Almost as if it expresses a desire for a particular kind of knowledge—a certainty in human affairs—that life cannot grant; almost as if it would avoid the restless anxiety that attends and underpins human freedom. All this is known, of course, and like the last paragraph should not come as news, but that is not to say that such knowledge effectively governs inquiries, policies, and actions. The concept of religion circulates in a tragic register (a condition that is not always acknowledged).

It may be the case that contemporary crises of religion and secularism (scholarly crises as well as practical, institutional, and political crises) index a collective intellectual incapacity to cope with the apparent changes to our world wrought by large-scale processes—including what goes under the names of modernization, secularization, globalization, capitalism, and neoliberalism. These processes are in turn intimately bound up with the American exception (in terms of wealth and power—both in turn, as scholars across disciplines are bringing into focus anchored in racial domination). These dynamic processes of transformation press concepts of secularism as separation, as well as the ideal of disestablishment more commonly contemplated by students of American religious history, into crises revealing new landscapes marked by policies and research that actively engage, shape, and mold religion. Policies addressed to religion are generally promoted and accepted as merely reconciling, harmonizing, or insulating religious and political practices, while these policies in fact profoundly reshape the contours of both. There are complex dynamics of change at work here that are obscured and sometimes redirected by the simplifying narratives typically applied to them.[11]

But for every confident pronouncement about the human capacity for knowledge and mastery in the history of philosophy, social science, and political thought, one might also find traces of minor traditions that acknowledge the limits of such mastery. Insofar as it can be linked through such a transnational constellation of canonical thinkers such as Max Horkheimer and Theodor Adorno, Ludwig Wittgenstein, Martin Heidegger, William James, Henri Bergson, and Friedrich Nietzsche, a tragic conception is linked in a rather substantial tradition. If human freedom—here, religious freedom—is sought, one might do well to ask if freedom is likely to be found in the authoritative mastery of circumstances or if it might instead emerge from the fleeting margins and recesses that elude authoritative grasp. Or, if those margins prove too inhospitable, if it is to be sought adverbially instead—as a distinctive practice of modifying authoritative actions and policies to inflect them with the hesitations, reservations, and anxieties of the margins, and to open them continuously to revision. This latter possibility would be one way of enacting a more anxious freedom, acknowledging both the need to act and the impossibility of mastering the consequences of one's actions.

What would it mean to enact a more anxious freedom as a way of inhabiting the American exception? While not the dominant mode, this is a distinct and recurrent possibility advocated and enacted within the history of American exceptionalism. Moving beyond operative conceptions of religious freedom, American freedom, and American exceptionalism toward a more anxious stance might, I think, require a conversion of interest and commitment accompanied by new narratives and sensibilities on the part of scholars, policymakers, activists and ordinary folks.[12] Even tinkering with the concepts of religion and American exceptionalism tends to produce shocks, and there is no guarantee about the outcome. Machiavelli's courage in the face of tragedy is pertinent here. There are, of course, many ways to respond to this predicament—one is not bound to the masculinized, militarized, classical virtues admired in Machiavelli's *Discourses*—but it is important to acknowledge that profound ethical and political predicaments emerge here at the precise limits of knowledge and threshold of tragedy.

I understand my work to intersect with the project of this volume in seeking to reflect upon a seeming paradox that has gained significant recognition among scholars: the concepts of religion and secularism are in many ways insufficient for the purposes of analyzing and intervening in the key contemporary problems they index, and yet these concepts appear indispensable, perhaps even inescapable. Religion, for example, is alternately—and sometimes even simultaneously—treated as a social phenomenon like all others and also as a domain qualitatively distinct from all others. In the U.S. context, for example, protestant Christianity is taken at once as the archetype of authentic religiosity and presumed to be a shared, nonreligious cultural background. While my first book was titled *Beyond Church and State*, the book I am currently writing may need to be titled, *Back to Church and State*—not so much because I was wrong the first time around but because of the tension implicit in our condition. In part, my argument in this new work is that the difficulties in coming to theoretical terms with religion and secularity stem from the fact that, in their modern formations, both religion and secularity are produced and reproduced as exceptions to existing political and social orders.

The figure of the exception appears frequently in the fields of politics, law, history, and theology. Contemporary scholarship, for example, continues to devote a great deal of attention to the lapidary formulation, "Sovereign is he who decides the exception" of Carl Schmitt's *Political Theology* (1922), which was taken up in Giorgio Agamben's *Homo sacer* (1998) and in a great deal of scholarship that has followed. Only a generation earlier, however, a quite different figure of the exception captured scholarly attention: the emergence of the United States as a superpower renewed interest in longstanding ideas of "American exceptionalism," which were first given expression in the rhetoric of the Puritan founding, later echoed in Alexis de Tocqueville's *Democracy in America* (1835) and since vigorously debated by social scientists and public intellectuals. Part of my aim is to uncover a variety of religious, secular, and political exceptionalisms irreducible to these better-known forms. Tracing what might be called patterns of ordinary exceptionality produced within the fabric of everyday life, my suspicion is that much of the work of religion, secularity, and democracy can be understood as interrelated processes that create, manage, and are complicated by exceptions. Another way of thinking about this research is to frame it as an investigation of more anxious freedoms and as an effort to think again about the possibilities of exceptionality (in part, but not exclusively, activating different possibilities of American exceptionalism implicit, but not dominant in that tradition)—I think the concepts most familiar to political theorists are insufficient to many of these tasks.

How sure should we be that we know what the legacy of American exceptionalism has been, is, and could be? In this volume's terms, what finds itself at home within a tradition of American exceptionalism, and how does this also include parts formerly omitted or excluded? I think we should be anxious about this legacy. In another essay that addresses this problem, and takes the current U.S. president's words as a point of departure, I take Donald Trump's avowed preference for Norwegian immigrants over people from "Shithole Countries" in the Caribbean and Africa as a starting point for reflecting on the philosopher Stanley Cavell's articulation of a critical, dissenting mode of American exceptionalism. Trump's preference for Norwegians becomes ironic to the extent that Helge Årsheim's contribution to this volume diagnoses the fragility of Norwegian national identity and the self-conscious initiatives undertaken to establish a normality that would anchor it. I argue in that essay that Trump's chauvinist, triumphal exceptionalism—encapsulated as "America First" and "MAGA," or "Make America Great Again"—might inadvertently draw our attention to a more promising, minor mode of exceptionalism, an exceptionalism that drawing on Cavell, drawing on Emerson, takes exception to itself. An exceptionalism that, less elliptically, is grounded in acknowledging past and current failures to attain our ideals as a way of renewing commitment to reach for those ideals in the present. An exceptionalism grounded in close inspection of America's legacies rather than as turn upward and away toward the future.

As I put it in my last effort, while Ralph Waldo Emerson, whom Cavell takes as his point of departure, is often interpreted as an American triumphalist, much of Cavell's thrust is to inoculate American exceptionalism against that impulse by insisting on the tragic dimension of America's unapproachability. Cavell suggests an exceptionalism in which the leading notes are those of determined criticism, rather than celebration; aspirational solidarity rather than historical or ethnic nationalism; dissent and resistance rather than a self-sacrificing love of country. The exhortation is addressed to Americans not because they are an especially worthy people but rather because when we ask Emerson's question—"where do we find ourselves?"—the answer is that we find ourselves in America, among a people who might yet become Americans. This remains an exceptionalism, but it is a severely chastened one such that enacting the American exception is bound up with acknowledging the failure (as yet) to attain America's promise. Despite the apparent dominance of chauvinistic white nationalisms in the history of American exceptionalisms, Cavell would remind us, there might be a minor though no less American tradition that takes exception to those dominant forms.[13]

In promising to "Make America Great Again," America's "shithole" presidency may yet, ironically, accomplish the task of focusing national attention on the ways that America's historical failures continue within its present and on the constant need to return to and remain with those failures with honesty and a commitment to address and redress them, rather than to continue a triumphant tradition that disavows and otherwise avoids them. Today's exceptionalism, arguably *through its triumphalist disavowals*, solicits these minor chords with intense urgency. Concerns about racism, growing inequality, and collapsing public institutions, too, are quite commonplace, not only within specialized scholarship but also among the newspaper-reading public, as seen for example in the pages of *The New York Times* in "The 1619 Project" and "The America we Need."[14]

Looking at these issues through an exceptionalist lens produces more particular and distinctive observations, however. Cavell had noted in a striking aside that "what seems to me evident is that Emerson's finding of founding as finding, say the transfiguration of philosophical grounding as lasting, could not have presented itself as a stable philosophical proposal before the configuration of philosophy established by the work of the later Heidegger and the later Wittgenstein." It is perhaps in the same way that it becomes possible to find new critical resources in old texts. And this is another reason to imagine, with some hopefulness, that we have not yet found the bottom of the tradition of American exceptionalism. And that we might yet find a way to go on with it.[15]

Between the time I completed that essay and the time I turned to completing this essay, Stanley Cavell passed away at the age of ninety-one, after some years of illness.[16] Something happens when contemporaries become predecessors, names in a tradition, part of an intellectual legacy. Much as one wonders what's involved and what's omitted in taking our sense of the epic voice from Homer, or the tragic predicament from Shakespeare (in both cases, *What of women?*, as we are more and more insistently asking), I have been wondering more pointedly about what's involved and what's omitted in taking a dissenting mode of American exceptionalism from Stanley Cavell. The political theorist George Shulman has asked similar questions and constructed probing answers in part by contrasting Cavell's conception of disavowal and failed acknowledgment with James Baldwin's critique of white innocence.[17]

As a generous, appreciative, and creative reader, Shulman's point is not to fault, undermine, or disqualify Cavell for failing to engage more directly with America's legacy of race and racism. One might do that, for over a long career reflecting on America, Cavell had next to nothing to say about race and racism. Instead, Shulman introduces an insistently political perspective on that philosophical legacy in order to complicate and extend the problematic of disavowal and failed acknowledgment that Cavell thematizes richly but incompletely. Shulman seeks to amend and augment Cavell's perspective by involving him in dialogue with a wider range of thinkers and problems—much like adding Barker and Miller to discussions of Homer. While I appreciate that kind of response, I would like to propose another one that I think is different in important respects but that I hope is no less generous, appreciative, and creative. My thought is to take a moment to acknowledge Cavell's shortcomings as such—as the flaws, blindnesses, and omissions endemic to all personalities, plans, and projects. If the tragic flaws in a philosopher induce anxiety in a reader, a natural response is to supplement and amend those flaws, but another possible response is to sit with the anxiety that appears here.

In a more anxious view, the legacy of American philosophy as it lands in Cavell's work is no less incomplete, no less compromised, no more sufficient than it had been landing in Emerson's writings. And it is no discredit to Baldwin, either, that a reader who has tarried long enough with him will find that he too stops short of reaching the depths, exhausting the problems, or teaching us what we would need to know. The legacies even of America, though they evolve, remain unapproachable. Could taking in that fact be one way of establishing an anxious or tragic relation to the tradition? Could it be related to the sensibility that informs Jay-Z's recording *4:44*, from which I drew this essay's title? Once again, Jay-Z is not an obscure musician, and *4:44* was a Grammy-nominated, Billboard-topping, platinum-selling album. These points are obvious, permeating popular culture, and broadly received, yet strangely enough still so often disavowed.

Jay-Z's "Legacy" refers both to the wealth and status he intends to bequeath to his children as well as the privation and pain that he himself inherited as a child. These are different but internally related inflections of a distinctly African American experience, pain and privation providing a drive and presenting obstacles to the achievement of wealth and status, captured in the popular refrain that Black Americans must work twice as hard and be twice as good to get by:

> Legacy, Legacy, Legacy, Legacy
> Black excellence, you gon' let 'em see
> Legacy, Legacy, Legacy, Legacy
> Black excellency, baby, let 'em see.

The legacy in question here depends not only on the transmutation of poverty into wealth but also on the persistence of the past's legacies in the present and their uncertain projection into the future:

> See how the universe works?
> It takes my hurt and help me find more of myself
> It's a gift and a curse
> That's called the Red Queen's Race
> You run this hard just to stay in place.

The queen's race is a reference to Lewis Carroll's *Through the Looking Glass*, and its point may be that America's legacies cannot be outrun. More specifically, Americans are obliged rather to run this hard to stay in place, and Black Americans are obliged to run twice as fast. As the queen tells Alice, "here, you see, it takes all the running you can do, to keep in the same place. If you want to get somewhere else, you must run at least twice as fast as that!" Most Americans at this point can probably see this, although most have for most of history looked away from it.

The America in the newspapers and on the radio is hard to see, but only in the sense that it embodies painful legacies, in the sense that it is hard to look at, and not in the sense that it is difficult to divine. Rather than addressing an America that is hard to see, there are so many voices in the American tradition that address what we can't possibly miss about America, unless we somehow find ways to avoid or look away from the legacies that stare us in the face. One problem is that we have always found ways to look away; another is learning to inhabit more anxious alternatives.

NOTES

1. See Courtney Bender, this volume. Robert Frost, "America Is Hard to See," in *Robert Frost: Collected Poems, Prose, and Plays*, ed. Richard Poirier and Mark Richardson (New York: Library of America, 1995), 430–32.
2. I think that, while our inquiries overlap in a number of places, Bender and I are pursuing different targets. And I want to be clear that while I am concerned that many of the gestures Bender examines are gestures that disavow violence and exclusion, those are features of her historical archive, not of her argument. Indeed, Bender clearly acknowledges the concern that "celebrations of American exceptionalism and visions of the nation's special role in history are built upon, and tend to perpetuate, a story that occludes histories of expansion, dispossession, and violence that undercut American exceptionalism's claims to its special relationship in creating democratic freedoms."
3. Joyce Appleby, "Recovering America's Historic Diversity: Beyond Exceptionalism." *The Journal of American History* 79, no. 2 (1992): 422.
4. While the nation-state situated between Canada and Mexico is more appropriately referred to as the "United States of America" rather than "America," my topic in this essay is more properly the latter construct, and the overweening metonymy is suggestive of the nature of that construct.
5. Appleby, "Recovering America's Historic Diversity," 428.
6. The project's more precise formulations ask: How is this exceptionalism produced? How are aspects of protestant Christian traditions transmitted through the encounters that produce and reproduce religious traditions? And, finally, how are the fields of domestic and foreign practice, while different in many ways, nonetheless profoundly interconnected?
7. Matthew Scherer, *Beyond Church and State: Democracy, Secularism, and Conversion* (Cambridge: Cambridge University Press: 2013).
8. Niccolò Machiavelli, *The Discourses*, Book One, Chapter Six (1517), in *Selected Political Writings*, ed. and trans. David Wootton. (Indianapolis: Hackett, 1994), 99.

9. Stanley Cavell, "'The Avoidance of Love:' Must We Mean What We Say?" (Cambridge: Cambridge University Press, 1976), 267–353.
10. Pat Barker, *The Silence of the Girls: A Novel* (New York: Doubleday, 2018); Madeline Miller, *Circe* (London: Bloomsbury, 2018); and Madeline Miller, *The Song of Achilles* (London: Bloomsbury, 2011).
11. For examples of work that examines these complex processes, see Winnifred Fallers Sullivan, *A Ministry of Presence: Chaplaincy, Spiritual Care, and the Law* (Chicago: University of Chicago Press, 2014); Elizabeth Shakman Hurd, *Beyond Religious Freedom: The New Global Politics of Religion* (Princeton, N.J.: Princeton University Press, 2015); Sylvester A. Johnson, *African American Religions, 1500–2000: Colonialism, Democracy, and Freedom* (Cambridge: Cambridge University Press, 2015); and Matthew Scherer, "The New Religious Freedom: Secular Fictions and Church Autonomy," *Politics and Religion* 8, no. 3 (2015): 544–64.
12. See Scherer, *Beyond Church and State*.
13. This paragraph also appears in my essay "A Yet Unapproachable America" in *Theologies of American Exceptionalism*, ed. Winnifred Fallers Sullivan and Elizabeth Shakman Hurd, eds. (Bloomington: Indiana University Press, 2021).
14. "The 1619 Project is an ongoing initiative from The New York Times Magazine that began in August 2019, the 400th anniversary of the beginning of American slavery. It aims to reframe the country's history by placing the consequences of slavery and the contributions of black Americans at the very center of our national narrative." *New York Times* magazine, August 14, 2019, https://www.nytimes.com/interactive/2019/08/14/magazine/1619-america-slavery.html. "The America We Need" editorial project "is exploring, and seeking to answer, basic questions about what the government owes its citizens, what corporations owe their employees and what we all owe each other. America was ailing long before the coronavirus reached its shores. Now we have the chance to make it better." *New York Times*, Opinion, various dates, https://www.nytimes.com/interactive/2020/opinion/america-inequality-coronavirus.html.
15. Stanley Cavell, "Finding as Founding," in *Conditions Handsome and Unhandsome: The Constitution of Emersonian Perfectionism* (La Salle, Ill.: Open Court, 1990), 139.
16. To be clear, while I have written about Cavell's work before, I only met Cavell once or twice, and I was not a student, intellectual intimate, or even interlocutor of his.
17. George Shulman, *American Prophecy: Race and Redemption in American Political Culture* (Minneapolis: University of Minnesota Press, 2008); and George Shulman, "Acknowledgment and Disavowal as an Idiom for Theorizing Politics," *Theory & Event* 14, no. 1 (2011), https://doi.org/10.1353/tae.2011.0003.

PART III
Inside/Outside

9
The Rule of Law

WINNIFRED FALLERS SULLIVAN

A number of years ago a part-time student in one of my classes came to tell me about his experience of being excommunicated from a local congregation after a "censure" hearing. It was not the substance of the judgment itself that bothered him so much. I believe in a sense he agreed with it—or that he understood the world in which the judgment had been made. He complained bitterly and at length, however, of the lack of what he called due process.

I was startled when he mentioned the lack of due process—although I should not have been. His expectation, as became clearer as we talked, was that he was entitled in this church judicatory to an *identical* set of procedural rights as he would be entitled to in a U.S. courtroom. He was, he believed, absolutely entitled to hear the charges against him, to be represented by counsel, and to have time to prepare a defense and cross-examine witnesses. Both the nature of the rights and his entitlement to have them granted and protected were in his mind exactly the same in the two contexts. They were for him inherent to law—at least law in the United States—and, in a way, considerably more important to him than the substantive law.

I am still trying to sort out why precisely it was so obvious to him both as a church-going Christian and as an American that he was entitled to due process in the church hearing. I am also interested in why his complaint surprised me—and perhaps surprises you. I have come to see this conversation as revealing an interesting and dramatic overlap in the nature of law in the two contexts. It was not just in *his* head, in other words, an idiosyncratic desire for procedural niceties. And it is not attributable, in my view, to ideological confusion on the part of conservative Christians about the United States being a Christian country governed by Christian law. What is revealed is a more thoroughly shared religio-legal history of the evolution of modern law, one that enjoys a specific intensification in the United States but that is also obscured in the United States by the institutional and conceptual displacement effected by constitutional disestablishment of religion.

For many today, I think, church courts and church law are very different entities from secular courts and secular law. Indeed, church courts and church law might be understood by most Americans not to be real courts or real law at all—but only anachronistic simulacra of courts and of law. They are, on this view, manifestly and irrevocably tainted and distorted by their association with religion—with the necessarily irrational and arbitrary nature of divine authority and revelation. Church courts, whether today or in the past, cannot, by this definition, be places of justice, substantive or procedural, in any absolute sense. Justice, procedural and substantive, we moderns believe, is firmly planted in the real world, the real secular world where, for Americans, due process is embodied in the Constitution and ultimately defined and defended by the U.S. Supreme Court.[1]

I have encountered a similar dismissal when I teach the fifteenth-century trial of Joan of Arc.[2] Even though she both possessed procedural rights and asserted them, my students assume that her trial by the Inquisition for heresy and war crimes was something like a kangaroo court presided over by the Queen of Hearts from *Alice in Wonderland*. It is difficult for them to accept it as law. Joan was not, of course, just banished, like my student was, so the posttrial hearing that found her first trial to have been procedurally irregular was posthumous and comforted only her family and friends. But that appeal, known as the trial of nullification, purported to vindicate a fidelity to the rule of law. For my student, although he had no appeal available as Joan's advocates did, due process was, as it was for her, necessary to religious as well as to secular law. He was, in a sense, a successor to Joan. (And, no doubt, his judges, like Joan's judges, had lawyers' answers for the charges concerning the denial of rights, answers that did not deny that they were real.)

In this essay I offer a beginning outline of how to think through the overlap of secular and religious legal cultures in the contemporary United States, substantive and procedural, and how that overlap enables the insider/outsider pivot that is a hallmark of the triumphal exceptionalism of the United States that we seek to identify and understand in this volume. The overlap between secular and religious legal cultures supports a religious understanding of law—of the rule of law—at home and abroad that is not exclusively American, but it is one that has specific U.S. causes and characteristics. The rule of law exhibits the same inside/outside characteristics, showing one face domestically and another extraterritorially. American religion is legal at home and not so abroad. Here I focus on the presence of "secular" law in a religious trial. Elsewhere, I and others have considered the presence of religion in secular courts.[3]

THE CASE

At the time of the proceeding, the congregation in question described itself as "protestant, reformed and evangelical." (I do not name the congregation to protect my student's privacy.[4]) On its website, the church announced that it subscribed to the post-reformation Westminster Confession of Faith (as adjusted for the United States after the Revolution) and to the Longer and Shorter Catechisms. These are well-known and long-established canonized descriptions of Christian doctrine subscribed to by a subset of protestant churches. The church in question was linked to church plantings in nearby cities and boasted both a Bible college with an undergraduate program described as symbiotic with a local public university and a small seminary program preparing pastors. The church had thirty pages of printed bylaws detailing its incorporation under state law, rules of membership, process for the election of officers, time and place of meetings, practices of record keeping, processes of conflict resolution, and finally guidelines for church discipline, each provision followed by a string of biblical cites to attest to their biblical foundation. In other words, these documents mixed authority from both secular and religious sources to underwrite its law. All of these documents were publicly displayed on the website.

To many outsiders this church might seem to have epitomized what is casually and misleadingly termed religious fundamentalism. Certainly some of its policies and actions could be read as having been both patriarchal and authoritarian. Pastoral ministry is limited to men, and it announced its mission to train pastors to "reprove, rebuke, exhort." But, as many have observed, "fundamentalism" is a word that obscures rather than clarifies. One of my objects in this piece is to disturb the hard line separating what are termed fundamentalists from other religious and nonreligious Americans specifically when it comes to their self-understanding in relation to American notions of legality and due process. By seeing conservative Christians as sharing a legal culture with other Americans, religious and secular, we may come to see the distinctiveness of the American religion/law project more clearly and perhaps bring law into focus without an immediate recourse to politics. We might also see some of the reasons why securing the rule of law, as a political goal, one that is prominent in both U.S. domestic and foreign policy, is a not an unambiguously positive objective.

It is important to acknowledge the attraction of these small bible-believing communities—at once of the world and not—as places of real belonging with a real capacity to help their members to negotiate a rapidly changing society, appealing to recurrent themes of word and love, promising support, purpose and conviction. The church in question invited new congregants by asking:

> What does it mean to be a Christian and a man or a woman in twenty-first century America? What does it mean to be a father or a mother or son or daughter or boss or employee or professor or a student? When do we speak out against the evils of our day and age, and how?
>
> Some of the Bible's answers to these questions are more popular than others. We want to preach them all with love—from the pulpit, and with our music, and in our lives and fellowship with one another. We're working to create a church culture that is in the world but not of the world. In this age, it can be tricky to do both. Right now, some of our folks wear t-shirts, and some of them wear suits. We have a rock band and we say the Apostle's Creed. We don't know how it will all end up, but we trust God to lead us on this journey.
>
> Won't you join us?

While apparently small and local, these particular churches are not simply a collection of people reading and interpreting the Bible on their own. They connect themselves in complex and thoughtful ways to the longer history of the Presbyterian Church in the United States and to its division in the early twentieth century as a result of the modernist controversies. Their theological home is the Westminster Seminary in Philadelphia rather than Princeton Seminary in New Jersey. While the theological divisions linger, the two church communities share much, and today they read many of the same texts and address a similar set of questions. Their understandings of law have been influential.[5]

Let us return to my former student. He had long been a member of this particular church, together with his wife and five children. Because of differences with the leaders of the church about their interpretation of scripture, he had been censured and expelled. He had also been separated from his family. (The case ran on a parallel track in state family court, with many of the same issues arising.[6] The process there was no more satisfactory to him.) He sent me a copy of the final judgment in his church discipline case. The judgment was as follows:

Following the trial on _____, and a meeting of the elders thereafter on _____, you have been found guilty of contumacy and divisiveness, and the censure of excommunication has been pronounced. Therefore, we no longer consider you a believer in Jesus Christ, and exhort you to seek salvation in Him. In addition, for the sake of the peace, unity, and purity of _____ Church, _____, we are indefinitely continuing our prohibition of your coming to the church property or to church events. For the benefit of your soul, we encourage you to attend a Bible-believing church, such as _____.

The language of this pronouncement eerily echoes Joan of Arc's sentence almost six centuries earlier: "We therefore lawfully declare you an excommunicate and heretic, as one obstinate and confirmed in these sins, faults and errors . . . you are to be abandoned to secular justice, lest you infect other limbs of Christ, and we do so abandon you. . . . And if you show true signs of repentance, you may receive the sacrament of penance."[7] My student, like Joan, was excommunicated, and, like Joan, he complained bitterly of the failure to supply him with a list of the charges against him and to allow him to be represented.[8] Each of them, untrained in the law, sought a due process each knew to be their right. Why did they have such expectations?

EXPLAINING THE OVERLAP

There are several accounts we could give of why, notwithstanding the by now longstanding modernist separation of church and state and a corresponding decline of formal ecclesiastical jurisdiction in North America, my student's legal consciousness, if you like, was not so divided on the matter. I begin with the level of the individual and then proceed to more general explanations. I exclude the possibility that this was an idiosyncrasy explained by the biography of the student. I assume that he stands in for a larger religio-secular legal phenomenon in the United States—one that is continuous with fifteenth-century France but that would refuse the connection.

One explanation that might be offered is that, as an American, my student had simply absorbed rights consciousness with his mother's milk, so to speak, and imported it into the church setting. On this reading, we might, with many Americans, see the procedural rights of the U.S. Constitution embodied in the phrase "due process of law" as granting a kind of global protection for individual

Americans in all institutional settings, public and private—something that is personal to them and travels with them *as Americans*. A particular dedication to the rule of law is, on this view, seen to be something peculiar to the United States—a dedication forged in the Revolution and the founding that today bleeds out from the civic realm and seeps into other domains—through carriers like my student—a form of what might be considered an aspect of popular constitutionalism.[9] There would be ethnographic support for this position. This tendency is something that has been observed by lawyers working with clients in other private institutional settings outside of civil courts such as universities. Americans often assume rights that are not actually afforded them in such settings.[10] Indeed, most (perhaps all) Americans—on the right and on the left—have inaccurate absolutist understandings of the process they are due and understand themselves to be in some sense anti-institutional.[11] Their right to due process, like other rights claimed through movements of popular constitutionalism, gives them rights against those institutions while ironically being utterly dependent on them.[12]

Another possible explanation for my student's sense of outrage is that attention to procedural rights by American Christians in particular is something that American churches themselves have undertaken, seeing themselves as constitutionally obligated to observe standards of due process in their ecclesiastical proceedings. This would be more like a corporate legal consciousness, one of the results of disestablishment—part of the bargain they have made with the state as a result of legal incorporation as a semisovereign.[13] Legal historians describe ecclesiastical jurisdiction, or what is sometimes called "church discipline," to have continued in the United States well into the nineteenth century. Gradually, secular courts took over most matters, although that has been a long and uneven process. Where secular courts did not pick up the slack, when a gap opened between church discipline and secular courts, other extrajudicial processes, including lynching, did.[14] We could understand this U.S. history as continuing a mimetic process of institutional development begun between church and state in the Middle Ages.[15]

In other words, we could tell a longer story that is much less specific to the United States. Legal historians might say that the elements of due process prevalent in various U.S. institutions, including churches, find their origins in Roman law standards, the reception of Roman law in medieval Europe, and the subsequent entwined histories of the development of ecclesiastical canon law and secular governance in various national and imperial legal histories.[16] Internal church standards of due process could be seen, on this account, to have long roots, possibly in Rome, or, in a somewhat shorter trajectory, beginning anew in the teachings of the Reformers.[17] One could trace various elements of procedural justice, then, through this long history of European law. Different church denominations would be seen to have different versions of the relationship of civil and ecclesiastical jurisdiction as well as different philosophies of law and of law's place in the Christian economy of salvation, but they would all be a part of this longer story. Conservative American Presbyterians, on this account, inherit a very specific and, one might say, legalistic tradition of church governance, one originating in Geneva but refined in Scotland.[18]

Legal philosophers might broaden the story considerably, saying that phenomenologically all law implies due process—that a certain minimum of procedural fairness is inherent to law. Due process on this account would be a part of natural justice. The integrity of law as a separate enterprise, whether secular or religious, depends on such an understanding. Lon Fuller's *The Morality of Law* outlines one version of this morality of the legal enterprise itself, including the need for clarity and transparency, the rejection of ex post facto legislation, and consistency of application.[19] Without these minimum standards, including some version of due process, according to Fuller, you do not have law. Legal anthropologists would likewise see legalism as universal, further lowering the stakes of the religious/secular divide.[20]

Together these stories go a long way toward explaining why litigants in both secular courts and church courts in the United States might have the same expectations of fairness. In other words, we can place my student's indignation in the stream of these overlapping narratives and see how his expectation of due process is at once very particularly a project of this particular church and its confession as well as being distinctively an invention of U.S. courts and legislatures, or we can widen out the lens and see how law's singularity as a domain of life enables him to inhabit an insider/outsider status with respect to law. He both owns the law, as sovereign participant in "we, the people" of both church and the state, and is subject to the law.

Law, particularly procedural law, in the United States is perhaps necessarily both secular and religious, both as a matter of historical development and as a philosophical and anthropological matter. Law cannot be thought without a horizon of natural justice.

THE RULE OF LAW IN THE UNITED STATES

How, then, do we explain our surprise at my student's indignation? Are we just blinded by secular dogmatism?

The surprise of which I spoke has two sources, I think. One is indeed a secularist prejudice against the possibility of justice and regularity in religious law and an overconfidence in its possibility in secular law. But another is the real ambivalence of Christians—perhaps particularly American Christians—toward law. Paul, in his letters to the early churches, is sometimes understood to have argued that law—Jewish law—is abrogated by the apocalyptic nature of Christian love, that Christians can and should live without law or separate from law. There are indeed American protestants who shun civil law altogether—seeking instead to settle differences through a kind of consensus or informal counseling and arbitration.[21] But mostly those Christians who are not living imaginatively in the end times (most Christians, in other words), are fond of law, civil law and church law, because they love order and believe God loves order. (For an exploration of protestant Christian theories of the state and of civil law, see Melani McAlister's essay in this volume.)

All Christians have doctrines that define the respective obligations of Christians to their churches, on the one hand, and to the larger society, on the other. These doctrines have evolved over time as Christians have found themselves in vastly different host societies, but the touchstone has been a return to biblical sources. One way to tell the story is that the early churches, living within the Roman Empire, understood Jesus to give a divided charge, one that obligated them to both the church and the secular authority but in different ways. In the synoptic gospels, Jesus is reported to have answered a question about the Jewish obligation to pay taxes with the sentence, "Render unto Caesar the things that are Caesar's, and unto God the things that are God's" (Mark 12:17). The precise scope of those things that are Caesar's and those things that are God's has been a matter of great debate. But with the Constantinian revolution and the Christianization of the Roman Empire, a mutual accommodation of the two missions is usually seen to have occurred, expressed in the high medieval doctrine of the two swords, and continuing until Martin Luther's break with the Church of Rome. Luther then developed a theology of two kingdoms, which once again separated the two domains, obligating Christians to be loyal to both church and state in the name of good order. John Calvin likewise insisted on a dual allegiance, although he and Luther differed on the actual governance and content of the respective jurisdictions. On the other hand, the Anabaptists, sometimes termed the radical reformation, largely withdrew from the authority of the state, rejecting the two swords and the two kingdoms. (All of these theories of Christian obligation also trace themselves in various ways to Augustine and *The City of God*.) The United States, as a destination for immigrant members of all versions of the Christian churches, has absorbed a wide range of ecclesiologies. All have changed their forms of governance and their understanding of church–state relations in the

U.S. context. Sorting out the peculiar mix of religious and legal consciousness specific to the United States is complicated.

My student's former church belongs to what is sometimes termed a neo-Calvinist strain in protestant theology. Neo-Calvinists inherit from the Reformers a specific understanding of the importance and authority of the civil magistrate. Their modern Dutch reformed theorists—Abraham Kuyper, Herman Dooyeweerd, Francis Schaeffer, R. J. Rushdoony, and others[22]—trace a lineage from Paul, Augustine, Luther, and Calvin, seeing law as necessary and as necessarily divided between the church and the civil magistrate. A vigorous conversation is under way just now among reformed protestants about how to read Luther and Calvin in this regard and about whether some understanding of "natural law," formerly seen as tainted by association with Catholic thinkers, is appropriate for protestant self-understanding. These theological debates are being conducted on the territory of U.S. law and law schools, in conversation with mainstream debates about law's domain.[23] Participants range from those urging Christians to live radically within a biblical eschatology to those urging a return to a shared division of labor between church and state with respect to our common lives.

As we think in this book about the pivot between inside and outside, between home and abroad, I urge consideration very specifically of how law, *qua* law, plays a role because religious freedom and the rule of law often travel together as if two sides of the same coin.[24] Religious freedom advocacy assumes the rule of law. Apparently assumed is the fact that the rule of law is necessarily the task of secular authorities. Yet to deny the legalism of religion—religion of all kinds, not just conservative Christianity—is to misread its challenge to the civil order.

In the terms of this essay, U.S. law is always both Christian and not Christian. That doubleness enables American exceptionalism in very specific ways. It is not just my student's expectation of due process in the church judicatory. Now a former law student, he also sees the conversation about law and justice in law school as continuous with the debates within bible-believing churches about common grace.[25]

Law and legal education themselves are arguably today threatened more by what is called economic analysis of the law and neoliberal techniques of population management (themselves, too, having a religious pedigree, of course) than by religious fundamentalism. Most religious and secular critical legal theorists of justice, ironically perhaps, actually speak the same language, both suspicious of the seductive hyper-rationalism of the secular enlightenment. Acknowledging rather than resisting that overlap might lead to greater understanding.

In a recent essay, Canadian legal scholar Benjamin Berger notes the distinctiveness of American dedication to the rule of law. Berger recalls the moment during the 2016 presidential campaign when Khizr Khan held up his pocket copy of the Constitution and spoke of his son's sacrifice in the Iraq war. Berger comments:

> What stands out to me from that speech is the remarkable moment in which Khan produces a copy of the U.S. Constitution, provoking an emotional eruption from the audience. It is a moment of great drama. And to a Canadian, and a comparative constitutionalist, it is truly exceptional. Something like this—waving a copy of the constitution at this pitched political moment—would simply not happen in Canada; or, if it did, it would fall flat as a piece of drama. In Britain, they would have nothing to waive, except perhaps a collection of statutes and volumes of the All England Law Reports.
>
> I struggle to put words to why this moment is so exceptional, why it captures something so unique to me as an observer. Why is this moment not only possible but so potent—so moving and effective—in the United States, whereas it would seem so inapt, so discordant, elsewhere?
>
> It seems to me that there is something in this moment that reflects a distinctive relationship with law. . . . In this holding out of the constitution there is an appeal to sacrality, one that exceeds the preciousness that flows from particularity by drawing on a felt proximity between law, truth, and vocation. It is that form of sacrality, it seems to me, that is distinctive. This moment impresses me as reflective of a political relationship to a constitution that is not just "ours" but also "true" (*self-evidently* so) and of a community with a political theology—and, with it, an exceptionalism—shaped by that conviction.[26]

CODA: LAW AND THE CATHOLIC SEX ABUSE CRISIS

The widening sex abuse scandal in the Catholic Church has garnered a variety of responses from scholars and other commentators inside and outside of the church. These interventions have focused on clerical culture, sexuality, institutional impulses to secrecy, seminary training, antiquated theologies of sex, mandatory celibacy, a male-only clergy, and a range of other matters. With respect to law, the most common view is that the solution is more secular law. "Call the cops."[27] The problem, it is assumed, is that a combination of deliberate efforts to protect priests from the reach of secular law, a reticence by secular authorities to charge priests, and antiquated statutory limitation provisions has inhibited the obvious solution—that is, prosecution and punishment by state authorities.

Like the story told here about due process, the default recourse to state law reflects a lack of understanding of the deeply entwined nature of religious and secular law as well as an abdication by church authorities of their responsibility under church law. It lets the church off the hook. By regarding church law as not law, it is beyond critique as law. My student's intuition about the shared space of religious and secular law might be the beginning of such a critique.

NOTES

1. The peculiar nature of U.S. attachment to the rule of law is helpfully highlighted in Benjamin L. Berger, "Two Theologies of Chosenness," in *Theologies of American Exceptionalism*, ed. Winnifred Fallers Sullivan and Elizabeth Shakman Hurd (Bloomington: Indiana University Press, 2021).
2. For an English-language translation of the account of the trial and an introduction to the trial and its aftermath, see Daniel Hobbins, ed., *The Trial of Joan of Arc* (Cambridge, Mass.: Harvard University Press, 2007).
3. Winnifred Fallers Sullivan, Robert Yelle, and Mateo Taussig-Rubbo, eds., *After Secular Law* (Stanford, Calif.: Stanford University Press, 2011).
4. My former student has given me permission to discuss his case. He also provided me with some of the legal documents in the case. I have worked hard to anonymize this case. I urge readers to forbear trying to locate the church or the case. It is in relevant ways similar to such churches across the United States.
5. The judge in the case I wrote about in *The Impossibility of Religious Freedom* (Princeton, N.J.: Princeton University Press, 2009) was a member of a Presbyterian Church. He was very comfortable mixing his reading of the Bible with his reading of the Florida statutes.
6. For a consideration of the religious history of family law, see Janet Jakobsen and Ann Pellegrini, *Love the Sin: Sexual Regulation and the Limits of Religious Tolerance* (New York: New York University Press, 2003); and Saba Mahmood, *Religious Difference in a Secular Age: A Minority Report* (Princeton, N.J.: Princeton University Press, 2015).
7. Hobbins, *The Trial of Joan of Arc*, 202.
8. Joan also claimed specific rights guaranteed in inquisitorial trials—to be guarded by women, not by men, and a right of direct appeal to the Pope. Hobbins, *Trial of Joan of Arc*, 23.
9. Popular constitutionalism is a much-debated phrase used by constitutional historians. See, for example, Sean Beienburg and Paul Frymer, "The People Against Themselves: Rethinking Popular Constitutionalism," *Law & Social Inquiry* 41 (2016): 242–66. I use it here to signal the divergence between judicial and lay interpretations

10. of the Constitution. My assumption is that judicial interpretations always interact with lay interpretations in complex ways that are incompletely understood.
10. See, for example, Jed Rubenfeld, "Privatization and State Action: Do Campus Sexual Assault Hearings Violate Due process?" *Texas Law Review* 96 (2017): 15–69.
11. For a classic critique of American "rights talk," see Mary Ann Glendon, *Rights Talk: The Impoverishment of Political Discourse* (New York: Free Press 1993). See also her *Abortion and Divorce in Western Law* (Cambridge, Mass.: Harvard University Press, 1989), in which she compares the deleterious effects on law of the more absolutist rights consciousness of the United States.
12. One current critic of the limits of such rights consciousness is Samuel Moyn. A collection of his publications is available at http://campuspress.yale.edu/samuelmoyn/publications/ (accessed April 8, 2020).
13. See, on church incorporation, Sarah Barringer Gordon, "The First Disestablishment: Limits on Church Power and Property Before the Civil War," *University of Pennsylvania Law Review* 162 (2014): 307–72; and Kellen Funk, "Church Corporations and the Conflict of Laws in Antebellum America," *Journal of Law and Religion* 32, no. 2 (2017): 263–84. See also Winnifred Fallers Sullivan, *Church State Corporation: Construing Religion in U.S. Law* (Chicago: University of Chicago Press, 2020).
14. See W. D. Blanks, "Corrective Church Discipline in the Presbyterian Churches of the Nineteenth Century South," *Journal of Presbyterian History* 44 (1966): 89–105; and Christopher Waldrep, "'So Much Sin': The Decline of Religious Discipline and the 'Tidal Wave of Crime'" *Journal of Social History* 23 (March 1990): 535–52.
15. See Harold J. Berman, *Law and Revolution [I]: The Formation of the Western Legal Tradition* (Cambridge: Harvard University Press, 1983); Harold J. Berman, *Law and Revolution II: The Impact of the Protestant Reformations on the Western Legal Traditions* (Cambridge: Harvard University Press, 1983); and Sullivan, *Church State Corporation*.
16. Most Americans begin the history of due process with the U.S. Constitution with occasional gestures to Magna Carta. For an account of American due process set in a longer history, see E. Thomas Sullivan and Toni M. Masaro, "Due Process Exceptionalism," *Irish Jurist* 46 (2011): 117–51. For a more capacious global account of law—or legalism, see Paul Dresch and Hannah Skoda, eds., *Legalism: Anthropology and History* (Oxford: Oxford University Press, 2012); and Paul Dresch and Judith Scheele, eds., *Legalism: Categories and Rules* (Oxford: Oxford University Press, 2015). For a gripping account of the development of the rule of law in the British empire see Keally McBride, *Mr. Mothercountry: The Man Who Made the Rule of Law* (Oxford: Oxford University Press, 2016).
17. Berman, *Law and Revolution [I]*, and Berman, *Law and Revolution II*.
18. See John Witte Jr., *Law and Protestantism: The Legal Teachings of the Lutheran Reformation* (Cambridge: Cambridge University Press, 2002); and John Witte Jr., *The Reformation of Rights: Law, Religion and Human Rights in Early Modern Calvinism* (Cambridge: Cambridge University Press, 2008)
19. Lon Fuller, *The Morality of Law*, rev. ed. (New Haven, Conn.: Yale University Press, 1969).

20. Mona Oraby and Winnifred Fallers Sullivan, "Law and Religion: Reimagining the Entanglement of Two Universals." *Annual Review of Law and Social Science* 16 (October 2020).
21. See, for example, Carol Greenhouse, *Praying for Justice: Faith, Order and Community in an American Town* (Ithaca, N.Y.: Cornell University Press, 1989). See also *Hosanna-Tabor Evangelical Lutheran Church and School v. EEOC*, 565 U.S. 171 (2012).
22. To understand the importance and impact of these writers, see, for example, the Lexham Press website devoted to Abraham Kuyper, https://abrahamkuyper.com/; the Wikipedia page for Herman Dooyeweerd, https://en.wikipedia.org/wiki/Herman_Dooyeweerd; the L'Abri website, http://www.labri.org/history.html (all accessed April 8, 2020).
23. See, for example, the work of John Witte, including "Faith in Law: The Legal and Political Legacy of the Protestant Reformations," in *The Reformation of the Church and the World*, ed. John Witte Jr. and Amy Wheeler, 105–38 (Louisville, Ky.: Westminster John Knox Press, 2018).
24. See, Winnifred Fallers Sullivan, "Religious Freedom and the Rule of Law: Exporting Modernity in a Postmodern World?" *Mississippi College Law Review* 22 (2003): 173–83.
25. Common grace is the grace that is experienced by all humans, not just Christians. See Abraham Kuyper, *Common Grace* (*De Gemene Gratie*, 1902–5).
26. Berger, "Two Theologies of Chosenness."
27. See Winnifred Fallers Sullivan, "Separationism and the Sex Abuse Crisis," *The Immanent Frame: Secularism, Religion, and the Public Sphere* (blog), July 20, 2012, https://tif.ssrc.org/2012/07/20/separationism-and-the-sex-abuse-crisis/.

10

Double Standards in a Tripartite World

JOLYON BARAKA THOMAS

Few people would think of Japan as a place where religious freedom is under threat. By the numbers, the country is one of the least religious in the world, with levels of professed belief and affiliation that rarely rise above about a quarter of the population. If asked about the current state of religious freedom in Japan, most professional observers would probably say that promoting religious freedom was a primary goal of the U.S.-led Allied Occupation of Japan (1945–1952) and that religious freedom has been firmly enshrined in Japan's postwar constitution since 1947. Unlike Myanmar, China, the Central African Republic, Syria, and Vietnam, Japan does not appear as a "country of particular concern" in the annual report produced by the United States Commission on International Religious Freedom (USCIRF). Indeed, the only two places where Japan appeared in the commission's 2017 report were in reference to regional concerns about North Korea, another country on the commission's list of bad actors.[1] It would seem that Japan is a pretty safe place for religion.

Nevertheless, some stakeholders regard recent moves by the Abe Shinzō administration as threats to religious freedom. In June 2017, for example, the Federation of New Religious Organizations of Japan submitted a complaint to Abe decrying proposed anti-conspiracy legislation as inimical to religious freedom and reminiscent of the 1925 Peace Preservation Law (Chian iji hō) that allowed the imperial Japanese state to crack down on minority religious movements.[2] The controversial bill passed in the Diet (Japan's parliament) later that month, with lawmakers citing global antiterrorism efforts and security concerns related to the upcoming 2020 Olympics as rationales for their votes in favor.[3]

"Trust us to do the right thing," they seemed to say, but religious groups and journalists greeted that message with justifiable suspicion.[4]

Prime Minister Abe's cozy relationships with conservative Shintō organizations have also attracted negative attention, and it is common to read that his personal politics presage a return to the so-called State Shintō of wartime Japan.[5] Abe's decision to host the 2016 G7 summit at the Ise Shrines seems to have been a brazen attempt to legitimize a nationalist variant of Shintō in the eyes of the international community, and his annual New Year's visits to those shrines link Shintō ritual to the public calendar and the theater of state.[6] People who study Japanese religion and politics have therefore eyed Abe's close connections with the Shintō Seiji Renmei (Shintō Association for Spiritual Leadership, or SAS) with suspicion.[7] They expect Abe and his cabinet to try to institute through constitutional revision something amounting to a reproduction of the wartime status quo, when shrines hosted compulsory civic rituals and Shintō mythology appeared as indisputable fact in history textbooks.[8]

Journalists have adopted this attractive narrative. A July 2016 article in the *Daily Beast* described Nippon Kaigi (the Japan Conference), another lobby with close ties to Abe and many Japanese legislators, as a secret "cult" designed to restore Japan's wartime past.[9] Revelations in late 2016 that the Osaka Prefectural Government gave a preferential land deal to the private education corporation Moritomo Academy under alleged pressure from Abe and his wife, Akie, further stoked concerns that Abe's goal is to erode the firm separation of religion from the state enshrined in Japan's postwar constitution. (The Moritomo Academy affiliate Tsukamoto Kindergarten fosters a habitus reminiscent of Imperial Japan; students venerate the emperor's portrait and recite the 1890 Imperial Rescript on Education.) Subsequent revelations that government officials doctored documents related to the controversial land deal to remove explicit references to the Abes and Nippon Kaigi prolonged the scandal, although Abe appears to have weathered the storm. He officially secured his party's support in September 2018, has weathered two other major scandals, and in the absence of any substantive or sustained political opposition has now become Japan's longest-serving prime minister.

Abe's patronage of Shintō institutions and his apparent support of nationalist academies have prompted questions about his ulterior motives, but the problem is really about how religion is defined, both in everyday conversation and in the law. Roughly 75 percent of Japanese people do not identify as religious, but nearly as many periodically engage in ritual practices that they tend to interpret as custom or habit. This terminological ambiguity allows Abe and organizations like SAS to portray shrine rites and imperial rituals as the core of Japanese culture, as repositories of national tradition, and as central to civic life.[10] Such majoritarian rhetoric prompts—some would say forces—minorities to adopt the language of religious freedom when they press their complaints with the government.

Religious freedom disputes are always fraught, but these issues are particularly complicated in Japan because the postwar Japanese constitution was written under military occupation at the end of World War II.[11] This historical fact has always left open the possibility that the constitution, despite the language of its preamble, was not freely chosen by the Japanese people.[12] More importantly, because the national charter explicitly includes the inherently *transnational* language of "fundamental human rights," there is always an open question about how individuals' right to religious freedom can be guaranteed by the Japanese state. The incoherence of Japanese religious freedom jurisprudence over the last several decades suggests that this problem has never been fully resolved.[13]

Questions about the definition and scope of religious freedom inform recent debates about how Japan's constitution might change. Chafing at the coercive circumstances under which the current constitution was drafted, Abe's ruling Liberal Democratic Party (LDP) describes constitutional revision as fundamental to party identity and as a central policy aim. The party advocates revision as a way of correcting the putatively "unnatural" language of the preamble, making the Self-Defense Forces a "normal" military by revising the famed Article 9 that renounces Japan's ability to wage war and advancing minor terminological revisions that would have major political effects, including changes to the postwar religion/state settlement. LDP-adjacent lobbying groups and political action committees contribute to the revisionist campaign. For example, a June 2015 SAS pamphlet called for the elimination of Clause 3 of Article 20 of the current constitution, and a November 2016 SAS pamphlet argued that strict separation of religion and the state does not accord with Japan's national character. (Clause 3 prohibits state support for religious education and other religious activities.)[14] The policy positions of this group deserve attention because hundreds of LDP politicians count as members.

Reactions to the LDP and SAS proposals from the political Left describe these initiatives as renascent militarism and as a revival of State Shintō, but it bears mentioning that the LDP proposals use classical liberal language (freedom, peace, rights) to advocate illiberal policy (strengthened authoritarianism and heightened interest in sovereignty and security). If one pairs the language of the LDP's 2012 constitutional draft with legal trial balloons such as the revised Fundamental Law on Education (2006) and the aforementioned Anti-Conspiracy Law of 2017, it seems clear that the party has been using freedom talk to construct a society premised on mutual obligations rather than on individual rights and liberties.[15] Legal changes already enacted and constitutional revisions the party proposes would effectively make shrine rites into national ceremonies rather than religion, would evacuate individuals' abilities to make rights claims at all, and would make security supersede liberty.

Although various sources of political drag make it unclear whether the LDP will actually push through constitutional revision, the legal changes that the party has already advanced have profound implications for the future of religious freedom in Japan.[16] By tweaking the constitutional definition of "religion" so that practices like imperial ritual and veneration of the war dead at the controversial Yasukuni Shrine become collective "social customs," the LDP eliminates the possibility that citizens might mobilize religious freedom claims against state expenditures on shrine rituals.[17] By defining public order very broadly and expanding the capacity of the state to surveil citizens in the name of security, the 2017 Anti-Conspiracy Law could easily be used to target religious minorities (e.g., Muslims) and other political groups (e.g., communists).[18] Moreover, because the 2012 draft constitution designated the fundamental legal unit of society the household rather than the individual, the ability for individuals to sue would essentially disappear if similar language were passed into law.

Setting aside the definitional problem of whether the LDP's actions are inimical to religious freedom, it is clear that legitimate concerns about political liberties exist. Schoolteachers have been penalized for their principled refusals to perform the national anthem on religious freedom grounds.[19] The Japanese Buddhist Federation held anxious lecture meetings in January 2015 about whether the December 2014 State Secrets Law would have a chilling effect on freedom of conscience.[20] Christian and Buddhist organizations have joined the Federation of New Religious Organizations of Japan in protesting the 2017 Anti-Conspiracy Law.[21] When Abe's office used social media to publicize his January 4, 2018, visit to the Ise Shrines, it drew complaints from legal activists and Christian denominations that he had infringed upon the constitutional injunction against using state funds for the promotion of a particular religion.[22] These protests are written in Japanese and therefore target a local audience, but their argumentation invariably appeals to international norms such as the human right to religious freedom. Thus, even as the Abe administration points to the threat of global terrorist conspiracies to justify restricting liberties, domestic groups use the transnational language of human rights to censure the administration's actions. Both look abroad to advocate changes at home.

What about observers overseas? What do international religious freedom advocates see when they think about Japan, religion, and rights? While Japan's regional neighbors have their own critical perspectives due to hotly contested memories of Japanese military adventurism and imperialism, the United States also has a vested interest in this topic. For one thing, triumphalist histories often claim that religious freedom only came to Japan due to America's postwar interventions, meaning that Japan's postwar record with religious freedom is a referendum on how well American reforms actually worked. Geopolitical dominance and military strategy are also key. The United States may be uniquely powerful in the post–World War II world, as Matthew Scherer suggests in his essay in this volume, but U.S. hegemony is predicated on the existence of allies like Japan that can mediate and project U.S. power in a region otherwise gripped with economic and military tensions. Japan's recent disputes over religious freedom would therefore presumably be of utmost importance to the United States, but it seems that Japan is quite hard for Americans to see when they scan the world looking for religious freedom problems (see Courtney Bender's chapter in this volume).

INTERNATIONAL RELIGIOUS FREEDOM AND THE U.S.–JAPAN ALLIANCE

International promotion of religious freedom has historically been a central point of U.S. foreign policy.[23] This commitment has been strengthened since passage of the International Religious Freedom Act in 1998 and has been further reinforced by the Frank R. Wolf Act of 2016.[24] The legislation requires the USCIRF to generate annual reports about the state of religious freedom worldwide. These reports include lists of "Countries of Particular Concern" that are allegedly guilty of violating religious freedom. While the instances of discrimination highlighted in the reports are indeed concerning, the reports focus on sensational, usually violent infringements on religious freedom in countries that are ideologically distant from the United States. Meanwhile, the reports are silent on religious freedom disputes *at* and *within* U.S. borders, and they say little about religious freedom complaints leveled against close U.S. allies. While the mandatory annual reports on religious freedom generated by the U.S. Department of State are more comprehensive than the "name and shame" USCIRF reports, they, too, downplay religious freedom issues when discussing close allies. For example, annual reports prepared by Japan-based foreign service officers are obvious cut-and-paste jobs that dutifully include a few token examples of minor complaints and obligatory documentation of the official

American response. Going by these reports, Japan seems pretty boring as far as religious freedom violations are concerned.

Despite the fact that Japanese religious organizations and individuals have very publicly stated their fears that the Abe administration's policies are inimical to religious liberty, the USCIRF and the State Department treat Japan as of little concern. This is probably because they are primed to look for certain types of infringements. Have people been hacked to death for their lack of religious belief, as in Bangladesh? Is the threat of terrorism being used as a rationale for incarcerating and "reeducating" alleged dissidents, as in China? Is a refugee crisis unfolding due to persecution of religious minorities, as in Myanmar? Because Japan today lacks sensational, violent oppression of the sort that happened in the 1930s and early 1940s, the LDP's legal machinations and the complaints they elicit fly under the American radar.

Why would Japan be so hard to see?

Sharing Noah Salomon's concern in his essay in this volume that the alluring notion of double standards may not fully encapsulate the complexities I aim to analyze, I contend that the dichotomous framing of "home" and "abroad" is necessary but insufficient for understanding differential applications of conceptions of rights and religion in U.S. foreign policy. Japan shows that between home and abroad lies the ambiguous space occupied by the enemy-turned-ally. Japan simultaneously resists, mediates, and represents U.S. visions for how the world abroad can be transformed. The LDP's proposed changes to the constitution and Abe's support for Shintō organizations push back against U.S. reforms that were specifically designed to eliminate the possibility that anything remotely akin to religious establishment might resurface. Simultaneously, Abe's habit of touting the "rule of law" in northeast Asia helps to project America-centric ideology into a region wracked with anxiety about territorial disputes, a newly muscular China, and a nuclear North Korea. Moreover, in some histories Japan still exemplifies the U.S. project of turning hostile enemies into docile allies through the promotion of American freedom, especially with the utter failure of the more recent state-building adventure in Iraq.[25]

The U.S.-led reforms that took place between 1945 and 1952 are certainly of historical interest, but not because they confirm the successful projection of American values overseas. Rather, the double standards that were operative during what I think of as the "long" Occupation (the decade from 1945 to 1955) highlight the differential application of the religious freedom principle at several different "homes" and "abroads." In the remainder of this chapter, I focus on Occupation-era debates regarding religious education because schooling is one place where recent and proposed revisions to Japanese national law have elicited concerns about the present and future of religious freedom in Japan.[26] This history elucidates why conservative Japanese groups now aim to bring "nonreligious" Shintō into public schools, why liberals decry such actions as potential violations of religious freedom, and why Americans don't seem to care.

TEACHING AND LEARNING HOW TO BE FREE

Although American occupiers tried to present a united front when advancing their postwar reforms, they were deeply divided regarding the relationship between religiosity and democracy. These ideological differences among Occupation personnel matched similar divides at home, where Christian majoritarians fought bitterly against those who espoused strict separation of religion from public school education.[27] The Occupation's Civil Information and Education Section housed two divisions that represented these competing views. On the one hand, the Religions and Cultural Resources Division (Religions Division, hereafter) had been created specifically to enact the hastily concocted policy of eliminating "National Shintō" in the fall of 1945. Division chief William K. Bunce was a fierce proponent of radical separation of religion from the state. As the author of the 15 December 1945 directive that officially disestablished State Shintō, he argued vehemently against the idea that religion had any place in public school education.

On the other hand, the Education Division was headed by Mark T. Orr, an administrator who was open to the idea that religious education had a place in Japanese schools. Orr's stance reflected the views of the aptly named United States Education Mission to Japan, which published a report in March 1946 outlining proposals for Japanese education reform.[28] Members of the mission had strong ties to the American Council on Education Studies, an organization that wanted to expand the presence of religion in public schools as an anticommunist measure. The mission's report accordingly posited a causal connection between religion and democracy and advocated using schools to help Japanese schoolchildren select "the good" and reject "the bad" among various religious offerings.[29]

Other parties influenced the debate. Paul H. Vieth of Yale Divinity School, a theologian specializing in religious education, advised the occupiers between 1947 and 1948. In a 1947 book called *The Church and Christian Education*, Vieth and his coauthors had argued that while constitutional separation of religion from the state had significant merits, religion nevertheless deserved a place in public schools: "Nothing short of the inclusion of religion in the curriculum of the public school will suffice," the authors wrote.[30] In Japan, Vieth advocated allowing religious groups to use schools during nonclassroom hours, a controversial practice that the Religions Division had initially prohibited.[31] Japanese actors also injected their agendas into the debate over religious education. Chairman of the Japanese Federation of Religions Andō Masazumi called for the introduction of religious education into Japanese public schools as a way of forestalling the rapid moral decline that allegedly followed Japan's defeat, while University of Tokyo professor of religious studies Kishimoto Hideo stressed the importance of religion/state separation even as he called for religious literacy training for children.[32]

With separationist and religious majoritarian stances represented in the two Occupation offices and the people who advised them, the stage was set for a showdown over religious education. Conflict erupted in November 1947, when a Ministry of Education pamphlet offering curricular guidance to principals and schoolteachers brought the issue to a head.[33] At issue was whether the pamphlet infringed upon the antiestablishment language of the American-drafted "Peace Constitution" (promulgated November 3, 1946; enacted May 3, 1947) and whether it violated the Japanese-drafted Fundamental Law on Education (enacted March 31, 1947).[34] Behind the dispute lay a question about how much Japanese people could be trusted to write their own laws. Bunce saw the Japanese-drafted Fundamental Law on Education as a sneaky way to smuggle religion back into schools; Orr saw the Fundamental Law on Education as a way to foster religious literacy that was a prerequisite for the religious freedom that Bunce held so dear.

Strikingly, each official made tactical use of "home" and "abroad" in his argument. Bunce argued that whatever worked in the United States in terms of "religious education" would not necessarily apply to Japan's more religiously diverse population. For his part, Orr made the case that it was difficult to promote religious liberty without talking explicitly about religion. The point, he argued, was that sectarian education needed to be avoided in Japan's public schools, but Japan's students nevertheless needed to learn about religion in order to be informed global citizens. The argument between the two branches of the Civil Information and Education Section grew contentious and decidedly uncivil. The two leaders agreed that an individual's ability to choose one religion from a range of options represented "real" religious freedom, but they fiercely disagreed about how public schooling could foster such an elective, exclusivist mindset. In the end, rapprochement came by offering strict guidance to the Ministry of Education that eliminated any possibility that schools could be used for what Orr called "sectarian education."

Just as the two branches of the Civil Information and Education Section were battling over the definition of religious education, Bunce's trusted consultant, Kishimoto, published an essay in the journal *Shakaiken* (The social sphere) entitled "The Relationship Between Religion and Education in America: A Comparative Glimpse at Japan."[35] In this piece written for a Japanese audience, Kishimoto argued that the United States and Japan were both confronting the problem of trying to protect religious freedom while simultaneously establishing the appropriate relationship between religion and public education. The situation was complicated because the two countries had different religious heritages. The United States was a Christian nation with a robust religious freedom tradition; in Japan, multifarious religious traditions had long coexisted, but Japanese people were only recently learning how to properly protect religious freedom.

Operating from the premise that cultivating religious sentiment and fostering general knowledge about religions was a desideratum in both countries, Kishimoto suggested that American religious organizations were well prepared to operate in a synergistic relationship with U.S. public schools. Citing a 1947 study published by the aforementioned American Council on Education Studies (and coauthored by Vieth), Kishimoto noted that there was a developing laudable trend in America to shift traditional Sunday school religious training to "weekday religious education."[36] Here Kishimoto referred to a short-lived experiment in which American schoolchildren were let out of school early on designated days so that they could go to their respective places of worship and receive formal confessional training in religion without official state involvement. While such a system worked well in the American context, Kishimoto argued, Japan's religious organizations were unprepared to take on such weighty responsibility. The only option remaining was to introduce basic "religious appreciation education" at the primary school level, to be followed by the incorporation of nonconfessional religious studies instruction at the middle and high school levels. Such training would support religious freedom in Japan's new postwar moment.

Kishimoto's fall 1947 essay is interesting because, in a reversal of the tactic adopted by Bunce and Orr, he used the situation abroad to make a case for instituting specific changes in public schooling at home. He used his facility with English and familiarity with U.S. practices to highlight the fact that even as the occupiers were busily stripping Japanese schools of all aspects of religion and ritual, U.S. municipalities were engaged in heated debates about the flag salute, release time for sectarian education, situations in which public monies were disbursed to parochial schools, and the necessity of introducing religious language into the Pledge of Allegiance recited daily by U.S. schoolchildren.[37] This activity reflected the politics of the early Cold War, as anxieties about juvenile delinquency and the allure of communism spurred U.S. politicians and educators to promote religious training however possible. Indeed, by 1954 the U.S. Congress voted to include the words "under God" into the Pledge of Allegiance. President Eisenhower enthusiastically signed the bill into law on Flag Day of that year.[38]

The change to the pledge must have looked bizarre from across the Pacific. Just a few short years prior, American-led occupiers had dictated that shrines be removed from school grounds, that students no longer venerate the imperial portrait, and that the practice of bowing toward the imperial palace be abolished. Courses in history, geography, and self-cultivation had all been temporarily discontinued until Japan's "real" history could be taught without the mythological trappings of the past. All of these changes had been instituted because Japan's schools had *too much* religion; the problem in the United States was that students did not have enough.

HERE, THERE, AND EVERYWHERE

Liberals and religious minorities in Japan today are lambasting what they see as threats to religious liberty. They see conservatives recoding cultural practices so that they fall outside of the legal scope of "religion," thereby making them immune to religious freedom claims. Political lobbies like SAS demand revision of the constitutional religious freedom clause so that shrine ceremonies can be subsidized with public funds and religion (or something like religion) can be taught in public schools.[39] Legal trial balloons like the 2006 revision of the Fundamental Law on Education prompted some religious studies scholars to advocate credentialing public school teachers in "religious culture education," an initiative that would fulfill Kishimoto's vision at long last.[40] As of April 2018, morality education enjoys a newly expanded place in the public school curriculum, including units in which students learn to properly respect "Japanese traditions." There is too much going on to summarize neatly, partly because all parties involved gerrymander "religion" and "not-religion" to prioritize the moral norms and modes of comportment they prefer.

At the risk of indulging in some ahistorical counterfactual speculation as I conclude, the Americans in charge of foreign policy in the mid-1940s would surely have found the contemporary Japanese state of affairs unacceptable. They would certainly have been quick to denounce recent changes to public school education as evidence of renascent State Shintō. Had it been available to them, they no doubt would have quickly slapped the label of "Country of Particular Concern" on Japan.

Three-quarters of a century later, the world is different. Japan is closer to "home" than "abroad." Our missiles are based there. Our ideals were implanted there. To admit that Japan has problems with religious freedom would be to admit that religious freedom has problems. Confronting those problems requires acknowledging the tripartite—not bifurcated—world that we inhabit. There's what we do at home, which is of course always right. There's what the bad guys do over there, which is of course always wrong. There's what our former enemies do right under our noses. And what's happening here, there, and everywhere reeks of inconsistency.

NOTES

Thanks to Elizabeth Shakman Hurd and Winnifred Fallers Sullivan for the invitation to participate in the "Home and Abroad" workshops and to fellow workshop participants for insightful feedback. This research was assisted by a grant from the Abe Fellowship Program administered by the Social Science Research Council and in cooperation with and with funds provided by the Japan Foundation Center for Global Partnership. The Center for Global Partnership and the Maureen and Mike Mansfield Foundation also facilitated thought-provoking discussions with policymakers, bureaucrats, and politicians in Tokyo and Washington, D.C.

1. *Annual Report of the U.S. Commission on International Religious Freedom 2017*, April 2017, http://www.uscirf.gov/sites/default/files/2017.USCIRFAnnualReport.pdf.
2. Motoyama Kazuhiro, Chair for the Committee on Religious Freedom of the Japanese Association of New Religious Organizations, open letter to Prime Minister Abe, June 5, 2017, http://www.shinshuren.or.jp/userfile.php?id=76&hash=f20863 6d1877da6f3cd4c0f4b69e7c38.
3. "Update: Diet Enacts Anti-Conspiracy Legislation After Hastening Vote," *Asahi Shinbun*, June 15, 2017, http://www.asahi.com/ajw/articles/AJ201706150014.html.
4. Colin P. A. Jones, "Conspiracy Theory Becomes Frightening Reality for Japan," *Japan Times*, June 14, 2017, https://www.japantimes.co.jp/community/2017/06/14/issues/conspiracy-theory-becomes-frightening-reality-japan/#.WrujxWaZMWp.
5. Thierry Guthmann, "Nationalist Circles in Japan Today: The Impossibility of Secularization." Trans. Aikek P. Rots. *Japan Review* 30 (2017): 207–25, https://www.jstor.org/stable/44259467?seq=1; and David McNeill, "Back to the Future: Shintō, Ise and Japan's New Moral Education," *Asia-Pacific Journal: Japan Focus* 11 iss. 50, no. 1 (2013), https://apjjf.org/2013/11/50/David-McNeill/4047/article.html. The phrase "State Shintō" that often appears in this body of work is

problematic. First, it reproduces the American occupiers' racist conceit that America had "real" religious freedom while Japan was in thrall to an oppressive state religion. Second, although commonly used as shorthand for the ideology of Imperial Japan, the phrase "State Shintō" fails to accurately capture Japanese governance in the period when Japan's first modern constitution was in effect (1890–1945, the height of Japanese imperialism). Japan had no national religion designated in constitutional law, but it did have a constitutional guarantee of religious freedom. The phrase "State Shintō" is therefore politically biased, of dubious historical accuracy, and of limited analytic use. Accordingly, in this chapter I only use the phrase when citing or summarizing others' ideas. For details, see Jolyon Baraka Thomas, *Faking Liberties: Religious Freedom in American-Occupied Japan* (Chicago: University of Chicago Press, 2019).

6. Justin McCurry, "G7 in Japan: Concern over World Leaders' Tour of Nationalistic Shrine," *Guardian*, May 24, 2016, https://www.theguardian.com/world/2016/may/25/g7-japan-world-leaders-tour-shrine-cameron-obama-abe; and Aike P. Rots, "Public Shrine Forests? Shintō, Immanence, and Discursive Secularization," *Japan Review* 30 (2017): 179–205, http://publications.nichibun.ac.jp/region/d/NSH/series/jare/2017-07-24/s001/s012/pdf/article.pdf.
7. Mark R. Mullins, "Secularization, Deprivatization, and the Reappearance of Public Religion in Japanese Society," *Journal of Religion in Japan* 1, no. 1 (2012): 61–82.
8. Mark R. Mullins, "Neonationalism, Religion, and Patriotic Education in Post-Disaster Japan." *Asia-Pacific Journal: Japan Focus* 14, iss. 20, no. 6 (2016), http://apjjf.org/-Mark-Mullins/4964/article.pdf.
9. Jake Adelstein and Mari Yamamoto, "The Religious Cult Secretly Running Japan," *Daily Beast*, July 10, 2016, https://www.thedailybeast.com/the-religious-cult-secretly-running-japan.
10. Rots, "Public Shrine Forests?"
11. Thomas, *Faking Liberties*.
12. There is a point of overlap with Greg Johnson's chapter in this volume: perceptions of religious freedom look different depending on whether one's allegiance is to the sovereign Kingdom of Hawai'i, to the state of Hawaii and the U.S. Constitution, or to broader international norms regarding heritage conservation.
13. Ernils Larsson, "Jinja Honchō and the Politics of Constitutional Reform in Japan," *Japan Review* 30 (2017): 227–52, http://publications.nichibun.ac.jp/region/d/NSH/series/jare/2017-07-24/s001/s014/pdf/article.pdf; and John Breen, "'Conventional Wisdom' and the Politics of Shintō in Postwar Japan," *Politics and Religion* 4, no.1 (2010): 68–82, https://www.ceeol.com/content-files/document-97571.pdf.
14. Shintō Seiji Renmei, *"Hokori aru Nihon o mezashite"* [Aiming for a proud Japan]. Tokyo: Shintō Seiji Renmei, June 1, 2015; and Shintō Seiji Renmei, *"Nihon koku kenpō no katachi"* [The shape of the Japanese constitution], Tokyo: Shintō Seiji Renmei, November 1, 2016.
15. The Fundamental Law on Education revision happened during Abe's first term as prime minister.
16. In addition to high-profile scandals surrounding the prime minister, the LDP's junior coalition partner Komeito is beholden to voters who are largely affiliated

with the mass religious movement Sōka Gakkai, whose members tend to oppose constitutional revision. See Levi McLaughlin, "Komeito's Soka Gakkai Protestors and Supporters: Religious Motivations for Political Activism in Contemporary Japan," *Asia-Pacific Journal: Japan Focus* 13, iss. 40, no. 1 (2015), https://apjjf.org/-Levi-McLaughlin/4386.

17. Rots, "Public Shrine Forests?"; and Larsson, "Jinja Honchō." There is some resonance here with the initiatives Helge Årsheim describes in his chapter on Norway, as conservatives aim to establish Shintō as a de facto national church that can legitimately receive taxpayer funds.

18. Jones, "Conspiracy Theory."

19. Mullins, "Neonationalism, Religion, and Patriotic Education," 5–7; and Isaac Young, "Shut Up and Sing: The Rights of Japanese Teachers in an Era of Conservative Educational Reform," *Cornell International Law Journal* 42, no. 1 (2009): 157–92, http://scholarship.law.cornell.edu/cilj/vol42/iss1/7.

20. Japanese Buddhist Federation, "Kore kara mo tekisetsu ni unyō sareteiru ka chūshi ga hitsuyō." http://www.jbf.ne.jp/assets/files/pdf/himitu.pdf (accessed May 30, 2020).

21. Tajima Kō (Shinshū Ōtani-ha Sect Representative [Shūmu Sōchō]), "Tero tō soshiki hanzai junbizai (kyōbōzai) hōan ni hantai suru seimei," May 17, 2017. http://www.higashihonganji.or.jp/news/declaration/19796/; and Komine Akira (Representative Board Member of the Reformed [Christian] Church in Japan), "'Kyōbōzai hō' (kaisei soshiki teki hanzai shobatsu hō) no kyōkō saiketsu ni kōgi shi, haishi o motomeru seimei," June 23, 2017, http://www.rcj-net.org/statement/statement_against_prime_minister_2017June23.pdf.

22. Kitō Masaki (@masaki_kito), "Kantei no Instagram de mo! Shikamo kochira wa Ise Jingū ni hashutaggu made tsukete. Mohaya seikyō bunri kakushinhan desu," Twitter, January 4, 2018, https://twitter.com/masaki_kito/status/948814691618365440. The Reformed [Christian] Church in Japan wrote to Abe, October 12, 2016, protesting his January 5 New Year's visit to the Ise Shrines and his shrine visit with G7 leaders in May of that year. http://www.rcj-net.org/statement/Protest_statement_against_Prime_Minister_Abes_visit_to_Ise_Shrine_and_guiding_leaders_°of_each_country_to_Ise_Shrine_at_the_Ise_Shima_Summit_2016Oct15.htm.

23. Anna Su, *Exporting Freedom: Religious Liberty and American Power* (Cambridge, Mass.: Harvard University Press, 2016).

24. Elizabeth Shakman Hurd, *Beyond Religious Freedom: The New Global Politics of Religion* (Princeton, N.J.: Princeton University Press, 2015).

25. Anna Su's account in her 2016 book *Exporting Freedom* veers close to this sort of claim. See Elizabeth Shakman Hurd's essay in this volume.

26. Ugo Dessì, "Shin Buddhism, Authority, and the Fundamental Law of Education." *Numen* 56, no. 5 (2009): 523–44, https://doi.org/10.1163/002959709X12469430260048.

27. This tense dynamic recalls Evan Haefeli's discussion in this volume of how unresolved internal divisions within the Anglican Church at "home" influenced the religious politics of the early American colonies "abroad."

28. George Stoddard, et al. *Report of the United States Education Mission to Japan*, trans. Akira Watanabe (Tokyo: Meguro Shoten, 1947). Courtesy of the Kokugakuin University D.C. Holtom Collection.
29. The occupiers' distinction between "political" and "religious" Shintō anticipated by several decades the "countering violent extremism" initiatives described by Elizabeth Shakman Hurd in this volume.
30. Paul H. Vieth, ed. *The Church and Christian Education* (St. Louis: Bethany Press for the Cooperative Publishing Association, 1947).
31. See, for example, "Paul H. Vieth to Chief of Religions and Cultural Resources Division: Memorandum on Ministry of Education's Proposed Directive," April 30, 1948, Religions and Cultural Resources Division Records, Civil Information and Education Section, Supreme Commander of the Allied Powers (RCR) Box #5789, Folder #20, National Archives and Records Administration, College Park, Maryland (NARA).
32. Otake Masuko, "Report on the [February 19, 1948] Conference on Religious Education under the Auspices of Shukyo Renmei (Personal Note for WPW [William P. Woodard])," February 24, 1948, RCR Box #5787, Folder #18, NARA.
33. Here and below I refer to a collection of documents from November 1947 gathered in William P. Woodard Papers, Special Collections and University Archives, Manuscripts and Archives (Coll 153), Box #23, Folder #2, University of Oregon Libraries, https://library.uoregon.edu/.
34. Article 9 of the 1947 Fundamental Law on Education read: "Religious tolerance and the important part religion plays in public life shall be valued in education. The state and public schools shall not engage in religious education or religious activities for the cause of any specific religion."
35. Kishimoto Hideo, "Shūkyō to kyōiku to no sōkan: Beikoku to Nihon to no hikaku teki hekiken" [originally "Amerika ni okeru shūkyō to kyōiku to no kankei: Nihon to no hikaku teki hekiken"], *Shakakiken* 1, no. 3 (December 1947), in *Kishimoto Hideo shū*, vol. 5, Wakimoto Tsuneya and Yanagikawa Keiichi, 279–90 (Tokyo: Keiseisha, 1976).
36. American Council on Education Studies, *The Relation of Religion to Public Education: The Basic Principles* (Washington, D.C., April 1947).
37. Many of these debates appear in Sarah Barringer Gordon, *The Spirit of the Law: Religious Voices and the Constitution in Modern America* (Cambridge, Mass.: Belknap Press of Harvard University Press, 2010), 40–95.
38. Gordon, *Spirit of the Law*, 47–55. See also Kevin M. Kruse, *One Nation Under God: How Corporate America Invented Christian America* (New York: Basic Books, 2015), 95–125.
39. Helge Årsheim's chapter in this volume documents similar initiatives in Norway.
40. Fujiwara Satoko, "On Qualifying Religious Literacy: Recent Debates on Higher Education and Religious Studies in Japan," *Teaching Theology & Religion* 13, no. 3 (2010): 223–36, https://doi.org/10.1111/j.1467-9647.2010.00615.x.

11

The Cultural Politics of Yoga in India and the United States

SUNILA S. KALE AND CHRISTIAN LEE NOVETZKE

In November 2015 a free yoga course at the University of Ottawa offered to around sixty students with disabilities was abruptly cancelled. One reason cited was a relationship to "cultural genocide." Here is the rationale provided by the Student Federation leaders who decided to discontinue the course: "Yoga has been under a lot of controversy lately due to how it is being practiced and what practices from what cultures (which are often sacred spiritual practices) they are being taken from. Many of these cultures are cultures that have experienced oppression, cultural genocide and diasporas due to colonialism and western supremacy, and we need to be mindful of this and how we express ourselves while practicing yoga."[1]

Although the press in India took little notice of this event in Canada, the news quickly entered the slipstream of viral media in the United States especially, which is arguably the commercial and cultural hub of modern postural yoga (MPY) today.[2] From introspective meditations to yoga studio teach-ins and political reflections from the yoga communities of the United States, for a brief moment a segment of the North American public sphere erupted with a debate about yoga and cultural appropriation. While some criticized the Student Federation as misguided by political correctness, the news of this course cancellation ignited a tinderbox of other critiques already in place regarding the practice of yoga in North America and the Global North more broadly, drawing on important questions of colonialism, capitalism, and racism in particular. Much of this critique settled on the idea that yoga, as it is now practiced in North America, and especially in the United States, is a form of cultural appropriation by white affluent America and that is also a version of neocolonialism.[3]

The term "cultural appropriation" names the annexation by a dominant culture of some key elements of a minority culture in a context of unequal power. A familiar form of cultural appropriation in the U.S. context is the use of Native American imagery for sports teams, and such issues of indigeneity and dignity resonate in this volume with the essays by David Maldonado Rivera on Puerto Rico and Gregory Johnson on Hawaii. Those making similar arguments about yoga posit that yoga has been appropriated by Western capitalism, dominated by a culture—almost homogenously white, upper middle class, capitalist, and consumerist—that valorizes a cisgender heteronormativity and is exemplified by an impossibly restrictive body type. In short: yoga has become controlled and corrupted by the most toxic of American cultural norms and, in the process, has lost its connections with the place of its origin, India. This form of domination in relation to yoga is often described in the language of colonialism, with yoga itself "colonized" by the Global North. A key feature of the argument that presents yoga as a form of cultural appropriation asserts an explicit link between the contemporary Western colonization of yoga and the colonization of India by European powers. In other words, the argument connects the unequal power relations represented in settler colonialism in the United States to the racialized social order of British imperialism in the Indian subcontinent. The criticism that yoga amounts to a form of cultural appropriation that is inherently colonial in its uses of power also often rests on the idea that colonialism created the means by which yoga could be "taken" from India, divested of its historical and cultural roots, and refashioned outside of India shorn of its Indic character. Cultural appropriation is thereby understood as a form of extractive colonialism.

In one dominant version of this idea, cultural appropriation shifts registers; it is not the territory of India that has been divested of yoga but rather the community of Hindus, both within India and without. For example, seven years before the course was cancelled in Ottawa, a group of Indian American activists organized as the Hindu American Foundation (HAF) launched a campaign to "Take Back Yoga." Dismayed that Americans did not understand yoga to be, at least in its origins, Hindu *and* Indian as HAF contended, HAF sought to resituate yoga within Hinduism and, by extension, within India as a Hindu majority nation-state.[4] Furthermore, they argued that mainstream ignorance or even rejection of the links between yoga and Hinduism amounted to a form of "Hinduphobia" in America. The project of HAF typifies this variation of the cultural appropriation argument regarding yoga in America today, although it is by no means the only diasporic voice in the debate.[5]

Certainly, the practice of yoga in the modern world has taken on forms of cultural appropriation, and yoga does exist in America in spaces dominated by a white racial hegemony that can generate profound discomfort for South Asians, Hindus, people with non-normative body types, and people of color. Our aim in this essay is to deepen the core value that we feel is expressed by people who make such critiques, which is a desire for greater clarity regarding yoga's history and a commitment to pointing out the spaces of social injustice that occur in how this history is told and remembered. We seek to extend the spirit of these debates about the cultural politics of yoga through an analysis of yoga between and within the United States and India today.[6]

Our engagement with this argument contains three focal points. The first attends to the idea of yoga's imbrication in colonialism. Rather than view yoga as a practice coopted by colonialism, we highlight yoga's history as a tool in the hands of Indians opposed to colonial rule. But we also point out that this use of yoga by Indian freedom fighters tended to erase the multireligious and multi-caste history and diversity of yoga, and relied on a flattened and singular Hindu normative culture. Our second point of focus is the movement of yoga from India to the United States, one that bore the marks of yoga's transformed presence in the early twentieth century—as a powerful anticolonial tool but also one that rested on a homogenized Indian identity built around a singular high-caste, upper-class Hindu archetype. Our third point observes demographic distinctions between India's population and its diaspora in the United States in terms of religion, caste, and class. Our aim is to reflect on the cultural politics of yoga in America, both past and present, in relation to both India and Hinduism in our age.

YOGA AND COLONIALISM IN INDIA

Arguably one of the first moments of armed resistance organized by Indians against British colonialism (in the form of Company rule) was an uprising of yogis in the region of Bengal. It began around 1763 and lasted until around 1802. This insurgency was undertaken by "warrior ascetics," as William Pinch terms them, organized groups of yogis and *fakīr*s (the Urdu-Islamicate term used to describe yogis in many Indian languages and in British English), who in addition to practicing various forms of yoga were warriors, traders, migrant farmers, and artisans. These were groups of Hindus and Muslims from across the spectrum of India's caste demographics who resisted Company rule. This loosely organized, religiously and ethnically heterogeneous group together raided the armies and outposts of the British East India Company in Bengal, the precursor of British imperial colonialism.[7] Their motivation was likely not that of a nationalist group, and indeed the uprising may have had much to do with systems of taxation and the giving of alms following the famine of 1770. Such military encounters with yogis and *fakīr*s, particularly those organized in monastic orders, were a source of anxiety for the British; they came to fear the yogi as a political force and actively vilified and even criminalized some groups associated with yoga. The yogi was denigrated in British imperial and Orientalist discourse as a "snake charmer" and a thief but also a character of antisocial and anti-imperial danger. Far from being a benign figure of wellness to be coopted by British culture, the yogi was someone to be feared, criminalized, and ostracized. Indeed, many groups of yogis were effectively "criminalized" in the colonial period by British authority, relegated to the category of anticolonial threat to British civil order.[8] As Pinch notes, British policy and imperial ideology saw the yogi as "an alternate locus of authority."[9] The yogi—and, by extension, yoga itself—was understood by the British to pose a challenge to colonialism, one that could not be coopted or controlled, and so had to be criminalized through the figure of the dangerous or "sinister" yogi.[10]

The heterogeneous nature of this group designated by the term "yogi" (or *fakīr* or *jogī*), spanning both caste difference and the distinctions of "Hindu" and "Muslim," indicate the rich and diverse history of yoga that was in place at the time of this uprising. Indeed, the history of yoga in India over millennia is a history of a practice not confined to any single religion but one that spans people of all religions and of none.[11] It was also a practice within everyday life in India for millennia used to address everything from minor physical discomfort as a form of medicine to deep existential transcendence as a form of religion. Although yoga as a psychophysical practice in everyday life is not restricted by caste, religion, class, or gender in India, the dominant textual traditions are restrictive in several ways. They are primarily composed in Sanskrit, a language historically produced by and limited to high-caste men, predominantly (but not exclusively) Hindu, Jain, and Buddhist. And within such yogic texts, women and low castes are sometimes objectified or ostracized. Yet the history of elite Sanskrit texts cannot be taken as a complete portrayal of the scope of yoga in the past or present. Such elite texts concern elite spheres, not the world of everyday life.

A half century after the rebellion of warrior ascetics and their subsequent imperial vilification, this uprising became an inspiration for revolutionary-minded Indians who opposed British rule. One can see this in the famous colonial-era novel *Ānandamaṭh*, written by Bankim Chandra Chatterjee in 1882, a work that produced the first two lines of India's national song *Vande*

Mātharam ("I praise you, Mother."). Even as the text hails yogis as proto-nationalist heroes, one can also observe the erasure of the heterogeneous nature of yoga in favor of a single unified "Hindu" and high-caste origin for yoga. The figure of the Muslim *fakīr* is absent, and the band of heroic Hindu yogi rebels are flattened along the axis of caste.[12] Yoga became a key feature of anticolonial political thought and action, but it was also subject to the homogenizing tendencies of anticolonial politics to collapse Hindu and Indian into a single category. Our aim here is to note the twin effects of colonialism's engagement with yoga. First, British imperial vilification of the yogi then made yoga and yogis available as a resource for anticolonial, anti-imperial, and proto-nationalist sentiment. Second, as yoga became a tool in the hands of Indian nationalists, it was flattened by the high-caste, mostly male Hindus at the vanguard of the nationalist movement to appear as a primarily high-caste and Hindu practice in contradistinction to its diverse history on the subcontinent.

The way in which the figure of the yogi as Hindu coalesced as both an object of British anxiety and a sign of Indian nationalist resistance can be explained metonymically by the figure of Mohandas K. Gandhi (1869–1948). Around 1921, as Gandhi's national and international fame was rising, two important things were strategically reconceived in Gandhi's political repertoire. First, he changed his clothes: from alternating between Western business suits and Gujarati urban middle-class clothing befitting his role as a lawyer and political leader in South Africa, Gandhi transitioned his public political persona into the sartorial resemblance of an ascetic and a renunciate—that is, a yogi. Indeed, when Winston Churchill in 1931 derided Gandhi as a "half-naked... fakir" during his visit to London, Gandhi agreed that he had spent a decade trying to be exactly that, a yogi/*fakīr* and thanked Churchill for his "compliment."[13] Around the same time, Gandhi was imprisoned for sedition by the British. The British allowed anticolonial agitators to bring with them behind bars books that were deemed "religious" as opposed to political works, which were banned. Gandhi, like many nationalists before and after, carried to prison in 1922 one of Hinduism's best-known Sanskrit texts, the *Bhagavad Gītā* (c. 400 BCE). This was likely the English translation (for Gandhi could not read the Sanskrit original at that time) published by the British Orientalist scholar Sir Edwin Arnold in 1885 as *The Song Celestial*.

The British, and even Sir Arnold himself, regarded the *Gītā* as a religious text, akin to the New Testament. Such a reading underestimated its explicitly political sentiments. Set in the midst of a mythic and ancient civil war, the *Gītā* is a conversation between a warrior, Arjuna, who refuses to fight a fratricidal battle, and his charioteer, Krishna, who tries to convince Arjuna that he must fight despite the fact that the war is a morally ambiguous and ultimately disastrous enterprise. The methods and theories that Krishna deploys to convince Arjuna to take up war are all called "yoga," a term in the text that means a discipline of action, and in this case in particular, action in the context of war and political contest. In other words, "yoga" in the *Gītā* comes to mean the moral and metaphysical rationalization to fight a war against one's enemies.[14] This is not primarily the yoga of physical postures or meditative practices, and the text predates the famous *Yogasūtras* of Patanjali by almost six centuries.[15] It was in the yoga of the *Gītā* that Gandhi found political inspiration. However, in adapting his political theory of yoga from a text that is largely seen as central to Hinduism, Gandhi further refined his yogi/*fakīr* image to emphasize the Hindu yogi while perhaps inadvertently obscuring the Muslim or other potential figure of yoga, a criticism Gandhi received repeatedly during his lifetime and after.[16]

Gandhi was not the first to see in the *Gītā* a yoga of political action. Before him, high-caste Hindu political figures like Lala Lajpat Rai (1865–1928), Aurobindo Ghose (1872–1950), and B. G. Tilak (1856–1920) had already developed an idea of karma yoga, or the yoga of political action.[17] Yet Gandhi's *karma yoga* took a unique form. Combining B. G. Tilak's articulation of the *Gītā*'s *karma yoga* as a call to direct action against the British, Gandhi replaced the idea of violent resistance with a theory of "selfless" non-violent political action.[18] Gandhi's yoga became both *anāsakti*, or "nonattached," and *ahiṁsā*, or "not harmful." Moreover, his most effective—and some would argue most potentially dangerous—mode of political action was a projection of the ascetic power associated with the yogi: Gandhi's willingness to take on a fast-unto-death. Gandhi used this political weapon effectively against the British but also sometimes against fellow Indian nationalists who disagreed with his politics around caste and Hinduism—such as Dr. B. R. Ambedkar, a key leader of India's "Untouchable" or Dalit community, primary architect of the Indian constitution, and an eventual convert to Buddhism.[19]

And so Gandhi combined the persona of a Hindu yogi through his public affect and a core political philosophy of *karma yoga*, drawn from the *Gītā* and the thoughts of fellow nationalists. Gandhi thus typifies how many Hindu-oriented leaders of India's independence movement reconstructed a modern theory of yoga as emancipatory political action beyond essentially psychophysical practices. And yet these actions also served to reinforce an idea of yoga as exclusively Hindu and high caste.

This anticolonial political theory of yoga, like the story of the yogi/*fakīr* uprising, also lost its interreligious and intercaste character in the process of its movement onto the center stage of Indian nationalist discourse. Here we can perhaps see colonialism's pernicious effects on the social demographics and presentation of yoga. As many have argued, colonialism telescoped and reified Indian culture through regimes of Orientalist knowledge, one feature of which was the elevation of the Western-educated high-caste male as the epitome of the modern Indian, a figure who nevertheless remained the subject of never-ending suspicion.[20] All the key figures who appropriated yoga in this political context were themselves high-caste (*savarṇa*) Hindus, including Gandhi. And the use of the *Gītā* as a core text for the development of karma yoga as a political theory further circumscribed the demographic space that surrounded this powerful concept to the field of Hinduism associated with India's demographically smallest upper-caste groups.[21] This may not have been the intentions of those nationalists who fought against British rule under the sign of karma yoga, but it is an effect of their efforts felt then and still today.

Alongside and in parallel to the emergence of yoga as anticolonial political theory, the psychophysical practices of yoga described from the time of the ancient *Yogasūtras* (ca. sixth century CE) through the medieval *Haṭha Yoga Pradīpikā* (ca. fifteenth century CE) began to transform in particular political locations in India into the modern postural yoga that is today simply called "yoga." Many of these political locations were known as "princely states" or indirectly ruled, semi-sovereign regions in a vassal-like relationship to the British Crown in colonial India. In this period, the key features of yoga as we know it now were created by Indians who were borrowing and adapting Western gymnastic physical culture to create a uniquely Indian mode of physical and mental strength. For example, Joseph Alter has traced how the signature *sūrya namaskār* was developed by the ruler of the princely state of Aundh not too far from the colonial center of Bombay in an effort to combine emerging ideas of Western-style physical education with traditional Indian exercise practices, and Mark Singleton has shown how the flowing *vinyāsa* form emerged from the royal Wadiyar court in the princely state of Mysore combining the same ideals of Western gymnastics with Indian classical hatha yoga.[22] Indeed, it was in Mysore, under the famed teacher Tirumalai Krishnamacharya, that the founders of MPY as a global phenomenon were trained: B. K. S. Iyengar (1918–2014), Pattabhi Jois (1915–2009), and the Russian émigré Indra Devi (1899–2002). All three were among the core creators and expounders of MPY in Europe and North America in the mid-twentieth century.[23] Iyengar and Jois, as two Brahmin teachers of the prince of Wadiyar, might represent the caste-narrowing of yoga in this period, and Indra Devi, erstwhile Eugenie Peterson, a white woman from Russia, perhaps exemplifies another plank of the cultural homogenization of MPY.

The origin of modern postural yoga within India's princely states is also imbricated in the emergence of Indian modernity across multiple spheres such as education, development, infrastructure, and science. At the same time that MPY was evolving in Mysore, the indirectly ruled state was also the site of key innovations in economics and politics, including early twentieth-century electrification, elected political representation, and industrial planning among other state-led initiatives.[24] A similar pairing of commitment to psychophysical yoga and novel forms of governance was evident in Aundh, where its ruler, inspired by Gandhi, created the first state constitution in 1939 that surrendered his kingdom to its people (another first in India), allowed universal suffrage, adopted elected village-level governance, and ensured freedoms of speech, religion, and the press. The creation of MPY and the creation of Indian political modernity and sovereignty were thus conjoined in the princely states, and so too were they linked in the outward broadcasting of this modernity to the world. One can see this in the yogic figure of Vivekananda (1863–1902), who typified this amalgam of modernity and Indian culture by linking yoga to both Hinduism and Western-style mysticism but also to rationality, health, science, and human freedom, particularly in speeches given during his travels to the United States in 1893 and 1899. As many scholars have subsequently recognized, Vivekananda's presentation of Hinduism as a highly ethical and rational religion to the Western world was also part of turning the tide of public sentiment against colonialism throughout the Global North in the nineteenth century.[25]

We have traced here one genealogy of yoga's emergence as anticolonial politics in India, which also became the avenue through which yoga spread throughout the world. At the same time, we have suggested that the price paid for this politics was an erasure of important kinds of diversity in Indian culture, such as the presence of non-Hindus—especially Muslims—as authentic yoga practitioners, the narrowing of modern yogic practices to a middle- and upper-class context, and the restriction of the great plethora of caste backgrounds that had long been a feature of yoga's practice in India. If yoga was adapted from its ancient roots by upper-caste and upper-class Hindu Indians who wanted to resist colonialism and construct new visions of a strong and sovereign Indian culture, then they also (perhaps, again, inadvertently) minimized and in some cases deleted the non-high-caste voices and non-Hindu perspectives that had also created these possibilities for yoga in the modern world. Yoga entered the modern world through an aperture through which it was reshaped into a predominantly high-caste Hindu practice.

THE CULTURAL POLITICS OF YOGA IN
THE UNITED STATES OF AMERICA

Although yoga originated in India, took its myriad forms, and proliferated on the subcontinent over more than two millennia, there is no doubt that the geographic center of yoga as a global commodity form today is not India but America.[26] One way to understand yoga in the late twentieth and early twenty-first centuries is as a capitalist endeavor, and this capital is located primarily in the West. As a result, a majority of those who profit from yoga are disproportionately white middle- or upper-class Americans. If the measure of cultural appropriation is the very fact that yoga as a global phenomenon appears to be a Western one at this stage in history, then yoga has been appropriated by the West, although often with the explicit efforts of Indians, such as Pattabhi Jois, B. K. S. Iyengar, Bikram Choudhury, and a thriving yoga tourism industry in India.[27] But the story of this appropriation, as we have shown, is more complicated than a legacy of colonial domination, economic exploitation, and the divestment of agency from either India or Indians. In this last section, we point out how India remains at the referential center of the global practice of MPY, even if as a kind of commodity fetish. In other words, yoga is still indelibly coded by and linked to "India" as both a place and an object imagined into being by contemporary Orientalism, colonialism, and postcolonial national identity. We agree with the charge to call out racism, sexism, and Orientalism in the practices and spaces of MPY in the United States. But we suggest that this impetus should be extended to address the inherited inequalities of caste and class that are telescoped into yoga as it has been transposed to U.S. shores through diasporic immigration. In other words, to understand any argument about the cultural politics of the modern iterations of yoga as we know it today requires that we engage with questions of caste, gender, class, religious exclusion, and historical erasure that may have deeper roots in yoga's migration out of India in the nineteenth and early twentieth centuries.

Although India is not the financial or demographic hub of MPY, India and Indian culture remain key markers of authenticity in the global practice of yoga today. MPY privileges Indian cultural forms, like Sanskrit and Indian music (or facsimiles of Indian music), in such a way as to invest these things with the cultural capital of "authenticity." The founding gurus and many of the current leaders of MPY are Indian, and the commodity sign of Indian-ness remains a key element of yoga branding, from the use of Sanskrit words like *"namaste," "mantra,"* and *"om"* to images easily identified with India (designs, motifs, the color saffron, Hindu deities, Sanskrit words, etc.). And it is still a requirement in almost all yoga training courses in America to study the classical texts of yoga, such as Patanjali's *Yogasūtras* and the *Haṭha Yoga Pradīpikā*. While this is in part the act of cultural appropriation identified by critics, it is also an adherence to authenticity that roots "real yoga" in Indian cultural forms, particularly Hindu ones, and a version of Hinduism strongly rooted in Sanskrit and Sanskritic cultural forms. The strong desire to associate Indian-ness with authenticity in the yoga sphere was satirized in the controversial documentary film *Kumaré* by Vikram Gandhi in 2011, in which Gandhi—an Indian American from New Jersey—takes on an Indian accent to fashion himself as a yoga guru while teaching a yoga practice he calls "blue light meditation" to white upper-middle-class spiritual seekers.

While the privileged cultural capital of India, Sanskrit, and Hinduism in the yoga industry may indeed amount to a form of Orientalism, it is still an Orientalism that focuses on Indic-Hindu authenticity and fixates on the genealogies of modern yoga that retain Indian men (for the most part) as their titular figures, often considered as "gurus" and founders, such as Iyengar, Krishnamacharya, Jois, Iyengar, Choudhury, and others. At the same time, actual Indian people—from India or diasporic Indians—constitute a very small portion of either yoga's teaching cadre outside India or its customer base. And so the numerical minority of Indians who are agents within the Western practice of yoga come to represent yoga's "authentic" Indian roots enacting a version of what Lisa Lau has called "re-Orientalism."[28] Indeed, this is tellingly represented in the conclusion to the story about yoga at the University of Ottawa that we described at the beginning of this essay. One year after the course was cancelled, the class was reinstated, but this time with a teacher of Indian origin. The newly hired teacher, Priya Shah, expressed some perplexity about this development, stating in an interview, "When I read about [the cancellation and reinstatement of classes], I was kind of thinking 'Did they hire me because I'm Indian?... I was born in Calgary, I grew up in Canada but my background is Indian and I've been there once before. I was there for about five months.'"[29] This apparent neo-Orientalist fetishization of Indian people and culture in the context of yoga reinforces a desire for "authenticity" across personhood, emblems, idols, incense, chanting, music, Sanskrit terms, and more, reflecting what Priya Shah and many others observe as a fetishized location within the yoga industry that privileges the Indic, an emblemization only rarely enacted as a privileging of Indians themselves. India, in the context of MPY, becomes part of yoga's commodity fetish, which employs a set of cultural references and associations that makes of yoga something more than a practice but rather an identifiable commodity, an "alternative lifestyle" in a global market that takes a fashioned aesthetic of "India" (chanting, Sanskrit, henna, "namaste," etc.) as a marker of its brand.[30]

The campaign in the United States to "take back yoga" initiated by the Hindu American Foundation was aimed at reinvesting yoga with a sense of its origins as Indian and Hindu simultaneously—that is, recentering yoga around another imagination of authenticity, India and Hindu culture. In India, this effort is somewhat at odds with the position of the Indian government over decades, even with the formal position of the current Hindu nationalist government of India. Moreover, HAF is actually in alignment with the position of those practitioners of yoga in the United States who have been charged with appropriating yoga. In other words, it is the impulse of largely non-Indian white American yoga practitioners to remain "authentic" that leads them to adopt and adhere to Indian and especially Hindu cultural forms in the yoga sphere, to consistently reinvest the practice of yoga in America with the cultural forms (as they interpret them) of Hinduism from India. Again, this does not mean empowerment, nor does it lead necessarily to a critique of racism or Orientalism. It remains the case that yoga spaces in the United States are dominated by white upper-middle-class people, yet such yoga spaces have also become a primary place where cultural forms of Hinduism and India take center stage in American society writ large—this imbalance is precisely the concern of the HAF, it seems; the "theft" of yoga is the shift of power outside of "Hindu" hands. This is a legacy of the colonial-era movement of yoga from India to the rest of the world, which was telescoped through the lens of a narrowly circumscribed vision of yoga as the practice of upper-caste, upper-class Hindus.

That yoga spaces must be "decolonized" in the sense of creating a more capacious social space for non-white, non-body-normative people, and especially for South Asians of all backgrounds, is beyond question. But how far can we extend this laudable call to address social injustices in the practice and perpetuation of yoga in contemporary America? How can some of the endemic issues of Indian social injustice—which the Indian state as a secular liberal democracy itself is in principle constantly seeking to remedy—be addressed through yoga spaces in America?

To understand what issues might be at stake, it is useful to compare the demographics of Indians in India with Indians in the United States. One recent study describes the Indian diaspora in America as the "other one percent," not only because they make up 1 percent of the U.S. population but because they are economically the wealthiest and best educated minority in the United States.[31] A call to address class inequity, in addition to race and sex, has been articulated by many organizations in the United States, such as the South Asian Americans Perspectives on Yoga group led by Roopa Singh.[32] In addition, the Indian American diaspora is disproportionately Hindu and upper caste.[33] To understand what this means, consider that, in class terms, India is a developing country, with over half its population living off of the equivalent of three U.S. dollars per day.[34] In terms of caste, 75–80 percent of India's population report their caste as "low" (Other Backward Classes, approximately 50 percent), "Untouchable"/ Dalit (Scheduled Castes, approximately 17 percent), or "tribal" (Scheduled Tribes 9 percent).[35] And India contains the world's third-largest Muslim population (15 percent or around 200 million people). By comparison, the Indian diaspora in the United States is wealthy, high caste, and Hindu. In other words, the demographic indicators tell us the Indian diaspora in the United States reflects only 15–20 percent of India's population in terms of caste, class, and religion. Even if we expand the diaspora to include previous generations of migrants from India and double-diaspora communities, it is still very unlikely to mirror the caste and class profile of India as a whole. It is thus a small proportion of India's population in terms of caste and class that make up the majority of the population of Indian Americans, which also supplies the key voice in the critique of yoga as cultural appropriation.

The lack of a proportionate representation of Indians in America to Indians in India is the result of many millennia of oppression around caste, class, region, religion, and race and is the focus of activist efforts to understand the nature of culture and power in the diaspora. For example, an Indian Dalit political activist in the United States, Prachi Patankar, wrote in her 2014 article "Ghosts of Yogas Past and Present":

> Many caste-privileged Hindus use such claims to cultural capital to dominate cultural norms in ways that oppress and even perpetuate violence against Muslims, Christians, Dalits, Bahujans [majority], and Adivasis [Indigene], altogether the vast majority of India's people. They have used this power to erase or appropriate from the richly-diverse indigenous and local spiritual practices of people into their Brahminical form of Hinduism. From the standpoint of the vast majority of South Asians, the cultural threat they face is not at all from "white people" practicing or "appropriating" yoga.[36]

Patankar, like many others, argues that the colonization of yoga, in a sense, may have occurred long ago, well before the British or other colonial powers entered South Asia. This is a cognate of colonialism, a kind of "deep colonialism" attributed to Brahmin, high-caste, and forward-caste people who, in the colonial period in particular, began producing what constitutes the global practice of yoga today.[37] While not disavowing the racism, body normativity, or class exclusions of contemporary yoga practice in America, cultural critics and activists like Patankar also point out that the history of yoga is not an "Indian" history in some inclusive sense but a history of a particular caste-oriented, gendered practice over millennia on the subcontinent that is also a history of exclusion. It reflects a culture dominated by a high-caste, well-educated, Westernized, and globalized elite formed since the end of the colonial period. There is a risk, as Patankar points out, that the critique of the cultural politics of yoga may inadvertently participate in a much larger and deeper appropriation of not only yoga but of Indian culture writ large. As recent studies have shown, although India's vast majority of Scheduled Castes and Tribes and Other Backward Classes have increased their political power in India, they nevertheless continue to experience marked prejudices in India that are now also translating into their experience as Indian Americans.[38] This is also a demographic that is growing in the Indian American community, bringing with them both the stigma of social inequity and the commitment to redressing this inequity.[39]

As proponents of the argument about the cultural politics of yoga importantly remind us, we must contend with race, class, and power, among many other things when assessing the current state of yoga in the world. The critical debate about the cultural politics of yoga in America cannot distance itself from the important history of yoga in India, particularly in the colonial period, nor can it remove itself from the complicated politics of caste and class that are at the core of the Indian American experience and remain essential to political and cultural life in India.

Yoga, as we have argued elsewhere, identifies a political viewpoint, the effect of which is determined by its user—there's no presupposed political endpoint to yoga itself.[40] This makes yoga politically powerful, but its power is directed by the intentions of its users. If yoga in the nineteenth and early twentieth centuries could offer a way to fight against the injustices of white racist British imperialism, then it is perhaps possible that the political practice of yoga could be recovered to address racism, classicism, sexism, body normativity, and Orientalism in yoga spaces in the Western world and to address the problems of casteism, religious prejudice, and class inequity that many Indians suffer today in India and increasingly in the United States as well.

NOTES

We would like to thank Winni Sullivan and Beth Hurd for the invitation to participate in this volume and thank our fellow participants for their input on this essay. Our thanks also to Jayadev Athreya, Radhika Govindrajan, and Shana Sippy for thoughtful comments on this article.

1. From an email cited widely in the media. See Aeden Helmer, "Free Ottawa Yoga Class Scrapped over 'Cultural Issues,'" *Ottawa Sun*, November 20, 2015. This was not the first accusation of this sort. A similar debate, which did not lead to a cancellation, occurred at Ryerson University in Canada in 2000. Tania Pereira, "Western Culture Stretches Eastern Traditions," *Eyeopener*, March 22, 2000, https://theeyeopener.com/2000/03/western-culture-stretches-eastern-traditions/.

2. For the most part, the Indian public sphere, and especially the English-speaking public, seemed not to register this debate as significant at all. By our count, we could find only a single story of some three hundred words that appeared in one of India's most widely circulating English-language newspapers, *The Times of India*, on November 24, 2015.

3. Recent engagements of this kind have included Enoch Page's provocative essay, "The Gender, Race, and Class Barriers: Enclosing Yoga as a White Public Space," in *Yoga, the Body, and Embodied Social Change: An Intersectional Feminist Analysis*, ed. Beth Berila, Melanie Klein, and Chelsea Jackson Roberts, 41–66 (Lanham, Md.: Lexington, 2016); and Shreena Gandhi and Lillie Wolff, "Yoga and the Roots of Cultural Appropriation," Praxis Center, December 19, 2017, https://www.kzoo.edu/praxis/yoga/. Although also see Andrea Jain's rebuttal of Gandhi and Wolff, "Fox News Controversy on Yoga and the White Supremacy Reveals Problem of Yoga Discussion," *Religion Dispatches* (blog), February 7, 2018, http://religiondispatches.org/fox-news-controversy-on-yoga-and-white-supremacy-reveals-problem-of-yoga-discussion/. See also the concept of "Decolonizing Yoga" in general and the many articles and videos that discuss how yoga has been appropriated and how individual seekers can "decolonize" their practice (the Decolonizing Yoga website, http://www.decolonizingyoga.com/ (accessed May 30, 2020); the South Asian American Perspectives on Yoga in America (SAAPYA) website, https://saapya.wordpress.com/ (accessed May 30, 2020); and the "Take Back Yoga" campaign of the Hindu American Foundation (HAF), https://www.hafsite.org/media/pr/takeyogaback (accessed January 30, 2020). Note that the HAF removed this link as of April 2020.

4. The Take Back Yoga campaign seems to have been initiated by an exchange between Aseem Shukla and Deepak Chopra on the *On Faith* blog associated with the *Washington Post* (see Paul Vitello, "Hindu Groups Stirs Debate Over Yoga's Soul," *New York Times*, November 27, 2010, https://www.nytimes.com/2010/11/28/nyregion/28yoga.html). As this debate made clear, Shukla feels yoga is fundamentally "Hindu" rather than simply "Indian."

5. One prominent diaspora voice that is explicitly critical of the HAF position is the Coalition Against Genocide, which reported their findings that the HAF has close

ties to India's Hindu Right political organizations. Coalition Against Genocide, *Affiliations of Faith: Hindu American Foundation and the Global Sangh*, Spotlight Series Report (2013), http://www.coalitionagainstgenocide.org/reports/2013/cag.15dec2013.haf.rss.pdf. In turn, the HAF created its own report declaring that the Coalition Against Genocide is a group of "Radical South Asian Leftists" and also "Hinduphobic." See *The Coalition Against Genocide: A Nexus of Hinduphobia Unveiled* (Washington, D.C.: Hindu American Foundation, March 7, 2013), https://www.hinduamerican.org/wp-content/uploads/2020/05/Coalition_Against_Genocide_A_Nexus_of_HinduphobiaUnveiled.pdf.

6. In the larger body of our work on yoga, we call for a definitional reframing of yoga as a political philosophy. Our interest in thinking about yoga in this way draws us to the political valences that surround and inflect yoga. For the purposes of clarity in this article, however, we use "yoga" to refer to postural and meditative practices, although they are embedded in politics, because it is this ubiquitous notion of yoga that is at the heart of the debate about cultural appropriation.

7. See W. R. Pinch, *Warrior Ascetics and Indian Empires* (Cambridge: Cambridge University Press, 2006), 82–102. Also see this recent article by Christine Marrewa-Karwoski, "Far from Hindutva, Yogi Adityanath's Sect Comes from a Tradition That Was Neither Hindu Nor Muslim," *Scroll In*, April 9, 2017, https://scroll.in/article/833710/far-from-hindutva-yogi-adityanath-comes-from-a-tradition-that-was-neither-hindu-nor-muslim.

8. David Gordon White, *Sinister Yogis* (Chicago: University of Chicago Press, 2009), 240.

9. Pinch, *Warrior Ascetics*, 25.

10. Colonial era texts on criminality abound in references to such figures through various terms, such as "yogi," "jogi," and "fakir." See, for example, William Crooke, *The Tribes and Castes of the North-western Provinces and Oudh*, 4 vols. (Calcutta: Office of the Superintendent of Government Printing, 1896). We should note, following the work of David Gordon White, that seeing yogis as outside or parallel to political orders is hardly an invention of the British but a feature of the long history of yoga on the subcontinent.

11. For a snapshot of this diversity, see David Gordon White, ed., *Yoga in Practice* (Princeton, N.J.: Princeton University Press, 2011); and J. Mallinson and M. Singleton, *The Roots of Yoga* (London: Penguin, 2017).

12. In terms of caste, *Ānandamaṭh* does suggest an anticaste sentiment in the idea that yogis must renounce caste, which in this case involves two high-caste figures (a Brahmin and a Kayastha).

13. See Churchill's address to the Council of the West Essex Unionist Association on February 23, 1931, and Gandhi's reply on July 17, 1944. See also Emma Tarlo, *Clothing Matters: Dress and Identity in India* (Chicago: University of Chicago Press, 1996).

14. There are references to the meditative and psychophysical aspects of yoga in the *Bhagavad Gītā*, such as chapter 6, but this is not the dominant meaning of the word in the text.

15. As noted, the *Gītā* does contain one extended engagement with meditative practices (chapter 6) and does contain some discussion of breathing techniques

(chapter 4), but these too are all in the service of compelling Arjuna to fight political enemies. For the dating of the *Pātañjalāya Yogaśāstra* to around the sixth century CE, see Philip Maas, *Samādhipāda: das erste Kapitel des Pātañjalayogaśāstra zum ersten Mal Kritisch ediert* (Aachen: Shaker, 2006). The *Kaṭha Upaniṣad* is often cited as the first text to describe yoga as psychosomatic practice in detail, but this text cannot be dated to a period earlier than the *Gītā* and was most likely composed around the same time. However, the *Kaṭha Upaniṣad* can hardly be described as a systematic text; it is more of a parable.
16. See Ayesha Jalal, *The Sole Spokesman: Jinnah, the Muslim League, and the Demand for Pakistan* (Cambridge: Cambridge University Press, 1985); and Eleanor Zelliot, *From Untouchable to Dalit: Essays on the Ambedkar Movement* (New Delhi: Manohar Publications, 1992).
17. After Gandhi, the term continued to have new interpreters among Indian nationalists, such as K. B. Hedgewar (1889–1940) and V. N. "Vinoba" Bhave (1895–1982).
18. These ideas are contained in Tilak's *Gītā Rahasya*, composed in 1915, which Gandhi may also have taken with him to prison, thus evading government censors.
19. Dalit is a self-designation of some of India's "Untouchable" communities; the word means "downtrodden" and is associated with the Dalit leader Dr. B. R. Ambedkar and his many followers and admirers.
20. We note here Macaulay's "Minute on Education" in 1935. Thomas Babington Macaulay and G. M. Young, *Speeches by Lord Macaulay, with His Minute on Indian Education* (London: Oxford University Press, H. Milford, 1935).
21. Although it is important to note that Gandhi was not a Brahmin but a high-caste Bania. Similarly, Aurobindo Ghose was a high-caste Kayastha. However, Rai, Tilak, Hedgewar, and Bhave were all Brahmins, as were most of India's many other nationalist leaders of Hindu origin.
22. Joseph S. Alter, *Gandhi's Body: Sex, Diet, and the Politics of Nationalism* (Philadelphia: University of Pennsylvania Press, 2000); and Mark Singleton, *Yoga Body: The Origins of Modern Posture Practice* (Oxford: Oxford University Press, 2010).
23. See Michelle Goldberg, *The Goddess Pose: The Audacious Life of Indra Devi, the Woman Who Helped Bring Yoga to the West* (New York: Vintage, 2016).
24. See Janaki Nair, *Mysore Modern: Rethinking the Region Under Princely Rule* (Minneapolis: University of Minnesota Press, 2011); and Chandan Gowda, "'Advance Mysore!' The Cultural Logic of a Developmental State," *Economic and Political Weekly* 45, no. 29 (July 2010): 88–95.
25. Michelle Goldberg recently argued in response to the Ottawa yoga course cancellation that many who see yoga as having been taken from India or from Hindus by Western colonialism ignore the fact that during the late colonial period the purposeful spread of yoga to the world was a way to combat, resist, and undermine Western colonialism, and was chiefly undertaken by Indians. See Goldberg, *The Goddess Pose*.
26. Each year the "yoga industry" in America grows steadily, far outstripping any yoga industry in any other nation-state, including India. From around $6.9 billion sales in 2015, yoga now generates around $10 billion yearly in revenue in the United States, projected to crest $12 billion by 2021. The majority of this revenue was

created by yoga classes in the United States rather than merchandise, like the infamous yoga pants. In 2008, around 18 million people reported practicing yoga in the last twelve months, and as of 2015 the number grew to 25 million. Yoga is both a career and a product in contemporary capitalist America. See Statista, "Our Research and Content Philosophy," https://www.statista.com/aboutus/our-research-commitment (accessed May 30, 2020).

27. Many scholars have begun to study yoga tourism in India. For example: J. P. S. Jammu, "Yoga Tourism in India," *International Journal of Information Movement* 1, no. 8 (2016): 1–6; Ewelina Telej and Jordan Robert Gamble, "Yoga Wellness Tourism: A Study of Marketing Strategies in India," *Journal of Consumer Marketing* 36, no. 6 (2019): 794–805; C. B. Maddox, "Studying at the Source: Ashtanga Yoga Tourism and the Search for Authenticity in Mysore, India," *Journal of Tourism and Cultural Change* 13, no. 4 (2015): 330–43; and N. Pangti, Sanjay Nainwal, and Uttaranchal Tourism Development Board, *Destination Wellness: Yoga, Meditation and Ayurveda in Uttaranchal* (Dehradun: [Uttaranchal Tourism Development Board]: Distributed by Natraj Publishers, 2004).

28. Lisa Lau, "Re-Orientalism: The Perpetuation and Development of Orientalism by Orientals," *Modern Asian Studies* 43, no. 2 (2009): 571–90; and Lisa Lau and Ana Mendes, *Re-Orientalism and South Asian Identity Politics the Oriental Other Within* (London; New York: Routledge, 2011).

29. Andrew Foote, "Free Yoga Class Returns to uOttawa Student Centre," CBC News. January 24, 2016. https://www.cbc.ca/news/canada/ottawa/free-yoga-class-returns-to-uottawa-student-centre-1.3417817.

30. Andrea R. Jain, *Selling Yoga: From Counterculture to Pop Culture* (Oxford: Oxford University Press, 2015).

31. Sanjoy Chakravorty, Devesh Kapur, and Nirvikar Singh, *The Other One Percent: Indians in America* (New York: Oxford University Press, 2017). Despite including a breadth of the data, criticism of the book notes that it perpetuates a "model minority myth" by leaving out or underrepresenting more working-class diaspora communities. For example, the book focuses on data in the wake of the 1965 rules that reordered U.S. immigration, leaving out the older diasporic communities from the late nineteenth and early twentieth centuries. Also left out are substantial double-diaspora communities, such as Indo-Caribbean and Indo-Fijjian immigrants. Despite such criticism, the work remains an important measure of demographics of the Indian diaspora in the United States.

32. See the SAAPYA blog, https://saapya.wordpress.com (accessed May 30, 2020).

33. See Chakravorty et al., *The Other One Percent*; and Devesh Kapur, *Diaspora, Development, and Democracy: The Domestic Impact of International Migration from India* (Princeton, N.J.: Princeton University Press, 2010).

34. See World Bank, "Poverty and Equity Brief, South Asia: India," April 2020, https://databank.worldbank.org/data/download/poverty/33EF03BB-9722-4AE2-ABC7-AA2972D68AFE/Global_POVEQ_IND.pdf.

35. The figures for Scheduled Tribes and Scheduled Castes are according to the 2011 census by the Indian government; the Other Backward Class figures are either

based on extrapolations from older census data or figures supplied by various state governments and commissions.
36. Prachi Patankar, "The Ghosts of Yogas Past and Present," *Jadaliyya*, February 26, 2014.
37. A version of this idea is at the core of the work of figures such as Jotirao Phule, Savitribai Phule, and Dr. B. R. Ambedkar, among many others.
38. See Maari Zwick-Maitreyi, Thenmozhi Soundararajan, Natasha Dar, Ralph F. Bheel, and Prathap Balakrishnan, *Caste in the United States: A Survey of Caste among South Asian Americans* (Equality Labs, USA, 2018); and Sonia Paul, "When Caste Discrimination Comes to the United States," *NPR*, April 25, 2018.
39. See the review essay by Ananya Chakravarti, "Caste Wasn't a British Construct— and Anyone Who Studies History Should Know That," *The Wire* (June 30, 2019).
40. See Sunila Kale and Christian Lee Novetzke, "Some Reflections on Yoga as Political Theology," *The Wire*, January 28, 2016; and Sunila Kale and Christian Lee Novetzke, "Yoga and the Means and Ends of Secularism," *The Wire* (June 21, 2017).

12

Border Religion

ELIZABETH SHAKMAN HURD

It is common for critics of U.S. imperialism to accuse religion and religious institutions of facilitating political domination while others applaud religion's role as a democratizing and pacifying agent, both domestically and in foreign affairs.[1] To varying degrees these rival accounts share an assumption that it is possible to differentiate religion from nonreligion, whether to condemn or celebrate its role in governance. This assumption is the hubris of secularism. An impressive amount of legal, moral, and political speech and action takes for granted an unquestioned boundary between religion and other domains. Traversing the political spectrum, inside and beyond the academy, this boundary is so deeply sedimented that it can be difficult to see.[2] Its capacity to span or erase the Right/Left political divide makes it nearly impossible to challenge.

This chapter examines this unstable distinction between religion and nonreligion in the contemporary United States. It brings it into sharper focus using three heuristics of the border between the "religious" and the "political": failure, submersion, and subterfuge. Each shows a different aspect of the uncertain frontier between the categories and the concerns that arise for state power and for the production of knowledge. The first involves the perception of *border failure* between the religious and the political in the politics of "countering violent extremism" (CVE). The second involves the fear of *border submersion* and religious impostorhood in religious asylum-seeking proceedings. The third involves disputes over *border subterfuge* and the concern that the religion/nonreligion boundary has been concealed in the interest of American power and should now be revealed to either celebrate or condemn religion's role in American imperialism. Many critics of American empire seek to "out" the role of religion in general, and American Protestantism in particular, as a nefarious force in American imperialism, while those celebrating American power and hegemony point to its positive contributions. While bordering practices around religion operate differently in each case, all rely on and contribute to the production of a stable religion / not religion boundary where it otherwise would not exist. All share an urgent sense that border work must be done.[3] This chapter explores that sense of urgency and the stakes attached to it. The ambiguity surrounding the border between religion and nonreligion is, I suggest, an important site of politics. It is at least in part through the politics of religion that Americans draw and maintain boundaries between domestic and foreign, home and abroad, and free and unfree.[4] The politics of the border are consistently elided, however, including by most historians and scholars of international relations, as important sites of authority at home, in foreign policy, and in jurisdictions considered "foreign in a domestic sense." What might it look like to study the United States in global context if we began with the assumption that the assignment of religiousness or nonreligiousness as qualities of actions, institutions, or policies is an *effect* of particular historically located patterns, habits, affects, and practices—and that these effects are deeply imbricated with the construction and reproduction of borders between domestic and foreign, citizen and alien, home and abroad?

BORDER FAILURE

Critics of CVE programs describe them as a solution in search of a problem. Yet, for many proponents, the problem is border failure, a failure to distinguish between proper religious identities and actions and their political or secular counterparts. This inability on the part of the impaired subject to mark and maintain a proper line between religion and not religion legitimates differential and discriminatory treatment at home, at border crossings, and, increasingly, all over the world.[5]

CVE programs are designed to manage the apparent risk that American Muslims (among others) may fail to discriminate between legitimate religion (that is: sincere faith) and illegitimate religion/politics (specifically: violent politics or extremism), which could result in a collapse of the appropriate boundary between religion and politics. This is the problem of border failure. In this view, a subject's incapacity to recognize when their faith or worldview is being illegitimately twisted and politicized is a symptom of border failure. It may be willful misrecognition or it may be intentional—it is difficult to say. In either case, the rational and reasonable subject is transformed into a "puppet" who is at risk of radicalization.[6] For the prospective reformer, then, border failure is a generalized pathology that inclines subjects toward anti-American views and perhaps even violence.

Attempts to remedy border failure abound in CVE interventions at home and abroad.[7] This thinking is brought to life in the FBI's interactive website to counter violent extremism, "Don't Be a Puppet: Pull Back the Curtain on Violent Extremism."[8] The Bureau defines violent extremism as "encouraging, condoning, justifying, or supporting the commission of a violent act to achieve political, ideological, religious, social, or economic goals." According to the Countering Violent Extremism Pilot Initiative Multidisciplinary Threat Assessment & Intervention Working Group, violent extremists are "individuals who support or commit ideologically motivated violence to further social and political goals."[9] CVE initiatives were on the rise long before the Trump administration took office: a 2008 budget request revealed the number of FBI informants to be at least fifteen thousand domestically, or roughly ten times the number of informants active during the era of J. Edgar Hoover and COINTELPRO.[10] In 2016 the Department of Homeland Security announced funding of nearly $1 billion for "state, local, tribal, and territorial efforts" through the Homeland Security Grant Program, with CVE designated as a domestic program priority.[11] The Obama administration "dramatically elevated CVE in the international agenda" in developing a "preventative, civilian-led framework."[12]

Proponents of CVE describe it as a social and psychological intervention that is neither theological nor political. The FBI has said, "It is not the role or goal of the SRC [shared responsibility committees, see below] to influence an individual's core political or religious beliefs."[13] Self-positioning above the political and religious fray and operating from an allegedly universal and a-cultural position, CVE projects emphasize rights, democracy, compassion, public health, tolerance, and peaceful dissent.[14] Focusing on what proponents describe as "concerning pre-criminal" social and psychological behavior, deradicalization programs are presented as standing apart from religion and politics. They depoliticize and dereligionize.[15] They present themselves as dealing with community health and welfare. The FBI, for instance, has sought to develop "shared responsibility committees," as mentioned above, that enlist local mental health professionals, religious leaders, teachers, local law enforcement, and social workers to develop strategies to counter violent extremism. The bureau is careful to specify that the goal of shared responsibility committees is "disengagement," defined as "the social and psychological process whereby an individual's commitment to violence is reduced to such an extent that he/she is no longer at risk of using violence as a solution to a grievance."[16] The aim is to shape behavior or, in the lingo of a Minneapolis CVE program that targets Somali Americans, to "build resilience to" violent extremism, and not to change beliefs.[17] The "core religious" aspects—presumably beliefs—remain untouched.

This framing upholds the opposition between good religion and bad religion that is at the core of these programs. The distinction is between good religion as legitimate faith, on one hand, and bad religion as distortions thereof culminating in undesirable forms of political dissent or even violence, on the other. In policing this distinction, CVE quietly pathologizes political dissent.[18] The failure to know the difference between a proper religion/politics distinction and a distorted, violent, or anachronistic one makes these programs appear necessary. By purporting to know and protect against the illegitimate politicization of religion ("don't be a puppet"), the FBI and its partners are the brokers of these borders. This appeals across the political divide, as Nadia Marzouki explains: "By upholding this opposition between religion as faith and political religion, the discourse of intellectuals and liberal lawyers of all religious backgrounds reinforces a certain 'teleological' conception of democracy and of the relation between religions in America. According to this narrative, all minorities were first the object of suspicion and attacks, but by progressively adapting to American culture, they were finally able to put these suspicions to rest."[19]

CVE combines this teleological conception of democracy with special concerns about Islam in relation to the border between safe religion and dangerous and distorted political religion. In its Americanized "good Muslim" mode, Islam is depicted as nonthreatening and defanged—a faith like any other.[20] In its "political religion" or "bad life choice" mode, it is depicted as a subversive social disorder that is prone to violence. In this view, Islam is no longer a religion, or no longer only a religion, but something more. Newt Gingrich and David Yerushalmi, leading anti-Sharia advocates, associate Islam with violent extremism and present it as a comprehensive (and threatening) political and legal system. As such, they suggest, it should be exempt in U.S. constitutional controversies from the free exercise protections of the First Amendment. They see it as a distorted and unwieldy form of pathological politics and not as religion in the sense of the term in the U.S. Constitution.[21]

CVE aims for a stable border between real religion, on the one hand, and unwelcome "political" religion, on the other. Remedies are built on this foundation. CVE positions itself as separate from legitimate religion and above politics, grounded in an American ideal of religious freedom. This is what allows liberals and conservatives alike to assert that CVE is compatible, and even complementary, with legal guarantees for religious freedom, despite its evident concern with the religious practices of its targets. In this view, CVE improves on the religious and political freedom of its subjects rather than negating it. It is a salutary intervention that ensures that the part of these subjects (Muslim, not Muslim, it doesn't have to be and perhaps cannot be specified) that is drawn to violence, anti-American, anti-Western, or pro-Palestinian politics is renounced as heretical.[22]

According to this narrative, the psychological element that allegedly inhabits radicals who sympathize with Black Lives Matter or with Palestinians living in the occupied territories simply cannot be isolated as *religious* belief. True religious belief locates and forms a kernel of truth that the state cannot and should not access or influence. It remains untouched. But the rest, the remainder, can and must be tamed, sculpted, and even converted into the naturalized and unmarked autonomous universal subject of disestablished American religious and political tolerance. This is the message of the FBI's interactive game: don't allow others to control your behavior. Don't allow your real self to be overtaken by outside forces that seek to rob you of your agency. Don't be a fanatic.

There are many critics of CVE, and they are vocal.[23] For Arun Kundnani, CVE is an unwelcome state attempt to control deviant or defiant citizens in accordance with the state's political agenda—it is about politics. CVE and other counter-radicalization programs, he argues, produce knowledge in the service of state security that is neither objective nor connected to the real causes of violence, which are difficult if not impossible to identify.[24] While there is something to this argument, Kundnani also misses something important: specifically, these projects *require* an idea of religion. A particular idea of religion authorizes the distinction between disestablished, tolerant, permissible American religion, on one hand, and foreign, overly politicized, distorted "bad life choice" extremism, on the other. Extremism, they say, is not religion. Real religion is free; it is pro-American; it does not resist the desires of the American government. This settlement authorizes the tame and defanged religion that speaks the language of CVE, interfaith harmony, and American religious freedom. It accords with the fluctuating religion / not religion distinction of disestablished protestant Christianity discussed in the introduction to this volume. It quietly marks out that which is disciplined and silenced. This unspoken residual is not and could never be part of one's legitimate "core religious and political beliefs" and so must be discarded. Once this potentially violent and unstable excess is excised, the reasonable and tolerant subject shorn of destabilizing religiopolitical zeal emerges naturally. The border between American religion and its others is secured. Everyone can exhale.

Self-authorizing as neither religion nor politics but as a teachable moment of American—even universal—values, CVE participates in a "scrum of fictions about authorizing presence and foundations for intervention."[25]

BORDER SUBMERSION

In religious asylum cases it is the prospect of border submersion that structures discourse around religion and its borders. In many of these cases, the line between religion and nonreligion is understood to be important but hidden from view. Religion or nonreligion is submerged in the individual subject. Professional tactics and training are required to unearth the subject's presumably stable religious or nonreligious identities and affiliations. Unlike CVE, in which the object is to police the proper border between religion and not religion (understood as extremist politics, psychological disorder, and so on) in religious asylum cases, the object is to surface and verify a submerged and often disputed religious or nonreligious identity. That identity matters because it serves as the alleged grounds for persecution. To claim religious asylum, authentic or sincere religiosity has to be named and brought into the light of day. Like CVE, the process both presupposes and establishes a border between authentic and imposter religion.

The religion / not religion border assumes different legal significance in different asylum proceedings. There is no hard and fast rule. Grounds for claiming asylum are complex and often inscrutable. They vary depending on jurisdiction, judge, and other factors. Yet, in these proceedings, the outcome can often hinge on whether the authorities are successful in ascertaining and authenticating the religious identity of the claimant. As a former U.S. asylum officer put it, "as an officer you can never be informed enough about all the religions and subgroups." But, she continues, if one is unsure, there may be other ways to determine what religious group a person belongs to, such as their name or choice of clothing, depending on which country they come from. If that is not the case, "we might ask about behavior or how they practice their religion."[26] Nailing it down is a matter of asking the right questions or observing clothing, class, and manners. But it must be done.

This methodical and even clinical search for submerged religion is at the center of Michael Nijhawan's excellent legal ethnography of the German asylum courts' treatment of the Sikh and Ahmadiyya diasporas.[27] Examining the sociolegal context in which German asylum judges adjudicate Ahmadi asylum claims, Nijhawan describes the decision-making processes that go into the establishment of the line between the religious and nonreligious subject. He explains that where such lines are understood to fall can determine whether an individual is granted asylum. Put simply, "to get asylum in Germany on religious grounds you have to be a person with a religious personality."[28] Religiosity, in turn:

> is assessed in the courts as an opaque state, entirely subjective and yet paradoxically in need of certainty for the legal process of granting Ahmadis asylum (based on religious persecution) to make sense. It becomes imperative for the courts to determine what counts as normalcy in religious terms and especially so when particular identities bear the mark of either too little or too much of such religion in the current immigration discourse.[29]

The need for certainty requires that courts undertake credibility assessments, which are at "the core of the judicial process." In international contexts in particular, he suggests, "the reference to credibility assessments (also known as "refugee status determination" or RSD) is especially contentious."[30] This is because "in scenarios of religious persecution, courts engage in RSD to make categorical distinctions between legitimate refugees and so-called religious impostors." Citing Michael Kagan, Nijhawan concludes that "when asylum adjudicators set out to decide whether to accept such refugee claims, they can quickly find themselves administering a process akin to a religious trial."[31]

Like their German counterparts, U.S. asylum courts also face dilemmas involving religious sincerity.[32] Immigration judges and appeals courts have to locate and authenticate religious identity in relation to a broader set of circumstances. In some cases, religious identities may be unclear or "submerged" in the individual, generating suspicion among judges who are on the lookout for fake, insincere, or "noncredible" claims. The risk of religious imposterhood haunts these proceedings. In a 1997 split decision concerning an Iranian who practiced Christianity in the United States, *United States v. Bastanipour*, the U.S. Seventh Circuit rejected the asylum claim on grounds of insincerity.[33] Kagan explains that although the applicant had regularly attended church services in the United States, "the immigration judge concluded that he was not genuine in his conversion to Christianity because he did not know the names of the twelve apostles." According to the Seventh Circuit, which reviewed the decision:

> With the Court's understanding that Christianity begins with the life and teaching of Jesus Christ in the New Testament, the 12 apostles have some of the most important, if not the most important, writings of Christianity.... The

respondent's knowledge about Christianity [was presented] to the Court in such general terms that any person of any religion can come up with that description of their religion, namely peace, tranquility, and love.[34]

Judge Marsha S. Berzon dissented, countering that the immigration judge had asked the wrong question. In her view, "the question is not what Toufighi believes but what Iran understands him to believe—or, more accurately, not to believe. It is thoroughly plausible that because he attends Christian services and belongs to a Christian church, Toufighi will be taken to have renounced Islam."[35] A stable and verifiable line between religion and not religion is essential to the authentication of the claimant's religious identity. "True conversion" matters, as the Seventh Circuit confirms:

> Certainly true conversion does matter in one sense. If one is a believer in a religious faith, one would presumably wish to practice that faith. Religious adherence could take the form of attending services, meeting with others of the same faith, personal prayer, or openly sharing one's belief, to name a few examples. If any activity necessary to a convert could trigger persecution in Iran, such a practice should be brought to the attention of the immigration judge. To evaluate the relevance of this practice to the life of the alien, the immigration judge should be satisfied with the sincerity of the alien's new religious commitment.[36]

The judges expressed concern about the "sincerity of the alien's new religious commitment." A commitment that is not verifiably religious or that is religious but insincere cannot serve as legitimate grounds for asylum.

Like CVE, religious asylum requires an idea of religion. What does it entail to be a sincere believer? What does it look like to be authentically religious? Or nonreligious?[37] Unlike CVE, however, in which the object is to patrol the boundary between true religion and false religion (with the latter conceived as extremist politics, psychological disorder, and so on), in the religious asylum context, the object is to surface and authenticate a submerged religious or nonreligious identity. A firm and verifiable religion / not religion border anchors these secular processes. One does not receive religious asylum for holding dissenting political views. The judge draws the line. This line does not precede these processes but is, at least in part, an effect of them, as claimants strive to present themselves in terms that are legible to the authorities. The politics of religious asylum, then, not only reflects but helps to create a border between religion and not religion. The designation of a particular individual as either authentically religious or as an impostor is a product of these proceedings.

BORDER SUBTERFUGE

The term "border subterfuge" refers to the conviction that the religion/nonreligion border has been intentionally hidden or obscured in the interest of American hegemony. Curiously, this idea is shared in various forms across the American political spectrum. Critics of U.S. empire seek to reveal the nefarious hidden power of religion in general, and Protestantism in particular, as a driving force in American global and imperial ambitions, while those who celebrate American power and hegemony pay tribute to the contributions made by religious traditions to liberty, security, and freedom at home and abroad.

Both narratives obscure the more complex realities of U.S. domestic and foreign religion policy and politics that are the subject of this volume. Both presume that religion can be cleanly distinguished from nonreligion and disembedded from its social, legal, and historical context. The religion/nonreligion border is taken for granted. The notion that Christianity in its various guises has driven and continues to direct behind the scenes American imperial practices at home and abroad unwittingly amplifies the arguments of those who celebrate protestant Christianity's supposedly unalloyed contributions to modernity, morality and freedom. The two sides face off and feed off each other in a kind of circular culture war. Both narratives contribute to creating a religion / not religion divide when in reality this boundary is often absent, amorphous, or Janus-faced. The presumption of an organized and ontologically fixed border between religion and not religion feeds the culture war as each side digs in. The prospect of border subterfuge and the need to either condemn or vindicate religion fuels the flames.

The real action lies elsewhere. In her book *Islam: An American Religion*, Nadia Marzouki offers a welcome alternative to the seesaw of either celebrating or condemning protestant Christianity in projects of American governance. Her ethnography of the affective politics of belonging to the Tea Party, antimosque, and anti-Sharia movements in the early twenty-first-century United States vividly captures the fluidity of the religion / not religion border. Meetings of these groups, she shows, are rituals that affirm particular forms of public solidarity that can only be reduced to "public Christianity" at significant cost:

> "Christian America" functions therefore as a floating signifier that refers to different conceptions of America and to diverse religious doctrines. The reiteration of allegiance to this floating signifier forges the unity of this movement. Events organized by the Tea Party, antimosque demonstrations, and anti-Sharia

demonstrations are not experienced as forums where one comes to debate or lecture but as rituals through which reaffirms solidarity with the group. One participates less out of a sense of belonging to a Christian doctrine and more to restate one's faith in America, in the sovereignty of "We the people," and in the Constitution.[38]

The religion / not religion demarcation is not especially relevant to the substance and texture of these affiliations, affects, and forms of solidarity. "One participates less out of a sense of belonging to a Christian doctrine," Marzouki writes, "and more to restate one's faith in America, in the sovereignty of 'We the people,' and in the Constitution."[39] Christian Novetske and Sunila Kale make a related point in this volume in their discussion of the politics of yoga. Conflicting and shifting transnational political and religious appropriations of yoga make it impossible to pin down what yoga actually "is" in any definitive sense. As they suggest, "the movement of yoga from India to the United States ... bore the marks of yoga's transformed presence in the early twentieth century—as a powerful anticolonial tool but also one that rested on a homogenized Indian identity built around a singular high-caste, upper-class Hindu archetype."

I became aware of the bipartisan appeal of the notion of border subterfuge and the political stakes attached to it after writing my book *Beyond Religious Freedom*. That book argues that global advocacy for religious freedom protects and privileges particular kinds of religious (believing and unbelieving) subjects and produces subjects and faith communities for whom choosing and believing are seen as the defining characteristic of what it is to be religious, and the right to choose to believe is seen as the essence of what it means to be free.[40] U.S. advocacy for religious freedom, then, is understood in terms of the rise of a particular economy of belief and unbelief and its imbrication with modern ideas of religion, American hegemony, and the free market. The discourse of religious freedom is a historically contingent economy of belief and unbelief that is simultaneously protestant and not protestant, American and universal.

Some critics have read this argument through the lens of border subterfuge as a condemnation of U.S. religious, and specifically protestant Christian, imperialism.[41] By interpreting what was intended as a study of the politics of religious freedom in all of its forms as an indictment of American religious imperialism *tout court*, these critics reduced the argument to an exercise in "naming and shaming" an unflattering history of U.S.-sponsored protestant hegemony traveling under the beneficent guise of religious freedom. In this reading, the book is little more than a thinly veiled attempt to call out border subterfuge—that is, the obscuring of the powerful role of religion in the interest of American power and hegemony. Depending on one's view, then, the book either successfully or unsuccessfully "outs" Protestantism in general, and protestant notions of religious freedom in particular, as a motivating force in American imperialism. This (mis)interpretation makes it easy to dismiss critics of American religious freedom advocacy as secular leftists who are out to scorn religion and scold religionists.

This is a mistaken reading of my book, and it relies on a fixed religion / not religion border that my work eschews. Religion is not just *there*, in my reading. It is neither uniformly a force for good nor a force for evil. The existence of the border between religion and nonreligion cannot go unquestioned. Focusing on the instability of this border, as I do in this chapter, suggests that some critics and defenders of American empire may share more than they realize in their approach to religion, with the former seeking to "out" religion as an engine of U.S. domestic and foreign imperialism and the latter celebrating it as a tool of benevolent hegemony and purveyor of political and economic freedom.

CONCLUSION: THE GREATER UNITED STATES

Over a century ago a group of historians at the University of Wisconsin coined the term "the greater United States" to gesture toward something beyond the logo map of the United States that most Americans learn to recognize in elementary school. August Ohman's 1904 pocket map depicts the greater United States between 1804 and 1904, including the Philippines, Alaska, Hawaii, Guam, Wake Island, American Samoa, Puerto Rico, and the Panama Canal Zone.

William Appleman Williams and the so-called Wisconsin school popularized the notion of the greater United States to include westward expansion, the acquisition of overseas territories, and overseas military bases. As historian Daniel Immerwahr explains, "Williams's school regarded 1898 as symptomatic rather than substantive: the small and visible tip of a much larger imperial iceberg. It was a moment when the United States briefly flirted with outright territorial conquest before turning toward other, harder-to-see forms of global power."[42]

Borders between religion and nonreligion are among these harder-to-see forms of power. They are real but constructed, elusive but ever-present, even—and perhaps especially—for those who rely on them to order the world. Borders between religion and nonreligion serve the aims of today's version of the greater United States in ways that are not well understood at home, abroad, or in jurisdictions

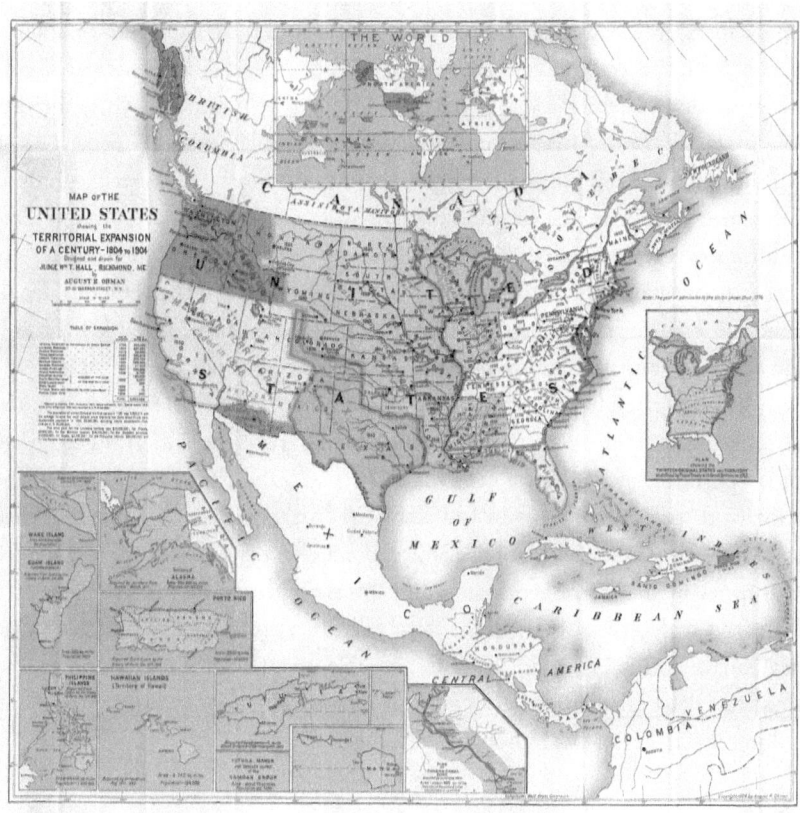

FIGURE 12.1 August Ohman 1904 pocket map.

David Rumsey Map Collection.

considered "foreign in a domestic sense."[43] Scholars of empire, counterterrorism advocates and experts, asylum judges and border officials, scholars of religion and law, and Indigenous religious rights activists all rely on these borders. The ambiguity that surrounds them is an important site of politics.[44]

Extolling freedom at home and regretting establishment abroad does not come close to capturing the politics of American religion at the intersection of the domestic and foreign. Borders around religion and borders around America work in tandem in ways that are not well understood. There is, however, a theological and teleological conviction in the United States that America as it really is, and as it should be, will come into clearer focus as these borders are clarified and secured. Earlier in this volume, Courtney Bender describes a future-oriented American political theology that lends force to this exceptionalist narrative: "This form of American exceptionalism is at its core religious. From the chapel and the mountaintop, from the jet window or the poem, its open-aired sublime renews a messianic aspiration for the nation. It activates a hope that no matter what, the real America is still coming into being, just beyond the visible horizon."

To unsettle the religion / not religion distinction allows us to catch a glimpse of this form of American exceptionalism. It allows us to rethink received understandings of Christianity as (or only as) a religion, following Gil Anidjar.[45] It teaches us to live with the blurriness of the edges between the religious, legal, economic, environmental, and political.[46] This can be uncomfortable for those who resist the political and religious uncertainties of nonseparationist ontologies. Yet many are already working in these spaces. Marzouki finds that evangelical Protestantism is "certainly an important part of the American religious landscape, but its power is not hegemonic."[47] In a study of the partial implementation of British colonial law in India and Sri Lanka, Keally McBride says that "it is interesting to study colonial legalities precisely because they are so evidently determined by the interests of power. But this is not the entire story to be told."[48] The essays collected in this volume also tell other stories. One could say that they "impossibilify" religion as a differentiable quantity that can influence the American project without being merged into it. There is no single recipe for striking this balance, but I know it when I see it.[49]

NOTES

1. On religion and religious institutions facilitating political domination, see, for example, Walter A. McDougall, *The Tragedy of U.S. Foreign Policy: How America's Civil Religion Betrayed the National Interest* (New Haven, Conn.: Yale University Press, 2018). To their credit, others refuse these terms entirely; see, for instance, Melani McAlister, *The Kingdom of God Has No Borders: A Global History of American Evangelicals* (Oxford: Oxford University Press, 2018); Emily Conroy-Krutz, *Christian Imperialism: Converting the World in the Early American Republic* (Ithaca, N.Y.: Cornell University Press, 2015); Andrew Preston, *Sword of the Spirit, Shield of Faith: Religion in American War and Diplomacy* (New York: Knopf, 2012); and Steven K. Green, *Inventing a Christian America: The Myth of the Religious Founding* (Oxford: Oxford University Press, 2015). On critiques of U.S. imperial power on Christian theological grounds, see Harold K. Bush Jr., "Christianity, Literature, and American Empire," *Christianity and Literature* 62, no. 3 (Spring 2013): 419–40.
2. This is evident in Anna Su's *Exporting Freedom*, which alternates between asserting that conflicting notions of religious freedom animated U.S. occupations of the

Philippines, Japan, and Iraq, and invoking an idealized notion of religious freedom to make generalizing claims about its role in U.S. diplomatic and military history. In the latter mode, and most notably in the chapter on the U.S. occupation of Japan, Su adopts a reverential discourse ("religious freedom finally emerged as a reality") that is at odds with the historical evidence she uses to develop her cases. Anna Su, *Exporting Freedom: Religious Liberty and American Power* (Cambridge, Mass.: Harvard University Press, 2016), 133.

3. I explore these questions in my current book project, *Religion on the Border*.

4. Paul Kramer writes that "the very terms 'domestic' and 'foreign' as actors' categories forged in struggles over space, sovereignty, and boundary-making, the work of cartographers and border guards, the tremendous power of which can only be apprehended if they are discarded as terms of art." Paul A. Kramer, "Power and Connection: Imperial Histories of the United States in the World," *American Historical Review* 116, no. 5 (December 2011): 1357, https://doi.org/10.1086/ahr.116.5.1348.

5. CVE travels under different names and is frequently renamed even as the interventions remain largely unchanged. The most recent (spring 2020) Department of Homeland Security programming in this area travels under the heading of "Targeted Violence and Terrorism Prevention."

6. "The concept of 'radicalisation' emerged as a vehicle for policy-makers to explore the process by which a terrorist was made and to provide an analytical grounding for preventative strategies that went beyond the threat of violence or detention," and "by 2004 the term had acquired its new meaning of a psychological or theological process by which Muslims move towards extremist views." Arun Kundnani, "Radicalisation: The Journey of a Concept," *Race & Class* 54, no. 2 (2012): 4, 7.

7. As of late 2017, an estimated two thousand Department of Homeland Security officials were deployed to more than seventy countries around the world. Ron Nixon, "Homeland Security Goes Abroad. Not Everyone is Grateful." *New York Times*, December 26, 2017. https://www.nytimes.com/2017/12/26/world/americas/homeland-security-customs-border-patrol.html.

8. The FBI's "Don't Be a Puppet" program "uses a series of interactive materials to educate teens on the destructive nature of violent extremism and to encourage them to think critically about its messages and goals. The site emphasizes that by blindly accepting radical ideologies, teens are essentially becoming the 'puppets' of violent extremists who simply want them to carry out their destructive mission—which often includes targeting or killing innocent people. The FBI encourages community groups, families, and high schools across the United States to use this site as part of their educational efforts. All Americans are asked to join the FBI in exposing the seductive nature of violent extremist propaganda and offering positive alternatives to violence."

Instructions for navigating the site are as follows: "Go through the five numbered sections in order. Free the puppet in each section and make all of the boxes turn white. Then you will earn an FBI certificate." "Don't Be a Puppet," FBI, https://www.fbi.gov/cve508.

9. From slides shown at a November 3, 2014, meeting organized by the U.S. Attorney's office in Boston. Waqas Mirza, "Boston Finds Muslim Surveillance Program

10. Cora Currier and Murtaza Hussain, "Letter Details FBI Plan for Secretive Radicalization Committees," *Intercept*, April 28, 2016, https://theintercept.com/2016/04/28/letter-details-fbi-plan-for-secretive-anti-radicalization-committees/. COINTELPRO, short for Counter Intelligence Program, refers to a series of covert surveillance, infiltration, disruption, and destabilization projects undertaken in the 1950s–1970s by the FBI against groups that had been deemed subversive by the U.S. government; see part 3 of Sylvester Johnson, *African American Religions, 1500–2000* (Cambridge: Cambridge University Press, 2015). On the 2008 budget request, see Steven Aftergood, "The FBI as an Intelligence Organization, *Secrecy News*, Federation of American Scientists," August 27, 2007, https://fas.org/blogs/secrecy/2007/08/the_fbi_as_an_intelligence_org/.

11. "Fiscal Year (FY) 2016 Funding for State and Local Government Programs for Countering Violent Extremism," U.S. Department of Homeland Security, Office of Community Partnerships (Washington, D.C., February 29, 2016), https://www.dhs.gov/sites/default/files/publications/FY2016%20Homeland%20Security%20Grant%20Program%20Fact%20Sheet_1.pdf.

12. Former undersecretary of state for civilian security, democracy, and human rights Sarah Sewell, cited in Naz Modirzadeh, "If It's Broke, Don't Make it Worse: A Critique of the U.N. Secretary-General's Plan of Action to Prevent Violent Extremism," *Lawfare* (blog), January 23, 2016, https://www.lawfareblog.com/if-its-broke-dont-make-it-worse-critique-un-secretary-generals-plan-action-prevent-violent-extremism.

13. The FBI letter is in Currier and Hussain, "Letter Details FBI Plan for Secretive Radicalization Committees."

14. There are many examples. For one illustration, see the website of the October 2018 World Summit on Countering Violence and Extremism, https://www.nonviolencesummit.org.

15. This point is made clearly by Shanifa Nasser, "If You Want to Deradicalize Muslim Youth, Talk More Politics, Less Religion, Say Critics," *CBC*, May 13, 2016. http://www.cbc.ca/news/canada/deradicalization-foreign-policy-1.3562405.

16. The quote comes from an undated FBI letter addressed to potential members of shared responsibility committees; https://www.documentcloud.org/documents/2815794-FBI-SRC-Letter.html. See also Cora Currier and Murtaza Hussain, "Letter Details FBI Plan for Secretive Radicalization Committees," *Intercept*, April 28, 2016, https://theintercept.com/2016/04/28/letter-details-fbi-plan-for-secretive-anti-radicalization-committees/.

17. See "Building Community Resilience Minneapolis-St. Paul Pilot Program A Community-Led Framework," United States Attorney's Office (Minneapolis, MN: February 2015), https://www.justice.gov/usao-mn/file/642121/download. On the impact of these interventions in the Minneapolis Somali-American community, see the forthcoming work of Ahmed Ibrahim of Carleton College. Ibrahim's dissertation is a historical ethnography of a Shari'a-based movement in Mogadishu after the disintegration of the central government in 1991. Ahmed Ibrahim, "The

Shari'a Courts of Mogadishu: Beyond 'African Islam' and 'Islamic Law'" (Ph.D. dissertation, City University of New York, 2018), CUNY Academic Works, https://academicworks.cuny.edu/gc_etds/2520/.

18. "Radicalization theory discounts politicized organizing as a valid response to oppression by the state or by dominant groups. It really flattens the roles and reality of state violence and delegitimizes resistance as nothing more than quote unquote grievances." Maya Dukmasova, "The Problem with the 'Public Health' Approach to Ideological Violence," *Chicago Reader*, December 10, 2018, https://www.chicago reader.com/chicago/the-problem-with-the-public-health-approach-to-ideological -violence/Content?oid=64917858&fbclid=IwAR0VYVp0S_nUOLU7Ufzhatfogu -3SDGctzeT_f_3JjY_8nrixqd3Hrh2om8.

19. Nadia Marzouki, *Islam: An American Religion* (New York: Columbia University Press, 2017), 136.

20. See Marzouki, *Islam*, noting that "the Protestant conception of what counts as a 'true' religion plays an important normative role in the evaluation of Islam, just as it did earlier when it came to the exclusion of Mormons, Catholics, and Jews. But there is no concomitant evangelical Protestant awakening—the reference to Protestant lineage represents only part of the nativist ideology; the rest is composed of a mix of the ideals of equality (but only for the 'elect'), popular sovereignty, civic engagement, and freedom" (154).

21. Nadia Marzouki, "Le mouvement contre le droit islamique et le droit étranger aux États-Unis," *Politique américaine* 1, no. 23 (2014): 37.

22. This helps explain the fierce opposition in the United States to the Boycott, Divestment, and Sanctions movement, a solidarity movement for Palestinian rights that is openly critical of the Israeli occupation, which has gathered political momentum in the United States in recent years. As of early 2019 twenty-seven states had passed measures opposing the movement, including five executive orders issued by state governors. According to the advocacy group Palestine Legal, since 2014 over one hundred measures targeting boycotts and other advocacy for Palestinian rights have been introduced in state and local legislatures and the U.S. Congress. For a list of antiboycott legislation in the United States, see "Anti-Boycott Legislation around the Country" on the Palestine Legal website, https://palestinelegal.org /righttoboycott.

23. Kundnani, "Radicalisation." For a critique of the assumptions underlying radicalization talk, see chapter 4, "The Myth of Radicalization," in Arun Kundnani, *The Muslims Are Coming! Islamophobia, Extremism, and the Domestic War on Terror* (New York: Verso, 2015), 115–52. For a call to abandon the discourse of radicalization due to incoherence, see Mark Sedgwick, "The Concept of Radicalization as a Source of Confusion," *Terrorism and Political Violence* 22, no. 4 (2010): 479–94.

24. I agree with Kundnani on the difficulty of isolating the causes of violence. On this point, see Laleh Kahdivi's beautifully written novel on the life of a young Iranian American from California who ends up fighting in Syria. Laleh Khadivi, *A Good Country* (New York: Bloomsbury, 2017). On the difficulty of assigning causation to collective violence and the preoccupation with motives in the context of the "war

on terror," see Talal Asad, *On Suicide Bombing* (New York: Columbia University Press, 2007).

25. Paul Christopher Johnson, Pamela Klassen, and Winnifred Fallers Sullivan, Introduction to *Ekklesia: Three Inquiries in Church and State* (Chicago: University of Chicago Press, 2018), 8.

26. Megan Brewer, cited in Antonia Blumberg, "Why Trump's Failed Attempt to Prioritize Christian Refugees Never Had a Chance," *Huffington Post*, March 10, 2017, http://www.huffingtonpost.com/entry/why-trumps-failed-attempt-to-prioritize-christian-refugees-never-had-a-chance_us_58bef9bae4b0d841663e3595?linkId=35434890.

27. Michael Nijhawan, *The Precarious Diasporas of Sikh and Ahmadiyya Generations: Violence, Memory, and Agency* (New York: Palgrave Macmillan, 2016).

28. Nijhawan, *Precarious Diasporas*, 131.

29. Nijhawan, *Precarious Diasporas*, 107.

30. Nijhawan, *Precarious Diasporas*, 108.

31. Nijhawan, *Precarious Diasporas*, 108, citing Michael Kagan, "Refugee Credibility Assessment and the Religious Imposter Problem: A Case Study of Eritrean Pentecostal Claims in Egypt," *Vanderbilt Journal of Transnational Law* 43 (2010): 1181.

32. Unlike most other domains, U.S. domestic law has been fairly closely aligned with international refugee and asylum law; see, further, Joan Fitzpatrick, "The International Dimension of U.S. Refugee Law," *Berkeley Journal of International Law* 15, no. 1 (1997): 1–26.

33. *United States v. Bastanipour*, 980 F.2d 1129, 1131 (7th Cir. 1992), cited in Kagan, "Refugee Credibility Assessment," 1220.

34. Cited in Kagan, "Refugee Credibility Assessment," 1222. Judges James K. Singleton and Sandra S. Ikuta upheld the denial of asylum but because of the standard of review in administrative law did not engage directly with the analysis that led to the negative credibility assessment.

35. Cited in Kagan, "Refugee Credibility Assessment," 1221.

36. Cited in Kagan, "Refugee Credibility Assessment," 1222n232.

37. These difficult questions are at the heart of secularism as a modality of governance. While writing this chapter I was contacted by a researcher with ACCORD, part of the Austrian Red Cross, which had been commissioned by the UNHCR to write a report on Iranian atheists for an asylum case. Email from Mag. Daisuke Yoshimura, Austrian Centre for Country of Origin and Asylum Research and Documentation (ACCORD), Österreichisches Sterreichisches Rotes Kruez, GeneralSekretariat, April 28, 2017.

38. Marzouki, *Islam*, 154.

39. Marzouki, *Islam*, 154.

40. Elizabeth Shakman Hurd, "After Religious Freedom?" *Journal of Politics, Religion & Ideology* 18, no. 1 (April 2017): 116; and Elizabeth Shakman Hurd, *Beyond Religious Freedom: The New Global Politics of Religion* (Princeton, N.J.: Princeton University Press, 2015).

41. Daniel Philpott, "Culture War or Common Heritage? On Recent Critics of Global Religious Freedom," *Lawfare*, June 30, 2016, https://www.lawfareblog.com/culture-war-or-common-heritage-recent-critics-global-religious-freedom.

42. Daniel Immerwahr, "The Greater United States: Territory and Empire in U.S. History," *Diplomatic History* 40, no. 3 (2016): 375.

> The conception of a "Greater United States" had largely vanished by the U.S. entry into the First World War. This can be most clearly seen in the realm of the law. In a series of cases from 1901 to 1922, known as the Insular Cases, the Supreme Court considered whether the territories were part of the "United States" as referred to in the Constitution, i.e., it asked whether the Constitution applied to them. Reasoning with a racist logic—the initial cases were decided by the same court that decided *Plessy v. Ferguson*—it concluded that the bulk of the territories were "unincorporated" into the political body of the United States. As one of the justices summarized the logic, the Constitution was "the supreme law of the land," but the territories were "not part of the 'land.'" (381).

See also Daniel Immerwahr, *How to Hide an Empire: A History of the Greater United States* (New York: Farrar, Straus and Giroux, 2019), in which the author explains that the "book's main contribution is not archival, bringing to light some never-before-seen document. It's perspectival, seeing a familiar history differently" (16).

43. Christina Duffy Burnett and Burke Marshall, eds. *Foreign in a Domestic Sense: Puerto Rico, American Expansion and the Constitution* (Durham, N.C.: Duke University Press, 2001).
44. There is always political potential associated with this discursive ambiguity, as Gil Hochberg suggests: "The difficulty of pinning down these terms' (Semitism, Semite, Semitic) meanings, and realizing their relevance to our present-day politics, should by no means discourage us or cause us to abandon them.... There is a great potential associated most directly with the terms' ambiguity; one that grants them a *discursive flexibility*, which I suggest we approach not as a scholarly problem to be solved but as a political opportunity to be sieged." Gil Z. Hochberg, "'Remembering Semitism' *or* 'On the Prospect of Re-Membering the Semites,'" *ReOrient* 1, no. 2 (Spring 2016): 201.
45. Gil Anidjar, "Christianity, Christianities, Christian," *Journal of Religious and Political Practice* 1, no. 1 (2015): 41.
46. Winnifred Fallers Sullivan, Robert A. Yelle, and Mateo Taussig-Rubbo, Introduction to *After Secular Law*, ed. Winnifred Fallers Sullivan, Robert A. Yelle, and Mateo Taussig-Rubbo (Stanford, Calif.: Stanford University Press, 2011), 6.
47. Marzouki, *Islam*, 42. On the dissenting religious left in the United States, see also Nadia Marzouki, "Etats-Unis: La nouvelle guerre de religion a commencé," *Bibliobs*, July 22, 2018, https://bibliobs.nouvelobs.com/idees/20180719.OBS9952/etats-unis-la-nouvelle-guerre-de-religion-a-commence.html.
48. Keally McBride, *Mr. Mothercountry: The Man Who Made the Rule of Law* (Oxford: Oxford University Press, 2016): 67.
49. For exemplary scholarship in this vein, see the work of Nandini Chatterjee, in particular her article "English Law, Brahmo Marriage, and the Problem of Religious Difference: Civil Marriage Laws in Britain and India," *Comparative Studies in Society and History* 52, no. 3 (July 2010): 524–52.

PART IV
Abroad

13
Established Authorities

Theology, the State, and the Apartheid Struggle

MELANI MCALISTER

Let everyone be subject to the governing authorities, for there is no authority except that which God has established. The authorities that exist have been established by God. Consequently, whoever rebels against the authority is rebelling against what God has instituted, and those who do so will bring judgment on themselves.

—Romans 13:1–3 (NIV)

The sufficient statement of the historical significance of the Baptists is this: The competency of the soul in religion.

—E. Y. Mullins[1]

A number of scholars of secularism have carefully analyzed the relationship that secular states imagine themselves to have with the religions that they claim to be separate from. As these scholars point out, in modern secular states, laws that promote religious freedom (and that claim neutrality in relationship to religion) are inevitably not neutral; they are in the business of defining what religion is and is not and thus regulate, select, and limit the practice of religion.[2]

This essay considers a related but different question: how have highly politicized religious actors theorized the state in relation to their practice of faith and politics? In particular, I explore the thinking of a set of evangelical Christians in the United States and South Africa during the apartheid era. In the 1980s Black and white evangelicals in both countries engaged in an intense set of conversations and practices that included a specific reckoning with whether, as evangelicals, they were obliged to show respect for, or to respect the laws of, the white South African government.

The question of what an individual owes their government, and in what circumstances, has animated the followers of Jesus since he commanded them to "render unto Caesar the things that are Caesar's" (Matt. 22:21). I argue that analyzing evangelical ambivalence about the state is crucial to understanding the transformations that have led us to a moment in the twenty-first century when white American evangelicals in particular seem to have few doubts about grasping whatever reins of state power they can find. However, when we consider U.S. evangelicals historically and then situate them in the context of the global religious formation of which they are just one part, evangelical relationships to the state are revealed as deeply fraught and distinctively complicated. In the case I explore here, Baptists play an outsized role, but the debates about theologies of the state are much broader, crossing a number of evangelical lines—national, racial, and denominational.

My argument is that U.S. and South African evangelical considerations of the problem of state power were negotiated in the 1980s through a conversation about biblical interpretation. That conversation, however, was also shaped by networks of relationships that (re)negotiated understandings of race, power, and politics through and within a transnational discussion about the Bible. In those deliberations, South Africa's apartheid policies were made relevant to Americans through a quiet but recognizable conversation about the history of racism and segregation in the United States. American evangelicals, Black and white, responded to debates over apartheid in part through the lens of their own histories. But these responses were not simply replications of the history of civil rights—where African American churches (particularly the mainline protestant churches) played a leading role in the movement and white evangelicals were actively resistant or relatively silent.[3] Instead, the debate about apartheid in the 1980s provided a space for U.S. evangelicals to quietly relitigate the 1960s, with a number of white and Black theologically conservative Christians taking stronger political stances against racism than they had done in their own U.S. contexts. I will argue that the "abroad" component is significant here: some American evangelicals were influenced by their global religious networks to take a stronger stance against apartheid. As Lauren Turek has shown, transnational connections also provided sustenance for those who wanted little or no action against apartheid, as connections between the religious Right in the United

States and the right wing of South African Christianity were solidified.[4] For Americans, no matter what their theological or political leanings, conversations about apartheid never happened outside the implicit context of the history of race and racism in the United States. That U.S. history, in turn, had resonances that shaped understandings of apartheid in South Africa itself, including among South African evangelicals.

The theoretical framework for this analysis is Bruno Latour's actor-network theory. Latour has argued that understanding networks requires first recognizing that they are made of many different types of actors (actants), from humans to animals to technologies to microbes. For Latour, we can consider a technology or a virus to be as significant as people to making the world because they, too, create impacts: "an actant can be literally anything provided it is granted to be the source of the action."[5] My actor-network analysis of evangelicals, then, includes Bible verses as actants, not because Bible verses have independent intent but because they are travelers that do things, crossing borders and demanding interpretation.

In addition, Latour argues, we must be cognizant of how fragile and constantly shifting networks actually are. It might be easy to think of certain networks as quite durable: Wall Street chief executives, many of whom went to the same Ivy League schools, seem like a solid network, as do, say, the network of people and dogs who show at national competitions. But Latour asks us to think about it differently, to see that the activity of making any group, any network, is a *process*, a matter of shifting ties that are forged and unmade, controversies announced and resolved—or not resolved—so that new groups form. Networks are not pathways that neatly link one set of people to another in a solid set of lines; they are associations of people and institutions and resources that take a great deal of work to maintain.

The process is messy, partial. Some people are always tracing boundaries to try to stabilize the group. Latour argues that every group has its unofficial officials, those who work to justify the group's existence and define its rules. (Theologians and Bible commentators, organizational leaders, TV pastors—these are a few of the unofficial officials of the unofficial network of global evangelicalism.) These boundary makers carry out their work as part of a contest, a process of legitimating members (creating nodes in a network) and strengthening ties (drawing the lines between nodes). Groups are not silent things, Latour says, "but rather the provisional product of a constant uproar made by the millions of contradictory voices about what ... pertains to what."[6] In other words, it is not just a matter of debating who is in the network and who is outside; boundary-marking matters, but it is just one component of actor networks. Networks are also made through the matter of deciding "what pertains to what." What Bible verses matter and in what situations? What methods of exposition are acceptable? What topics are "political" and which are "moral?" Who has the authority to speak about politics?

With the loud conversation, heated debates, and shifting terms of the global evangelical network, and with the constant expansion and contraction of its decidedly ragged borders, we can begin to construct the people, institutions, texts, and technologies that matter. Any map we can etch of a living network will look less like those nice drawings we have all seen, of clean lines between stable nodes, and more like the motion of light on water, captured in one instant, transformed in the next.[7] In this essay, I partially trace a set of connections that capture one part of a contentious network that includes institutions of global and national evangelicalisms, the South African state, racist power(s), and the meanings of a cultural text—in this case, the biblical verses of Romans 13:1–7, where the New Testament's vision of a relationship between believers and the state is most fully articulated.

ROMANS 13

Theology is not destiny, but theology matters, not least in the hothouse of doctrine clarification that is evangelical life. The theology of the state that appears in the book of Romans is one of the mostly frequently evoked and politically fraught sites for evangelicals (and other Christians) who want to analyze religion and politics. In general, Paul's letter to the Romans is, in the words of the evangelical theologian John Stott, "the fullest, plainest and grandest statement of the gospel in the New Testament."[8] The importance of the book overall only heightens the complexity that attends verses 1–7 of chapter 13, in which Paul provides advice to the church in Rome about how to respond to "the authorities." There are relatively few other texts in the New Testament that speak to the state, and none do so at such length, with such seeming enthusiasm for the rightfulness of state power. The circulation of Romans 13, in a variety of settings and across a number of boundaries, provides one entrée into the ways that evangelicals have tried to understand what they owe "the authorities that exist" in any given historical moment.

Many recent American commentators on Paul's letter to the Romans have seen it, overall, as simultaneously a statement of the importance of salvation through faith alone and as a discourse about the equality of Jews and Gentiles before God. In this long epistle, Paul lays out a set of arguments about whether it matters to adhere to Jewish law or not, but he also flags tensions that seem to have emerged between Jewish and Gentile believers in the early church. His goal is to link these two components of the text: to show Jews and Gentiles in the Roman church that they should "be devoted to one another in love" (Rom. 12:10, NIV) because God has saved them all, and equally, only through the sacrifice of Jesus.

But Paul goes on to comment, in Romans 13, that believers must nonetheless be subject to the power of the government: "Let everyone be subject to the governing authorities, for there is no authority except that which God has established." Paul goes on: "Consequently, whoever rebels against the authority is rebelling against what God has instituted" (Rom. 13:1–2, NIV). Not surprisingly, these verses have been the subject of a great deal of commentary regarding Christian views of the state. Most commonly, these passages historically have been seen as the basis for a theology of the state—any state—as instantiation of a divinely ordained social order. The text is always fraught, however, since elsewhere in the New Testament the followers of Jesus seem to set themselves apart from, or in opposition to, governmental power. Could it really be that Paul was arguing that all states are ordained by God? Are Christians inevitably beholden to obedience?

Liberal protestants had long argued that Paul was simply telling the Christians of his day that they could not live solely in an otherworldly fashion, that political authority did matter, and they were not entirely exempt from earthly rules. And the *New Oxford Annotated Bible*, for example, argues that Paul's exhortation to obey government was specifically responding to a rising tide of anti-Jewish feeling in the Roman world, and that he was anxious to avoid the kind of civic violence that had roiled some Roman cities and in which Jews were particularly vulnerable.[9]

But believers of various stripes have long used Romans 13 to demand that Christians obey their government, whatever it may be. In North America of the eighteenth and nineteenth centuries, Paul's words were used to insist that the colonists should not rise up against the king, that slaves should not disobey their masters, and pacifists should submit to conscription.[10] Not surprisingly, in the twentieth century, many white segregationists found reasons to quote Romans 13 to African American civil rights activists. (Less well known is that liberals in the Southern Baptist Convention used Romans 13 in the late 1950s to stipulate to their fellow believers that they should comply with government authority in the case of *Brown v. Board*.[11])

Those Christian thinkers who wanted to argue that Christians could and sometimes should disobey the government would often draw upon other scripture, including the chapters on violent and oppressive governments in Revelation. But nearly every major theologian who addresses the state has considered Romans 13 at length; it simply is not possible to think through the state systemically and "read around" Paul's commentary in Romans. Dietrich Bonhoeffer discusses the text in the *Cost of Discipleship*, published in 1937 in Germany. Bonhoeffer's book was a theorization of what it meant for Christians to live under an evil government. In it, he describes Paul as making an argument for Christians to work against evil always by doing good. Paul is making *no* statement, he insists, about the rightness of established government, only the necessity of reacting to such government in a way that does not see secular power as having final authority over Christian life. "No state is entitled to read into St. Paul's words a justification of its own existence," Bonhoeffer wrote.[12] Bonhoeffer's actions were true to his interpretation: *Cost of Discipleship* was one of the last major works Bonhoeffer wrote before being imprisoned and ultimately executed for a planned assassination attempt against Hitler.

At the turn of the twenty-first century, there was a small theological industry around Paul in general and the book of Romans in particular, in which both liberal and conservative theologians struggled to contextualize Paul's seeming embrace of state authority as inherently "of God."[13] Most commentators, including the highly admired evangelical theologian John Stott, insisted that Paul did not demand acquiescence to state power. To say that rulers are "established by God" is only to say that no power on earth exists except under God's dominion—all human authority is derived from God's ultimate authority. Yet there is no question, Stott says, that Paul puts the state in general in highly positive light, and so, in general, Christians must recognize that the state, except in some circumstances, has authority and is owed Christian duty. Christians must do more than tolerate it; they must "submit to its authority, honour its representatives, pay its taxes and pray for its welfare."[14] And yet the overall context of the Bible and the specific context of Paul's letter mean that it is more than just an apology for the state.

> The statement that rulers commend those who do right and punish those who do wrong is not of course invariably true, as Paul knew perfectly well. . . . So, in depicting rulers in such a good light, as commending the right and opposing the wrong, he is stating the divine ideal, not the human reality. Yet the requirement of submission and the warning of rebellion are couched in universal terms. For this reason they have constantly been misapplied by oppressive right-wing regimes, as if Scripture gave rulers carte blanche to develop a tyranny and to demand unconditional obedience.[15]

But the Bible, Stott says, gives many examples of people justly refusing to follow the orders of evil governments. There is no reason to say that Romans 13 was universal, even if it was general.

CIRCULATION IN SOUTH AFRICA

In South Africa in the apartheid era (1948–1994), Romans 13 was quoted frequently by supporters of the white government, both in the United States and in South Africa, as apologists for apartheid connected to each other through a miasma of faithful language. Indeed, verses 1–7 were a favorite of South African president P. W. Botha who, when he was in office in the 1980s, often quoted them in attempts to silence anti-apartheid activists via the Christian rhetoric that permeated much of South African cultural life.

In 1985, for example, the white evangelical Anglican anti-apartheid activist Michael Cassidy attended what he hoped might be a breakthrough meeting with President Botha. In the midst of a crisis in the townships and rising anti-apartheid activism globally, Cassidy imagined that Botha might be willing to consider genuine reforms. Instead, when Cassidy walked into the room for their meeting, Botha stood up and started reading to him from Romans 13.[16]

Several months earlier, when Botha had been invited to speak to the Zion Christian Church—a renowned Black church and one of the largest churches in South Africa, with more than 2 million members—he exhorted the crowd to obey governing authority, again citing Romans.[17] The Zion Christian Church was itself an influential conservative force among Black South Africans, one with its own transnational networks. The church was important enough that when independent Baptist minister Jerry Falwell went to South Africa in the fall of 1985, he met with Zion Christian Church bishop Joseph Lekhanyane.[18] Lekhanyane told Falwell that it was frustrating that the international media focused so much on pastors like Desmond Tutu and Allan Boesak, the activist anti-apartheid leaders who were affiliated with the World Council of Churches and who, Lekhanyane said, did not speak for his (far more pietistic) members. After that meeting, Falwell felt emboldened enough to denounce Desmond Tutu to the media as a "phony." That comment cost Falwell dearly in the U.S. media, undermining his attempt to establish his own authority for speaking on the topic of apartheid.[19]

Romans 13 was cited so often and with such fervor in South Africa that Christian anti-apartheid activists could not ignore it. As anti-apartheid activism quickened in the mid-1980s, a group of mostly liberal South African Christians, Black and white, produced the Kairos Document, an extensive critique of the role of Christians in supporting, or in failing to adequately oppose, apartheid. The statement, which emerged largely from churches associated with the South African Council of Churches, responded to the intensifying violence by the South African Defence Force and the increasing desperation and violence in the townships.[20] Titled *A Challenge to the Church*, the document was exactly that. The Kairos writers insisted that the church in South Africa had failed to stand sufficiently for justice.

The problem, according to Kairos, was that Christians in South Africa had been captured by two different failed theologies, which the authors linked to two kinds of failures of political vision. The first of these, "state theology," was one of obedience to authority. The white branch of the Dutch Reformed Church—what commentators often described as the "National Party at Prayer"—was guilty of using the Bible to justify the status quo of "racism, capitalism, and totalitarianism." The authors addressed at some length state theology's frequent use of Romans 13. (The scripture was assumed to be so familiar that the Kairos Document did not even quote it.) The Kairos theologians insisted that Romans 13 must be read in context, and that Paul was simply warning the Christians to whom he was writing that they must expect to be subject to some sort of state authority, at least until Jesus returned. For the Kairos authors, the goal was to make quick work of the cynical use of Romans 13 to justify apartheid.[21]

The Kairos critique that hit closer to home, however, was the critique of "church theology," which the authors understood to be the official theology of the English-speaking churches, including the member churches of the liberal South African Council of Churches. This church theology, the authors said, had offered a "limited, guarded, and cautious" critique of apartheid. But when it came to suggesting solutions, the liberal churches had fetishized a few "stock ideas" from the Christian tradition. In particular, they were enamored of "reconciliation" and nonviolence. These fine-sounding terms, the document argued, were used to separate the churches from their responsibility, which was to stand for justice.

Reconciliation, in particular, had been the hallmark term of liberal church anti-apartheid activism in South Africa. It was the language of political liberals like Michael Cassidy, the Anglican activist who met with Botha and who, in the early 1970s, had played a leading role in bringing Billy Graham to South Africa to speak to integrated audiences. Cassidy was well-known in global evangelical circles as the voice of "moderate" white South African Christians and was widely embraced by the theologically conservative and racially moderate factions of the white U.S. evangelical world—those associated with groups like the Billy Graham Evangelical Association and *Christianity Today* magazine. In South Africa, reconciliation was central to the language of the South African Council of Churches, made up largely of mainline protestant denominations. Reconciliation, according to Kairos, implied that both "sides" had some repenting to do. It was a stance "carved in the space between Afrikaner nationalist and liberationist discourses," where God's people called on spiritual power to heal a political culture that seemed irrevocably torn asunder.[22] In some conflicts, however, there was no morally righteous middle ground. "Nowhere in the Bible or in Christian tradition," Kairos argued, "has it ever been suggested that we ought to try to reconcile good and evil."[23] In those circumstances, to call for such reconciliation was a sin.

The Kairos Document was signed by scores of people from the liberal protestant churches, including Methodists, Presbyterians, and Anglicans as well as some Catholics. Even though it implicitly criticized the South African Council of Churches, the document was understood to be linked to those churches and the global World Council of Churches, which since the 1960s had been a leading global voice against apartheid. By the time Kairos was published in 1985, the World Council of Churches had been funding Southern African liberation movements, including the African National Congress, for well over a decade.[24] Over the course of following several years, Kairos would become the most widely quoted church statement about apartheid. Its influence abroad would be less, perhaps, than Bishop Desmond Tutu's statements and sermons, but it was widely discussed, and the World Council of Churches and a number of global Christian bodies circulated thousands of copies around the world.[25]

It is perhaps no surprise that the liberal protestant churches (eventually) took such a vocal and influential stance against apartheid, although Kairos came relatively late—almost ten years after the 1976 massacres at Soweto. But more unexpected was the fact that, in short order, the Black evangelical churches in South Africa took a similar stance—and this stance would shape a conversation among evangelicals globally. A few weeks after Kairos was published, a group of evangelicals based in Soweto began to craft their own anti-apartheid statement, which would eventually become the groundbreaking *Evangelical Witness in South Africa*.

The leadership for that evangelical project came in part from the Kairos Document. The stark lines that existed in the United States between liberal protestants and evangelicals were not nearly as strong in South Africa (or in most countries in Africa). The Black South African Pentecostal minister Frank

Chikane, for example, was one of the lead authors of Kairos. A few other people who were deeply linked to the evangelical tradition in South Africa had also signed.

One of those signatories was a young Black evangelical preacher named Caesar Molebatsi, who became a driving figure behind the publication *Evangelical Witness in South Africa*. Molebatsi had been converted by white American missionaries in the 1960s, and he had attended Wheaton College in the United States before returning to South Africa in the mid-1970s. When Molebatsi was there, Wheaton college was a hothouse for an emerging transnational evangelical Left. Important alumni include John Gatu, an East African who had proposed a transnational moratorium on missionaries to Africa; Pius Wakatama from Rhodesia, author of *Independence for the African Church* (1976); and Latin American theologian René Padilla, who was known as the leader of an insurgent "social concern" faction among a younger generation of global evangelicals.[26] During his student days at Wheaton, Molebatsi engaged in many long discussions with other young African Christians, usually about the role of First World churches in the Third World. He began to believe that missionaries in South Africa had "stayed beyond their usefulness, accepting the reigning political philosophy of apartheid without challenging its inherent evil."[27]

He returned to South Africa just after the Soweto uprisings in June 1976 and became an outspoken anti-apartheid activist. Although it took a number of years to gather up like-minded Black evangelicals in what was a traditionally pietistic community, Molebatsi and others were determined not to see social justice arguments dominated only by theological liberals. Molebatsi was more friendly than many South African evangelicals to the South African Council of Churches, but he made clear that he would not compromise his biblical literalism. He became one of the instigators of *Witness* to traverse the boundary between theological conservativism and a strong anti-apartheid stance.

Witness was a haunting jeremiad that offered a specifically Black and evangelical voice, drawing on many of the arguments of Kairos but deploying them in an evangelical register. The document positioned itself as a confession of the sins of evangelical believers, criticizing the "structural conformity" of South African evangelical churches, including Black churches. It came out a year after Kairos, and, like that statement, *Witness* spent a fair amount of time attacking those who wielded Romans 13 against activism. "Theologians of the status quo, or State Theology, can be characterized by their use and misuse of Romans 13. Whenever victims of oppression try to raise their voices or resist the oppression, Romans 13 is thrown into their faces by beneficiaries of those oppressive systems. Romans 13 is used therefore to maintain the status quo and to make

Christians feel guilty when challenging injustices in society."[28] It was time for evangelicals to take a hard look at their own history, including what the writers called the two primary evangelical "sins": racism on the part of whites and complacency by Blacks.

Witness noted that both sins involved acceptance of the status quo, wryly commenting, "Whereas there is a general tendency of the church to conform to the norms and values of the society of its time even when they are at variance with the gospel of the Lord Jesus Christ, the evangelical tradition excels in this regard."[29] Failing to read the whole Bible fully, evangelicals had failed themselves and their country. "The problem is that Jesus was a radical and we are moderates," they wrote.[30]

Witness reserved special opprobrium for white American Christians who had come to South Africa to offer up their gospel of complacency. The televangelist Jimmy Swaggart, for example, was exceptionally popular with South Africans. Swaggart, who was a minister in the Assemblies of God church, had the second-largest television ministry in the United States after Oral Roberts. He was an influential figure on the U.S. religious Right. In South Africa, Swaggart's books and tapes sold very well among both Black and white Christians.[31] During his 1985 tour through the country, Swaggart had preached to integrated audiences and proudly proclaimed that his multiracial crowds were proof that "apartheid is dead." Swaggart's revivals were broadcast on South African state television, and many Black South Africans were furious. How could a "foreigner," the *Witness* writers asked, announce "that apartheid is dead when we know that it is alive and well, and that it kills."[32]

> For us who are brutalized by white Christians in South Africa, with the western tradition of oppression and exploitation, for us who are oppressed and exploited by white Christians who are supported by the so-called Christian West, for us who have been called "communists" because we resisted apartheid, for some of us who have been detained in solitary confinement under the so-called "Terrorism" Act just for raising our voices against apartheid, for us this motive [for declaring apartheid dead] can only be seen to be coming from the devil.[33]

Couched as a confession, *Witness* was a full-out assault on the evangelical norm, both in South Africa and the United States. Copies of *Witness* circulated not only in South Africa but in the rest of Africa, the United States, the United Kingdom, and other parts of Europe. It was translated into several European languages and circulated there as well. In the United States, the document was reprinted by the evangelical publisher Eerdmans.

SOUL FREEDOM AND THE STATE

South Africans often felt that the question of Christians' relationship to the state was one of the most profound political and theological issues of their day. They were not alone: In the 1960s and 1970s, Latin American evangelical theologians had taken a lead in calling for global evangelicals to consider themselves as being in solidarity with the poor and against the power of the state. Many of those views had been embraced in the United States by the evangelical Left—whose members founded the magazine *Post-American* in the 1960s.[34]

Still, the question of how to view the state was a fraught one for many international evangelicals. Throughout the Cold War, there were Christians from around the Global South who faced despotic state power; in locales from Egypt to Estonia, evangelicals understood themselves to be in a minoritized position, facing oppressive governments, a hostile dominant culture, or both. In the United States, on the other hand, evangelicals, particularly white evangelicals, had moved rapidly into positions of cultural and political power over the course of the 1970s and 1980s. By the time of the intensified U.S. debates over apartheid in the mid-1980s, most evangelicals had long moved away from any reluctance to engage in politics. (In reality, such a reluctance was never as thorough as many commentators have presumed.) Although the rhetoric of demanding that believers focus on personal salvation rather than politics remained easily at hand among evangelicals, the reality, both before and after the rise of the Moral Majority, was that American believers had allied themselves with a broad range of political positions, including a fairly close identification with U.S. foreign policies during the Cold War. Evangelicals of color tended to be far less enamored of the policies of the U.S. state abroad, but Black evangelical churches did take political positions, including on issues of foreign policy. Those sometimes challenged U.S. policy, as with the African Methodist Episcopal Church's open criticism of U.S. policy in Congo in the early 1960s. Or they sometimes offered modest support, as with Black churches' support for Christians in the Soviet Union in the 1970s or, later, their support for U.S. policy toward southern Sudan in the 1990s.[35]

But even for the most powerful white American evangelicals, the relation of Christianity to the U.S. state was understood to be complicated, in theory if not always in practice. Billy Graham, for example, pastor to the presidents and embodiment of a state-identified form of evangelical Christianity, found himself forced to reconsider his ties. In 1974, just as his friend Richard Nixon was about to be impeached, Graham told the Lausanne International Congress on

Evangelization that "to tie the Gospel to any political system, secular program, or society is dangerous." Graham promised that he would move beyond nationalism: "When I go to preach the Gospel, I go as an ambassador of the kingdom of God—not America."[36]

This was hardly the political vision put forward by many on the religious Right, who consistently were willing and able to ally themselves with U.S. power globally and to engage that power for their own domestic agendas as well. But that vision was never unchallenged or unproblematic from the perspective of evangelical institutions, both in the United States and especially internationally, which were traversed by controversy about the degree of their engagement with "the world." Apartheid was just one arena in which the global evangelical community faced the reality that some of their own had identified strongly with an oppressive state power, while others made it their task to confront that identification.

In the United States, Christian opposition to apartheid was led by the mainline liberal protestant churches and, at times, the Catholic Church. The Episcopal Church was an early leader, for example, having supported divestment since the 1960s. Evangelical institutions were split: World Vision and *Christianity Today* were outspoken against apartheid but generally not willing to support anything other than slow, nonviolent, church-led moves toward change. The Southern Baptist Convention (SBC), by far the largest of evangelical denominations in the United States, was generally quietist; in the 1980s its publications opposed apartheid but expressed a great deal of concern about "radicalism" and violence among South Africa's Black population. (By the 1970s almost no one short of the Far Right in the United States would say anything positive about apartheid; the debate was always over how far and fast to push opposition, given the anticommunist credentials of the apartheid government.) Exceptions to the SBC's quietist "moderation" emerged from the liberal-leaning members of the Christian Life Commission and a few others who were active in the 1980s in trying (unsuccessfully) to get the denomination to divest.

However, there was one SBC-supported organization in the United States that did speak out strongly against apartheid. The Baptist Joint Committee on Public Affairs had started in 1939 as a shared program of the Northern Baptist and Southern Baptist Conventions. By the mid-1980s it was a coalition of eight Baptist denominations, including two, the National Baptist Convention, USA, and the smaller National Baptist Convention of America, that were largely

African American. The largely white SBC was by far the largest of the denominations in the joint committee and its largest financial contributor.

In 1980, the Southern Baptist pastor James Dunn became the new executive director of the Baptist Joint Committee on Public Affairs and used it as a site for challenging the conservative resurgence in the SBC that was transforming the denomination in the late 1970s and early 1980s. He did so by mobilizing an alternative network of Baptists and by drawing heavily on what he claimed as traditional Baptist doctrines about individual conscience. In doing so, Dunn became one of the most important liberal Southern Baptists of the late twentieth century, operating as both an antiracist and as a strong supporter of church/state separation.

Dunn was an energetic and, in some ways, traditional southern preacher. He liked to declare himself a "Texas-bred, Spirit-led, Bible-teaching, revival-preaching" Baptist.[37] Dunn was famously a social liberal on issues of race. But he came to the joint committee after twelve years as head of the Christian Life Commission of the Texas Baptist Convention, where he campaigned against the alcohol industry, obscenity, and other "traditional" moral issues as well as against racism.

Dunn was also a prominent advocate of "soul freedom"—the idea that each individual Christian was responsible for interpreting the will of God for herself or himself, separate from any position taken by their church. This was not inherently a radical belief: after all, a version of the doctrine was part of the basis of the protestant Reformation. But the idea of such competency of the individual soul was taken up with particular enthusiasm by Baptists in the United States, who saw themselves as democratic, congregational, and independent. The idea of "soul competency" as a distinctively Baptist belief was articulated most notably for Americans by Edgar Young Mullins, whose 1908 *Axioms of Religion: A New Interpretation of Baptist Faith* was one of the most influential books among U.S. Baptists of all varieties in the twentieth century. God created humans so that they are capable of knowing God directly through the revelation of the scriptures, Mullins argued. Thus, "all men have an equal right and direct access to God."[38] For Baptists, traditionally, this meant that there could be little that was dictated by the church in terms of belief. When the Southern Baptist Convention was founded in 1845, its organizers stated: "We have constructed for our basis no new creed; acting in this matter upon a Baptist aversion to all creeds but the Bible."[39] And, indeed, it was one of the hallmarks of the SBC that, with a few exceptions, for much of the twentieth century there was little push for doctrinal agreement beyond a generically stated high view of the authority of scripture.

By the time of the right-wing takeover of the SBC in the late 1970s, this anti-creedalism was being called into question. Some Baptists had begun asking whether this notion of "soul competency" did not lead to the freedom to believe pretty much anything. As the Baptist historian Winthrop Hudson had suggested in 1959, "the practical effect of the stress upon soul competency as the cardinal doctrine of Baptists was to make everyone's hat their own church."[40] With no borders to acceptable belief, critics argued, undisciplined individual experience became immune from theological debate.

In theory, a concern over excessive focus on individual interpretation might be something shared by both moderates and conservative Baptists (or, indeed, by believers of almost any denomination). In practice, however, the SBC's agitation over the "excesses" of soul competency was spearheaded by conservatives and emerged prominently in debates about biblical interpretation that galvanized the SBC in the 1960s and 1970s. In 1961 a professor at Midwestern Seminary had published *The Message of Genesis*, which argued that the creation stories in Genesis might not be historically accurate accounts.[41] These were unremarkable claims among seminarians, but they evoked a firestorm of criticism in the SBC, leading the convention into a process of producing its second Statement of Baptist Faith and Message. (The first was in 1925). The 1963 Faith and Message statement reaffirmed the Bible as "having truth without any mixture of error for its matter." This was officially not a "creed" but a "confession"—not a requirement for membership but a description of what Baptists supposedly already believed. In reality, it was an attempt to assert some limits on biblical interpretation, to insist that Baptists must hold to what conservatives began to describe as "inerrancy."[42] Conservatives' interpretation of the Faith and Message statement was that it disallowed any liberal contextualizing of biblical accounts. It was no coincidence, then, that conservative SBC activists began to organize in the early 1970s as the "Baptist Faith and Message Fellowship." That group monitored SBC institutions for their adherence to the principles of inerrancy while planning for what would become the conservative takeover of the SBC in the next decade.[43]

James Dunn emerged from the liberal Baptist networks that were generally opposed to what they insisted was "creedalism" in the SBC. But by the time he joined the Baptist Joint Committee, Dunn was also establishing his own base of power. And he was not shy about using the accusation of creedalism as a kind of "more traditional than thou" claim against SBC conservatives. Indeed, both sides in the intensifying conflicts within the SBC made claims to authentic Baptist-ness: moderates highlighted the longstanding statements about individual conscience; conservatives highlighted the longstanding statements about biblical authority.

It is within this context that Dunn made an unyielding affirmation of the importance of "separation of church and state" into a central activity of the Baptist Joint Committee. If Baptists did not trust their own denomination to dictate creed, it stood to reason, according to Dunn and others, that they should have no interest in seeing the U.S. state either support or oppose statements of religious belief. Indeed, this has been exactly the position of the SBC through the late nineteenth and most of the twentieth centuries, when the convention still tended to view with suspicion any moves to by the U.S. government to privilege one religion over the other—particularly, but not only, if such moves might benefit Catholics. In this vein, Southern Baptists and a range of other evangelicals had, for example, opposed early policies that allowed the Peace Corps to place volunteers with religious organizations. "We have long criticized the Peace Corps," *Christianity Today* editors wrote in 1965, "for staffing sectarian-sponsored enterprises with volunteers whose salaries are paid out of public funds."[44] In the 1960s Baptists were stalwarts of the organization Protestants and Other Americans United for the Separation of Church and State.[45]

From the time he took the helm of the Baptist Joint Committee in 1980, Dunn saw his mission as supporting religious liberty. This, he argued, was one of the shared theological and political positions that could unite Baptists, Black and white, liberal and conservative. At first this worked out well, and the joint committee's positions followed most of the SBC's own stances very closely. Both groups opposed a U.S. ambassador to the Vatican, supported equal access for religious groups to the use of school grounds after hours, and fought any attempts to require churches to pay taxes. But it was on the issue of school prayer that Dunn separated the joint committee from its most powerful denomination.

In the first fifteen years following the 1962 *Engle v. Vitalae* Supreme Court decision that banned state-sponsored prayer in the schools, the SBC had consistently supported the ban, reiterating that position in eight separate resolutions. But the denomination's position on prayer changed after the 1979 election of Adrian Rogers as president of the convention and the right-wing takeover of the SBC. In 1982 the "messengers" (delegates) at the SBC annual convention voted to support President Ronald Reagan's proposed school prayer amendment.[46] The Baptist Joint Committee, however, refused to join the call, instead issuing a statement that cited the SBC's previous resolutions on the matter. Dunn declared that religious liberty was always endangered when "religion is made the handmaiden of a particular ideology. God is minimized in any marriage of religion and politics. We wind up making God the national mascot and that's civil religion at its worst."[47] Never one to pull his punches, he declared that for a Baptist to support for "state-sponsored religion in public schools" was a heretical position because it denied freedom of individual conscience.[48] Here we see the complexity or perhaps even incoherence of the way that Dunn wielded the idea of soul freedom: declaring that people cannot be Baptists unless they believe in soul competency made such competency into a doctrine that people were not free to disavow.

Dunn's strong view of religion as ideally distant from the state did not mean that he was opposed to putting religion into politics. Dunn liked to say that "mixing politics and religion is inevitable but merging church and state is inexcusable."[49] In fact, one hallmark of Dunn's thinking (and that of a number of other Baptists) was that his commitment to soul freedom, dubiousness about the state, and liberal politics of race were intimately intertwined.

Not surprisingly, then, in the 1980s Dunn joined the many others who had produced biblical commentary on Romans 13. His was published in 1986—just as anti-apartheid activism was escalating in the United States. Dunn's argument was a now standard one for theological discourse on Romans, although it was still controversial in the ordinary theology of many evangelical believers. He argued that Paul's exhortations about the need to heed one's rulers was specific to the Christian community living in Rome at the time he wrote. In the late 50s AD, the new Christian communities—still largely seen as sects of Judaism—were in danger. The insistence that Jews and Gentiles needed to redraw the boundaries of sanctified community to include each other equally also meant that these communities were even more vulnerable to Roman power. If Paul made clear that the rulers were "servants of God," he was also arguing that they would ultimately have to answer to God. Thus, Rome's early Christians should pay their taxes and keep their heads down while not trying to withdraw into some separated community as Jews had once done. "Political realism for Paul meant living within the political system even if that meant living to a large extent within the terms laid down by that system." Political quietism was Paul's advice to the Romans, but Dunn insisted that this was specific, not generalized, advice. People in democracies have different expectations about what influence they can have. And, Dunn wrote, echoing Bonhoeffer, "when a government was *not* serving God for the good of its citizens, any appeal to this passage as a way of maintaining their subservience would be a complete distortion and an abuse both of Paul's purpose and of its continuing scriptural significance."[50]

Over the course of the 1980s, Dunn was increasingly at odds with the rightward turn of the SBC, but he used his platform on the Baptist Joint Committee to advocate for causes he believed in. The committee's *Report from the Capital* was a monthly digest of news and opinion that covered national and international issues, often from a distinctively liberal slant. Its April 1985 cover, for example, showed a group of people marching with anti-apartheid signs; by that point the daily protests at the South African embassy organized by TransAfrica were already widely covered in the press. In the *Report from the Capital* story, two men are in the foreground of the cover photo; one is Black, one white, both carrying signs that declare that "American Baptists" support justice in South Africa. The accompanying story, "Churches Act to Thwart Apartheid," is a paean to divestment, declaring that religious groups were leading the anti-apartheid movement. (This excess of enthusiasm was not exactly accurate. The secular activists at TransAfrica and the student protestors at campuses had already taken significant leadership in the movement.) The story explains that both the SBC and the United Methodists opposed divestment, but the Presbyterians had already shed holdings in Mobil, Texaco, and a few other corporations. (The United Methodist Church would divest the following year.) The story ends by reminding readers that the South African Council of Churches had recently taken the risky and illegal move of asking churches in other countries to divest, saying that the pressure was needed to help bring about fundamental change.[51]

Indeed, this was true, and in South Africa in the mid-1980s it was no longer just the liberal churches of the South African Council of Churches that were making the call. In October of 1985, as the authors of *Evangelical Witness* were composing their document, the South African Baptist Union issued an outspoken statement against apartheid—a new position for the historically quiescent (racially mixed but mostly white) denomination. The South African vote was reported enthusiastically in the SBC's *Baptist Press* wire service.[52] The anti-apartheid stances of South African Baptists were echoed in statements by the Baptist World Alliance, as the SBC found itself under increasing national and international pressure to take more active stands against apartheid.

Indeed, although Dunn's pro-divestment stances were not broadly popular among Southern Baptists, there was a small but vocal liberal contingent, based largely in the SBC's Christian Life Commission, that supported his position and, in 1985, called for the denomination to divest. (That group included one white South African, John Jonsson, who was a seminary professor at Southern Baptist Theological Seminary in Kentucky. Jonsson had been active against apartheid both before and after he left South Africa in 1982 and later worked in South Africa to help found the group Concerned Baptists, an ally and counterpart of Concerned Evangelicals.)

Ultimately, Dunn was pushed out of the SBC but not because of his anti-apartheid work. It was his anti–school prayer positions, along with his generally combative stance regarding the religious Right overall, that put Dunn in the sights of the rising conservative leadership in the SBC. "There was no other staff member in the entire SBC bureaucracy the fundamentalists would rather fire," commented one observer.[53] Dunn was undeterred, even though he lost badly in a series of conflicts that ended with the SBC defunding the Baptist Joint Committee in 1991 and starting a separate SBC Religious Freedom Committee. (That new SBC committee ultimately combined with the remnants of the Christian Life Commission to become the Ethics and Religious Liberty Commission, run for twenty-five years by culture warrior Richard Land.) As long as Dunn was the executive director of the Baptist Joint Committee—he stayed until 1999—he made frequent use of the bully pulpit that he was offered and played a role in highlighting for a range of Baptists, Black and white, the concept of "soul freedom" and the limits of state power.

CONCLUSION

Apartheid in South Africa provided an important ground for discussions of evangelicals' doctrinal assumptions about the state. The conversations did not happen just in South Africa or just in the United States but within and across the transnational networks that linked American and South African evangelicals in complex and sometimes contradictory ways.

The lessons to be gleaned from this complex story are several. First, using Latour to highlight multiple actants and noisy networks, this approach challenges nationalist histories as well as any neat division between the process of biblical interpretation and the construction of social power. Takings seriously the "hybrid" nature of the world as we live it means attending to what Latour describes as the associations that "mix up knowledge, interest, justice, and power ... heaven and earth, the global stage and the local scene."[54] I have highlighted the people, institutions, arguments, and Bible verses that played some role in shaping the transnational conversation about apartheid among a subset of evangelicals. In bringing Romans 13 into the story, I am not suggesting that people just "grab" the Bible interpretation that is most convenient to their other, "real" needs. Instead, treating Bible verses as actants is designed to show the ways in which those verses exert power on believers who take them seriously, even as their meaning is shifting and negotiated.

I have intentionally highlighted here the wariness with which some protestants (a great many of them, in fact) have viewed the state, including the U.S. state. Although it can seem as if some evangelicals are simply instrumental and cynical in their evocations of the state—whether seeing it as totalitarian and dangerous or as organized and bequeathed by God—there are real struggles over what the state in general *is*, much less how any specific, given state is to be viewed. Evangelicals have a thick and weighty history of discussion about the state and its claims on them, as well as their claims on it.

This is not to say that, both before and after the apartheid era, ordinary ministers in the United States and beyond were disinclined to quote Romans 13 as if it were a stand-alone truth that justified whatever a favored president chose to do. In the twenty-first century, the verses have been used in support of the Iraq War under George W. Bush and in favor of war against Korea in the case of Trump advisor and Baptist pastor Robert Jeffress.[55] I only insist that such users must shout noisily in a busy field of evangelical cultural/political/intellectual production, against the grain of a good bit of scholarship and tradition. Thus, I hope I have shown there is weight and heft in networks, meaning that evangelicals can make their claims about the Bible, but they do not make them just as they please, rather under networked circumstances, at messy intersections, forging memory and forgetfulness, allies and enemies, interpretations and assumptions in the process.

NOTES

1. Edgar Young Mullins, *The Axioms of Religion: A New Interpretation of the Baptist Faith* (1908; repr., n.p.: Forgotten Books, 2017), 64.
2. The literature on the origins and limits of secularism as a state practice is vast, but some of the most important overall texts are Winnifred Fallers Sullivan, *The Impossibility of Religious Freedom* (Princeton, N.J.: Princeton University Press, 2005); Elizabeth Shakman Hurd, *The Politics of Secularism in International Relations* (Princeton, N.J.: Princeton University Press, 2008); Matthew Scherer, *Beyond Church and State: Democracy, Secularism, and Conversion* (Cambridge: Cambridge University Press, 2013); and Saba Mahmood, *Religious Difference in a Secular Age: A Minority Report* (Princeton, N.J.: Princeton University Press, 2015). Other compelling discussions of secularism focus less on the state than on the larger meaning of "secularism" as a distinctly modern way of being in the world. For William Connolly, one of the serious drawbacks of the secular sensibility is that it is hyper-rational, disallowing the passions, the nonrational senses, as legitimate parts of the public sphere; Talal Asad discusses secularism as an organizing strategy of modernity. Charles Hirschkind offers an excellent discussion of Connolly and Asad. William E. Connolly, *Why I Am Not a Secularist* (Minneapolis:

University of Minnesota Press, 2000); Talal Asad, *Formations of the Secular: Christianity, Islam, Modernity* (Stanford, Calif.: Stanford University Press, 2003); and Charles Hirschkind, "Is There a Secular Body?," *Cultural Anthropology* 26, no. 4 (November 1, 2011): 633–47.

3. I argue for a more complex understanding of white evangelical responses to civil rights in Melani McAlister, *The Kingdom of God Has No Borders: A Global History of American Evangelicalism* (New York: Oxford University Press, 2018). See also Mark Newman, *Getting Right with God: Southern Baptists and Desegregation, 1945–1995* (Tuscaloosa: University of Alabama Press, 2001); Alan Scot Willis, *All According to God's Plan: Southern Baptist Missions and Race, 1945–1970* (Lexington: University Press of Kentucky, 2004); and David L. Chappell, *A Stone of Hope: Prophetic Religion and the Death of Jim Crow* (Chapel Hill: University of North Carolina Press, 2005).

4. Lauren Frances Turek, *To Bring the Good News to All Nations: Evangelical Influence on Human Rights and U.S. Foreign Relations* (Ithaca, N.Y.: Cornell University Press, 2020).

5. Bruno Latour, "On Actor-Network Theory: A Few Clarifications," *Soziale Welt* 47, no. 4 (1996): 373.

6. Bruno Latour, *Reassembling the Social: An Introduction to Actor-Network-Theory* (Oxford: Oxford University Press, 2005), 31.

7. "The motion of light in water" is the title of Samuel Delaney's autobiography. Samuel R. Delany, *The Motion of Light in Water: Sex and Science Fiction Writing in The East Village* (Minneapolis: University of Minnesota Press, 2004).

8. John Stott, *The Message of Romans: God's Good News for the World* (Downers Grove, Ill.: IVP Academic, 1994), 19.

9. Michael D. Coogan, Marc Z. Brettler, Carol Newsom, and Pheme Perkins, eds., *The New Oxford Annotated Bible with Apocrypha: New Revised Standard Version*, 4th ed. (New York: Oxford University Press, 2010), 1975.

10. Mark A. Noll, *In the Beginning Was the Word: The Bible in American Public Life, 1492–1783* (New York: Oxford University Press, 2015).

11. Newman, *Getting Right with God*, 28.

12. Dietrich Bonhoeffer, *The Cost of Discipleship* (New York: Touchstone, 1995), 262.

13. Among liberals who wrote about Romans 13, see, John Howard Yoder, *The Politics of Jesus* (Grand Rapids, Mich.: Eerdmans, 1972); and Neil Elliott, *Liberating Paul* (Minneapolis: Augsburg Fortress Publishers, 2006). Other evangelical authors include N. T. Wright, *Romans* (Downers Grove, Ill.: IVP Connect, 2009); Timothy Keller, *Romans 8–16 for You* (Purcellville, Va.: Good Book Company, 2015); and John F. MacArthur, *Romans: Grace, Truth, and Redemption* (2007; repr., Nashville, Tenn.: Thomas Nelson, 2015).

14. Stott, *Message of Romans*, 347.

15. Stott, *Message of Romans*, 341.

16. Michael Cassidy, *The Passing Summer: A South African's Response to White Fear, Black Anger, and the Politics of Love* (Ventura, Calif: Regal, 1990), 299.

17. Paul Freston, *Evangelicals and Politics in Asia, Africa and Latin America* (Cambridge: Cambridge University Press, 2004), 172–73; and Tracy Kuperus,

"The Political Role and Democratic Contribution of Churches in Post-Apartheid South Africa," *Journal of Church and State* 53, no. 2 (Spring 2011): 299–302. A useful study of the Zion Christian Church in terms of its theology and practice is Victoria Morongwa Peagler, "Blow the Trumpet in Black Zion: A Phenomenological Exploration of the Zionist Christian Church of South Africa" (Ph.D. diss., Fuller Theological Seminary, School of Intercultural Studies, Pasadena, California, 2010).

18. Falwell's church began paying dues to the Southern Baptist Convention in 1996 and he attended his first Southern Baptist Convention in 1998. "Long an Independent, Jerry Falwell Joins Southern Baptist Fold," Religion News Service, January 1, 1996, https://religionnews.com/1996/01/01/top-story-falwell-realigns-long-an-indenpendent-jerry-falwell-joins-southern/; and Michael Foust, "Jerry Falwell Dead at 73," *Baptist Press*, May 15, 2007, https://www.baptistpress.com/resource-library/news/jerry-falwell-dead-at-73-2/.

19. Robert Pear, "Falwell Denounces Tutu as a 'Phony,'" *New York Times*, August 21, 1985, http://www.nytimes.com/1985/08/21/world/falwell-denounces-tutu-as-a-phony.html; Jerry Falwell, "An Interview with Jerry Falwell," *Transformation* 3, no. 2 (April 1986): 36; and Beth Spring, "Falwell Raises a Stir by Opposing Sanctions Against South Africa," *Christianity Today*, October 4, 1985. Some of the following discussion is drawn from chapter 7 of my book, McAlister, *The Kingdom of God Has No Borders*.

20. In the vast scholarship on anti-apartheid activism, see in particular Francis Njubi Nesbitt, *Race for Sanctions: African Americans Against Apartheid, 1946–1994* (Bloomington: Indiana University Press, 2004); and Adrian Guelke, *Rethinking the Rise and Fall of Apartheid: South Africa and World Politics* (Houndmills, Basingstoke, Hampshire: Palgrave Macmillan, 2005). On the earlier period, see Thomas Borstelmann, *Apartheid's Reluctant Uncle: The United States and Southern Africa in the Early Cold War* (New York: Oxford University Press, 1993).

21. Kairos Theologians, *The Kairos Document: Challenge to the Church, A Theological Comment on the Political Crisis in South Africa*, ed. John W. de Gruchy (Grand Rapids, Mich.: Eerdmans, 1986), quote on page 17. They are drawing in part on the work of German theologian Ernst Käsemann, who, like Bonhoeffer, was part of the anti-Nazi movement in the German church, and Oscar Cullman, whose work on theology of the state has been very broadly influential. Ernst Käsemann, *Commentary on Romans*, trans. Geoffrey W. Bromiley (Grand Rapids, Mich.: Eerdmans, 1980); and Oscar Cullmann, *The State in The New Testament* (New York: Scribner, 1956).

22. Glen Thompson, "'Transported Away': The Spirituality and Piety of Charismatic Christianity in South Africa (1976–1994)," *Journal of Theology for Southern Africa*, no. 118 (March 2004): 131.

23. Kairos Theologians, *The Kairos Document*, 26.

24. The funding went through the Programme to Combat Racism. Claude Emerson Welch, "Mobilizing Morality: The World Council of Churches and Its Programme to Combat Racism, 1969–1994," *Human Rights Quarterly* 23, no. 4 (2001): 863–910.

25. Kairos Theologians, *The Kairos Document*. On the document's impact, see John W. De Gruchy, "The Church and the Struggle for South Africa," *Theology Today* 43,

no. 2 (July 1, 1986): 229–43; Bonganjalo Goba, "The Kairos Document and Its Implications for Liberation in South Africa," *Journal of Law and Religion* 5, no. 2 (January 1, 1987): 313–25; and Brian M. Du Toit, "Theology, Kairos, and the Church in South Africa," *Missiology* 16, no. 1 (January 1, 1988): 57–71.

26. David R. Swartz, *Moral Minority: The Evangelical Left in an Age of Conservatism* (Philadelphia: University of Pennsylvania Press, 2012).
27. David Virtue, *A Flame for Justice* (Oxford: Lion, 1991), 84. On Wheaton alums, see Swartz, *Moral Minority*, 121–22.
28. Concerned Evangelicals, *Evangelical Witness in South Africa: A Critique of Evangelical Theology and Practice* (Grand Rapids, Mich.: Eerdmans, 1987), 28–29.
29. Concerned Evangelicals, *Evangelical Witness*, 32.
30. Concerned Evangelicals, *Evangelical Witness*, 23.
31. Kate Bowler, *Blessed: A History of the American Prosperity Gospel* (New York: Oxford University Press, 2013), 105.
32. Concerned Evangelicals, *Evangelical Witness*, 40.
33. Concerned Evangelicals, *Evangelical Witness*, 39.
34. See David Kirkpatrick, *A Gospel for the Poor: Global South Christianity and the Latin American Evangelical Left* (Philadelphia: University of Pennsylvania Press, 2019); Swartz, *Moral Minority*; and Melani McAlister, "The Global Conscience of American Evangelicalism: Internationalism and Social Concern in the 1970s and Beyond," *Journal of American Studies* 51, no. 4 (November 2017): 1197–220.
35. See chapters 1, 6, and 9 in McAlister, *The Kingdom of God Has No Borders*.
36. Billy Graham, "Why Lausanne?," in *Let the Earth Hear His Voice: The Complete Papers from the International Congress on World Evangelization*, ed. James Dixon Douglas (Minneapolis: World Wide Publications, 1975), 30.
37. Aaron Douglas Weaver, *James M. Dunn and Soul Freedom* (Macon, Ga.: Smyth & Helwys, 2011), 3.
38. Mullins, *Axioms of Religion*, 88. For a thorough analysis of Baptist history and theology across lines of race, see Thomas Kidd and Barry Hankins, *Baptists in America: A History* (New York: Oxford University Press, 2015).
39. SBC Annual (1845), 19, quoted in Bill J. Leonard, *God's Last and Only Hope: The Fragmentation of the Southern Baptist Convention* (Grand Rapids, Mich.: Eerdmans, 1990), 78.
40. Winthrop Still Hudson, "Shifting Patterns of Church Order in the Twentieth Century," in *Baptist Concepts of the Church* (Philadelphia: Judson Press, 1959), 215. Also cited in Weaver, *James M. Dunn and Soul Freedom*, 71.
41. Ralph Elliott, *The Message of Genesis* (Nashville: Broadman Press, 1961).
42. Nancy Tatom Ammerman, *Baptist Battles: Social Change and Religious Conflict in the Southern Baptist Convention* (New Brunswick, N.J.: Rutgers University Press, 1990), 64–65.
43. Leonard, *God's Last and Only Hope*, 135.
44. "Peace Corps in Cameroon," *Christianity Today*, January 1, 1965, p. 29.
45. Bill J. Leonard, *Baptists in America* (New York: Columbia University Press, 2005), 157–82.

46. Dorothy Schleicher, "A History and Analysis of the Role of the Baptist Joint Committee, 1972–Present" (Master's thesis, Baylor University, Waco, Texas, 1993), 129–42; and William Martin, *With God On Our Side: The Rise of the Religious Right in America* (New York: Broadway, 2005), 232–34.
47. Schleicher, "History of Baptist Joint Committee," 150.
48. Ammerman, *Baptist Battles*, 100.
49. Weaver, *James M. Dunn and Soul Freedom*, 74.
50. James D. G. Dunn, "Romans 13:1–7: A Charter for Political Quietism?," *Ex Auditu* 2 (1986): 67, 68.
51. James Owens, "Churches Act to Thwart Apartheid," *Report from the Capital*, February 1985.
52. Rev. W. Lukhele, "Call Me Not a Pastor," October 1985, AR 138-2: 55.15, Southern Baptist Historical Library and Archive (hereafter, SBHLA), Nashville, Tennessee; Baptist Union of South Africa, "Open Letter to Pres. Botha," October 21, 1985, AR 138-2: 164.18, SBHLA; and Robert O'Brien, "South African Baptists Urge End of 'Evil' Apartheid" (Baptist Press, October 22, 1985), SBHLA. The Baptist Union's 1986 statement was more muted, probably in response to right-wing criticism. David Walker, "Evangelicals and Apartheid: An Inquiry into Some Predispositions," *Journal of Theology for Southern Africa*, no. 67 (June 1989): 49; Christopher Alan Lund, "A Critical Examination of Evangelicalism in South Africa, with Special Reference to the Evangelical Witness Document and Concerned Evangelicals" (Master's thesis, University of Cape Town, Cape Town, South Africa, 1988), 46.
53. Ammerman, *Baptist Battles*, 240.
54. Bruno Latour, *We Have Never Been Modern*, trans. Catherine Porter (Cambridge, Mass: Harvard University Press, 1993), 3. Here Latour is rhetorically and sarcastically saying that we "must not" mix these things.
55. Sarah Pulliam Bailey, "'God Has Given Trump Authority to Take Out Kim Jong Un,' Evangelical Adviser Says," *Washington Post*, August 9, 2017, https://www.washingtonpost.com/news/acts-of-faith/wp/2017/08/08/god-has-given-trump-authority-to-take-out-kim-jong-un-evangelical-adviser-says/?utm_term=.124d77af8494.

14

In Search of Normcore?

Religion at Home and Abroad in Norway

HELGE ÅRSHEIM

Norway is a small country at the outskirts of Europe, its independence and sovereignty premised on strong international order and extensive interactions with neighboring countries. Continuously negotiating the relative youth of its modern independence from Sweden in 1905 with a widely held self-understanding of its prehistory as a mighty, sovereign realm in the early stages of the European Middle Ages, Norwegian discourses on its role and destiny in the world have yet to come into their own. Variously enthroning the Viking, the peasant, the fisherman, the missionary, and the humanitarian as icons of "Norwegian-ness" in different stages following independence, the lack of an overarching, shared narrative of what it means to be Norway and to be Norwegian constitutes something of a national trauma.

The extent of this trauma is illustrated time and again, as in the recent debate following a proposal from the ruling Conservative Party to establish a "cultural canon" for Norway. According to the minister of education, who fronted the proposal, the canon was necessary due to present "shortsightedness" and a tendency to forget important cultural expressions. The initiative was intended to "visualize our culture, not only to future generations, but also to our new citizens."[1] The ensuing debate re-rehearsed a number of arguments that featured in a 2013 debate on "Norwegian culture" that erupted following the appointment of Hadia Tajik, a Muslim, Norwegian-born daughter of Pakistani immigrants, as minister of culture. This in turn echoed the successive, introspective discussions that shook Norway following the 2011 terrorist attacks at the Norwegian Labour Youth camp at Utøya and the office block housing the Norwegian government, which again rehearsed earlier arguments about different dichotomies between "us" and "them" that can be traced back to the very beginnings of Norwegian nationhood, when the Constitutional Assembly at Eidsvoll in 1814 ratified article §2 of the Constitution, prohibiting entry to the realm for Jews, Jesuits, and members of Catholic monastic orders. Taken together, Norwegian debates on self-identity have been strongly related to these notions of difference, of distinctions between "us" and "them." As is often the case, the determination of "them" has always been more sharply delineated than the often vacuous and implicit "us."

While Norwegian self-identities and perceptions of others certainly rely on the identification of differences, it is less prone to the U.S.-style "exceptionalism" alluded to in the introduction to this volume. Rather, I would propose that Norway, and dominant notions of Norwegian-ness, hinge on *normalism*. Not to be confused with normativity, normalism, in Jürgen Link's reading, can be characterized as a regulatory principle whose early antecedents in the thinking of Auguste Comte constituted "the brake for the engine of modernity, which is at risk of exploding."[2] Unlike normativity or exceptionalism, both of which presuppose the identification of *rules*, normalism requires the identification and production of *data*, from which averages and approximate standards may be derived and applied as yardsticks for the "not normal" against which it defines itself. In this particular reading, ideas of the "normal" are specific products of modernity, distinct both from the more colloquial concept of normalcy and from its usage in the hard sciences, in particular in the mental health professions.

Viewed through the lens of normalism, the often vague and implicit conceptions of self embedded in distinctions between "us" and "them" in constructions of Norway and Norwegian-ness come into sharper relief. Bereft of the moral high ground or manifest destiny implied in normative or exceptionalist accounts of identity, Norwegian notions of "us" and "them" rely on the assistance of more or less clearly elucidated "standards" or statistical averages. Indeed, debates on distinctions between cultural and religious insiders and outsiders in Norwegian society and politics frequently center on more or less specific baselines, whether in terms of acceptable dress, available dietary requirements, or participation in everything from the labor force to social events. These baselines are clearly not "normative" in the sense of prescribing specific boundaries, nor are they "neutral" in the sense of not taking a stand—rather, Norwegian discourses of normalism presuppose the existence and availability of a set of standards that can act as approximate measurements of sameness and otherness.

A vital component of the Norwegian penchant for normalism is the co-occurrence of Norwegian independence and growing sense of self-understanding, on the one hand, and the growth of the modern regulatory state as the ideal template of state organization over the course of the twentieth century, on the other. Norway came into its own intertwined with the tumultuous events of the "short" twentieth century, or the "age of extremes" identified by Eric Hobsbawm. From independence in 1905 and to the turn of the millennium, Norwegian conceptions of itself and of the world developed in fits and starts as an incipient cultural, political, and legal complex formed and tried to keep abreast of the monumental changes in its surroundings. Norway in 1905 was a semi-industrialized country whose integration with international economic and political developments was rapidly changing, while altered socioeconomic conditions led to heightened cultural, political, and religious tensions.[3] The dissolution of the union with Sweden was largely premised on these changes, as Norwegian politicians and businessmen wanted Norwegian sovereignty over foreign policy issues in order to manage the rate and direction of industrial and economic development.

Throughout the formative years of the Norwegian state, the figures dominating its development were drawn almost exclusively from the legal and socioeconomic professions that combined their research efforts with their evolving views of governance and modernization. In the nineteenth century the kernel of the later state machinery was established by a fairly exclusive clique of scholars associated with the fledgling University of Oslo, which was founded in 1811. This clique has later been characterized as the "professor politicians" because of their penchant for the splicing of the instrumental rationality of the Enlightenment and the ideals of romanticism to provide the foundations for policymaking.[4] The Norwegian penchant for government-appointed commissions drawn from a wide range of academics and actors from civil society in order to map policy areas to assess their potential reform found its early beginnings in this time period, as the professor politicians sought to take Norwegian society into the modern age through the aid of scientific knowledge. The legal profession in particular saw an upturn in these early years of Norwegian sovereignty, laying the foundations for a German-style Rechtsstaat, in which former allegiances and traditions from agrarian society were replaced by ostensibly neutral state institutions. Taken together, the strong involvement of scientific measurement with statecraft and the growing trust in the expertise of public institutions engendered by legal abstractions have provided ideal conditions for the specific type of Norwegian normalism, which are still heartfelt today.

HOME IS WHERE THE CHURCH IS

A search for a Norwegian approach to religion "at home" as something that is distinctive and to some extent different from religion "abroad" necessarily starts with a closer examination of the Church of Norway (CoN). Unlike the U.S. understanding of religion at home as "tamed and free in a way not yet achieved by religion elsewhere," as observed in the introduction to this volume, the Norwegian understanding of religion "at home" is one of control, restraint, and order, in line with the importance of normalism in society as a whole. The historical role and influence of the CoN in imprinting this conception of religion on Norwegian society can hardly be overestimated. Predating the modern Norwegian state by almost eight hundred years, the history of the CoN arguably represents a singular unbroken institutional "chain of memory." From the establishment of Nidaros as an archdiocese in 1152, via the Lutheran Reformation in 1536, to the adoption of the Norwegian Constitution in 1814, the CoN has been inextricably linked to the granting and exercise of political power and the formulation of religious and cultural orthodoxy. While the majority of the prerogatives of the CoN have been stripped away in constitutional reforms over the course of the twentieth century, the Church still exercises considerable "soft power" influence, facilitated by its nationwide staff and congregations, its multiple voices in public debates, and its institutionalized access to political and bureaucratic circles.

Despite being recently "disestablished," the Church, to which 72.9 percent of the population is affiliated, enjoys broad constitutional privileges, including the right to financial support from the state.[5] Unlike the other Nordic countries, where funds for the national churches are collected through a specific church tax reserved for members, the CoN is financed through a lump sum in the national budget. Hence, the activities of the CoN are sponsored by every taxpayer, whether they are members of the church or not. While this support has also been available to other religious organizations since the passing of the 1969 Act Relating to Religious Communities on a per capita basis, the remunerations for the CoN are consistently larger due to special transfers kept out of the ordinary budget, an imbalance that is defended with the particular economic challenges facing the CoN as a "national church" with maintenance and personnel costs for parishes across the country.

The amount and rationale behind the financial subsidies to religious communities is currently going through substantial revisions and have become a battleground issue for divisions between religious "insiders" and "outsiders."

According to one line of reasoning, the subsidies allotted to religious communities beyond the CoN are purely compensatory and paid only to be able to fund the majority church while simultaneously avoiding violations of international human rights law.[6] Another approach sees the financial support to religious communities through a broader lens, arguing that the interaction between the Norwegian state and a variety of religious communities amounts to an actively supportive policy toward religion that hinges on a view of religion as a distinctive form of "welfare benefit," a term coined by Norwegian theologian Oddbjørn Leirvik.[7] According to Leirvik, the shift from compensation to active support took place in the early 2000s, as several government-appointed commissions sought to develop a consistent policy on religion, a process that is still far from completed. Throughout the reports issued by such commissions, religious communities have been portrayed as foundational not only to the formation of personal identities but also to the development and maintenance of fellowship and community in wider society.

Arguably, this sentiment, whereby communal religion acts as a conduit for the recognition of both "self" and "other," has a long pedigree in the Norwegian public sphere, as policymakers have sought to tackle the combined pressures of gradual unchurching, the rapid secularization of social institutions, and increasing religious diversity with a religious engagement policy, not unlike the instrumentalist approach to "religion abroad" in U.S. foreign policy.

When the system of religious education in Norwegian public schools was overhauled in the mid-1990s, a government-appointed commission suggested a new subject that would pay attention to the fundamental threats to identity formation posed by the influx of "postmodernism" whereby the development of a sound, personal identity was jeopardized by relativism and cultural polyphony. To secure the personal moorings of each student, the school subject should not only provide something to think *about* but also *somewhere* from which to think. This "somewhere" was provided by the creation of a mandatory school subject with a clear majority of instruction in Christianity, with smaller proportions allotted to other religions.[8]

While the idea that state support for religion can be characterized as a form of welfare benefit is fairly recent, the notion that certain forms of religion are conducive to social organization and a well-functioning society while others are not is arguably part and parcel of Norwegian concepts of sovereignty and nationhood and echoes sentiments from the other pieces gathered in this volume. In the Norwegian setting, this consistent "othering," which has only begun to be discussed critically over the course of the last decades, has been concentrated around the CoN and its followers, with potential faults and dangers of religion associated with adherents and organizations of other religious traditions. This association is not only cultural and social but has also been a consistent legal principle. Although the 1814 Constitution was strongly inspired by the liberal principles of the Atlantic revolutions, its original provisions on the preeminence of the Evangelical Lutheran faith—which was legally protected from criticism and denigrations, in which parents were obligated to raise their children, and to which members of the government were required to pay allegiance—had more in common with the recent history of Denmark–Norway with absolutism.

Remnants of absolutist rule, under which the sovereign was head of both church and state, could be traced long after its formal dissolution. The death penalty for blasphemy was only abolished with the adoption of the 1842 Criminal Act, which kept the prohibition but lessened the penalty to hard labor or a short prison sentence.[9] Unlicensed preaching remained prohibited until the passing of the Act on Christian Dissenters in 1845, and then only for a limited number of congregations. The constitutional prohibition on the entry of Jews to the realm was lifted in 1851, while monastic orders and Jesuits were allowed in 1897 and 1956, respectively. Then, as part of the celebrations of its 150-year anniversary in 1964, the Constitution was furnished with a clause guaranteeing the "free exercise" of religion.

While these legal changes have certainly benefited the Jewish community and Christian denominations, which have gradually been considered less of a threat against the body politic, other minorities have been less fortunate. From the mid-nineteenth century and to the 1970s, ethnic minorities were subject to a range of assimilationist policies, targeting everything from traditional practices and means of subsistence to cultural expressions, education, and, in particular, language. Throughout the assimilationist period, Travelers, Roma, Kven, Finns, and Sami were considered inferior and in need of developmental assistance. In these civilizational missions, Christian churches played key roles, sending missionaries and running schools and hospitals while eradicating remnants of pre-Christian religious views. Although language was the main battleground issue in the assimilationist policies, the role of religion as a key component of the civilizational mission can hardly be overestimated, and today Sami spirituality and religiosity is largely based on imported notions of "pan-indianism" and the shared spiritual attachment to land shared by indigenous peoples around the world.[10] Although assimilationism was officially abandoned in the late 1970s, tensions persist in and around areas with Sami majority communities, relating in particular to land rights and to language rights.[11]

Over the last decades, the "othering" of these "old" minorities has largely been replaced by a heated public debate on the role of Islam and Muslims, ranging from the accommodation of their various religious practices and their perceived ability to follow the laws of the land, and to their potential collusion with terrorism, both domestically and abroad. Over the course of the 2000s the Norwegian public sphere has seen waves of discussion on everything from the acceptability of the Muslim call to prayer in public space, the cartoon crisis, the perpetual debates on the hijab and the niqab at work in schools and in public, to the proper length of the beards of Muslim men, the certification of halal products, the provision of halal food in prisons, the gendered division of swimming lessons, the regulation of male circumcision, and the public training and certification of imams.

Alongside clearly demarcated religious "others," however, Norway has also seen increasing numbers of religious "nones." Measured in terms of stated belief in God, the proportion of Norwegian nones (46 percent) outnumbered the number of believers (34 percent) in a survey from 2017.[12] Measured in terms of formal affiliation, the nones (15.1 percent) are still dwarfed by the CoN (72.9 percent), but have clearly surpassed members of other registered denominations (12 percent). The striking imbalance between the proportion of the population that believes in God and the membership in the CoN underscores how nones continue to take part in the religious mainstream. The participation of nones in this mainstream can also be seen in the case of the Norwegian Humanist Association, which has been an active and important voice in the ongoing debate on the accommodation of religious and nonreligious outsiders since its foundation in 1956. Since 1981 the association has received the same per capita financial support and legal capacities to conduct weddings and funerals as religious communities.

Taken together, the demarcation between insiders and outsiders of religion "at home" in Norway is characterized more by apprehension toward religious outsiders than a tendency to generalize or neutralize the "religiousness" of the majority religious tradition, whose strong association with state authority has made it virtually indistinguishable from other public institutions. While there is certainly a tendency to "culturalize" the trappings of the majority religion according to the same patterns observed by Lori Beaman in the much-discussed *Lautsi* decision of the European Court of Human Rights, the imprint of the "1000 year Christian cultural heritage" that makes the rounds every election season is still unmistakably *religious* in orientation.[13] Religion, as long as it is "normal" in the sense of conforming to more or less clearly defined standards and averages, is seen as a public good to which the state should offer its support.

Religious doctrines, practices, or organizations that fail to conform to the implicit standards of normality, on the other hand, have become subject to increasing political attention and resistance over the course of the last decades. This attention has gone through the same subtle shift observed across Europe, from discussions concerning immigration, culture, and traditions that dominated public debate in the 1990s to an alarmist discussion that relates strongly to religion. While this "religionized" attention has so far been concentrated around Islamic practices and communities, the recent disestablishment of the CoN will likely affect its standing in the face of public opinion as it becomes free to find its own way in the world. Bereft of the normality implied by its association with state power, the newly minted organization of the CoN will have to face up to difficult questions on its finances, its political role, its views of gender equality, and its role as a religious hegemon in an increasingly unchurched and religiously plural society. Hence, while the main rationale for the maintenance of a bond between state and church in the new §16 of the Constitution was to secure the continued nationwide presence and influence of the CoN, the legal guarantees put in place in order to achieve these purposes may inadvertently contribute to the gradual weakening of its position.

ON THE ROAD

From their very earliest steps on the international arena in the late nineteenth century, the self-perception of Norwegian diplomats and politicians has been one of representing a peaceful nation in the world.[14] This self-perception has been bolstered by affirmations from international society, ranging from the decision by Alfred Nobel to leave the award of his Peace Prize to a committee appointed by the Norwegian Parliament, to the international recognition of the work for displaced peoples in Europe following World War I by Norwegian explorer, diplomat, and author Fridtjof Nansen, and to the appointment of the Norwegian politician Trygve Lie as the first secretary-general of the United Nations. The origins of the idea of Norway as a peacemaker in international affairs are complex and not sufficiently researched. One theory points to centuries of subjugation at the hands of Denmark and Sweden and the corresponding lack of a nationalist elite with the militaristic traditions of the more powerful neighboring states, both of which participated heavily in successive major conflicts on the European continent. Whatever its origins, Norwegian diplomats have been entangled in several peace and reconciliation processes across the world from the 1970s onward, from Thailand to Timor and Sri Lanka to Colombia, albeit with fairly mixed results.[15]

Parallel to its peacemaking efforts, Norwegian foreign policy has been dominated by an interest in the development of strong international legal institutions, both to provide security and to foster increased trade relationships. As a small country on the outskirts of the major centers of power, Norway has always relied on the creation and utilization of legal instruments to promote its interests in the international sphere. During the interwar years, Norway was a founding member of the League of Nations while also pursuing an expansionist strategy through the legal system established by the league, by securing custodianship over the Arctic archipelago Svalbard in the treaty negotiations at Versailles in 1919, and by unsuccessfully seeking sovereignty over Eastern Greenland at the International Court of Justice in 1933. Following German occupation during World War II, Norway became a founding member of NATO in 1949 and of the Council of Europe the same year. Recognizing the need for legal clarification of its maritime exclusive economic zone, Norwegian diplomats have successfully negotiated treaties that secure Norway, as a country that occupies 1 percent of the European landmass, the exclusive rights to exploit one-third of the European maritime area.[16]

The penchant for normalism in domestic politics can also be detected in the Norwegian foreign policy approaches to the environmental consequences of its extractive industries. As one of the largest providers of oil and natural gas in the world, Norway carries a heavy responsibility for its carbon emissions and faces the persistent risk of oil spills, both in the high seas near the fragile Arctic and in zones ever closer to the coastline, where it could endanger both fisheries and marine wildlife. The political approach to this responsibility was developed during the oil boom in the 1970s, which co-occurred with the ascendancy of the environmental protective agenda at the United Nations and in countries around the world. Realizing the damages the environmental risks of its oil production could do to its international standing, Norwegian politicians quickly jumped on the bandwagon, appointing the world's first governmental post dedicated specifically to the protection of the environment in 1972. In 1983 former prime minister Gro Harlem Brundtland spearheaded the UN environmental commission bearing her name, which coined the term "sustainable development" when it submitted its report and recommendations, entitled *Our Common Future*, in 1987. Ever since, Norwegian foreign policy has persistently pursued a strong environmental engagement in the international sphere, donating considerable funds to the UN Environmental Agency, participating in international treaty mechanisms like the Kyoto Protocol, and promoting environmental protective measures through its development aid schemes.

The irony of taking on a leading role internationally in promoting the protection of the environment while simultaneously being responsible for and cashing in on a substantial amount of carbon emissions is not lost on Norwegian politicians or the chief executives of the state-run Norwegian oil company Statoil (recently reinvented as "Equinor," to shed its newfound interest in renewables from associations with its oil-tinged past and present). Addressing the issue of environmental degradation, the plot line developed among the executives overseeing the extractive industries has been to consistently refer to the statistical evidence for the *relative* purity and low emissions from Norwegian oil and gas extraction compared with more polluting alternatives, in a not-so-subtle version of the well-established rhetorical strategy of whataboutism.

A similar pattern can be detected in the discussions surrounding the management of the Government Pension Fund Global, the world's largest sovereign wealth fund, which currently owns 1.3 percent of all the shares in the world, to the tune of US$1 trillion.[17] Since its establishment in 1990, the management of the fund, including guidelines for which industries its investments can or should be targeting, has been a recurrent topic of political debate in Norway. The establishment of an advisory council on ethics in 2004 marked an important step toward increasing transparency, but news stories on the fund's involvements in businesses involved in anything from arms trade and gross human rights violations to nuclear energy continue to emerge as the fund becomes involved with an ever-growing number of transnational business conglomerates around the world. The management of the fund, which was established to ensure that oil revenues would be made available to future generations, encapsulates the dilemma at the heart of the Norwegian oil age: on the one hand, the fund acts as a responsible investor and secures the stability and predictability of the Norwegian economy for decades to come. On the other hand, the entire value of the fund comes at the expense of carbon emissions that damage the environment and at the risk of oil spills.

THE MISSIONARY POSITION

Notions of Norway and Norwegian-ness abroad have been developed in the relative tension between an idealistic self-image as a peaceful nation seeking to help those less fortunate, but doing so in order to clean up after its darker side as a pragmatic rent-seeker using whichever legal opportunity that can potentially bolster its international standing or increase its income. In its pursuit of both of these objectives and the space in between, Norwegian diplomats and policymakers have relied extensively on the cooperation with religious organizations and, in particular, their leaders. Norwegian religious leaders have been used as peace brokers in the Middle East and on East Timor and were sent on reconciliation missions to Pakistan following the cartoon crisis in 2006.

Parallel to the influence of religious leaders, Norwegian foreign policy, particularly in the area of development aid, has relied extensively on the competence and networks of religious organizations. Development issues became a theme of political interest for Norway in the 1960s as part of the country's obligations under its membership in the Organization for Economic Co-Operation and Development and as a strategic goal for the NATO alliance to fight communism. Lacking colonial, trade, or political connections to impoverished nations while having sent more Christian missionaries than any other country relative to population size, the know-how of missionary organizations became decisive to the geographical distribution and thematic orientation of early Norwegian development aid. Christian development aid organizations receive by far the largest proportions of the aid budget, which currently amounts to approximately US$4 billion, or 1 percent of the Norwegian gross national income. The proportion of state support for missionary activity has never been higher than at present, as state funding has gradually replaced the funds made available by private donations in earlier decades.

As social anthropologist Marianne Gullestad has observed, Norwegian missionary efforts have engendered and thrived on a subtle sense of superiority, under which the impression that the world, and Africa in particular, is in need of saving has become both believable and a moral imperative to act. These sentiments have been made possible by the dominant self-understanding of Norway as an "innocent, humane, tolerant, anti-racist and peace-loving society that is committed to help the needy" that is a strong undercurrent in Norwegian public discourse.[18] These conceptions of self and other clearly resemble the notion of being "more evolved" than the rest of the world, as noted for the U.S. approach to religion by Courtney Bender and Elizabeth Hurd in this volume. However, in the Norwegian setting, the idea of being "more evolved" does not stop at religion but is arguably a much broader and pervasive sentiment that stretches into most aspects of society.

Historian Terje Tvedt has characterized this self-image as a national "do-gooder regime" under which any form of criticism leveled against morally infused dilemmas becomes silenced and impossible, driving moralist development aid goals that have been hopelessly unrealistic and based on little or no understanding of local conditions in receiving countries.[19] Whatever the exactitude of these diagnoses, the strong international engagement of Norwegian civil society and diplomats in missionary efforts, environmental protection, and development aid is subject to perpetual discussions in which blunt moralism persistently provides the decisive backdrop.

Despite the already strong and sustained relationship between Norwegian development aid and religious organizations, aid organizations have recently called for a further strengthening of the involvement with religion in the distribution of aid money on the ground, on the presumption that some actors in the aid community, and particularly in the Ministry of Foreign Affairs, tend to avoid entanglement with religious actors in other countries for fear of getting involved in entrenched local conflicts. The call for more attention to the role of religion in development has led to calls for more "religion knowledge," both for diplomats and for bureaucrats working in the aid and development sector, from, among others, the Oslo Center for Peace, Democracy and Human Rights, headed by former prime minister Kjell Magne Bondevik.

The Norwegian Ministry of Foreign Affairs has also been targeted by Norwegian civil society and members of the European Parliament from the Christian Democratic Party to step up efforts to protect religious minorities abroad. While the concern for religious minorities abroad has a long history in Norwegian religious civil society originating in initiatives to protect the rights of Christians behind the Iron Curtain during the Cold War, the 2000s saw a more sustained effort that culminated in the appointment of a special ambassador for the protection of religious minorities in 2011. The mandate, which has never really gained traction in the Ministry of Foreign Affairs, has since been redefined to cover religious freedom more generally, albeit still with an emphasis on minorities. Concrete projects and results from these efforts have so far not materialized beyond a small earmarked funding for civil society to document the plight of Christians in the Middle East and the issuance of a guidance note for embassy staff on how to deal with religious minorities in their day-to-day work. Importantly, the note carefully connects the notion of religious freedom to surrounding rights like the freedom of expression and the freedom of association. As such, Norway appears to side with the European approach to religious freedom that dismisses the enthroning of the right as a unique and foundational right that some U.S. proponents favor.

CONCLUDING REMARKS

At first sight, Norwegian approaches to religion at home and abroad appear to be unconnected, as the dominance of the CoN at home leaves no particular trace upon the more utilitarian management of "religion" abroad. Upon closer inspection, however, domestic demarcations between "us" and "them" can also be traced in the continuum between idealism and utilitarianism that shapes Norwegian foreign policy. Underpinning both dichotomies is the idea that "normal" religion, properly framed and harnessed, can and should be exploited and used to further the interests of state and society. Importantly, however, neither the domestic nor the foreign policy approach to religion developed in Norway is unique to religion but can be generalized to most major political issues, all of which tend to be processed by the machinery of statistical averages, careful predictions, and instrumental analysis—in short, through normalism.

In the determination of what constitutes "normal" religion, discourses of Norway and Norwegian-ness appear primarily to rely on religious organizations like the CoN and its leaders as trusted arbiters and conversation partners in the continuous identification of the standards of normality toward which the "others," whether at home or abroad, may be measured toward. The dichotomy between "normal" and other forms of religiosity resembles the emerging division between "good" and "bad" religion in international relations identified by Elizabeth Shakman Hurd. On this reading, "good" religion should be protected and promoted because it contributes to relief efforts, nation-building, and the moral foundations of international public life, while "bad" religion should be contained and suppressed because it fosters intolerance, gender and sexual inequality, fanaticism and terrorism, and easily slips into violence.[20] However, unlike the good/bad schema identified by Hurd, which is premised on the recent, dawning realization among scholars of international relations that religion may be a relevant issue after all, Norwegian approaches to religion at home and abroad are parts of much longer historical arcs. The beginnings, curvatures, and potential endpoints of these arcs are only now becoming visible, as scholars have started drawing "religion" into the equation in their analyses of Norwegian policymaking, both at home and abroad. Until very recently, the normality of the hegemony of the CoN and the coextensions between missionary efforts and development aid were so embedded in Norwegian images of self and others that they were practically invisible. Until scholars like Marianne Gullestad, Torkel Brekke, and Terje Tvedt started writing on the ideologies and presuppositions that underpin Norwegian conceptions of self and of others at the end of the 1990s, the presumption was that the internal and external management of "religion" were completely unrelated.

This should come as no surprise, as the CoN up until the very near present both constituted and acted the part of just another branch of the Norwegian civil service. Only through legal changes that came into effect on January 1,

2017, did the Church gain legal personality and its ministers lose their status as civil servants. What remains to be seen—not least due to the ambiguous status of the Church in the amended Constitution—is who will be given the difficult task of shaping the new religious normal in Norwegian society in the years to come.

NOTES

1. "Høyre vil ha en norsk kulturkanon," Norwegian Public Broadcasting, January 3, 2017, https://www.nrk.no/kultur/hoyre-vil-ha-en-norsk-kulturkanon-1.13303178.
2. Jürgen Link, "On the Contribution of Normalism to Modernity and Postmodernity" *Cultural Critique* 57 (Spring 2004): 33–46, 38.
3. Berge Furre, *Norsk historie 1905–1940* (Oslo: Samlaget, 1971).
4. Rune Slagstad, *De nasjonale strateger* (Oslo: Pax, 1998).
5. As noted by Winnifred Sullivan and Lori Beaman, "establishment" is a tricky concept with many different interpretational layers. Winnifred Fallers Sullivan and Lori Beaman, eds., *Varieties of Religious Establishment* (Aldershot, U.K.: Ashgate, 2013). This is most certainly also the case in the Norwegian setting, where constitutional amendments adopted by parliament in order to separate the Church of Norway from the state pronounces that the Church will "remain the established church of Norway." For a further explanation of this paradox, see Helge Årsheim, "Imagine There's No Religion—and No State Church Too?" *Religion: Going Public* (blog), February 27, 2017, http://religiongoingpublic.com/archive/2017/imagine-theres-no-religion-and-no-state-church-too.
6. Ingunn Folkestad Breistein, "En helhetlig tros- og livssynspolitikk—ønskelig og mulig?" *Teologisk Tidsskrift* 2, no. 4 (2013): 314–36.
7. Oddbjørn Leirvik, "Religion som velferdsgode?" *Kirke og Kultur* 120, no. 4 (2016): 309–11.
8. The school subject has since been revised several times and has been the subject of criticism both from the UN Human Rights Committee (*Leirvåg and Others vs. Norway*, CCPR/C/82/D/1155/2003, November 23, 2004) and from the Grand Chamber of the European Court of Human Rights (*Folgerø and Others vs. Norway*, Application no. 15472/02, 2007).
9. Blasphemy remained prohibited in under gradually lessening penalties until 2015, when §142 of the 1902 Penal Act was formally abolished. See Årsheim, "Imagine There's No Religion."
10. Siv Ellen Kraf and Cato Christensen, "Religion i Kautokeino-opprøret: En analyse av samisk urfolksspiritualitet," *Nytt Norsk Tidsskrift* 28, no. 1 (2011): 18–27.
11. These tensions have recently run particularly high, as the Norwegian Supreme Court has dismissed two major cases concerning Sámi rights claims—one (Sara) related to an enforced reindeer cull, the other (Nesseby) concerning usage rights and ownership to land in Finnmark, the northernmost province in Norway. The

decisions are available in English translation at the Supreme Court of Norway website, https://www.domstol.no/en/Enkelt-domstol/supremecourt/rulings/ (accessed September 2, 2020).

12. Ipsos MMI: *Ukens tall*, https://www.ipsos.com/nb-no/ukenstall-flere-tror-ikke-pa-gud, (accessed April 3, 2018).
13. Lori G. Beaman, "Battles over Symbols: The 'Religion' of the Minority Versus the 'Culture' of the Majority," *Journal of Law and Religion* 28, no. 1 (2013): 67–104.
14. Halvard Leira, "'Hele vort folk er naturlige og fødte fredsvenner': Norsk Fredstenkning Fram Til 1906." *Historisk Tidsskrift* 83, no. 2 (2004): 153–80.
15. Iver B. Neumann, "Fred og forsoning som norsk utenrikspolitikk," *Internasjonal politikk* 70, no. 3 (2012): 362–71.
16. Aage Thor Falkanger, "Noen folkerettslige problemstillinger i Nordområdene—i fortid og nåtid," *Lov og rett* 46, no. 6 (2007): 323–44.
17. "Norway's Sovereign-Wealth Fund Passes the $1trn Mark," *Economist*, September 23, 2017, https://www.economist.com/news/finance-and-economics/21729458-5m-odd-norwegians-own-more-1-all-shares-world-norways.
18. Marianne Gullestad, "Normalising Racial Boundaries. The Norwegian Dispute About the Term Neger," *Social Anthropology* 13, no. 1 (2005): 27–46.
19. Terje Tvedt, "International Development Aid and Its Impact on a Donor Country: A Case Study of Norway," *European Journal of Development Research* 19, no. 4 (2007): 614–35.
20. Elizabeth Shakman Hurd, "International Politics After Secularism," *Review of International Studies* 38, no. 5 (2012): 943–961.

15

When Home Becomes Abroad, and Abroad Becomes Home

Thinking American Empire Through a New Sudan

NOAH SALOMON

On July 9, 2011, South Sudanese living in Khartoum came home from a long day of work only to find that their houses had been transferred to a foreign land. Walking up the dirt roads to their residences, what was most odd about this realization was that, despite this, everything looked eerily the same as when they had left for work in the morning. The walls that surrounded their domiciles—some stately, others very simple—still stood, and even the living quarters themselves behind those walls were still there, looking very much as they had left them. Their furniture was arranged the way they remembered; their cupboards still had most of the food that was in them before they left. Yet the ground underneath their homes had shifted, or so they were told. At around noon that day, 1,200 miles away in the city of Juba, James Wani Igga, Speaker of the South Sudanese parliament, had declared the independence of his country at a ceremony attended by dignitaries from across the world, including the Sudanese president, Omar al-Bashir, who wistfully bid the South Sudanese farewell after having fought them so bitterly for so many years. With that most powerful performative locution, what had been home for many South Sudanese living in the north (some only in more recent decades following displacement, others for their entire lives) was now constituted as a foreign land, and the far-off lands of Juba, Malakal, Nimule, and Bor, on which many had never before set eyes, were now their "homes."[1] In subsequent months and years, a lengthy process of repatriation (or in many cases, simply, patriation) began, a process that produced significant tension, as those who had remained on the ground in the south during the civil war came to see these returnees as usurpers, having relinquished "home" when the times were tough and seeking it back when there was money and status to gain. Exactly where one could call home and where abroad was difficult to pin down, as much for those who returned as for those who had stayed.

Within a volume that explores the nature of "home" and "abroad" as categories that differentially organize both political commitments and the identities of those who hold them, the question must be asked whether such categories have the stability and tenacity we often give them. Even if they have served as particularly powerful frames in which U.S. law and foreign policy have unfolded, as the volume editors so cogently argue, should we, as scholars, accept their coherence? For example, is the way that religion is governed at home and abroad actually as distinct as it might at first seem, evidence of double standards, a place where the Establishment Clause does not stand, or rather might our practice abroad be evidence of tensions raised at home, and vice versa? Although, to ask these questions, I use an example from what may seem a distant "abroad," I hope it may nevertheless push back at examples from our purported home, the United States, the geographic and conceptual space from which this volume is framed.

On closer examination, home and abroad appear less as distinct places than as discursive constructions that make certain kinds of political practice possible. For example, the U.S. encounter with Islam abroad makes the construction of surveillance projects at home seem necessary, while the purported existence of freedom of worship at home makes arguments that foreign projects do not unfairly target Muslims abroad seem plausible. The home is inextricable from the abroad in both cases. The publications of the U.S. State Department on Muslims in America produced for foreign consumption, which one encounters in the waiting rooms of embassies in Muslim-majority countries and beyond, is a small but clear example of the ways the domestic context is used as a device to help frame the war on terror abroad, helping it to draw a seemingly clean line between the *religion* that the U.S. protects and the *politics* it finds intolerable.[2] Elizabeth Shakman Hurd's insightful and urgent essay in this volume insists on the need for thinking of U.S. engagement *on the border*, and thus not separated *by a border*, as a dichotomous rendering of "at home and abroad" might otherwise suggest.[3] Hurd's examples in her chapter of Department of Homeland Security employees stationed in seventy countries around the world and of the new government conceptions of the borderlands moving increasingly inland into the U.S. mainland make us further cognizant that the state of exceptions to constitutional norms often tolerated on foreign territory are increasingly "at home," while the enforcement of U.S. law is increasingly stationed abroad. Hurd provocatively asks, creatively situating the border between religion and nonreligion in conversation with the border between home and abroad: "What might it look like to study the United States in global context if we began with the assumption that the assignment of religiousness or nonreligiousness as qualities of actions, institutions or policies is an *effect* of particular, historically located patterns, habits, affects, and practices—and that these effects are deeply imbricated with the construction and reproduction of borders between domestic and foreign, citizen and alien, home and abroad?" The same sort of question can be asked about the putative border between the two Sudans.

Indeed, the emergence of the two Sudans represents both an exceptional case—a country going through the process of partition and redefining national identity on both sides of the border in the process—and one all too familiar, particularly given the alarming rise of xenophobic nationalism these days in the West at a rate unseen since the end of World War II. In both cases, home is deeply tied to ethnicity, and the claim that "we were all immigrants" is lost on those who insist, "yes, but not *those* kinds of immigrants." In some sense, the fact that the internationally mediated peace process that led to Sudanese partition relied on and reinscribed notions of home and nation on an ethnic and religious basis (these tribes belong north of the border, these other tribes south) is evidence of the not-yet-ready for the liberal promise that Mark Twain cites (and that scholars like Uday Mehta have discussed at length[4]). Yet in a very real sense too, they are examples of processes that occur "at home" as well, whether through the dehumanization and extrajudicial execution of Black men that underlies the trigger-happy practices of American law enforcement or through the implementation of "countering violent extremism" programs that seek to reform American Muslims.[5] That is to say, the very idea that America is constituted as a domestic exception to a foreign policy of ethnic politics and religious establishment would likely be lost on a great deal of the American population itself and thus emerges from a very limited, and privileged, subject position. Still, the U.S. role in the partition of the Sudans is certainly evidence of the "at home" and "abroad" *logic* that sustains and makes possible U.S. intervention the world over, one in which clear-cut boundaries are often explicitly organized around race and religion. And while South Sudanese independence was posed as a benign example of this logic, couched in the language of "self-determination" (without any real interrogation of who the "self" is that is doing the determining), its results have been equally, if not more, bloody than those that were not.

The example of Sudanese partition also forces us to ask: how do categories of home and abroad shift throughout time? What other instances can we think of where home became abroad and abroad became home, and what exactly does the change in these designations mark? While the case of Sudan's partition may be an extreme one, in that it reverses the signifiers of "home" and "abroad" literally between the morning and nightfall on one fateful day, I wonder if the lesson it teaches us—on the instability and artifice of the categories of "home" and "abroad"—might be more generally applicable than we might at first think.[6] If we are to destabilize American exceptionalism as both a political and a scholarly endeavor (that is, one to which our own writing also contributes), seeing how a case from a putative abroad might be generative in understanding our home and its imperial adventures may be a particularly useful and productive task.

It is, moreover, important to note that the Sudans are not just *any* abroad, but one that the United States (and earlier imperial powers) was essential in delineating both geographically and demographically. The Comprehensive Peace Agreement (CPA) of 2005 that laid out a blueprint for splitting Sudan on ethnic lines was often deemed one of George W. Bush's only foreign policy victories—that is, before the country slipped back into unrelenting civil war in December of 2013. Ironically, that war is often analyzed as ethnically motivated (this time between the Dinka and Nuer, rather than African and Arab, as in the Sudanese civil war of 1983–2005), evidence that "ethnic difference" is a cell that has the ability to divide itself infinitely and thus is a problem that no border can solve.

In the years following the signing of the CPA, the United States Agency for International Development (USAID), from its base in Nairobi, began a lengthy project of solidifying South Sudan's governmental infrastructure. In governance capacity formation projects such as these, it seems "abroad" is less the other to "home" than a vision of "home's" creation, projected on a distant land. Here, the goal was less reproducing the structure and institutions of the imperial power abroad than it was playing out that power's own tensions overseas in ways that would never be possible at home. So, in the case of U.S.–South Sudan relations, the tensions between the U.S. allergy toward international law on its own soil and its "firm commitment to human rights" can be juxtaposed with the harmony of the mission statements of the ministries that USAID helped set up in South Sudan with relevant UN mechanisms. Another example here would be the United States' own inability to address deficits on gender equality through executive power at home contrasted by its playing a leading a role in supporting a "Ministry of Gender" in South Sudan.[7] As a helpful parallel, we might look at Keally McBride's recent *Mr. Mothercountry*, which traces the story of a colonial administrator in Britain as he helped to establish rule of law across the empire, not *because* Britain was so well run, she argues, but *in spite of* it.[8]

Might we come to understand our home better by exploring its deepest and darkest fantasies as they play out in the very real situation of the countries to which they are exported? What does a foreign policy based on ethnicity and communal identity tell us about the lingering, unsettled nature of race and religion in our own country, assumptions borne out of decades of unaddressed strife? That is, might what America promotes abroad not be the "other" to its own peculiarities of race and religion but in fact its realization?[9] It is my hope that through an examination of one set of individuals caught in the in-between of this border drawing process, we might begin to answer some of these questions.[10]

On July 28, 2011, a mere three weeks after South Sudanese independence, I met Abdullah Deng Nhial at a garden hotel bar in Juba. With the smooth jazz horns of Wham's "Careless Whispers" wafting through the warm summer air, Nhial told me a story that was anything but carefree. Indeed, Nhial was in the midst of a transformation that was nothing short of a metamorphosis. Abdallah Deng Nhial Ayom was born in Anglo-Egyptian Condominium Sudan in 1954, two years before Sudan would declare its independence and only one year before the First Sudanese Civil War (between north and south) began. He was born in the town of Bor in Jonglei to a Dinka family of the same ethnic subgroup as the leader of the South Sudanese resistance during the Second Sudanese Civil War, John Garang. Nhial's family left Bor early on, and he grew up in Upper Nile State, in Renk, his first schooling being at a Qur'anic *khalwa*, even though neither of his parents were Muslim (his father was Christian, his mother followed traditional practices). Renk at that time (as it still was at the time of my research) was a heavily Muslim city, and Nhial described himself as deeply influenced by his surroundings. As a young man he converted to Islam. Extremely successful in his schooling, he managed to get a prized acceptance into the most famous classical center of Islamic learning in the world, Al-Azhar University in Cairo, where he studied in the School of Arabic Language. There he became active in the Sudanese Student Union, which at that time, in the mid-1970s, was heavily influenced by what was called *al-ittijah al-islami* (the Islamic trend), a collection of organizations loosely affiliated with the Muslim Brotherhood. After his time in Egypt, he returned to Sudan, first teaching Arabic in Renk and then, after getting master's degree at the University of Khartoum, teaching at the University of Juba.

The mid-1980s are a little opaque in my interview, but somehow Nhial had risen in the ranks of the National Islamic Front (NIF), an Islamist political party made up primarily of Northern Riverian elite that in the 1980s was desperately trying to diversify its ranks, as T. Abdou Maliqalim Simone's mesmerizing book *In Whose Image? Political Islam and Urban Practices in Sudan* details in a firsthand account.[11] Only days after the NIF took over Sudan in a bloodless coup in 1989, Nhial was appointed national minister of religious guidance and direction (*wazir al-irshad wa-l-tawjih*) in Khartoum. Despite various personnel reshuffling, throughout the early 1990s, Nhial remained at the highest echelon of government and party service, first as minister of peace and reconstruction and then as governor of White Nile state (in the north) in the early 1990s, and finally as parliamentary whip. In 1999, when the parliament was suspended by the president and Hasan al-Turabi, the mastermind behind the president's Islamist coup, was dismissed, Nhial joined the new party that al-Turabi subsequently founded (first called NIF-Popular Congress and then, simply, the Popular Congress Party), rising to the rank of assistant secretary general. Indeed, the way he came into my consciousness was that he was the Popular Congress Party candidate for the presidency in the 2010 national elections, back when national unity was still a theoretical possibility. Indeed, he was distinguished as being the only southern Sudanese candidate in those elections.[12] Since the winds were blowing in the direction of secession already, the Sudan People's Liberation Movement (SPLM), the chief representatives of southern Sudan, had fielded a northern candidate, Yasir Arman, as a coded reference that partition was inevitable and that southerners were no longer interested in a presidency based in Khartoum. Yet, the Islamist Popular Congress Party, in a show of support for national unity, chose Nhial as their candidate. By July of 2011 when I met him, however, he was no longer a member of the Popular Congress Party since he was now a citizen of South Sudan, with the very province he had once ruled as governor no longer a part of his country.

In between bites of a late dinner, Nhial told me,

> I, as a Muslim, and [the Islamist parties of which I was a member] called for the application of Islam in general life. And we believed that Islam is a religion and a state. Islam is the guide of the Muslim in all [aspects] of his life: economically, socially, culturally, in terms of sports, the arts, all of it. . . . I served in the role of assistant secretary general [of the Popular Congress Party that supported this position] until July 9, 2011. . . . At this point, I resigned because we became a country and it is forbidden for a foreigner to be part of a political party in another country.

And just like that, a career that started with Islamist political activities as part of the Sudanese Student Union at al-Azhar University in Cairo, continued with rising to the highest ranks of the NIF government and then to playing a major role in the Islamist opposition, ended between sunrise and sunset on one fateful day.

When I met him in 2011 Nhial was entering into a process of reinvention. South Sudan had banned any parties with a religious color under its emergent brand of secularism and Nhial, although he told me that secularism is "a fantasy invented by some academics and embraced by simple people in the third world," recognized that he could not agitate for Islam being both religion and state in his new country.[13] Rather, he had to hope for a gradual progression of Islam that might someday lead to a demographic majority. His former home (a unified Sudan) and two-thirds of its territory had become a foreign land, and he was trying to make this new political space of South Sudan into a new home, imagining what his career might look like under these circumstances, but often losing the thread.

The last I heard of Nhial was that he was very briefly appointed minister of environment in the South Sudanese government in 2013 but that he was quickly dismissed from that post after engaging in a fistfight with a parliamentarian over the status of the disputed (between Sudan and South Sudan), oil-rich region of Abyei. Abyei is the only Dinka-dominant area that had not been given to South Sudan after partition but remained under a special administrative status. At least partially under the logic of ethnic affinity, however, South Sudan still claims it as its own. According to a report concerning the fistfight, Nhial thought Abyei a lost cause for South Sudan, indelibly part of the north, clearly still refusing a definition of Sudan and South Sudan based on ethnicity alone.[14] Although Nhial told me that he had voted for secession since he felt that this was the will of the people and he did not want to be opposed to the voice of the majority (he is a politician, after all), it seemed he had never left behind the idea of a home that embraced both north and south.[15] "A Muslim is the brother of a Muslim the world over," he told me, but in the "at home and abroad" logics of the powers that supported the Comprehensive Peace Agreement, home had been determined solely by ethnic origin. Thus, it was not merely that the *location* of home and abroad had shifted for Nhial but that the very *definition* of what constitutes home and abroad was itself contested with new political realities forcing new imaginings: his own a somewhat amorphous vision in terms of the location of home that based solidarity on creed versus the new territorial reality based on ethnicity.

Nhial was not at all alone in the predicament of reinvention. Many far more average South Sudanese were also grappling with the drastic reversal of fortunes they faced. South Sudanese Muslims faced a particular challenge in this regard. As Muslims, they felt they had suddenly been deemed internal foreigners, no longer authentically South Sudanese in a country now attempting to define itself away from its past as part of a nation couched as an Islamic state. Like the protagonist in the well-known Urdu short story I reference in note 10, "Toba Tek Singh," they had planted their feet "on the border," refusing to move into either side of the space divided between "home" and "abroad," as they were currently constituted. Despite that on the whole they supported—indeed, deemed necessary—secession,[16] such individuals felt that their fellow non-Muslim citizens saw them as insufficiently South Sudanese. One young Muslim in Malakal asked me, "How do we change the perception that Islam is the religion of *jallaba* [a derogatory term for northerners]?" Or as another put it:

> Anyone who wants to serve Islam in the South they say he is working for the NCP [the name that the ruling party in the North took on in the late 1990s], that he is working for the North. Everyone concerned with Islamic issues in the South, they say he is working for the North. Today if any Muslims say we want to participate in governing the South, they will be characterized as working for the North, that they want to turn the country into an Islamic region.... In order to change the understanding of Southerners on Islam and Muslims in the South ... we should open up different channels of communication other than those with the North, we should connect outside, for example with the countries of the Gulf, with Saudi Arabia, with Muslims in America ... in order to change their understanding and tell them "we are not with the North."

While it is unclear that such an effort would have any chance of success, the urgency that southern Muslims felt in decoupling Islam from the painful history with the north and inserting it into a global history was striking. The fact that the south was split from the north on both religious and ethnic lines, under the logic of self-determination from Arab and Islamic excesses, made this decoupling particularly difficult for South Sudanese Muslims, as their existence muddled those clear categories and the clean breaks upon which independence itself was predicated. But South Sudanese Muslims had little choice otherwise. They had become foreigners in a double sense: in the north, legally speaking since they were ethnically southern, and in the south, culturally speaking since they were religiously Muslim. There was no nostalgia among South Sudanese Muslims for a home in the north, as fellow South Sudanese often assumed, but rather they expressed a desire to think in new ways about the kinds of solidarity to which they might be party, on distinctly transnational lines.[17]

The fact that the construction of this new home in South Sudan would require a new kind of religious identity was not lost on these individuals either. The privatization of Islam that was being required of the Muslim community as a result of the government's secularization process was deeply troubling to many young Muslims. One told me:

> We have so many Muslim organizations in the South now and what is required of them is to push against the closing of mosques.[18] Why are they saying "well, man, we've become the underclass, we're small in number, we can just pray at home not at mosques?" Why have they accepted this? This is exactly the problem. Who will defend us if not these organizations? [These leaders] should demand the opening of all closed mosques in the South, and the practicing of Islam with full freedom, and *da'wa* (proselytization) in the public square, not just in mosques.... These days, one is too timid to wear the *jallabiyya* so no one classifies him as Muslim. This is a problem. [The Muslim], rather than announcing his religion, has begun to hide it. These days, when one goes to Friday prayer, he wears a shirt and pants, while in the old days he would wear a *jallabiyya* and turban.

Another person in the room continued:

> When we met with the advisor to the president on religious affairs ... he said that he wanted the Muslims to back-off from several things: that there should be no concept of apostasy, that the Muslim should be able to change his religion as he likes ... the punishments for alcohol, the punishments for adultery, the rulings on divorce: these things Muslim must back away from in a clear way.... He also said that Arabic will not be an official language here. And if the Muslims want to open a private school, it could only happen under the heading of the Islamic Council that the state set up.

In both of these articulations, my interlocutors express difficulty coming to terms with their new home, for the new home requires not just relocation but the formation of a new ways of being Muslim. While legal citizenship can change overnight, religious identity inheres in more sedimented ways, thus ostensibly requiring more time to shake free of former attachments. While these South Sudanese Muslims did not long to return to the north, or to a situation of northern rule, they could not quite figure out how to be *at home* in their new home. The secular model that South Sudan had adopted (often referred to as "American secularism," in that its proponents felt it protected religious freedom while guarding against establishment, but in reality perhaps closer to French secularism, in that it established a state-sanctioned Muslim hierarchy and restricted organization on the basis of religion) was understood as a mechanism of exclusion for the Muslims who encountered it. For both Abdallah Deng Nhial and these Muslim youth, the changes required when home became abroad and abroad tried to fashion itself as home were difficult to inhabit indeed.

It is important to note that the idea that an SPLM victory would lead to the necessity of such acrobatics was never a fait accompli. This is a point worth mentioning if only to push back against the notion that the differences that divided south and north were in some sense atavistic, universally accepted, or that they required a border line in order to be policed. Indeed, the intensity of the violence within the borders of South Sudan and Sudan following partition should be evidence enough that such an argument is spurious. Although the reality of the present has a tendency to create an amnesia of the past, we know that John Garang, the SPLM's founder and *the* "founding father" of South Sudan, with his bust on its currency, supported the idea of a new Sudan, reformed from its northern to its southern borders, and its western to its eastern reaches, and not a separate state, a splitting of Sudan into "homes" and "abroads," south and north. In Garang's writings and speeches, we see an example of a postcolonial intellectual pushing back against the exportation of paradigms of home and abroad advocated by Western powers, the very paradigms, one might argue, adopted in the partition of Sudan.

In a document entitled "First Statement by John Garang to the Sudanese People on 10 August 1989; Following the Military *coup d'état* of 30 June 1989," Garang sets out the vision he would hold until his untimely death in a helicopter crash on July 30, 2005. It is worth quoting here as, although it imagines *a home*, it rejects the idea of a *homeland*, a *volkisch* vision tied to ethnic identity. "If the junta is to be of any use to the Sudan," he wrote in outlining his response to a coup whose agenda was still (perhaps intentionally) not clear,

> it must discard this perception of a Southern problem and think with the rest of us, think with the march of history, not with the archaic past.[19] According to this archaic perception Omer [al-Bashir, leader of the junta, and president of Sudan until April of 2019] thinks that he is the Sudanese nationalist and we in the SPLA are his Southerners, and according to him all that which is required is for him to sit down with Dr. John Garang, representing the South, and him representing the Sudan, and in his words talk soldier to soldier to solve his

Southern Problem. Has Brig. Omer el Bashir bothered to ask the question as to what is it that makes him the Sudanese and makes Dr. John Garang his southerner?[20]

In one stroke, Garang destabilizes the very hypothesis that was to underlie *both* northern and southern separatism *and* the international efforts that encouraged them: the very idea of a "Southern problem" or of a necessary minority condition altogether. The 2011 declaration of independence that was proclaimed in a square that bears his name, housing a tomb that holds his earthly remains, seems to reject the very premise of his vision as he framed it. Although Garang agreed in 2005 to a peace agreement that would allow for secession if unity was not made attractive for southerners, he never advocated for it in principle.[21] In Garang's "Statement of 10 August 1989," he argues that secessionism is in fact an agenda of the government of Sudan in order to rid itself of its "southern problem," far more so than it is (or should be) a goal of "the southerners." He continues: "We have reason to believe that the junta has a hidden agenda to partition the country. El Bashir himself has said so in various forms at least three times in the last 40 days.... [I] want to assure the Sudanese people that the Movement [SPLM] is totally against separation. In this connection, it is to be recalled that the first blood shed by the SPLA was not against the Sudanese Army, the first battles were against the separatists within the SPLA."[22] Instead, Garang argues, quoting the SPLM founding manifesto, "The principle objective of the SPLM/SPLA is not separation for the South. The South is an integral and inseparable part of the Sudan. Africa has been fragmented sufficiently enough by colonialism and neo-colonialism and further fragmentation can only be in the interest of her enemies."[23]

I cite Garang here simply to illustrate the very much contingent ways in which notions of home and abroad settle in the worlds we occupy. While the point might seem obvious that the borders we draw between these designations are arbitrary, political, and thus never predetermined, few cases both allow us to see the arguments (for and against) that lie behind their construction and the effects of their adoption on diverse populations. This I observed in my meetings with the wide range of South Sudanese Muslim activists I quote above and see as evident in the subsequent history of both Sudans.

So what might we learn from these Sudanese cases about the nature of the categories of "home" and "abroad" as frames for how we conduct our political practice and academic endeavors, as scholars working at institutions based in the American hegemon? How might South Sudan, as a uniquely situated "abroad" to the United States, help us to reflect on tensions at home? It seems to me that three points are worth mentioning here, although I mean them not as any sort of conclusions but rather as ideas to be explored further.

1. The instability of the categories of home and abroad are not unique to citizens of a country going through partition but rather are shared by many figures in our fractured present: from the migrant to the mercenary, from the advocate of global governance to the purveyor of global finance. Moreover, of course, historically speaking, though perhaps not as quickly as the South Sudanese case, notions of home and abroad change across time, but it is usually longue durée time. Engaging with South Sudanese interlocutors on the redefinitions required when the ground shifts beneath them in real time offers a rare opportunity to view the effects of a changing at home and abroad frame on modes of government, on senses of self, and, not insignificantly, on the politics of religion. If we view at home and abroad less as fixed spaces and more as constantly shifting indexes, what then do we make of attempts to contest their definitions among the people about whom we write? Could a political praxis of at home and abroad (like that of Garang, for example) be written for our own era and our own American location? In this age of rising American ethnonationalism, how might we contest the clarity of America in a similar way to which Garang interrogates "Sudan," recognizing the salience of our global location and thus resisting the temptation to frame things as either domestic or foreign?

2. South Sudan (and likely many other places) is perhaps not exactly an "abroad" to us here in the United States, at least in the othering way that this word is often used. Rather, its birth came about, in part, as the result of U.S. power and a fantasy about South Sudan as a bulwark that could stop the Muslim advance across the tenth parallel.[24] This is the reason that so many American evangelicals supported the southern rebels during the Sudanese civil war.[25] The case of South Sudan forces us, then, to look at the "abroad" less as a space where the liberal promise offered at home is suspended than as a place where the very fantasies that sustain that liberal promise (here in its enduring fear of the Islamic threat to who we think we are) play out. How might such a realization change the way we approach Sudan and parallel cases?

3. Finally, and relatedly, the South Sudanese case forces us to question the role of scholars in sustaining and rigidifying the categories of "home" and

"abroad," as the introduction to this volume so thoughtfully asks us to do. By studying America within its borders, or South Sudan as a foreign space, do we not reinscribe the very fiction of home and abroad that our work otherwise destabilizes? This is a question relevant not only to our scholarship but to our roles at the colleges and universities at which we teach, reliant still on outdated area studies models. Where is America not? The case of South Sudan shows us that not only are home and abroad two sides of the same coin, one a fantasy of the other, but if the tensions baked into their delineations are left unresolved, they can produce explosive results. The apocalyptic violence that took place in South Sudan following partition, structured as it was around the ethnic politics of the homeland, exhibits this point in vivid colors.

NOTES

To avoid any confusion, this particular "new Sudan" to which I refer in the title is that of the Republic of South Sudan, founded in 2011. The essay that comprises this chapter was written in the spring of 2017, prior to a whole host of transformational historical events in both Sudan and South Sudan, upon which many further "new Sudans" proliferated. I write on these newer developments in subsequent essays.

1. Nicki Kindersley's 2016 PhD dissertation, "The Fifth Column? An Intellectual History of Southern Sudanese Communities in Khartoum, 1969–2005" (Durham University, Durham, England, 2016), is the only study I know to discuss the complex identity of this community, although she ends her study some years before independence. In the following I introduce readers to some of the individuals I met who had "returned" to the South following partition.
2. Photos displayed in the State Department document "Being Muslim in America" illustrate this point: https://photos.state.gov/libraries/korea/49271/dwoa_122709/being-muslim-in-america.pdf (accessed May 30, 2020). The emerging work of anthropologist Ahmed Sharif Ibrahim that takes a multisited ethnographic approach to the global war on terror to argue for a shared space of U.S. engagement with Islam, spanning the U.S. and Somalia, is the first horizontal study of this problematic of which I am aware, clearly showing the inseparability of America's home and abroad across two key field sites.
3. Hurd suggests that contrasting freedom and disestablishment at home with a case-by-case state of exception abroad not only obscures complex realities of domestic and foreign religious governance but also reproduces narratives about the United States in relation to a series of internal and external others that are, in fact, in need of interrogation.
4. As Sullivan and Hurd quote in the introduction: "Is it, perhaps, possible that there are two kinds of Civilization—one for home consumption and one for the heathen

market?" Mark Twain, "To the Person Sitting in Darkness" (1901). See Uday Mehta, *Liberalism and Empire: A Study in Nineteenth Century British Liberal Thought* (Chicago: University of Chicago Press, 1999).
5. Again, see Hurd's essay in the present volume.
6. For isn't such instability of home and abroad present in everything from the changing identity of domestic foreigners (Japanese Americans to Muslim Americans), to the presence of U.S. outposts and Green Zones during recent military adventures, to the status of Puerto Rico?
7. A thorough description of USAID's support for gender mainstreaming projects in southern/South Sudan can be found in Judy A. Benjamin, *Gender Assessment: USAID/Southern Sudan*, October 2010, https://pdf.usaid.gov/pdf_docs/PNADT679.pdf. The website of the ministry showing its harmonization with international mechanisms that the United States itself has not ratified—such as the Convention on the Elimination of All Forms of Discrimination against Women (CEDAW)—is archived at https://web.archive.org/web/20190320123124/http://mgcswss.org/directorates/directorate-gender/. In Joan Scott's brilliant *Sex and Secularism* (Princeton, N.J.: Princeton University Press, 2017), she argues that gender equality in particular emerges as an enshrined value of the secular only through critical tension with the Western encounter with Islam, a point not irrelevant in South Sudan as it (with the help of its international friends) sought to disentangle itself from the Islamic mode of governance under which it lived prior to independence. With this history in mind, we can imagine why such work on gender might have seemed necessary to U.S. officials in southern/South Sudan at this particular juncture.
8. Keally McBride, *Mr. Mothercountry: The Man Who Made the Rule of Law* (Oxford: Oxford University Press, 2016). I thank Winnifred Fallers Sullivan for bringing this book to my attention.
9. The sustenance of the Darfur conflict through the projection of U.S. racial politics into an African versus Arab frame—as discussed by Mahmood Mamdani in his *Saviors and Survivors: Darfur, Politics and the War on Terror* (New York: Doubleday, 2010) and in Hisham Aidi's "Slavery, Genocide and the Politics of Outrage: Understanding the New Racial Olympics," *Middle East Report* 35, no. 264 (Spring 2005): 40–56—is another example of such a projection.
10. Conversations with Christian Novetzke at the working group for this volume's second gathering regarding parallels between the case of the Sudans and that of the partition of India were illuminating on this and several other points. (They were also evidence for me that someone, someday, needs to put together a book on comparative partitions, particularly bringing together those like Sudan, India, and Yugoslavia, where the specter of religious, and particularly Muslim, difference plays such a significant role). On the question of the in-betweens, Novetzke pointed me to the wonderful short story "Toba Tek Singh" by Saadat Hasan Manto, in *The Oxford Book of Urdu Short Stories*, trans. Amina Azfar (Oxford: Oxford University Press, 2009), which discusses the transfer of insane asylum patients between India and Pakistan as a device to point out the insanity of the arbitrariness of the designation of homeland. The story ends with the protagonist refusing any such

designation and dying in the neutral land on the border between the two countries. Kale and Novetzke's own wonderful essay for this volume equally troubles the borders between home and abroad by looking critically at the debates on cultural appropriation in which designations of (authentic) homes and (fabricated) abroads are too often taken at face value.

11. T. Abdou Maliqalim Simone, *In Whose Image? Political Islam and Urban Practice in Sudan* (Chicago: University of Chicago Press, 1994).
12. "Sudan's Main Presidential Candidates," Reuters, January 29, 2010, http://www.reuters.com/article/sudan-elections-idAFMCD94197720100129.
13. For a study of South Sudan's secular project, see Noah Salomon, "Religion After the State: Secular Soteriologies at the Birth of South Sudan," *Journal of Law and Religion* 29, no. 3 (October 2014): 447–69.
14. "Salva Kiir Dismisses Environment Minister After Fight," *Sudan Tribune*, November 27, 2013, http://sudantribune.com/spip.php?article48962 (accessed May 30, 2020).
15. Nhial told me that it was the ruling party in the north that made anything but secession impossible, seeming to argue (along with many I met, in fact, who often cited the reunification of Germany even only days after partition) that the two-state solution was only a temporary one, until the ruling party was out of power in the north. This theme has partially returned in popular discourse following the Sudanese Revolution of 2018–2019, when the ruling party was indeed deposed, but it has not caught on in any official policy circles as of yet.
16. Indeed, many South Sudanese Muslims came to argue that separation merely illustrated an already existing reality. One young activist in Juba told me in 2011:

    [Back in the days in which I lived in the North], there were people who said that a southerner could not pray in front of a northerner. And if you became an Imam and someone found that he was praying behind you, he'd go pray again. . . . Of course, in religious doctrine these words can nowhere be found, but the problem was with individual northerners. Sudan was already separated into two parts [even before partition]. Even the Muslims would say, "these are our southern brothers" [not that "these are Sudanese"]. . . . And we as Southerners in the North would eat and drink and stay only among ourselves [with very little social contact with Northerners]. . . . And even in the organizations that were supposed to help Southern Muslims, the directors would just say "come tomorrow" every time we came until we gave up. So we lost our trust in Muslim northerners. . . . Until now, there are those who try to create a fabric between Northern and Southern Muslims, but I reject this idea. This is now an independent country and we should . . . make the beginning as new, from zero. . . . Southerners don't want to deal with Arabs . . . we know their morals and their ways because we lived with them. But Southerners recognize Europeans, Kenyans, even Latin Americans. They are good people who don't like oppression. So perhaps we can change the channels of our relationships as Muslims to the west, not to north [Sudan].

17. That is, there was no nostalgia for the north "as home": as the euphoric moment of 2011's independence appeared smaller and smaller in the rearview mirror, South Sudanese who had moved to the south from the comparative comfort of Khartoum, regardless of religious identity, often expressed nostalgia for their lives in the north, despite the discrimination they faced there.

18. Mosques on government property were being shuttered at the time (2011–12) due to the desire of the government to secularize public space. I discuss this at more length in Salomon, "Religion After the State."
19. Garang writes elsewhere in this document, "We diagnosed the problem not as a 'Southern Problem' but as the 'Problem of Khartoum,' that is, the problem of power in Khartoum. We therefore resolved to struggle for a radical restructuring of power in Khartoum to bring about a new commonality, a new identity, a new socio-political formation, a socio-political formation which we call the New Sudan" (258).
20. The document is published in John Garang, *The Call for Democracy in Sudan* (London: Kegan Paul International, 1992), 241.
21. See, e.g., Simon Allison, "Was the Secession of South Sudan a Mistake?" *Daily Maverick*, January 7, 2014, https://www.dailymaverick.co.za/article/2014-01-07-analysis-was-the-secession-of-south-sudan-a-mistake/#.Wsuzpy-ZOL8.
22. Garang, *Call for Democracy*, 253.
23. Garang, *Call for Democracy*, 253.
24. It strikes me here that fantasies about the Sudans being untenable due to their diversity—and thus the idea that the reduction thereof is the key to their stability (a situation of course belied by the exponential increase in instability following partition)—itself sustains the fantasy of American exceptionalism as the one country able to assimilate its diversity into a workable whole. "America is hard to see," Bender reminds us in her insightful essay in this volume, due in part to its endless spiritual expanse, a horizon infinitely expanding out of view. It is ironic, perhaps, that the present essay begins with a Sudan that is hard to see for precisely the opposite reason: a truncation of possibility (to be both southern and Sudanese) that reminds us how American confidence in its own capaciousness is so often juxtaposed with the limits assumed to inhere everywhere else (I thank Christian Novetzke for pushing me to think about these contrasts).
25. Melani McAlister outlines this in her article "U.S. Evangelicals and the Politics of Slave Redemption as Religious Freedom in Sudan," *South Atlantic Quarterly* 113, no. 1 (2014): 87–108. Christopher Tounsel has written on how the partnership with American evangelicals led to a "martial theology" among Southerners during the Civil War. Christopher Tounsel, "Khartoum Goliath: SPLM/SPLA Update and Martial Theology during the Second Sudanese Civil War," *Journal of Africana Religions* 4, no. 2 (July 2016): 129–53. McAlister's latest book, *The Kingdom of God Has No Borders: A Global History of American Evangelicals* (Oxford: Oxford University Press, 2018), discusses evangelical involvement in South/southern Sudan at more length.

Afterword: Double Vision, Double Cross

American Exceptionalism, Borders, and the Study of Religion

PAMELA E. KLASSEN

"Where is America not?" asks Noah Solomon. "America is hard to see," says Courtney Bender. Both everywhere and ghostly, America is a powerful idea, a prophetic vision, and a very material infrastructure that stretches around, within, and above the earth. The United States of America became a homeland by drawing and redrawing the borders of "settler sovereignty" on top of already existing Indigenous visions of the land.[1] And then it articulated its encompassing global reach through political speech, legal writ, financial transactions, and blockbuster movies as much as through underwater cables, satellite surveillance, and drone strikes. A place-based distinction of "home" and "abroad" for understanding America, then, is at once exceedingly necessary and dangerously misleading. Necessary, because the juxtaposition of home and abroad motivates attachments to nation, both ambivalent and jingoistic, with powerful effects that require careful analysis. Dangerous, because such a juxtaposition, if overly naturalized, risks making even more nebulous the ubiquity of America and even more obscured the resistance to and refusal of this ubiquity by all those who do not call it home.

The essays gathered in *At Home and Abroad* work to bring their readers to see America and to recognize its limits. To orient the reader, the editors take two intersecting approaches in the introduction, one categorical and one historical. The first approach lists pairs of categories that the essays both utilize and problematize: inside/outside, religion/politics, home/abroad. The second approach crosscuts these pairs by way of four "historical moments," each of which reveals how "specific conceptions of, and shifting relations between, 'home' and 'abroad,' 'religion' and 'politics' have enabled a distinctively American national project whose implications cannot be accurately described if we continue to privilege divides between domestic and foreign while holding religion constant." Inspired and haunted by claims and "theologies" of American exceptionalism (the subject of a companion volume), the book is an argument via historical exemplar and category critique that religion, largely in a protestant Christian instantiation, is key to the power and the illusion of such exceptionalism.

Reading the book, one is urged to cultivate a practice of double vision by looking both "at home" and "abroad" to see how the malleability of religion, especially when manifested as religious freedom, has contributed to the making of American power. Each of the introduction's four historical moments couples an outward-facing illustration of how the discursive power of Christian-inflected American religious freedom was exported abroad with an inward-looking example of how "churchstateness," often by way of religious freedom, was in play at home.[2] In each case, however, the outward-facing and inward-looking examples trouble the very distinction of home and abroad. America is akin to an imperial virus that spread through invading other peoples, their laws, and their religious organizations and then incorporating them both metaphorically and literally. As David Maldonado Rivera (this volume) quotes in his essay on church incorporation in Puerto Rico, the United States was able to "possess" other lands and jurisdictions, such as Puerto Rico, through a sleight of hand that rendered these lands "foreign ... in a domestic sense."[3]

The first historical examples twinned by the editors occur in the early nineteenth century. One the one hand, the outward thrust of new protestant evangelization societies during the early republic, including the American Colonization Society's attempt to resettle African slaves in Liberia and the intensification of Christian missions to Indigenous peoples, center Christian visions of civilization as a tool of state expansion. On the other hand, within U.S. jurisdictions there were increasing efforts on the part of (largely white) citizens to disestablish Christianity in search of freedom from religion. The second twinned moment focuses on American protestant imperialism at the turn of the twentieth century, as exemplified by the annexation of the Philippines and the continued breaking of treaties with Indigenous nations through a process of annexation or allotment, at the same time that Bible reading in U.S. public schools was increasingly outlawed state by state. The third moment is framed by the mid-twentieth-century Cold War, an era in which to be anti-Communist abroad was also to be pro-Christianity (which by this point included Catholicism). At the same time, religious freedom laws grew in scope within the United States, especially at the federal level. In all of these examples, Americans debated their right to be free of state-based religious ordinances within their nation, while their nation-state faced the world with a Christian civilizing mission as its raison d'être.

We are living in the fourth historical moment, which is encapsulated by the ongoing twenty-first-century "war on terror," a time when Americans have deployed both their military and their laws, including the International Religious Freedom Act of 1998, against Muslims and in favor of Christians around the world. At the same time, domestically, in a recursive move that should surprise no one, American courts are giving increasing autonomy to Christian churches and Christian-identified corporations to exempt themselves from state laws they consider to threaten their religious freedom. This includes exemptions from laws requiring them to follow workplace nondiscrimination rules or to provide employees with access to contraception. Religious freedom at home, it turns out, is a useful concept for the U.S. courts to valorize a specifically Christian kind of separation of church and state.

Picking four historical moments by which to organize an argument, let alone a set of essays, is of course risky, but it is also a familiar rhetorical approach. Robert Bellah's classic and speculative 1967 essay "Civil Religion in America" was an attempt to render visible the ways that a biblical yet nondenominational, not-necessarily-Christian "civil religion" coalesced in the rendering of "the American vision."[4] Bellah's essay also turned to historical moments, with reference to three "times of trial" that marked the United States, all characterized by violence: (1) the Revolutionary War as a response to British "tyranny"; (2) the Civil War and the ongoing reckoning with the "offense" of slavery; and (3) the Vietnam war, which was ongoing as he wrote, and the challenge it posed to "responsible action in a revolutionary world."[5]

The genesis of Bellah's essay was his need to respond to alarming events around him, as he understood his nation to be on the precipice of a "chasm" that would not only betray its vision but also have devastating global and domestic consequences. His attempt to name and place civil religion as "at its best a genuine apprehension of universal and transcendent religious reality as seen in or, one could almost say, as revealed through the experience of the American people" was rooted in well-worn narratives of a noble kind of American exceptionalism that he feared was turning arrogant, overweening, and tragic.⁶ As he wrote of the postrevolutionary nation: "Our democratic republic rebuked tyranny by merely existing."⁷ At the same time that Bellah valorized and naturalized the early republic as an inherent adversary of tyranny, he also warned about the hazards of civil religion, crosscutting the exceptionalist vision of America with narratives of its failures as a slaveholding, imperialist aggressor. He lamented, more than fifty years ago: "Gradually but unmistakably, America is succumbing to that arrogance of power which has afflicted, weakened and in some cases destroyed great nations in the past."⁸ Perhaps, he mused, "a world civil religion" would be a remedy for American arrogance: "Indeed, such an outcome has been the eschatological hope of American civil religion from the beginning. To deny such an outcome would be to deny the meaning of America itself."⁹ Overflowing the borders of America, a world civil religion would require asking again, where is America not?

Across the essays that make up *At Home and Abroad*, the authors write with voices at once chastened and emboldened by America, a home that most of the authors claim as their own. The essays build from sources scaled from the intimately domestic—a map of a bedroom (Imhoff) and the food in a kitchen cupboard (Salomon)—to the vertiginously planetary—the view from a jet window (Bender) and a telescope to the galaxies (Johnson). Collectively, they posit that religion, as both category and practice, is key to understanding the formidable mix of everywhereness and elusiveness that has made America seem exceptional.

The global reach of America, whether through its drones or its dollar, its jurists, celebrities, or missionaries, extends from deeply held convictions that it is the home of freedoms that need to be exported, sometimes by persuasion and sometimes by force. As the editors write in the introduction: "We suggest that disestablishment enhances the capacity of protestant Christianity to operate in American history both as a religion and not as a religion—that is, its capacity to not be a religion in disestablished mode but to be a religion in free exercise mode, to use the rubrics of the First Amendment to the U.S. Constitution, which enables certain political and religious possibilities." None of these essays come close to endorsing the possibility of "a genuine apprehension of universal and transcendent religious reality," in the tenor of Bellah. I would hazard, however, that many, if not most of them, are motivated by similar perceptions of living in a time of crisis and chasm that requires critique.

Is *At Home and Abroad* an analysis of civil religion in another key? Not exactly, but the "legacy" of the concept is nevertheless in the air (Scherer, this volume). The arrogance of American power is profoundly rooted in a protestant, and wider Christian, "repertoire" of metaphor, justification, ritual, and authoritative knowledge (see Harriss, and see Kale and Novetzke, this volume). At the same time, critique of this power has often—but as these essays show not always or only—been motivated by traditions of self-critique practiced by protestants and Catholics themselves.[10]

Unsurprisingly, Bellah's essay is treated more as a primary source than a theoretical lodestar in this book. He merits a brief footnote in Courtney Bender's chapter, where she describes him as an "apophatic speaker," one among the many who saw in the seeds of a nondenominational American civil religion the possibility for a critical harmony that could encompass the world. She also describes how Charles Long, Bellah's contemporary, critiqued the "epistemic limits of civil religion" already in 1974, noting that for Black and Indigenous peoples, civil religion was a very white and very European concept of "racial nationalism."[11] The framework of "at home and abroad" also depends on borders that are epistemically unstable but operationally real; America is a nation built on jurisdictional uncertainty that has never gone away (see Hurd and see Johnson, this volume).

Even for white protestants, as Evan Haefeli's chapter shows, America was a nation built on ecclesiastical diversity verging on anarchy: "The United States thus began as a fragment of a global and religiously diverse empire that stretched from Canada to India, a parochial leftover of a cosmopolitan feast. This internally divided character made the Constitution's chary attitude toward a national religious establishment inevitable" (Haefeli, this volume). Drafting a Constitution, however, did not fully alleviate the tension between vesting the authority and legitimacy of the United States of America in a brand-new jurisdiction—speaking new laws over an old land—and vesting this legitimacy in previous promises that the Dutch, British, Spanish, and French empires made with Indigenous nations during centuries of treaties, ceremony, and diplomacy. To understand the repertoire of American religion, scholars need to understand its formative grounding on these layers of ceremony and law, grounds on which we continue to think and write.[12]

Both the notion of home and abroad and Bellah's concept of civil religion exemplify what Cooper Harriss, writing in this volume about Muhammad Ali, Bellah's contemporary, calls the double cross. For Harriss, the double cross is an illuminating bodily and moral metaphor that comes out of the physical moves and the betting jargon of the sport of boxing. A double cross is when a boxer lands a surprise punch from the same hand. But it is also the action of a boxer who doubles his money by accepting a pre-match bribe to lose the match but instead goes on to win, thus securing the prize money as well. Harriss applies this metaphor to Muhammad Ali's shifting loyalties over his life, arguing that "the long view affords one larger-scale attempt to negotiate this excess, a kind of exceptionalist double cross that emphasizes certain accumulations of identities through a lifetime of conversions (not just his conversion to Islam in 1964 but the wide range of racial and religious contradictions that complicate the arc of this more singular conversion: his racial treachery toward the likes of Ernie Terrell and Joe Frazier in the 1960s and 1970s, his endorsement of Ronald Reagan in 1984, and so many other instances)." Harriss also notes briefly Wendy Doniger's discussion of the theatrical idea of the double (and triple) cross as performed in plays and movies whose plot depends on cross-dressing and assumed identities. Doniger's discussion focuses in part on gendered depictions of marital betrayal in Hindu myth and Hollywood movies, for example, in stories within stories of a queen imitating her husband's mistress to win him back, only to end up having to share the king.[13] In boxing, theater, and perhaps even scholarly performance, the double cross is a "cliché of ambivalence"—a performance of fidelity and betrayal operationalized through violence and love.[14]

The first historical moment that the editors peg to the inside/outside story of *At Home and Abroad*—namely, the founding of the American Colonization Society in 1816—occurs at the same time that the still-expanding nation is confronting the ongoing challenge of multijurisdictional sovereignty in relation to Indigenous nations, using both warfare and legal rulings. As Winni Sullivan shows in a blog post for the theologies of exceptionalism wing of this same scholarly project, the double cross was at the heart of Supreme Court Justice John Marshall's ruling in *Johnson v M'Intosh*. The new republic claimed its sovereignty not through rebuking the tyranny of the Crown but through claiming it: "One sees in Marshall's opinion the fancy legal footwork at the heart of the American project, one that claims fidelity to the rule of law and to the law of nations while acting as an outlaw—an outlaw whose justification in subjugating savages is in her claim to being Christian and civilized in a new and very special way." Sullivan goes on to recommend: "Taking exception to the story told by Marshall demands attention and commitment to other ways of knowing and other understandings of living in the land."[15] Claiming the land of Indigenous inhabitants via the Christian doctrine of discovery and then presenting itself to the world as bastion of religious freedom, America is in more ways than one the land of the double cross.

For scholars of religion to take exception to this story of America without becoming double and triple crossers (or more) is likely impossible. Scholars have many lessons to learn from the ways love and betrayal have often gone hand in hand, as Jennifer Graber has shown in her work on Quakers who helped to effect the colonization of Kiowa land through the guise of being "Friends of the Indians."[16] Many of the authors in this volume register their concern about how far or how deep scholarly critique may go. Jolyon Baraka Thomas argues in this volume that a doubled vision—and the notion of a "double standard"—does not go far enough: "I contend that the dichotomous framing of 'home' and 'abroad' is necessary but insufficient for understanding differential applications of conceptions of rights and religion in U.S. foreign policy. Japan shows that between home and abroad lies the ambiguous space occupied by the enemy-turned-ally. Japan simultaneously resists, mediates, and represents U.S. visions for how the world abroad can be transformed." In another register, Sunila Kale and Christian Novetzke analyze the ongoing debate in Canada, the United States, and India about yoga and cultural appropriation as a problem of historicity, in which yoga, as both a political and bodily practice is remembered, renarrated, and reclaimed across time, place, and bodies. Connecting the politics of yoga to questions of North American settler colonialism, they argue that scholars must attend to class identity as much as to religious or racialized identities. In my own work, I have found it helpful to think about the specificity of *ritual* appropriation as a way to analyze yoga as a site in which body, religion, and sovereignty intersect within and across colonial borders.[17]

One important way to acknowledge, if not avoid, the double cross is to attend to the myriad multijurisdictional ways of knowing and governing the land. Nancy Buenger offers in this volume a fascinating analysis of equity courts as tools of progressive reformers concerned with women's rights and Indigenous recognition while also showing how "progressive jurists cherished equity's Christian heritage, and the boundary between the court's temporal and spiritual authority was obscure." Considering movements for "Home Rule" in both Chicago and American-occupied Philippines, Buenger shows how equity was a tool of governance and justice formed in the intersection of Christianity and empire within the U.S. and abroad. Similarly, Greg Johnson's discussion of *iwi* (bones) and *'āina* (land) in Hawaii shows that "spiritual jurisdiction" is at play in both American legal orders and in native Hawaiian resistance and refusal of such jurisdiction.[18]

The stakes of "jurisdictional uncertainty" are critical for both Indigenous sovereignty activists and scholars of religion.[19] Johnson writes in this volume: "It is one thing to improvise tactics of inherent jurisdiction on the ground; it is quite another to launch and sustain a movement that seeks a thoroughgoing revolution and maximal sovereignty. It should be an urgent agenda for scholars of Indigenous religions and law to track and understand moments and movements that evince bridgework from the former to the latter." Elizabeth Shakman Hurd echoes this challenge in her essay: "The politics of the border are consistently elided, however, including by most historians and scholars of international relations, as important sites of authority at home, in foreign policy, and in jurisdictions considered 'foreign in a domestic sense.'"

Getting a handle on the politics of borders requires seeing them from multiple sides. Helge Årsheim writes in this volume of a Christian-inflected religious "normalism" in Norway, showing how comparing national histories of church establishment, xenophobia, and global outreach are an excellent tool for deflating exceptionalism. Like Årsheim's, my perspective on double vision and the double cross comes from a different home—namely, Canada—which shares with the United States an overlapping yet distinct history of jurisdictional uncertainty. Thinking comparatively across a border that is sometimes fortified and sometimes simply a river or even a ditch, I have found taking a land-based approach particularly helpful. To make a homeland of the United States or, as the Canadian national anthem puts it, to sing of "our home and native land," took not only the tools of property such as treaties and deeds but also the accrual of stories that made the theft of Indigenous lands into purchase and squatting into home ownership.

The U.S.–Canadian border was stitched together on top of centuries of treaties, signed in Europe and negotiated with Indigenous nations and colonial officials. A good portion of the Canada–U.S. border is based on an imaginary line—the forty-ninth parallel—a circle of latitude drawn with the help of the earth's magnetism. According to one "rather dubious but popular account," it came to be called the "medicine line," in reference to what the Sioux and the Cree took to be its "magical political power."[20] Whether or not the medicine line is a settler trope or an Indigenous epithet, it is regularly invoked in scholarly accounts as part of a broader spiritually based Indigenous critique of U.S. and Canadian sovereignty: "The Great Spirit makes no lines."[21] Indigenous refusals of the rigid dualism of colonial borders continues.[22]

In a time of pandemic, when viruses cross borders and bodies even when ports of entry are shut down, we are afforded yet another angle of vision for seeing how the medicine line is at once powerful and powerless. Even land—in its solidity, its wateriness, and in what geophysicists call its "secular variations"—seems to resist borders as nation-states try to fix them. Rock-hard land erodes, erupts, and burns. Rivers and lakes carry pollution from one shore to the next regardless of the fixity of the border. And secular variations—or changes in the earth's core that happen over many years—cause the earth's magnetic fields to drift westward, messing in an underground way with the fixity of the parallel lines drawn by treaties.[23] Thinking about land in this way—how it is never quite captured by the borders that are laid, staked, and literally built into it, is helpful for destabilizing the very fixity of what counts as home and abroad. Letting the land—in its long-term secular variations—challenge the fixity of home and borders is perhaps most easily done with contiguous land masses such as North America. The persistence and resurgence of Indigenous sovereignty movements and their understanding of North America as Turtle Island, however, is another kind of challenge: they have refused to leave their land, even as it changes around them.[24] Legal pluralism, multijurisdictional orders, or jurisdictional uncertainty: whatever concept one uses, the United States is a land, people, and nation that rests on double crosses all the way down.

NOTES

1. Lisa Ford, *Settler Sovereignty: Jurisdiction and Indigenous People in America and Australia, 1788–1836* (Cambridge, Mass.: Harvard University Press, 2010).
2. Paul Christopher Johnson, Pamela E. Klassen, and Winnifred Fallers Sullivan, *Ekklesia: Three Inquiries in Church and State* (Chicago: University of Chicago Press, 2018).
3. *Downes v. Bidwell*, 182 U.S. 244 (1901), at 341.
4. Robert N. Bellah, "Civil Religion in America," in *The Robert Bellah Reader*, ed. Steven M. Tipton and Robert N. Bellah (Durham, N.C.: Duke University Press, 2006).
5. Bellah, "Civil Religion," 243.
6. Bellah, "Civil Religion," 238.
7. Bellah, "Civil Religion," 243.
8. Bellah, "Civil Religion," 244.
9. Bellah, "Civil Religion," 245.
10. Pamela E. Klassen, *Spirits of Protestantism: Medicine, Healing, and Liberal Christianity* (Berkeley: University of California Press, 2011), 209–18.
11. See Charles H. Long, "Civil Rights—Civil Religion: Visible People and Invisible Religion," in *American Civil Religion*, ed. Russell E. Richey and Donald G. Jones, 211–21 (New York: Harper & Row, 1974); and Leilah Danielson, "Civil Religion as Myth, Not History," *Religions* 10, no. 6 (2019): 377, https://doi.org/10.3390/rel10060374.
12. Pamela E. Klassen, "Back to the Land and Waters: Futures for the Study of Religions," *Religion* (October 23, 2019): 1–7, https://doi.org/10.1080/0048721X.2019.1681106.
13. Wendy Doniger, *The Woman Who Pretended to Be Who She Was: Myths of Self-Imitation* (Oxford: Oxford University Press, 2004), 33–34.

14. Doniger, *The Woman Who Pretended*, 224.
15. Winnifred Fallers Sullivan, "Comments on Johnson v M'Intosh," in "Theologies of American Exceptionalism," *The Immanent Frame* (blog), February 17, 2017, http://tif.ssrc.org/2017/02/17/marshall-and-morgan/.
16. Jennifer Graber, *The Gods of Indian Country: Religion and the Struggle for the American West* (Oxford: Oxford University Press, 2018).
17. Klassen, *Spirits of Protestantism*, esp. chapters 3 and 5.
18. Pamela E. Klassen, "Spiritual Jurisdictions: Treaty People and the Queen of Canada," in *Ekklesia: Three Inquiries in Church and State*, ed. Paul Christopher Johnson, Pamela E. Klassen, and Winnifred Fallers Sullivan, 107–74 (Chicago: University of Chicago Press, 2018).
19. Nan Goodman, *Banished: Common Law and the Rhetoric of Social Exclusion in Early New England* (Philadelphia: University of Pennsylvania Press, 2012).
20. Kate Morris, "Running the 'Medicine Line': Images of the Border in Contemporary Native American Art," *American Indian Quarterly* 35, no. 4 (2011): 571, https://doi.org/10.5250/amerindiquar.35.4.0549; and Beth LaDow, *The Medicine Line: Life and Death on a North American Borderland* (New York: Routledge, 2002), 40.
21. LaDow, *The Medicine Line*, 42.
22. Audra Simpson, *Mohawk Interruptus: Political Life Across the Borders of Settler States* (Durham, N.C.: Duke University Press, 2014); Richard Wagamese, "First Nations Face Border Struggles," *Canadian Geographic*, July 1, 2010, https://www.canadiangeographic.ca/article/first-nations-face-border-struggles; and Louise Erdrich, *Books and Islands in Ojibwe Country* (Washington, D.C.: National Geographic, 2003).
23. Ingo Wardinski, "Geomagnetic Secular Variation," in *Encyclopedia of Geomagnetism and Paleomagnetism*, ed. David Gubbins and Emilio Herrero-Bervera, 346–49 (Dordrecht: Springer Science & Business Media, 2007).
24. Simpson, *Mohawk Interruptus*.

Bibliography

ARCHIVAL MATERIAL

Archbishop Blenk, Puerto Rico I and II. Archives, Archdiocese of New Orleans, Louisiana.
Barrows, David P. Papers. Bancroft Library, University of California, Berkeley.
Kaplan, Mordecai. Papers, SC-6102. American Jewish Archives, Cincinnati, Ohio.
Olson, Harry. Papers. Northwestern University Archives, Evanston, Illinois.
Packard, Samuel W. Papers. In Walter Eugene Packard Papers. Bancroft Library, University of California, Berkeley.
Sampter, Jessie. Papers. A219. Central Zionist Archives, Jerusalem.
Taft, William H. Papers. Washington, D.C.: Library of Congress, 1969.
Wigmore, John H. Papers. Northwestern University Archives, Evanston, Illinois.

PUBLISHED WORKS

Addams, Jane. *The Excellent Becomes the Permanent.* New York: Macmillan, 1932.
———. *My Friend Julia Lathrop.* 1935. Reprint, Urbana: University of Illinois Press, 2004.
Adelstein, Jake, and Mari Yamamoto. "The Religious Cult Secretly Running Japan." *Daily Beast,* July 10, 2016. https://www.thedailybeast.com/the-religious-cult-secretly-running-japan.
Aidi, Hisham. "Slavery, Genocide and the Politics of Outrage: Understanding the New Racial Olympics." *Middle East Report* 35, no. 234 (Spring 2005): 40–56.
Alter, Joseph S. 2000. *Gandhi's Body: Sex, Diet, and the Politics of Nationalism.* Philadelphia: University of Pennsylvania Press.
Alonso-Alonso, Rev. A. "Religious Progress in Porto Rico." *Catholic World* 76 (1903): 446–52.
American Bar Association. "Report of the Committee on Uniform Judicial Procedure." *American Bar Association Journal* 1–6 (1915–1920).
American Council on Education Studies. *The Relation of Religion to Public Education: The Basic Principles.* Washington, D.C.: American Council on Education Studies, 1947.
American Political Science Association. "Papers and Discussions." *Proceedings of the American Political Science Association* 1 (1904): 35–249.
Ammerman, Nancy Tatom. *Baptist Battles: Social Change and Religious Conflict in the Southern Baptist Convention.* New Brunswick, N.J.: Rutgers University Press, 1990.

Anidjar, Gil. *Blood: A Critique of Christianity.* New York: Columbia University Press, 2014.
——. "Christianity, Christianities, Christian." *Journal of Religious and Political Practice* 1, no. 1 (2015): 39–46.
Antler, Joyce. *The Journey Home: Jewish Women and the American Century.* New York: Free Press, 1997.
Appleby, Joyce. "Recovering America's Historic Diversity: Beyond Exceptionalism." *The Journal of American History* 79, no. 2 (1992): 419–31.
Aquinas, Thomas. *Summa theologiae.* Vol. 41. Ed. Thomas Gilby. London: Blackfriars, 1961.
Årsheim, Helge. "Imagine There's No Religion—and No State Church Too?" *Religion: Going Public* (blog), February 27, 2017. http://religiongoingpublic.com/archive/2017/imagine-theres-no-religion-and-no-state-church-too.
Asad, Talal. *Formations of the Secular: Christianity, Islam, Modernity.* Stanford, Calif.: Stanford University Press, 2003.
——. *On Suicide Bombing.* New York: Columbia University Press, 2007.
Ayala, César J., and Rafael Bernabe. *Puerto Rico in the American Century: A History Since 1898.* Chapel Hill: University of North Carolina Press, 2007.
Ayau, Edward Halealoha, and Ty Kāwika Tengan. "Ka Huaka'i O Nā 'Ōiwi: The Journey Home." In *The Dead and Their Possession: Repatriation in Principle, Policy and Practice*, ed. Cressida Fforde, Jane Hubert, and Paul Turnbull, 171–89. London: Routledge, 2002.
Badt-Strauss, Bertha. *White Fire: The Life and Works of Jessie Sampter.* New York: Arno, 1956.
Bakhtin, Mikhail. "Forms of Time and of the Chronotope in the Novel." In *The Dialogic Imagination: Four Essays.* Trans. Caryl Emerson and Michael Holquist. Austin: University of Texas, 1981.
Barron, David J. "Reclaiming Home Rule." *Harvard Law Review* 116 (2003): 2255–386.
Barrows, David P. "The Governor-General of the Philippines Under Spain and the United States." *American Historical Review* 21 (1916): 288–311.
Bartelme, Mary. "The Opportunity for Women in Court Administration." *Annals of the American Academy of Political and Social Science* 52 (1914): 188–90.
——. "Spendthrift Trusts." *Albany Law Journal* 50 (1894): 6–11.
Baylen, Joseph O. "Stead, William Thomas." *Oxford Dictionary of National Biography.* Oxford University Press, 2010. https://doi.org/10.1093/ref:odnb/36258.
——. "A Victorian's 'Crusade' in Chicago, 1893–1894." *Journal of American History* 51 (1964): 418–34.
Beaman, L. G. "Battles over Symbols: The 'Religion' of the Minority Versus the 'Culture' of the Majority." *Journal of Law and Religion* 28, no. 1 (2013): 67–104.
Beienburg, Sean, and Paul Frymer. "The People Against Themselves: Rethinking Popular Constitutionalism." *Law & Social Inquiry* 41 (2016): 242–66.
Belknap, Michal R. *To Improve the Administration of Justice.* Chicago: American Judicature Society, 1992.
Bellah, Robert N. "Civil Religion in America." *Daedalus* 96 no. 1 (1967): 1–21.
——. "Civil Religion in America." In *The Robert Bellah Reader*, ed. Steven M. Tipton and Robert N. Bellah. Durham, N.C.: Duke University Press, 2006.
Bender, Courtney. "No Horizon: Some Considerations on the Standpoint of the Secular." Paper prepared for the workshop Anthropology Within and Without the Secular Condition. CUNY Graduate School, New York, September 2017.
——. "Pluralism and Secularism." In *Religion on the Edge: De-Centering and Re-Centering the Sociology of Religion*, ed. Courtney Bender, Wendy Cadge, Peggy Levitt, and David Smilde, 137–58. New York: Oxford, 2011.
——. "The Power of Pluralist Thinking." In *Politics of Religious Freedom*, ed. Winnifred Fallers Sullivan, Elizabeth Shakman Hurd, Saba Mahmood, and Peter G. Danchin, 66–77. Chicago: University of Chicago Press, 2015.
Bender, Courtney, and Pamela Klassen, eds. *After Pluralism: Reimagining Religious Engagement.* New York: Columbia University Press, 2010.

Berger, Benjamin L. "Two Theologies of Chosenness." In *Theologies of American Exceptionalism*, ed. Winnifred Fallers Sullivan and Elizabeth Shakman Hurd, Bloomington: Indiana University Press, 2021.
Berman, Harold J. *Law and Revolution [I]: The Formation of the Western Legal Tradition*. Cambridge: Harvard University Press, 1983.
———. *Law and Revolution II: The Impact of the Protestant Reformations on the Western Legal Traditions*. Cambridge: Harvard University Press, 1983.
Bhandar, Brenna. *Colonial Lives of Property: Law, Land, and Racial Regimes of Ownership*. Durham, N.C.: Duke University Press, 2018.
Blackford, Mansel. "Environmental Justice, Native Rights, Tourism, and Opposition to Military Control: The Case of Kahoʻolawe." *Journal of American History* 91, no. 2 (2004): 544–71.
Blackstone, William. *Commentaries on the Laws of England*. 2 vols. Chicago: Callaghan, 1884.
Blanks, W. D. "Corrective Church Discipline in the Presbyterian Churches of the Nineteenth Century South." *Journal of Presbyterian History* 44 (1966): 89–105.
Bloom, Nicholas. *The Metropolitan Airport: JFK International and Modern New York*. Philadelphia: University of Pennsylvania Press, 2015.
Blount, James H. "The Founding of Civil Government of the Philippines." *Green Bag* 20 (1908): 360–65.
———. "Some Legal Aspects of the Philippines." *American Lawyer* 14 (1906): 495–98.
Blume, William Wirt. "Chancery Practice on the American Frontier: A Study of the Records of the Supreme Court of Michigan Territory, 1805–1836." *Michigan Law Review* 59 (1960): 49–96.
Boles, John B. "Turner, the Frontier, and the Study of Religion in America." *Journal of the Early Republic* 13 no. 2 (1993): 205–16.
Bonhoeffer, Dietrich. *The Cost of Discipleship*. New York: Touchstone, 1995.
Bonney, Charles C. "The Powers of Non-Resident Guardians, and Incidentally the Authority of the Probate Court." *Chicago Legal News* 1 (1868): 102.
Borah, Woodrow. *Justice by Insurance: The General Indian Court of Colonial Mexico and the Legal Aides of the Half-Real*. Berkeley: University of California Press, 1983.
Borstelmann, Thomas. *Apartheid's Reluctant Uncle: The United States and Southern Africa in the Early Cold War*. New York: Oxford University Press, 1993.
Bowers, Amy, and Kristen Carpenter. "Challenging the Narrative of Conquest: The Story of *Lyng v. Northwest Indian Cemetery Protective Association*." In *Indian Law Stories*, ed. Carole Goldberg, Kevin Washburn and Philip P. Frickey, 489–533. New York: Foundation Press, 2011.
Bowler, Kate. *Blessed: A History of the American Prosperity Gospel*. New York: Oxford University Press, 2013.
Bradwell, James B. "Women Lawyers of Illinois." *Chicago Legal News* 32 (1900): 339–46.
Bramen, Carrie Tirado, *The Uses of Variety: Modern Americanism and the Quest for National Distinctiveness*. Cambridge, Mass.: Harvard University Press, 2009.
Brau, Salvador. *Ecos de Batalla*. Puerto Rico: Imprenta y Librería de Jose Gonzalez Font, 1886.
Breckinridge, Sophonisba P., and Edith Abbott. *The Delinquent Child and the Home*. New York: Charities Publication Committee, 1912.
Breen, John. "'Conventional Wisdom' and the Politics of Shintō in Postwar Japan." *Politics and Religion* 4, no. 1 (2010): 68–82. https://www.ceeol.com/content-files/document-97571.pdf.
Breistein, Ingunn Folkestad. "En helhetlig tros- og livssynspolitikk—ønskelig og mulig?" *Teologisk Tidsskrift* 2, no. 4 (2013): 314–36.
Brown, Adrienne. *The Black Skyscraper: Architecture and the Perception of Race*. Baltimore: Johns Hopkins University Press, 2018.
Brown, Herbert W. *Latin America: The Pagans, the Papists, the Patriots, the Protestants and the Present Problem*. New York: Fleming H. Revell Company, 1901.
Brown, Marie Alohalani. "*Mauna Kea: Hoʻomana Hawaiʻi* and Protecting the Sacred." *Journal for the Study of Religion, Nature, and Culture* 10, no. 2 (2016): 150–69.

Bureau of Statistics. *Colonial Administration 1800–1900.* 2 vols. Washington, D.C.: Government Printing Office,1903.
Burlingame, Lettie Lavilla. *Lettie Lavilla Burlingame: Her Life Pages, Stories, Poems and Essays.* Joliet, Ill.: J. E. Williams, 1895.
Burnett, Christina Duffy, and Burke Marshall, eds. *Foreign in a Domestic Sense: Puerto Rico, American Expansion, and the Constitution.* Durham, N.C.: Duke University Press, 2001.
Burnham, Daniel H., and Edward H. Bennett. *Plan of Chicago.* Ed. Charles Moore. Chicago: Commercial Club, 1909.
Bush, Harold K., Jr. "Christianity, Literature, and American Empire." *Christianity and Literature* 62, no. 3 (Spring 2013): 419–40.
Butler, Jon. *Awash in a Sea of Faith: Christianizing the American People.* Cambridge, Mass.: Harvard University Press, 1990.
Cadge, Wendy. "The Evolution of American Airport Chapels: Local Negotiations in Religiously Pluralistic Contexts." *Religion and American Culture* 28, no. 1 (2018): 135–65.
Carey, Patrick W. *People, Priests, and Prelates: Ecclesiastical Democracy and the Tensions of Trusteeism.* Notre Dame, Ind.: University of Notre Dame Press, 1987.
Carrington, Paul D. "Freund, Ernst." *American National Biography Online.* Oxford University Press, 2000. https://doi.org/10.1093/anb/9780198606697.article.1100314
Carroll, Henry K. *Report on the Island of Porto Rico.* Washington, D.C.: Government Printing Office, 1899.
Carson, Penelope. *The East India Company and Religion, 1698–1858.* Woodbridge, Suffolk, U.K.: Boydell, 2012.
Cassidy, Michael. *The Passing Summer: A South African's Response to White Fear, Black Anger, and the Politics of Love.* Ventura, Calif.: Regal, 1990.
Castañeda, Anna Leah Fidelis T. "Spanish Structure, American Theory: The Legal Foundations of a Tropical New Deal in the Philippine Islands, 1898–1935." In *Colonial Crucible: Empire in the Making of the Modern American State,* ed. Alfred W. McCoy and Francisco A. Scarano, eds., 365–374. Madison: University of Wisconsin Press, 2009.
Cavell, Stanley. "'The Avoidance of Love': Must We Mean What We Say?" Cambridge: Cambridge University Press, 1976.
———. "Finding as Founding," in *Conditions Handsome and Unhandsome: The Constitution of Emersonian Perfectionism.* La Salle, Ill.: Open Court, 1990.
———. *This New Yet Unapproachable America.* Chicago: University of Chicago Press, 1989.
Chakravorty, Sanjoy, Kapur, Devesh, and Singh, Nirvikar. *The Other One Percent: Indians in America.* New York: Oxford University Press, 2017.
Chappell, David L. *A Stone of Hope: Prophetic Religion and the Death of Jim Crow.* Chapel Hill: University of North Carolina Press, 2005.
Chatterjee, Nandini. "English Law, Brahmo Marriage, and the Problem of Religious Difference: Civil Marriage Laws in Britain and India." *Comparative Studies in Society and History* 52, no. 3 (July 2010): 524–52.
Chicago New Charter Movement. *Why the Pending Constitutional Amendment Should Be Adopted.* Chicago: New Charter Campaign Committee, 1904.
Chidester, David. *Savage Systems: Colonialism and Comparative Religion in Southern Africa.* Charlottesville: University of Virginia Press, 1996.
Chitty, Joseph. *A Practical Treatise on the Criminal Law.* 2 vols. London: A. J. Valpy, 1816.
Clapp, Elizabeth J. *Mothers of All Children: Women Reformers and the Rise of Juvenile Courts in Progressive Era America.* University Park: Pennsylvania State University Press, 1998.
Clayton, Henry D. "Popularizing Administration of Justice." *American Bar Association Journal* 8 (1922): 43–51.
Cleland, McKenzie. "The New Gospel in Criminology." *McClure's* 31 (1908): 358–62.
Coalition Against Genocide. "Affiliations of Faith: Hindu American Foundation and the Global Sangh." Spotlight Series Report, 2013. http://www.coalitionagainstgenocide.org/reports/2013/cag.15dec2013.haf.rss.pdf.

Coates, Benjamin Allen. *Legalist Empire: International Law and American Foreign Relations in the Early Twentieth Century.* New York: Oxford University Press, 2016.
Cogley, Richard W. *John Eliot's Mission to the Indians Before King Philip's War.* Cambridge, Mass.: Harvard University Press, 1999.
Cohen, Andrew Wender. *The Racketeer's Progress: Chicago and the Struggle for the Modern American Economy, 1900–1940.* Cambridge: Cambridge University Press, 2004.
Concerned Evangelicals. *Evangelical Witness in South Africa.* Grand Rapids, Mich.: Eerdmans, 1987.
Connolly, William E. *Why I Am Not a Secularist.* Minneapolis: University of Minnesota Press, 2000.
Conroy-Krutz, Emily. *Christian Imperialism: Converting the World in the Early American Republic.* Ithaca, N.Y.: Cornell University Press, 2015.
Coogan, Michael D., Marc Z. Brettler, Carol Newsom, and Pheme Perkins, eds. *The New Oxford Annotated Bible with Apocrypha.* New Revised Standard Version. 4th ed. New York: Oxford University Press, 2010.
Corn, John. *Winged Gospel: America's Romance with Aviation.* Baltimore: Johns Hopkins University Press, 2002.
Corn, Wanda. *The Great American Thing: Modern Art and National Identity, 1915–1935.* Berkeley: University of California Press, 1999.
Corrigan, John. *Emptiness: Feeling Christian in America.* New York: Oxford University Press, 2015.
Creviston, Vernon P. "'No King Unless It Be a Constitutional King': Rethinking the Place of the Quebec Act in the Coming of the American Revolution." *Historian* 73 no. 3 (2011): 463–79.
Crooke, W. *The Tribes and Castes of the North-western Provinces and Oudh.* 4 Vols. Calcutta: Office of the Superintendent of Government Printing, 1896.
Cullmann, Oscar. *The State in The New Testament.* New York: Scribner, 1956.
Cunningham, Charles H. *The Audiencia in the Spanish Colonies as Illustrated by the Audiencia of Manila (1583–1800).* Berkeley: University of California Press, 1919.
Curbelo, Silvia Alvaraz. *Un país del porvenir.* San Juan: Ediciones Callejón, 2001.
Curry, Thomas J. *The First Freedoms: Church and State in America to the Passage of the First Amendment.* Oxford: Oxford University Press, 1986.
Curtis, George B. "The Checkered Career of *Parens Patriae*: The State as Parent or Tyrant?" *DePaul Law Review* 25 (1976): 895–915.
Danielson, Leilah. "Civil Religion as Myth, Not History." *Religions* 10, no. 6 (2019): 374–89. https://doi.org/10.3390/rel10060374.
Darian-Smith, Eve. *Religion, Race, Rights: Landmarks in the History of Modern Anglo-American Law.* Oxford: Hart, 2010.
"Day Law Class for Women." *Chicago Legal News* 39 (1906): 91.
De Gruchy, John W. "The Church and the Struggle for South Africa." *Theology Today* 43, no. 2 (July 1, 1986): 229–43.
de Roover, Jakob, and S. N. Balagangadhara. "Liberty, Tyranny, and the Will of God: The Principle of Religious Toleration in Early Modern Europe and Colonial India." *History of Political Thought* 30 no. 1 (2009): 111–39.
Delany, Samuel R. *The Motion of Light in Water: Sex and Science Fiction Writing in the East Village.* Minneapolis: University of Minnesota Press, 2004.
Dessì, Ugo. "Shin Buddhism, Authority, and the Fundamental Law of Education." *Numen* 56, no. 5 (2009): 523–44. https://doi.org/10.1163/002959709X12469430260048.
Decision of the Supreme Court of Porto Rico and Dissenting Opinion in the Case of the Roman Catholic Apostolic Church vs. the People Porto Rico. Washington, D.C.: Government Printing Office, 1909.
Dignan, Patrick Joseph. *A History of the Legal Incorporation of Catholic Church Property in the United States (1784–1932).* New York: P. J. Kennedy and Sons, 1937.
Doniger, Wendy. *The Woman Who Pretended to Be Who She Was: Myths of Self-Imitation.* New York: Oxford University Press, 2004.

Dorsey, Jennifer. "Conscription, Charity, and Citizenship in the Early Republic: The Shaker Campaign for Alternative Service." *Church History* 85, no. 1 (2016): 140–49.

Drachman, Virginia G. *Women Lawyers and the Origins of Professional Identity in America: The Letters of the Equity Club, 1887–1890*. Ann Arbor: University of Michigan Press, 1993.

Drakopoulou, Maria. "Law and the Sacred: Equity, Conscience and the Art of Judgment as Ius Aequi et Boni." *Law/Text/Culture* 5 (2000): 345–74.

Dresch, Paul, and Judith Scheele, eds. *Legalism: Categories and Rules*. Oxford: Oxford University Press, 2015.

Dresch, Paul, and Hannah Skoda, eds. *Legalism: Anthropology and History*. Oxford: Oxford University Press, 2012.

Dressler, Markus, and Arvind-Pal S. Mandair, eds. *Secularism and Religion-Making*. New York: Oxford University Press, 2011.

Du Toit, Brian M. "Theology, Kairos, and the Church in South Africa." *Missiology* 16, no. 1 (January 1, 1988): 57–71.

Dunn, James D. G. "Romans 13:1–7: A Charter for Political Quietism?" *Ex Auditu* 2 (1986): 55–68.

Edmunds, Palmer D., ed. *Federal Rules of Civil Procedure*. 2 vols. Chicago: Callaghan, 1938.

Eig, Jonathan. *Ali: A Life*. New York: Houghton Mifflin Harcourt, 2017.

Elliott, Neil. *Liberating Paul*. Minneapolis: Augsburg Fortress, 2006.

Elliott, Ralph. *The Message of Genesis*. Nashville: Broadman Press, 1961.

Erdrich, Louise. *Books and Islands in Ojibwe Country*. Washington, D.C.: National Geographic, 2003.

Erman, Sam. *Almost Citizens: Puerto Rico, the U.S. Constitution, and Empire*. Cambridge: Cambridge University Press, 2018.

Esbeck, Carl H., and Jonathan Den Hartog, eds. *Disestablishment and Religious Dissent: Church-State Relations in the New American States, 1776–1833*. Columbia: University of Missouri Press, 2019.

Estes, Nick. *Our History Is the Future: Standing Rock Versus the Dakota Access Pipeline and the Long Tradition of Indigenous Resistance*. New York: Verso, 2019.

Falkanger, Aage Thor. 2007. "Noen folkerettslige problemstillinger i Nordområdene—i fortid og nåtid." *Lov og rett* 46, no. 6: 323–44.

Falwell, Jerry. "An Interview with Jerry Falwell." *Transformation* 3, no. 2 (April 1986): 36.

Far Eastern American Bar Association. *Twenty Years in the Judiciary*. Shanghai: Oriental Press, 1922.

Farr, Thomas. "Cold War Religion." Review of William Inboden III, *Religion and American Foreign Policy, 1945–1960: The Soul of Containment* (Cambridge: Cambridge University Press, 2008) in *First Things*, June 2009. https://www.firstthings.com/article/2009/06/cold-war-religion.

Farrelly, Maura Jane. *Anti-Catholicism in America, 1620–1860*. Cambridge: Cambridge University Press, 2017.

Fee, James Alger. "The Proposed New Rules for Uniform Procedure in the Federal District Courts." *Oregon Law Review* 16 (1937): 103–20.

Feliú, Vicenç. "Corporate 'Soul': Legal Incorporation of Catholic Ecclesiastical Property in the United States—A Historical Perspective." *Ohio Northern University Law Review* 40 (2013): 441–65.

Fessenden, Tracy. *Culture and Redemption: Religion, the Secular, and American Literature*. Princeton, N.J.: Princeton University Press, 2007.

Fine-Dare, Kathleen. *Grave Injustice: The American Indian Repatriation Movement*. Lincoln: University of Nebraska Press, 2002.

Fish, Peter G. "William Howard Taft and Charles Evans Hughes: Conservative Politicians as Chief Judicial Reformers." *Supreme Court Review* (1975): 123–45.

Fitzpatrick, Joan. "The International Dimension of U.S. Refugee Law." *Berkeley Journal of International Law* 15, no. 1 (1997): 1–26.

Forbath, William E. *Law and the Shaping of the American Labor Movement*. Cambridge, Mass.: Harvard University Press, 1991.

Ford, Eugene. *Cold War Monks: Buddhism and America's Secret Strategy in Southeast Asia*. New Haven, Conn.: Yale University Press, 2017.

Ford, Lisa. *Settler Sovereignty: Jurisdiction and Indigenous People in America and Australia, 1788–1836*. Cambridge, Mass.: Harvard University Press, 2010.

Frampton, Ward. "The Uneven Bulwark: How (and Why) Criminal Jury Trial Rates Vary by State." *California Law Review* 100 (2012): 198–200.

Freston, Paul. *Evangelicals and Politics in Asia, Africa and Latin America*. Cambridge: Cambridge University Press, 2004.

Freund, Ernst. "Some Legal Aspects of the Chicago Charter Act of 1907." *Illinois Law Review* 2 (1908): 427–39.

Friesen, Steven, ed. *Ancestors in Post-Contact Religion: Roots, Ruptures and Modernity's Memory*. Cambridge, Mass.: Harvard University Press, 2001.

Frost, Robert. "America Is Hard to See." In *Robert Frost: Collected Poems, Prose, and Plays*, ed. Richard Poirier and Mark Richardson. New York: Library of America, 1995.

———. "And All We Call American." In *The Poetry of Robert Frost: The Collected Poems, Complete and Unabridged* ed. Edward Connery Latham, 416–17. New York: Henry Holt and Company, 1979.

Fujiwara Satoko. "On Qualifying Religious Literacy: Recent Debates on Higher Education and Religious Studies in Japan." *Teaching Theology & Religion* 13, no. 3 (2010): 223–36. https://doi.org/10.1111/j.1467-9647.2010.00615.x.

Fuller, Lon. *The Morality of Law*, rev. ed. New Haven, Conn.: Yale University Press, 1969.

Funk, Kellen. "Church Corporations and the Conflict of Laws in Antebellum America." *Journal of Law and Religion* 32, no. 2 (July 2017): 263–84.

Furre, Berge. *Norsk historie 1905–1940*. Oslo: Samlaget, 1971.

Galanter, Marc. "The Vanishing Trial: An Examination of Trials and Related Matters in Federal and State Courts." *Journal of Empirical Legal Studies* 1 (2004): 459–570.

Garang, John. *The Call for Democracy in Sudan*. Edited by Mansour Khalid. London: Kegan Paul International, 1992.

García Leduc, José M. *¡La pesada carga! iglesia, clero y sociedad en Puerto Rico (Siglo XIX): Aspectos de su historia*. San Juan, P.R.: Ediciones Puerto, 2009.

Gerbner, Katharine. *Christian Slavery: Conversion and Race in the Protestant Atlantic World*. Philadelphia: University of Pennsylvania Press, 2018.

Ghosh, Amitav. *The Great Derangement*. Chicago: University of Chicago Press, 2018.

Gilbert, Hiram T. *The Municipal Court of Chicago*. Chicago: printed by the author, 1928.

———. "New Municipal Court System." *Chicago Legal News* 38 (1906): 296.

———. *New Municipal Court System: Address Delivered before the Union League Club of Chicago*. Chicago: unknown, 1906.

Gilpin, William. *The Cosmopolitan Railway: Compacting and Fusing Together all the World's Continents*. San Francisco: History Company, 1890.

Glasson, Travis. *Mastering Christianity: Missionary Anglicanism in the Atlantic World*. New York: Oxford University Press, 2012.

Glendon, Mary Ann. *Abortion and Divorce in Western Law*. Cambridge, Mass.: Harvard University Press, 1989.

———. *Rights Talk: The Impoverishment of Political Discourse*. New York: Free Press, 1993.

Go, Julian. *American Empire and the Politics of Meaning: Elite Political Cultures in the Philippines and Puerto Rico during U.S. Colonialism*. Durham, N.C.: Duke University Press, 2008.

Goba, Bonganjalo. "The Kairos Document and Its Implications for Liberation in South Africa." *Journal of Law and Religion* 5, no. 2 (January 1, 1987): 313–25.

Goldberg, Michelle. *The Goddess Pose: The Audacious Life of Indra Devi, the Woman Who Helped Bring Yoga to the West*. New York: Vintage, 2016.

Goodman, Nan. *Banished: Common Law and the Rhetoric of Social Exclusion in Early New England*. Philadelphia: University of Pennsylvania Press, 2012.

Goodnow, Frank J. "Municipal Home Rule." *Political Science Quarterly* 10 (1895): 1–21.

———. "Municipal Home Rule." *Political Science Quarterly* 21 (1906): 77–90.

Goodyear-Kaʻōpua, Noelani. "Protectors of the Future, Not Protestors of the Past: Indigenous Pacific Activism on Mauna a Wākea." *South Atlantic Quarterly* 116, no. 1 (2017): 184–94.

Goodyear-Kaʻōpua, Noelani, Ikaika Hussey, and Erin Kahunawaika'ala Wright, eds. *A Nation Rising: Hawaiian Movements for Life, Land, and Sovereignty*. Durham, N.C.: Duke University Press, 2014.

Gordon, Sarah Barringer. "The First Disestablishment: Limits on Church Power and Property Before the Civil War." *University of Pennsylvania Law Review* 162, no. 2 (2014): 307–72.

———. *The Spirit of the Law: Religious Voices and the Constitution in Modern America*. Cambridge, Mass.: Belknap Press of Harvard University Press, 2010.

Gorski, Philip. *American Covenant: A History of Civil Religion from the Puritans to the Present*. Princeton, N.J.: Princeton University Press, 2017.

Gowda, Chandan. "'Advance Mysore!:' The Cultural Logic of a Developmental State." *Economic and Political Weekly* 45, no. 29 (July 2010): 88–95.

Graber, Jennifer. *The Gods of Indian Country: Religion and the Struggle for the American West*. Oxford: Oxford University Press, 2018.

Graham, Billy. "Why Lausanne?" In *Let the Earth Hear His Voice: The Complete Papers from the International Congress on World Evangelization*, ed. James Dixon Douglas, 22–38. Minneapolis: World Wide Publications, 1975.

Graziano, Michael. "William Donovan, the Office of Strategic Services, and Catholic Intelligence Sources During World War II." *U.S. Catholic Historian* 33, no. 4 (Fall 2015): 79–103.

Green, Steven K. *Inventing a Christian America: The Myth of a Religious Founding*. Oxford: Oxford University Press, 2015.

———. *The Second Disestablishment: Church and State in Nineteenth-Century America*. Oxford: Oxford University Press, 2010.

Greene, Mary A. *The Woman's Manual of Law*. New York: Silver, Burdett, 1902.

Greenhouse, Carol. *Praying for Justice: Faith, Order and Community in an American Town*. Ithaca, N.Y.: Cornell University Press, 1989.

Grinnell, Frank W. "The Common Law History of Probation: An Illustration of the 'Equitable Growth' of Criminal Law." *Journal of Criminal Law and Criminology* 32 (1941): 15–34.

Guelke, Adrian. *Rethinking the Rise and Fall of Apartheid: South Africa and World Politics*. Houndmills, Basingstoke, Hampshire: Palgrave Macmillan, 2005.

Gullestad, Marianne. "Normalising Racial Boundaries. The Norwegian Dispute about the Term Neger." *Social Anthropology* 13, no. 1 (2005): 27–46.

Guthmann, Thierry. "Nationalist Circles in Japan Today: The Impossibility of Secularization." Trans. Aike P. Rots. *Japan Review* 30 (2017): 207–25. https://www.jstor.org/stable/44259467?seq=1.

"Habitual Drunkards." *Chicago Legal News* 1 (1869): 2.

Haefeli, Evan. *Accidental Pluralism: America and the Religious Politics of English Expansion, 1497–1662*. Chicago: University of Chicago Press, 2021.

———, ed. *Against Popery: Britain, Empire, and Anti-Catholicism*. Charlottesville: University of Virginia Press, 2020.

———. "Delaware: Religious Borderland." In *Disestablishment and Religious Dissent: Church–State Relations in the New American States, 1776–1833*, eds. Carl H. Esbeck and Jonathan Den Hartog, 37–54. Columbia: University of Missouri Press, 2019.

———. "How Special Was Rhode Island? The Global Context of the 1663 Charter." In *The Lively Experiment: Religious Toleration in America from Roger Williams to the Present*, ed. Chris Beneke and Chris Grenda, 21–36. Lanham, Md.: Rowman and Littlefield, 2015.

———. "Pennsylvania's Religious Freedom in Comparative Colonial Context." In *The Worlds of William Penn*, ed. Andrew Murphy and John Smolenski, 333–54. New Brunswick: Rutgers University Press, 2019.

———. "Toleration and Empire: The Origins of American Religious Diversity." In *British North America in the Seventeenth and Eighteenth Centuries*, ed. Stephen Foster, 103–35. Oxford History of the British Empire series. Oxford: Oxford University Press, 2013.

Hale, William Bayard. "A Court That Does Its Job." *World's Work* 19 (1910): 12695–703.
Hall, Dana Nāone. *Life of the Land: Articulations of a Native Writer*. Honolulu: 'Ai Pohaku Press, 2017.
Harlow, Luke E. "The Long Life of Proslavery Religion." In *The World the Civil War Made*, ed. Gregory P. Downs and Kate Masur, 132–58. Chapel Hill: University of North Carolina Press, 2015.
Harris, Susan K. *God's Arbiters: Americans and the Philippines, 1998–1902*. Oxford: Oxford University Press, 2013.
Harriss, M. Cooper. "The Cinematic Secularization of Muhammad Ali." In *Muslims in the Movies: A Global Anthology*, ed. Kristian Petersen. Cambridge, Mass.: ILEX/Harvard University Press, 2021.
Hartog, Hendrik. "Mrs. Packard on Dependency." *Yale Journal of Law & the Humanities* 1 (1988): 79–103.
Harvey, George R. "The Administration of Justice in the Philippine Islands." *Illinois Law Review* 9 (1914): 73–97.
Haselby, Sam. *The Origins of American Religious Nationalism*. New York: Oxford University Press, 2015.
Haskett, Timothy S. "The Medieval English Court of Chancery." *Law and History Review* 14 (1996): 245–313.
Hatch, Nathan O. *The Democratization of American Christianity*. New Haven, Conn.: Yale University Press, 1989.
Haynes, Sam W. "Manifest Destiny and the American Southwest." In *A Companion to the Era of Andrew Jackson*, ed. Sean Patrick Adams, 549–68. Malden, Mass.: Wiley-Blackwell, 2013.
Heckman, Wallace. *The Extent of Necessary Constitutional Amendment*. Chicago: Barnard & Miller, 1901.
Helmholz, R. H. *The Spirit of Classical Canon Law*. Athens: University of Georgia Press, 1996.
Henderson, John Greene. *Chancery Practice with Especial Reference to the Office and Duties of Masters in Chancery*. Chicago: T. H. Flood, 1904.
Hepburn, Charles M. *The Historical Development of Code Pleading in America and England*. Cincinnati: W. H. Anderson, 1897.
Hernández Aponte, Gerardo Alberto. *La iglesia católica en Puerto Rico ante la invasión de Estados Unidos de América*. San Juan, P.R.: UPR DEGI, 2013.
Herzog, Jonathan P. *The Spiritual-Industrial Complex: America's Religious Battle Against Communism in the Early Cold War*. Oxford: Oxford University Press, 2011.
Herzog, Tamar. *Upholding Justice: Society, State, and the Penal System in Quito (1650–1750)*. Ann Arbor: University of Michigan Press, 2004.
Heyrman, Christine Leigh. *American Apostles: When Evangelicals Entered the World of Islam*. New York: Hill & Wang, 2015.
Hilado, Serafin P. "A Comparative Study of the Adoption Law Under the Spanish Civil Code and the Code of Civil Procedure." *Philippine Law Journal* 4 (1918): 313–23.
Hill, Edward Judson. *Chancery Jurisdiction and Practice*. Chicago: E. B. Myers, 1873.
Hines, Thomas S. "The Imperial Façade: Daniel H. Burnham and American Architectural Planning in the Philippines." *Pacific Historical Review* 41 (1972): 33–53.
Hirschkind, Charles. "Is There a Secular Body?" *Cultural Anthropology* 26, no. 4 (November 1, 2011): 633–47.
Hobbins, Daniel, ed., *The Trial of Joan of Arc*. Cambridge, Mass.: Harvard University Press, 2007.
Hochberg, Gil Z. "'Remembering Semitism' or 'On the Prospect of Re-Membering the Semites.'" *ReOrient* 1, no. 2 (Spring 2016): 192–223.
Hoffer, Peter Charles. *The Law's Conscience: Equitable Constitutionalism in America*. Chapel Hill: University of North Carolina Press, 1990.
Horwitz, Morton J. *The Transformation of American Law 1780–1860*. Cambridge, Mass.: Harvard University Press, 1977.
———. *The Transformation of American Law 1870–1960*. New York: Oxford University Press, 1992.
Howe, Frederic C. *The City: The Hope of Democracy*. New York: Charles Scribner's, 1914.

Howe, Nicholas, *Landscapes of the Secular: Law, Religion, and American Sacred Space*. Chicago: University of Chicago Press, 2016.

Hudson, Winthrop Still. "Shifting Patterns of Church Order in the Twentieth Century." In *Baptist Concepts of the Church*. Philadelphia: Judson Press, 1959.

Hull House. *Hull-House Maps and Papers*. New York: Thomas Y. Crowell, 1895.

Howe, Frederic C. *The City: The Hope of Democracy*. New York: Charles Scribner, 1914.

Hurd, Elizabeth Shakman. "After Religious Freedom?" *Journal of Politics, Religion & Ideology* 18, no. 1 (April 2017): 112–16.

———. *Beyond Religious Freedom: The New Global Politics of Religion*. Princeton, N.J.: Princeton University Press, 2015.

———. "International Politics After Secularism." *Review of International Studies* 38, no. 5 (2012): 943–51.

———. *The Politics of Secularism in International Relations*. Princeton, N.C.: Princeton University Press, 2008.

Hurley, Timothy D., ed. *Origin of the Juvenile Court Law: Juvenile Courts and What They Have Accomplished*. Chicago: Visitation and Aid Society, 1907.

Hutchinson, William R. *Religious Pluralism in America: The Contentious History of a Founding Ideal*. New Haven, Conn.: Yale University Press, 2003.

Ibrahim, Ahmed. "The Shari'a Courts of Mogadishu: Beyond 'African Islam' and 'Islamic Law'." Ph.D. dissertation, City University of New York, 2018. CUNY Academic Works. https://academicworks.cuny.edu/gc_etds/2520/.

Illinois. *Illinois Circuit Court Reports*. Ed. Francis E. Matthews and Hal Crumpton Bangs. 3 vols. Chicago: T. H. Flood, 1907–1909.

———. *Revised Statutes of the State of Illinois*. Ed. Harvey B. Hurd. Chicago: Chicago Legal News, 1904, 1908.

Illinois State Bar Association. "Report of Special Committee on Masters in Chancery." *Chicago Legal News* 47 (1915): 579–82, 584–86.

Immerwahr, Daniel. "The Greater United States: Territory and Empire in U.S. History." *Diplomatic History* 40, no. 3 (2016): 373–91.

———. *How to Hide an Empire: A History of the Greater United States*. New York: Farrar, Straus and Giroux, 2019.

Ingersoll, Henry H. "Confusion of Law and Equity." *Yale Law Journal* 21 (1911): 58–71.

"Installation of Municipal Court Judges." *Chicago Legal News* 39 (1906): 138.

Ireland, Alleyne. *The Far Eastern Tropics: Studies in the Administration of Tropical Dependencies*. Westminster: Archibald Constable, 1905.

Jain, Andrea R. "Fox News Controversy on Yoga and the White Supremacy Reveals Problem of Yoga Discussion." *Religion Dispatches* (blog), February 7, 2018. http://religiondispatches.org/fox-news-controversy-on-yoga-and-white-supremacy-reveals-problem-of-yoga-discussion/.

———. *Selling Yoga: From Counterculture to Pop Culture*. Oxford: Oxford University Press, 2015.

Jakobsen, Janet, and Ann Pellegrini. *Love the Sin: Sexual Regulation and the Limits of Religious Tolerance*. New York: New York University Press, 2014.

Jalal, Ayesha. 1985. *The Sole Spokesman: Jinnah, the Muslim League, and the Demand for Pakistan*. Cambridge: Cambridge University Press.

James, Henry. *American Scene*. 1907. Reprint, New York: Penguin Classics, 1994.

Jammu, J. P. S. "Yoga Tourism in India." *International Journal of Information Movement* 1, no. 8 (2016): 1–6.

Jay-Z. *Legacy*. Roc Nation / UMG Recordings Inc, 2017.

Johnson, Courtney. "Understanding the American Empire: Colonialism, Latin Americanism, and Professional Social Science, 1898–1920." In *Colonial Crucible: Empire in the Making of the Modern American State*, ed. Alfred W. McCoy and Francisco A. Scarano, 175–90. Madison: University of Wisconsin Press, 2009.

Johnson, Greg. "Courting Culture: Unexpected Relationships Between Religion and Law in Contemporary Hawai'i." In *After Secular Law*, ed. Winnifred Fallers Sullivan, Robert A. Yelle and Mateo Taussig-Rubbo, 282–301. Palo Alto: Stanford University Press, 2011.

Johnson, Paul Christopher, Pamela Klassen, and Winnifred Fallers Sullivan, eds. *Ekklesia: Three Inquiries in Church and State*. Chicago: University of Chicago Press, 2018.

Johnson, Sylvester A. *African American Religions, 1500–2000: Colonialism, Democracy, and Freedom*. Cambridge: Cambridge University Press, 2015.

"Judge Tuley Memorial Services." *Chicago Legal News* 38 (1906): 177–79.

Julián de Nieves, Elisa. *The Catholic Church in Colonial Puerto Rico (1898–1964)*. Rio Piedras: Editorial Edil, 1982.

Kaeppler, Adrienne, Markus Schindlbeck, and Gisela Speidel, eds. *Old Hawai'i: An Ethnography of Hawai'i in the 1880s*. Berlin: Ethnologisches Museum Berlin, 2008.

Kagan, Michael. "Refugee Credibility Assessment and the Religious Imposter Problem: A Case Study of Eritrean Pentecostal Claims in Egypt." *Vanderbilt Journal of Transnational Law* 43, no. 5 (2010): 1179–233.

Kagan, Richard L. *Lawsuits and Litigants in Castile 1500–1700*. Chapel Hill: University of North Carolina Press, 1981.

Kairos Theologians. *The Kairos Document: Challenge to the Church, A Theological Comment on the Political Crisis in South Africa*. Edited by John W. de Gruchy. Grand Rapids, Mich.: Eerdmans, 1986.

Kameʻeleihiwa, Lilikalā. *Native Land and Foreign Desires: Pehea Lā E Pono Ai?* Honolulu: Bishop Museum Press, 1992.

Kanahele, Pualani Kanakaʻole. *Ka Honua Ola: The Living Earth*. Honolulu: Kamehameha, 2011.

Kapur, Devesh. *Diaspora, Development, and Democracy: The Domestic Impact of International Migration from India*. Princeton, N.J.: Princeton University Press, 2010.

Käsemann, Ernst. *Commentary on Romans*. Trans. Geoffrey W. Bromiley. Grand Rapids, Mich.: Eerdmans, 1980.

Katz, Stanley N. "The Politics of Law in Colonial America: Controversies over Chancery Courts and Equity Law in the Eighteenth Century." In *Law in American History*, ed. Donald Fleming and Bernard Bailyn, 257–84. Boston: Little, Brown, 1971.

Kauanui, J. Kēhaulani. *Hawaiian Blood: Colonialism and the Politics of Sovereignty and Indigeneity* (Durham, N.C.: Duke University Press, 2008)

———. "Precarious Positions: Native Hawaiians and U.S. Federal Recognition." In *Recognition, Sovereignty Struggles, and Indigenous Rights: A Sourcebook*, ed. Amy E. Denouden and Jean M. O'Brien, 314–36. Chapel Hill: University of North Carolina Press, 2013.

Keller, Timothy. *Romans 8–16 for You*. Purcellville, Va.: Good Book Company, 2015.

Kessler, Amalia D. *Inventing American Exceptionalism: The Origins of American Adversarial Legal Culture, 1800–1877*. New Haven, Conn.: Yale University Press, 2017.

Khadivi, Laleh. *A Good Country*. New York: Bloomsbury, 2017.

Kidd, Thomas. *God of Liberty: A Religious History of the American Revolution*. New York: Basic Books, 2010.

Kidd, Thomas, and Barry Hankins. *Baptists in America: A History*. New York: Oxford University Press, 2015.

Kindersley, Nicki. "The Fifth Column? An Intellectual History of Southern Sudanese Communities in Khartoum, 1969–2005." PhD diss., Durham University, 2016.

Kirkpatrick, David. *A Gospel for the Poor: Global South Christianity and the Latin American Evangelical Left*. Philadelphia: University of Pennsylvania Press, 2019.

Kishimoto Hideo, "Shūkyō to kyōiku to no sōkan: Beikoku to Nihon to no hikaku teki hekiken" [originally "Amerika ni okeru shūkyō to kyōiku to no kankei: Nihon to no hikaku teki hekiken], *Shakakiken* 1, no. 3 (December 1947), in *Kishimoto Hideo shū*, vol. 5, ed. Wakimoto Tsuneya and Yanagikawa Keiichi, 279–90. Tokyo: Keiseisha, 1976.

Klassen, Pamela E. "Back to the Land and Waters: Futures for the Study of Religions." *Religion* 50, no. 1: 1–7. https://doi.org/10.1080/0048721X.2019.1681106.

———. *Spirits of Protestantism: Medicine, Healing, and Liberal Christianity*. Berkeley: University of California Press, 2011.

———. "Spiritual Jurisdictions: Treaty People and the Queen of Canada." In *Ekklesia: Three Inquiries in Church and State*, ed. Paul Christopher Johnson, Pamela E. Klassen, and Winnifred Fallers Sullivan, 107–74. Chicago: University of Chicago Press, 2018.

———. *The Story of Radio Mind: A Missionary's Journey on Indigenous Land*. Chicago: University of Chicago Press, 2018.

Kraft, Siv Ellen, and Cato Christensen. "Religion i Kautokeino-opprøret: En analyse av samisk urfolksspiritualitet." *Nytt Norsk Tidsskrift* 28, no.1 (2011): 18–27.

Kramer, Paul A. *The Blood of Government: Race, Empire, the United States, & the Philippines*. Chapel Hill: University of North Carolina Press, 2006.

———. "Power and Connection: Imperial Histories of the United States in the World." *American Historical Review* 116, no. 5 (December 2011): 1348–91. https://doi.org/10.1086/ahr.116.5.1348.

Kruse, Kevin M. *One Nation Under God: How Corporate America Invented Christian America*. New York: Basic Books, 2015.

Kundnani, Arun. *The Muslims Are Coming! Islamophobia, Extremism, and the Domestic War on Terror*. New York: Verso, 2015.

———. "Radicalisation: The Journey of a Concept." *Race & Class* 54, no. 2 (2012): 3–25.

Kuperus, Tracy. "The Political Role and Democratic Contribution of Churches in Post-Apartheid South Africa." *Journal of Church and State* 53, no. 2 (Spring 2011): 278–306.

LaDow, Beth. *The Medicine Line: Life and Death on a North American Borderland*. New York: Routledge, 2001.

Lahav, Pnina. *Judgment in Jerusalem: Chief Justice Simon Agranat and the Zionist Century*. Berkeley: University of California Press, 1997.

Langbein, John H. "The Disappearance of Civil Trial in the United States." *Yale Law Journal* 122 (2012): 522–72.

Langbein, John H., Renée Lettow Lerner, and Bruce P. Smith. *History of the Common Law: The Development of Anglo-American Legal Institutions*. New York: Aspen, 2009.

Langston, Paul. "'Tyrant and Oppressor!' Colonial Press Reaction to the Quebec Act." *Historical Journal of Massachusetts* 34, no. 1 (2006): 1–17.

Larsson, Ernils. 2017. "Jinja Honchō and the Politics of Constitutional Reform in Japan." *Japan Review* 30: 227–52. http://publications.nichibun.ac.jp/region/d/NSH/series/jare/2017-07-24/s001/s014/pdf/article.pdf.

Latour, Bruno. "On Actor-Network Theory: A Few Clarifications." *Soziale Welt* 47, no. 4 (1996): 369–81.

———. *Reassembling the Social: An Introduction to Actor-Network-Theory*. Oxford: Oxford University Press, 2005.

———. *We Have Never Been Modern*. Trans. Catherine Porter. Cambridge, Mass.: Harvard University Press, 1993.

Lazarus, Emma. "The New Colossus." In *Emma Lazarus: Selected Poems and Other Writings*. Peterborough, Ont.: Broadview Press, 2002.

Lau, Lisa. "Re-Orientalism: The Perpetration and Development of Orientalism by Orientals." *Modern Asian Studies* 43, no. 2 (2009): 571–90.

Lau, Lisa., and Ana Cristina Mendes. *Re-Orientalism and South Asian Identity Politics the Oriental Other Within*. London: Routledge, 2011.

"Law Made by Man, for Man." *Chicago Legal News* 1 (1869): 220.

"The Law Providing for a Municipal Court in Chicago." *Chicago Legal News* 38 (1906): 398, 400–401.

Laycock, Douglas. "The Triumph of Equity." *Law and Contemporary Problems* 56 (1993): 53–82.

Lee, Tahirih V. "The United States Court for China: A Triumph of Local Law." *Buffalo Law Review* 52 (2004): 923–1075.

Leeson, Cecil. *The Probation System*. London: P. S. King, 1914.
Leira, Halvard. 2004. "'Hele vort folk er naturlige og fødte fredsvenner': Norsk Fredstenkning Fram Til 1906." *Historisk Tidsskrift* 83 (2): 153–80.
Leirvik, Oddbjørn. "Religion som velferdsgode?" *Kirke og Kultur* 120, no. 4 (2016): 309–11.
Leonard, Bill J. *Baptists in America*. New York: Columbia University Press, 2005.
———. *God's Last and Only Hope: The Fragmentation of the Southern Baptist Convention*. Grand Rapids, Mich.: Eerdmans, 1990.
Levensohn, Lotta. *Vision and Fulfillment*. New York: Greystone, 1950.
Link, Jürgen. "On the Contribution of Normalism to Modernity and Postmodernity." *Cultural Critique* 57 (Spring 2004): 33–46.
Lobingier, Charles Sumner. "Blending Legal Systems in the Philippines." *American Review of Reviews* 32 (1905): 336–38.
———. "Civil Law Rights Through Common-Law Remedies." *Juridical Review* 20 (1908): 97–108.
———. "Judicial Superintendent in China." *Illinois Law Review* 12 (1918): 403–8.
———. "Las Siete Partidas and Its Predecessors." *California Law Review* 1 (1913): 487–98.
———. "A Spanish Object-Lesson in Code-Making." *Yale Law Journal* 16 (1907): 411–16.
Locke, John. *A Letter Concerning Toleration*. Huddersfield, U.K.: Printed by J. Brook, 1796.
Lockmiller, David A. "The Settlement of the Church Property Question in Cuba." *Hispanic American Historical Review* 17, no. 4 (1937): 488–98.
Long, Charles. "Civil Rights—Civil Religion: Visible People and Invisible Religion." In *American Civil Religion*, ed. Russell E. Richey and Donald G. Jones, 211–21. New York: Harper & Row, 1974.
Lund, Christopher Alan. "A Critical Examination of Evangelicalism in South Africa, with Special Reference to the Evangelical Witness Document and Concerned Evangelicals." Master's thesis, University of Cape Town, South Africa, 1988.
Maas, Philip. *Samādhipāda: Das erste Kapitel des Pātañjalayogaśāstra zum ersten Mal Kritisch ediert*. Aachen: Shaker, 2006.
MacArthur, John F. *Romans: Grace, Truth, and Redemption*. 2007. Reprint, Nashville, Tenn.: Thomas Nelson, 2015.
Macaulay, Thomas Babington, and G. M. Young. *Speeches by Lord Macaulay, with His Minute on Indian Education*. London: Oxford University Press, H. Milford, 1935.
Mack, Edwin S. "The Revival of Criminal Equity." *Harvard Law Review* 16 (1903): 390–403.
Mack, Julian W. "The Juvenile Court." *Harvard Law Review* 23 (1909): 104–22.
Maddox, C. B. "Studying at the Source: Ashtanga Yoga Tourism and the Search for Authenticity in Mysore, India." *Journal of Tourism and Cultural Change* 13, no. 4 (2015): 330–43.
Madison, James. "Memorial and Remonstrance Against Religious Assessments." In *The Writings of James Madison: Comprising His Public Papers and His Private Correspondence, Including Numerous Letters and Documents Now for the First Time Printed*, ed. James Madison and Gaillard Hunt. New York: G. P. Putnam's Sons, 1900.
Mahmood, Saba. *Religious Difference in a Secular Age: A Minority Report*. Princeton, N.J.: Princeton University Press, 2015.
Makdisi, Ussama. *Artillery of Heaven: American Missionaries and the Failed Conversion of the Middle East*. Ithaca, N.Y.: Cornell University Press, 2007.
Malcolm, George A. "Philippine Law." Parts 1 and 2. *Illinois Law Review* 11 (1916): 331–50; 11 (1917): 387–401.
Mallinson, J., and M. Singleton. *The Roots of Yoga*. London: Penguin, 2017.
Mamdani, Mahmood. *Good Muslim, Bad Muslim: America, the Cold War, and the Roots of Terror*. New York: Doubleday, 2005.
———. *Saviors and Survivors: Darfur, Politics and the War on Terror*. New York: Doubleday, 2010.
Mancall, Peter C. *Envisioning America: English Plans for the Colonization of North America, 1580–1640*. Boston: Bedford/St. Martin's, 1995.

Manto, Saadat Hasan. "Toba Tek Singh." In *The Oxford Book of Urdu Short Stories*. Trans. Amina Azfar. Oxford: Oxford University Press, 2009.

Martin, William. *With God on Our Side: The Rise of the Religious Right in America*. New York: Broadway, 2005.

Martínez, Anne M. *Catholic Borderlands: Mapping Catholicism onto American Empire, 1905–1935*. Lincoln: University of Nebraska Press, 2014.

Marzouki, Nadia. *Islam: An American Religion*. New York: Columbia University Press, 2017.

———. "Le movement contre le droit islamique et le droit étranger aux États-Unis." *Politique américaine* 1, no. 23 (2014): 33–53.

Mason, Mary Ann. *From Father's Property to Children's Rights*. New York: Columbia University Press, 1994.

Masuzawa, Tomoko. *The Invention of World Religions: Or, How European Universalism was Preserved in the Language of Pluralism*. Chicago: University of Chicago Press, 2005.

Matarese, Susan. *American Foreign Policy and the Utopian Imagination*. Boston: University of Massachusetts, 2001.

McAlister, Melani. "The Global Conscience of American Evangelicalism: Internationalism and Social Concern in the 1970s and Beyond." *Journal of American Studies* 51, no. 4 (November 2017): 1197–220.

———. *The Kingdom of God Has No Borders: A Global History of American Evangelicalism*. New York: Oxford University Press, 2018.

———. "One Black Allah: The Middle East in the Global Politics of African American Liberation, 1955–1970," *American Quarterly* 51, no. 3 (September 1999): 625–56.

———. "U.S. Evangelicals and the Politics of Slave Redemption as Religious Freedom in Sudan." *South Atlantic Quarterly* 113, no. 1 (2014): 87–108.

McBride, Keally. *Mr. Mothercountry: The Man Who Made the Rule of Law*. Oxford: Oxford University Press, 2016.

McBride, Spencer. "Was the Constitution the Problem? The Politics of Religious Intolerance in Nineteenth-Century America." Presented at the Symposium on Religious Pluralism and Democracy, Utah Valley University, March 30, 2018.

———. "When Joseph Smith Met Martin Van Buren: Mormonism and the Politics of Religious Liberty in Nineteenth-Century America." *Church History* 85, no. 1 (2016): 150–58.

McConnell, Michael W. "Schism, Plague, and Late Rites in the French Quarter: The Strange Story Behind the Supreme Court's First Free Exercise Case." Stanford Public Law Working Paper No. 1675213. https://ssrn.com/abstract=1675213.

McDougall, Walter A. *The Tragedy of U.S. Foreign Policy: How America's Civil Religion Betrayed the National Interest*. New Haven, Conn.: Yale University Press, 2018.

McGreevy, John T. *Catholicism and American Freedom: A History*. New York: Norton, 2004.

McLaughlin, Levi. "Komeito's Soka Gakkai Protestors and Supporters: Religious Motivations for Political Activism in Contemporary Japan." *Asia-Pacific Journal: Japan Focus* 13, iss. 41, no. 1 (2015). https://apjjf.org/-Levi-McLaughlin/4386.

McNeill, David. "Back to the Future: Shintō, Ise and Japan's New Moral Education." *Asia-Pacific Journal: Japan Focus* 11, iss. 50, no. 1 (2013).

Mead, Sidney. *The Lively Experiment: The Shaping of Christianity in America*. Eugene, Ore.: Wipf & Stock, 1963.

Mehta, Uday. *Liberalism and Empire: A Study in Nineteenth Century British Liberal Thought*. Chicago: University of Chicago Press, 1999.

Merry, Sally Engle. *Colonizing Hawai'i: The Cultural Power of Law*. Princeton, N.J.: Princeton University Press, 2000.

Miller, Perry. *The Life of the Mind in America*. New York: Harcourt, Brace & World, 1965.

Minger, Ralph Eldin. "William H. Taft and the United States Intervention in Cuba in 1906." *Hispanic American Historical Review* 41 (1961): 75–89.

Mitchell, Kerry, *Spirituality and the State: Managing Nature and Experience in America's National Parks.* New York: New York University Press, 2016.

Mode, Peter G. *The Frontier Spirit of American Christianity.* New York: Macmillan, 1923.

Modirzadeh, Naz. "If It's Broke, Don't Make It Worse: A Critique of the U.N. Secretary-General's Plan of Action to Prevent Violent Extremism." *Lawfare* (blog), January 23, 2016. https://www.lawfareblog.com/if-its-broke-dont-make-it-worse-critique-un-secretary-generals-plan-action-prevent-violent-extremism.

Morris, Henry C. *The History of Colonization from the Earliest Times to the Present Day.* 2 vols. New York: Macmillan, 1900.

———. "A New Phase of Municipal Regulation." *World To-day* 19 (1910): 760–68.

———. "Some Effects of Outlying Dependencies upon the People of the United States." *Proceedings of the American Political Science Association* 3 (1906): 194–209.

Morris, Henry C., Theodore Marburg, and W. W. Willoughby. "Discussion." *Proceedings of the American Political Science Association* 1 (1904): 139–43.

Morris, Kate. "Running the 'Medicine Line': Images of the Border in Contemporary Native American Art." *American Indian Quarterly* 35, no. 4 (2011): 549–78.

Moses, Bernard. "Colonial Policy with Reference to the Philippines." *Proceedings of the American Political Science Association* 1 (1904): 88–116.

———. *The Establishment of Spanish Rule in America.* New York: G. P. Putnam, 1898.

Mullins, Edgar Young. *The Axioms of Religion: A New Interpretation of the Baptist Faith.* 1908. Reprint, n.p.: Forgotten Books, 2017.

Mullins, Mark R. "Neonationalism, Religion, and Patriotic Education in Post-Disaster Japan." *Asia-Pacific Journal: Japan Focus* 14, iss. 20, no. 6 (2016).

———. "Secularization, Deprivatization, and the Reappearance of Public Religion in Japanese Society." *Journal of Religion in Japan* 1, no. 1 (2012): 61–82.

Nair, Janaki. 2011. *Mysore Modern: Rethinking the Region under Princely Rule.* Minneapolis: University of Minnesota Press.

Nesbitt, Francis Njubi. *Race for Sanctions: African Americans Against Apartheid, 1946–1994.* Bloomington: Indiana University Press, 2004.

Neuman, Gerald L. *Reconsidering the Insular Cases: The Past and Future of the American Empire.* Cambridge, Mass.: Human Rights Program, Harvard Law School, 2015.

Neumann, Iver B. "Fred og forsoning som norsk utenrikspolitikk," *Internasjonal politikk* 70, no. 3 (2012): 362–71.

Newman, Mark. *Getting Right with God: Southern Baptists and Desegregation, 1945–1995.* Tuscaloosa: University of Alabama Press, 2001.

Nijhawan, Michael. *The Precarious Diasporas of Sikh and Ahmadiyya Generations: Violence, Memory, and Agency.* New York: Palgrave Macmillan, 2016.

Noll, Mark A. *In the Beginning Was the Word: The Bible in American Public Life, 1492–1783.* New York: Oxford University Press, 2015.

Norris, W. F. "The Criminal Code of the Philippines." *Green Bag* 15 (1903): 433–35.

Novak, William J. "Enjoining Immorality: Considerations of Justice and Public Policy." Unpublished manuscript in author's possession, 1985.

———. "Police Power and the Hidden Transformation of the American State." In *Police and the Liberal State,* ed. Markus D. Dubber and Mariana Valverde, 54–73. Stanford, Calif.: Stanford University Press, 2008.

Nye, David. *American Technological Sublime.* Boston: MIT Press, 1996.

O'Donnell, Catherine. "John Carroll and the Origins of an American Catholic Church, 1783–1815." *William and Mary Quarterly* 68, no. 1 (2011): 101–26.

"Of Judicial and Execution Sales." *Chicago Bench and Bar* 3 (1873): 97–120.

Olson, Harry. "The Municipal Court of Chicago—Its Organization and Administration." *Central Law Journal* 92 (1921): 81–92.

———. "The Proper Organization and Procedure of a Municipal Court." *Proceedings of the American Political Science Association* 7 (1910): 78–96.
Owens, James. "Churches Act to Thwart Apartheid." *Report from the Capital*, February 1985.
Owensby, Brian P. *Empire of Law and Indian Justice in Colonial Mexico*. Stanford, Calif.: Stanford University Press, 2008.
Packard, Elizabeth P. W. *The Prisoners' Hidden Life, or Insane Asylums Unveiled*. Chicago: printed by the author, 1868.
Packard, Samuel W. *The Great Prohibition Decision*. New York: Funk & Wagnalls, 1888.
Page, Enoch. "The Gender, Race, and Class Barriers: Enclosing Yoga as a White Public Space." In *Yoga, the Body, and Embodied Social Change: An Intersectional Feminist Analysis*, ed. Beth Berila, Melanie Klein, and Chelsea Jackson Roberts, 41–66. Lanham, Md.: Lexington, 2016.
Palmer, John M. *The Bench and Bar of Illinois*. Chicago: Lewis, 1899.
Pangti, N., Sanjay Nainwal, and Uttaranchal Tourism Development Board. *Destination Wellness: Yoga, Meditation and Ayurveda in Uttaranchal*. Dehradun: [Uttaranchal Tourism Development Board]: Distributed by Natraj Publishers, 2004.
Paras, Corazon L., Oscar L. Paras Jr., and Ma. Corazon P. Villanueva. *The Chief Justices of the Supreme Court of the Philippines. An Update*. Queson City, Philippines: Giraffe, 2008.
Parker, Donna Grear, and Edward M. Wise. "Wigmore, John Henry." *American National Biography Online*. Oxford University Press, 2000. https://doi.org/10.1093/anb/9780198606697.article.1100915.
Pasternak, Shiri. *Grounded Authority: The Algonquins of Barrier Lake Against the State*. Minneapolis: University of Minnesota Press, 2017.
Peagler, Victoria Morongwa. "Blow the Trumpet in Black Zion: A Phenomenological Exploration of the Zionist Christian Church of South Africa." Ph.D. diss., Fuller Theological Seminary, School of Intercultural Studies, Pasadena, California, 2010.
Pease, Theodore Calvin, ed. *The Laws of the Northwest Territory 1788–1800*. Springfield: Illinois State Historical Library, 1925.
Peterson, Merrill D., and Robert C. Vaughan. *The Virginia Statute for Religious Freedom: Its Evolution and Consequences in American History*. Cambridge: Cambridge University Press, 1988.
Philbrick, Frances S., ed. *The Laws of Indiana Territory 1801–1809*. Springfield: Illinois State Historical Library, 1930.
Phillips, Kevin. *The Cousins' Wars: Religion, Politics, & the Triumph of Anglo-America*. New York: Basic Books, 1999.
Philpott, Daniel. "Culture War or Common Heritage? On Recent Critics of Global Religious Freedom." *Lawfare*, June 30, 2016. https://www.lawfareblog.com/culture-war-or-common-heritage-recent-critics-global-religious-freedom.
Pinch, W. R. *Peasants and Monks in British India*. Berkeley: University of California Press, 1996.
———. *Warrior Ascetics and Indian Empires*. Cambridge: Cambridge University Press, 2006.
Pomeroy, John Norton. *The "Civil Code" in California*. New York: Bar Association, 1885.
———. *A Treatise on Equity Jurisprudence, as Administered in the United States of America*. 3 vols. San Francisco: A. L. Bancroft, 1881.
Poole, Reginald L. *Lectures on the History of the Papal Chancery Down to the Time of Innocent III*. Cambridge: Cambridge University Press, 1915.
Porter, V. Mott, ed. *Official Report of the Universal Congress of Lawyers and Jurists*. St. Louis: Executive Committee, 1905.
Post, Robert C. "Judicial Management: The Achievements of Chief Justice William Howard Taft." *OAH Magazine of History* 13 (1998): 24–29.
Pound, Roscoe. "The Organization of Courts." *Journal of the American Judicature Society* 11 (1927): 69–82.
Powell, M. C., ed. "Mr. Hu I-ku (Wenfu Yiko Hu)." In *Who's Who in China*, 369–70. Shanghai: China Weekly Review, 1925.
Power, Will. *Fetch Clay, Make Man: A Play*. New York: Overlook Duckworth, 2016.

Preston, Andrew. *Sword of the Spirit, Shield of Faith: Religion in American War and Diplomacy.* New York: Knopf, 2012.
Puterbaugh, Sabin D. *Puterbaugh's Chancery Pleading and Practice.* Chicago: Callaghan, 1888.
Qafisheh, Mutaz M. *The International Law Foundations of Palestinian Nationality: A Legal Examination of Palestinian Nationality Under the British Rule.* Vol. 7. Leiden: Brill, 2008.
Quillen, William T. Summer. "Constitutional Equity and the Innovative Tradition." *Law and Contemporary Problems* 56 (1993): 29–52.
Rafael, Vicente L. "The Afterlife of Empire: Sovereignty and Revolution in the Philippines." In *Colonial Crucible: Empire in the Making of the Modern American State*, ed. Alfred W. McCoy and Francisco A. Scarano, 342–52. Madison: University of Wisconsin Press, 2009.
Raustiala, Kal. *Does the Constitution Follow the Flag? The Evolution of Territoriality in American Law.* Oxford: Oxford University Press, 2011.
Reeve, Tapping. *The Law of Baron and Femme; of Parent and Child; of Guardian and Ward; of Master and Servant; and of the Powers of Courts of Chancery.* New Haven, Conn.: Oliver Steele, 1816.
Reuter, Frank T. *Catholic Influence on American Colonial Policies 1898–1904.* Austin: University of Texas Press, 1967.
Rice, Daniel F. "Niebuhr's Critique of Religion in America." In *Reinhold Niebuhr Revisited: Engagements with an American Original*, ed. Daniel Rice, 317–37. Grand Rapids, Mich.: Eerdmans, 2009.
Richey, Russel, ed. *American Civil Religion.* New York: Harper and Row, 1974.
Richland, Justin. "Jurisdiction: Grounding Law in Language." *Annual Review of Anthropology* 42 (2013): 209–26.
Rivera Ramos, Efrén. *The Legal Construction of Identity: The Judicial and Social Legacy of American Colonialism in Puerto Rico.* Washington, D.C.: American Psychological Association, 2001.
Robinson, Lelia Josephine. *The Law of Husband and Wife.* Boston: Lee and Shepard, 1889.
Rodríguez, Antonio Angel Ruiz. *La Real Chancillería de Granada en el siglo XVI.* Granada: Diputación Provincial de Granada, 1987.
Rogers, Howard J., ed. *Congress of Arts and Science, Universal Exposition, St. Louis, 1904.* Vol. 7, *Economics, Politics, Jurisprudence, Social Science.* Boston: Houghton, Mifflin, 1906.
Root, Elihu. *The Military and Colonial Policy of the United States. Addresses and Reports by Elihu Root.* Edited by Robert Bacon and James Brown Scott. Cambridge: Harvard University Press, 1916.
Rots, Aike P. "Public Shrine Forests? Shintō, Immanence, and Discursive Secularization." *Japan Review* 30 (2017): 179–205.
Rosenfeld, Paul. *Port of New York: Essays on Fourteen American Modernists.* New York: Harcourt Brace, 1924.
Rubenfeld, Jed. "Privatization and State Action: Do Campus Sexual Assault Hearings Violate Due Process?" *Texas Law Review* 96 (2017): 15–69.
Runstedtler, Theresa. *Jack Johnson: Boxing in the Shadow of the Global Color Line.* Berkeley: University of California Press, 2013.
Ruskola, Teemu. "Colonialism Without Colonies: On the Extraterritorial Jurisprudence of the U.S. Court for China." *Law & Contemporary Problems* 71 (2008): 217–42.
Rusling, James. "Interview with President William McKinley." *Christian Advocate*, January 22, 1903. Reprinted in Daniel Schirmer and Stephen Rosskamm Shalom, eds. *The Philippines Reader.* Boston: South End Press, 1987, 22–23.
Saenz, Michael. "Economic Aspects of Church Development in Puerto Rico." Ph.D. diss., University of Michigan, 1961.
Sai, David Keanu. *Ua Mau Ke Ea—Sovereignty Endures: An Overview of the Political and Legal History of the Hawaiian Islands.* Honolulu: Pu'a Foundation, 2011.
Salmon, Marylynn. *Women and the Law of Property in Early America.* Chapel Hill: University of North Carolina Press, 1986.
Salomon, Noah. "Religion After the State: Secular Soteriologies at the Birth of South Sudan." *Journal of Law and Religion* 29, no. 3 (October 2014): 447–69.

Sampter, Jessie. *A Course on Zionism*. New York: Federation of American Zionists, 1915.
———. *The Great Adventurer*. New York: R. Kerr Press, 1909.
———. "I Told You So." *Maccabaean* (March 1918).
———. *Seekers*. New York: Mitchell Kennerley, 1910.
Samuel, Herbert. *An Interim Report on the Civil Administration of Palestine*. London: H.M. Stationery Office, 1921.
Schäfer, Axel R. *American Progressives and German Social Reform, 1875–1920*. Stuttgart: Steiner, 2000.
Scherer, Matthew. *Beyond Church and State: Democracy, Secularism, and Conversion*. Cambridge: Cambridge University Press: 2013.
———. "The New Religious Freedom: Secular Fictions and Church Autonomy." *Politics and Religion* 8, no. 3 (2015): 544–64.
———. "A Yet Unapproachable America." In *Theologies of American Exceptionalism*, ed. Winnifred Fallers Sullivan and Elizabeth Shakman Hurd. Bloomington: Indiana University Press, 2021.
Schleicher, Dorothy. "A History and Analysis of the Role of the Baptist Joint Committee, 1972–Present." Master's thesis, Baylor University, 1993.
Schmidt, Leigh. *Consumer Rites: The Buying and Selling of American Holidays*. Princeton, N.J.: Princeton University Press, 1987.
Schmitt, Carl. *Political Theology*. Trans. George Schwab. Chicago: University of Chicago Press, 1985.
Schofield, Henry. "Equity Jurisdiction to Abate and Enjoin Illegal Saloons as Public Nuisances." *Illinois Law Review* 8 (1913): 19–41.
Schultz, Rima Lunin, and Adele Hast, ed. *Women Building Chicago 1790–1990*. Bloomington: Indiana University Press, 2001.
Schurman, Jacob G. "The Philippines." *Yale Law Journal* 9 (1900): 215–22.
Schweninger, Loren, ed. *The Southern Debate over Slavery*. Vol. 2, *Petitions to Southern County Courts, 1775–1867*. Urbana: University of Illinois Press, 2008.
Scott, Joan. *Sex and Secularism*. Princeton, N.J.: Princeton University Press, 2017.
Scott, Samuel Parsons, trans. *Las Siete Partidas*. 5 vols. Chicago: Commerce Clearing House, 1931.
Sedgwick, Mark. "The Concept of Radicalization as a Source of Confusion." *Terrorism and Political Violence* 22, no. 4 (2010): 479–94.
Seeley, Samantha. "Beyond the American Colonization Society." *History Compass* 14, no. 3 (March 2016): 93–104.
Segal, Hyman. *The Book of Pain Struggle, Called: The Prophecy of Fulfillment*. New York: self-published, 1911.
Sehat, David. *The Myth of American Religious Freedom*. New York: Oxford University Press, 2011.
Shea, Nina. U.S. Congress, House. Prepared Statement of Ms. Nina Shea, Director, Center for Religious Freedom, Freedom House. "In Defense of Human Dignity: The International Religious Freedom Report." Hearing before the Subcommittee on Africa, Global Human Rights and International Operations of the Committee on International Relations. 109th Cong., 1st Session, November 15, 2005.
Shelton, Thomas W. "Progress of the Proposal to Substitute Rules of Court for Common Law Practice." *Annals of the American Academy of Political and Social Science* 73 (1917): 178–88.
Sherman, Thomas. "A Month in Porto Rico." *Messenger of the Sacred Heart of Jesus* 33 (January–December 1898).
Sherwood, Samuel. *A Sermon, containing Scriptural Instructions to civil rulers . . . Also, an appendix stating the heave grievances the colonies labour under . . . By Rev. Ebenezer Baldwin*. New Haven, Conn.: T. and S. Green, 1774.
Shulman, George. "Acknowledgment and Disavowal as an Idiom for Theorizing Politics." *Theory & Event* 14, no. 1 (2011). https://doi.org/10.1353/tae.2011.0003.
———. *American Prophecy: Race and Redemption in American Political Culture*. Minneapolis: University of Minnesota Press, 2008.

Silva Gotay, Samuel. *Soldado Católico en guerra de religión.* Río Piedras, P.R.: Publicaciones Gaviota, 2012.
Silverman, David. *Faith and Boundaries: Colonists, Christianity, and Community Among the Wampanoag Indians of Martha's Vineyard, 1600–1871.* Cambridge: Cambridge University Press, 2007.
Simmons, Erica. "Playgrounds and Penny Lunches: American Social Welfare in the Yishuv." *American Jewish History* 92, no. 3 (September 2004): 263–97.
Simone, T. Abdou Maliqalim. *In Whose Image? Political Islam and Urban Practice in Sudan.* Chicago: University of Chicago Press, 1994.
Simpson, Audra. *Mohawk Interruptus: Political Life Across the Borders of Settler States.* Durham, N.C.: Duke University Press, 2014.
Singleton, Mark. *Yoga Body: The Origins of Modern Posture Practice.* Oxford: Oxford University Press, 2010.
Slagstad, Rune. *De nasjonale strateger.* Oslo: Pax, 1998.
Slotkin, Richard. *The Fatal Environment: The Myth of the Frontier in the Age of Industrialization 1800–1890.* Tulsa: University of Oklahoma Press, 1985.
Sparrow, Bartholomew H. *The Insular Cases and the Emergence of American Empire.* Lawrence: University Press of Kansas, 2006.
Spence, George. *The Equitable Jurisdiction of the Court of Chancery.* 2 vols. Philadelphia: Lea and Blanchard, 1846–1850.
Spring, Beth. "Falwell Raises a Stir by Opposing Sanctions Against South Africa." *Christianity Today*, October 4, 1985.
St. Clair, Arthur. *The St. Clair Papers.* Ed. William Henry Smith. 2 vols. Cincinnati: Robert Clarke, 1882.
Stoddard, George, et al. *Report of the United States Education Mission to Japan.* Trans. by Akira Watanabe. Tokyo: Meguro Shoten, 1947.
Stead, William T. "The Civic Church." In *The World's Parliament of Religions.* Vol. 2. Ed. John Henry Barrows. Chicago: Parliament, 1893.
———. *If Christ Came to Chicago!* Chicago: Laird & Lee, 1894.
Stevens, Laura M. *The Poor Indians: British Missionaries, Native Americans, and Colonial Sensibility.* Philadelphia: University of Pennsylvania Press, 2004.
Stevens-Arroyo, Anthony M. "Taking Religion Seriously: New Perspectives on Religion in Puerto Rico." *Centro Journal* 18, no. 11 (2006): 214–23.
Stiles, Ezra. *The United States Elevated to Glory and Honor: A Sermon.* New Haven, Conn., 1783.
Stinchcombe, William C. *The American Revolution and the French Alliance.* Syracuse, N.Y.: Syracuse University Press, 1969.
Story, Joseph. *Commentaries on Equity Jurisprudence: as Administered in England and America.* 2 vols. Boston: Hillard, Gray, 1836.
Stott, John. *The Message of Romans: God's Good News for the World.* Downers Grove, Ill.: IVP Academic, 1994.
Strauch, Tara Thompson. "Open for Business: Philadelphia Quakers, Thanksgiving, and the Limits of Revolutionary Religious Freedom." *Church History* 85, no. 1 (2016): 133–39.
Strayer, Joseph R. *On the Medieval Origins of the Modern State.* Princeton, N.J.: Princeton University Press, 1970.
Su, Anna. *Exporting Freedom: Religious Liberty and American Power.* Cambridge, Mass.: Harvard University Press, 2016.
Suárez, Francisca. *Refutación al Vicario Capitular.* Mayagüez: Tipografía Comercial, 1899.
Subrin, Stephen N. "How Equity Conquered Common Law: The Federal Rules of Civil Procedure in Historical Perspective." *University of Pennsylvania Law Review* 135 (1987): 909–1002.
Sullivan, E. Thomas, and Toni M. Masaro, "Due Process Exceptionalism." *Irish Jurist* 46 (2011): 117–51.
Sullivan, Winnifred Fallers. *Church State Corporation: Construing Religion in U.S. Law.* Chicago: University of Chicago Press, 2020.

———. "Comments on Johnson v M'Intosh." In "Theologies of American Exceptionalism." *Immanent Frame* (blog), February 17, 2017. https://tif.ssrc.org/2017/02/17/marshall-and-morgan/.
———. "Exporting Religious Freedom." *Commonweal*, February 26, 1999, reprinted in *CSSR Bulletin* 28, no. 2 (April 1999), and *Context* 31, no. 11 (1999).
———. *The Impossibility of Religious Freedom*. Princeton, N.J.: Princeton University Press, 2005.
———. *A Ministry of Presence: Chaplaincy, Spiritual Care, and the Law*. Chicago: University of Chicago Press, 2014.
———. *Prison Religion: Faith-Based Reform and the Constitution*. Princeton, N.J.: Princeton University Press, 2009.
———. "Religious Freedom and the Rule of Law: Exporting Modernity in a Postmodern World?" *Mississippi College Law Review* 22 (2003): 173–83.
Sullivan, Winnifred Fallers, and Lori Beaman, eds. *Varieties of Religious Establishment*. Aldershot, U.K.: Ashgate, 2013.
Sullivan, Winnifred Fallers, and Elizabeth Shakman Hurd, eds. *Theologies of American Exceptionalism*. Bloomington: Indiana University Press, 2021.
Sullivan, Winnifred Fallers, Elizabeth Shakman Hurd, Saba Mahmood, and Peter G. Danchin, eds. *Politics of Religious Freedom*. Chicago: University of Chicago Press, 2015.
Sullivan, Winnifred Fallers, Robert A. Yelle, and Mateo Taussig-Rubbo, eds. *After Secular Law*. Stanford, Calif.: Stanford University Press, 2011.
Swartz, David R. *Moral Minority: The Evangelical Left in an Age of Conservatism*. Philadelphia: University of Pennsylvania Press, 2012.
Taft, William H. "The Administration of Criminal Law." *Yale Law Journal* 15 (1905): 1–17.
———. "The Attacks on the Courts and Legal Procedure." *Kentucky Law Journal* 5 (1916): 3–24.
———. "The Delays of the Law." *Yale Law Journal* 18 (1908): 28–39.
———. "Inequalities in the Administration of Justice." *Green Bag* 20 (1908): 441–48.
———. "Possible and Needed Reforms in Administration of Justice in Federal Courts." *American Bar Association Journal* 8 (1922): 601–7.
———. "Recent Criticism of the Federal Judiciary." *Annual Report of the American Bar Association* 18 (1895): 237–74.
Tanenhaus, David S. *Juvenile Justice in the Making*. Oxford: Oxford University Press, 2004.
Tarlo, Emma. *Clothing Matters: Dress and Identity in India*. Chicago: University of Chicago Press, 1996.
Taylor, Diana. *The Archive and the Repertoire: Performing Cultural Memory in the Americas*. Durham, N.C.: Duke University Press, 2003.
Telej, Ewelina, and Jordan Robert Gamble. "Yoga Wellness Tourism: A Study of Marketing Strategies in India." *Journal of Consumer Marketing* 36, no. 6 (2019): 794–805.
Tengan, Ty Kāwika. *Native Men Remade: Gender and Nation in Contemporary Hawaiʻi*. Durham, N.C.: Duke University Press, 2008.
Teves, Stephanie Nohelani. *Defiant Indigeneity: The Politics of Hawaiian Performance*. Chapel Hill: University of North Carolina Press, 2018.
Thomas, Brook. "A Constitution Led by the Flag: The Insular Cases and the Metaphor of Incorporation." In *Foreign in a Domestic Sense: Puerto Rico, American Expansion, and the Constitution*, ed. Christina Duffy Burnett and Burke Marshall, 82–103. Durham, N.C.: Duke University Press, 2001.
Thomas, Jolyon Baraka. *Faking Liberties: Religious Freedom in American-Occupied Japan*. Chicago: University of Chicago Press, 2019.
Thompson, Glen. "'Transported Away:' The Spirituality and Piety of Charismatic Christianity in South Africa (1976–1994)." *Journal of Theology for Southern Africa*, no. 118 (March 2004): 128–45.
Thompson, Winfred Lee. *The Introduction of American Law in the Philippines and Puerto Rico 1898–1905*. Fayetteville: University of Arkansas Press, 1989.
Tiffany, Walter C. *Handbook on the Law of Persons and Domestic Relations*. St. Paul, Minn.: West, 1896.
Tolley, Michael. "Goodnow, Frank Johnson." *American National Biography Online*. Oxford University Press, 2000. https://doi.org/10.1093/anb/9780198606697.article.1400233.

Tounsel, Christopher. "Khartoum Goliath: SPLM/SPLA Update and Martial Theology During the Second Sudanese Civil War." *Journal of Africana Religions* 4, no. 2 (July 2016): 129–53.
Tous Soto, José. "Estudio comparativo entre el régimen autonómico español y la ley Foraker." *El Aguila*, July 25, 1907.
Trías Monge, José. *Puerto Rico: The Trials of the Oldest Colony in the World*. New Haven, Conn.: Yale University Press, 1997.
Tuley, Murray F. "Equity Maxims." *Chicago Legal News* 35 (1903): 424–39.
———. *McKinley and the Philippines: Imperialism*. Chicago: Iroquois Club, 1900.
Turek, Lauren Frances. *To Bring the Good News to All Nations: Evangelical Influence on Human Rights and U.S. Foreign Relations*. Ithaca, N.Y.: Cornell University Press, 2020.
Turner, Frederick *The Frontier in American History*. New York: Henry Holt, 1921.
Tvedt, Terje. "International Development Aid and Its Impact on a Donor Country: A Case Study of Norway." *European Journal of Development Research* 19, no. 4 (2007): 614–35.
Twain, Mark. "To the Person Sitting in Darkness." *North American Review* 172 (February 1901): 161–76.
U.S. Department of Homeland Security. "Fiscal Year (FY) 2016 Funding for State and Local Government Programs for Countering Violent Extremism." Office of Community Partnerships. Washington, D.C., February 29, 2016.
Valverde, Mariana. *Chronotopes of Law: Jurisdiction, Scale, and Governance*. New York: Routledge, 2015.
Veenswijk, Virginia Kays. *Coudert Brothers: A Legacy in Law: The History of America's First International Law Firm, 1853–1993*. New York: Truman Talley Books/Dutton, 1994.
Vieth, Paul H., ed. *The Church and Christian Education*. St. Louis: Bethany Press for the Cooperative Publishing Association, 1947.
Villamor, Ignacio. *Criminality in the Philippine Islands*. Manila: Bureau of Printing, 1909.
———. "Propensity to Crime." *Journal of the American Institute of Criminal Law & Criminology* 6 (1916): 729–45.
Virtue, David. *A Flame for Justice*, Oxford: Lion, 1991.
Waldrep, Christopher. "'So Much Sin:' The Decline of Religious Discipline and the 'Tidal Wave of Crime.'" *Journal of Social History* 23 (March 1990): 535–52.
Walker, David. "Evangelicals and Apartheid: An Inquiry into Some Predispositions." *Journal of Theology for Southern Africa*, no. 67 (June 1989): 46–61.
Walker, Peter. "The Bishop Controversy, the Imperial Crisis, and Religious Radicalism in New England, 1763–1774." *New England Quarterly* 90, no. 3 (2017): 306–43.
Walton, Clifford Stevens, trans. *The Civil Law in Spain and Spanish-America*. Washington, D.C.: W. H. Lowdermilk & Co., 1900.
Wardinski, Ingo. "Geomagnetic Secular Variation." In *Encyclopedia of Geomagnetism and Paleomagnetism*, ed. David Gubbins and Emilio Herrero-Bervera, 346–49. Dordrecht: Springer Science & Business Media, 2007.
Washington, George. *George Washington: A Collection*. Ed. by W. B. Allen. Indianapolis: Liberty Fund, 1988.
Watkins, Mel. *Stepin Fetchit: The Life and Times of Lincoln Perry*. New York: Vintage, 2006.
Weaver, Aaron Douglas. *James M. Dunn and Soul Freedom*. Macon, Ga.: Smyth & Helwys, 2011.
Weiss, Gunther A. "The Enchantment of Codification in the Common-Law World." *Yale Journal of International Law* 25 (2000): 435–532.
Welch, Claude Emerson. "Mobilizing Morality: The World Council of Churches and Its Programme to Combat Racism, 1969–1994." *Human Rights Quarterly* 23, no. 4 (2001): 863–910.
Wenger, Tisa. *Religious Freedom: The Contested History of an American Ideal*. Chapel Hill: University of North Carolina Press, 2017.
West, Geoffrey. *Scale: The Universal Laws of Growth, Innovation, Sustainability, and the Pace of Life in Organisms, Cities, Economies, and Companies*. New York: Penguin, 2017.
Wheeler, Rachel M. *To Live upon Hope: Mohicans and Missionaries in the Eighteenth-Century Northeast*. Ithaca, N.Y.: Cornell University Press, 2008.

White, David Gordon. *Sinister Yogis.* University of Chicago Press, 2009.
——, ed. *Yoga in Practice.* Princeton, N.J.: Princeton University Press, 2011.
Wigmore, John H. "A Model Report on Crime from an Attorney-General's Office." *Journal of the American Institute of Criminal Law & Criminology* 4 (1913): 479–80.
——. *A Treatise on the Anglo-American System of Evidence in Trials at Common Law.* 5 vols. Boston: Little, Brown, 1923.
Wilfley, Lebbeus R. "The New Philippine Judiciary." *Ohio Law Bulletin* 49 (1904): 404–12.
Willard, Frances E. *Home Protection Manual.* New York: Independent, 1879.
Willard, John. *A Treatise on Equity Jurisprudence.* New York: Banks, 1875.
Willis, Alan Scot. *All According to God's Plan: Southern Baptist Missions and Race, 1945–1970.* Lexington: University Press of Kentucky, 2004.
Willrich, Michael. "The Case for Courts: Law and Political Development in the Progressive Era." In *The Democratic Experiment: New Directions in American Political History,* ed. Meg Jacobs, William J. Novak, and Julian E. Zelizer, 198–221. Princeton, N.J.: Princeton University Press, 2003.
——. *City of Courts: Socializing Justice in Progressive Era Chicago.* Cambridge: Cambridge University Press, 2003.
Witte, John, Jr. "Faith in Law: The Legal and Political Legacy of the Protestant Reformations," in *The Reformation of the Church and the World,* ed. John Witte Jr. and Amy Wheeler, 105–38. Louisville, Ky.: Westminster John Knox Press, 2018.
——. *Law and Protestantism: The Legal Teachings of the Lutheran Reformation.* Cambridge: Cambridge University Press, 2002.
——. *The Reformation of Rights: Law, Religion and Human Rights in Early Modern Calvinism.* Cambridge: Cambridge University Press, 2008.
Witte, John, Jr., and Amy Wheeler, eds. *The Reformation of the Church and the World.* Louisville, Ky.: Westminster John Knox Press, 2018.
Wright, N. T. *Romans.* Downers Grove, Ill.: IVP Connect, 2009.
Wuthnow, Robert. *Inventing American Religion: Polls, Surveys, and the Tenuous Quest for a Nation's Faith.* New York: Oxford University Press, 2015.
Yelle, Robert. *The Language of Disenchantment: Protestant Literalism and Colonial Discourse in British India.* Oxford: Oxford University Press, 2013.
Yoder, John Howard. *The Politics of Jesus.* Grand Rapids, Mich.: Eerdmans, 1972.
Young, Isaac. "Shut Up and Sing: The Rights of Japanese Teachers in an Era of Conservative Educational Reform." *Cornell International Law Journal* 42, no. 1 (2009): 157–92. http://scholarship.law.cornell.edu/cilj/vol42/iss1/7.
Zelliot, Eleanor. *From Untouchable to Dalit: Essays on the Ambedkar Movement.* New Delhi: Manohar Publications, 1992.
Zollman, Carl. *American Civil Church Law.* New York: Columbia University, 1917.
Zwick-Maitreyi, Maari, Thenmozhi Soundararajan, Natasha Dar, Ralph F. Bheel, and Prathap Balakrishnan. *Caste in the United States: A Survey of Caste among South Asian Americans.* Equality Labs, USA, 2018.

Contributors

Helge Årsheim is guest researcher at the faculty of theology at the University of Oslo and commissioning editor for Open Access titles at the Scandinavian University Press.
Courtney Bender is professor in the Department of Religion at Columbia University.
Nancy Buenger is an independent scholar in Philadelphia, Pennsylvania.
Evan Haefeli is associate professor of history at Texas A&M University.
M. Cooper Harriss is associate professor of religious studies and adjunct professor of folklore and ethnomusicology at Indiana University Bloomington.
Elizabeth Shakman Hurd is professor of political science and Crown Chair in Middle East studies at Northwestern University.
Sarah Imhoff is associate professor of religious studies at Indiana University Bloomington.
Greg Johnson is professor of religious studies and director of the Walter H. Capps Center for the Study of Ethics, Religion, and Public Life at the University of California, Santa Barbara.
Sunila S. Kale is associate professor and chair and director of the South Asia Studies Center at the Jackson School of International Studies at the University of Washington.
Pamela E. Klassen is professor in the Department for the Study of Religion at the University of Toronto.
David Maldonado Rivera is assistant professor of religious studies at Kenyon College.
Melani McAlister is professor of American studies and international affairs at George Washington University.
Christian Lee Novetzke is College of Arts & Sciences Term Professor in the South Asia Program, the Comparative Religion Program, and the International Studies Program at the Jackson School of International Studies at the University of Washington.
Noah Salomon is associate professor of religion and the Irfan and Noreen Galaria Chair in Islamic Studies at the University of Virginia.
Matthew Scherer is associate professor of government and politics at George Mason University.
Winnifred Fallers Sullivan is Provost Professor in the Department of Religious Studies and director of the Center for Religion and the Human at Indiana University Bloomington.
Jolyon Baraka Thomas is assistant professor of religious studies at the University of Pennsylvania.

Index

"The 1619 Project," 175, 179n14

Abe Shinzō, 196–209
"abroad," 8, 115–18; as frame for practice, 298–99; instability of categories, 290–91, 299–300, 301n6; in Japan's religious freedom debates, 203–5; religion abroad, 127–28, 277; scale and, 116–18; South Africa and evangelical Christians, 250; Sudan and, 289; as term, 5. *See also* "abroad of a different home"; "at home and abroad" logics; "home"
"abroad of a different home," 130, 136–38, 141–44
Abyei region (Sudan/South Sudan), 294
Act on Christian Dissenters (1845), 278
actor-network theory, 251–52, 267
Act Relating to Religious Communities (Norway, 1969), 276
Addams, Jane, 61, 62, 63, 69, 74, 84n48
Adler, Felix, 120
affect, 117, 122, 126
African Methodist Episcopal Church, 260
African National Congress (ANC), 257
Africans, in early republican America, 20–21, 25–26, 170
Agranat, Simon, 128n5
Air Age Education Research program, 94–96, *95*
air globe, 94–96, *95*, 109n7
Al-Azhar University (Cairo), 292
Ali (film), 131
Ali, Muhammad, 5, 117, 130–47, 308–9; "abroad of a different home" and, 130, 136–38; "double cross," 131, 144, 145n1; exceptionalist identities of, 130–31, 145n1; films about, 131, 146n3; as global American religious figure, 144; military conscription refused by, 131; multiple conversions in tension, 130–31; performance and, 137, 139, 144; as persona, 137, 144; repertoire of identity and, 140–44; scope, considerations of, 131–37; secularization of, 132, 135, 143. *See also Fetch Clay, Make Man* (Power)
al-ittijah al-islami (the Islamic trend), 292
Allied Occupation of Japan (1945–1952), 196, 198, 201–4, 241n2; Civil Information and Education Section, 202–4; Religions and Cultural Resources Division, 202
Aloha 'Āina (love the land) movement, 156–57
Alter, Joseph, 216
Ambedkar, B. R., 215
American Airlines, 94–96, *95*
American Bar Association (ABA), 66, 75
American Bible Society, 27
American Civil War, 19, 29, 32, 119
American Colonization Society, 9, 305, 309
American Council on Education Studies, 202, 203
American exceptionalism, 1–3, 305; "Americanization," 38; anxious stance as possibility, 173–74, 176–78; arrogance, concerns about, 306–8; chronotopes, 92–94, 98–99, 107, 108n2; cultural mode of being narrative, 92; doubleness of, 191; durability of, 92; episteme and, 91–92, 106–7; future-tense, 91–99, 102, 106–8, 108–9n5, 178n2, 239–40; minor, 175; as "not religious," 94; perfection of religion, 3; political imaginary of, 91, 107; produced by looking away from history, 167,

American exceptionalism (*continued*) 170, 177–78; religion as both tamed and free, 1, 123, 136, 232, 276; religious claims for, 94; resistance to in Hawaii, 155; stability of practices across domestic constituencies, 1; triumphal, 174–75, 184, 200; violence necessary to narrative of, 92, 109n10; wealth and power of United States as, 168–69, 172. *See also* legacies of American exceptionalism; United States
American Historical Review, 65
American Indian Religious Freedom Act (1978), 151
American Judicature Society, 74–75
American Political Science Association, 70
American Revolution, 20–21, 26, 306
American Technological Sublime (Nye), 100–101, 110n20
"The America we Need" project, 175, 179n14
Anabaptists, 190
Ānandamaṭh (Chatterjee), 213–14, 225n12
Andō Masazumi, 203
Anglicans, 23, 208n27
anti-Catholicism, 27–30
Anti-Conspiracy Law of 2017, Japan, 196–97, 198, 199
anti-popery, 28–30, 32–34, *33*
apartheid, South Africa, 6, 117, 249–72; Christian anti-apartheid activists, 255–56; divestment, 261, 266; liberal protestant churches, stance of, 257, 261; reconciliation, critique of, 256–57; Romans 13 and evangelical Christians, role of, 249, 252–55, 265, 267–68; transnational connections and, 5, 250–51, 255–57. *See also* evangelical Christians
apocalyptic Christianity, 190
Appleby, Joyce, 168–70
The Archive and the Repertoire (Taylor), 137, 143
Arellano, Cayetano, 51, 65, 69
Arman, Yasir, 293
Arnold, Edwin, 214
Assemblies of God church, 259
assimilation: exclusions from, 97–98, 109n10; Norway, 278; religious pluralities as sign of cooperation, 97; required of Native Americans, 26
asylum-seeking proceedings, 228, 233–35
"at home and abroad," 13, 308; Ali's relationship to, 130, 132, 137; border subterfuge and, 236; CVE interventions and, 230; equity and, 53, 56, 76; Norway and, 284–85; rule of law and, 184; scale for studying, 117–18; South Sudan and, 289, 294, 299; U.S. imperial practices, 236; what counts as religion, 1–2, 6–7, 9
Atlantic crossing, 99–100
audiencia territorial (Philippines), 79n14. *See also real audiencia chancillería* (Philippines)
Augustine of Hippo, 190
authority, 249; in Romans 13, 249, 252–55; of scripture, 262–63; "state theology" and, 256, transcendent, 55
auto-jurisdiction, 149–50, 152–54, 160–61
Autonomic Charter of 1897 (Puerto Rico), 37
Axioms of Religion: A New Interpretation of Baptist Faith (Mullins), 262
Ayau, Halealoha, 152–54

Baldwin, Ebenezer, 29–30
Baldwin, James, 176–77
Balfour Declaration (1917), 127
Baltimore, Lord, 23
Baptist Faith and Message Fellowship, 263
Baptist Joint Committee on Public Affairs, 261–67
Baptist Press wire service, 266
Baptists: England, 22; liberal, 263; in South Africa, 250. *See also* evangelical Christians; Southern Baptist Convention (SBC)
Baptist World Alliance, 266
Barker, Pat, 171, 176
Barlin v. Ramírez (U.S.), 44, 49n24
Baron v. Baltimore (U.S.), 30
Barrows, David, 65, 69–70
Bartelme, Mary, 56, 61
al-Bashir, Omar, 288, 297–98
Bay Area Black Nationalists, 135
"belief," 119
benefit of clergy, 62, 73
Bengal, 212–13
Berlin, Leah, 122, 125–26
Berzon, Marsha S., 235
Bhagavad Gītā, 214–16, 224–25n15, 224n14
Bhandar, Brenna, 38
Bible verses, as actants, 251–52, 267
"Bible wars" litigation, 9
Bill of Rights, U.S., 4, 30
Bittenbender, Ada, 61
Black Lives Matter, 232
Blenk, James H., 44, 46
Bloom, Nicholas, 111n30
Blount, James, 66
Board of Education of Cincinnati v. Minor (U.S.), 10–11

Boesak, Allan, 255
Bondevik, Kjell Magne, 283
Bonhoeffer, Dietrich, 7, 254, 265, 270n21
The Book of Pain-Struggle (Segal), 121
borders (religion/politics distinction), 228–45, 289–90, 311; border failure, 228, 229, 233; border submersion, 228, 233–35; border subterfuge, 228, 236–38; Canada–U.S. border, 311; "countering violent extremism" (CVE), 228, 229–33, 241n5, 290; "imposterhood," religious, 228, 234–35
Boston Globe, 70
Botha, P. W., 255, 256
boundaries, 94–99, 106
Boycott, Divestment, and Sanctions movement, 243n22
Bradwell, James, 60–61
Bradwell, Myra, 60–61
Brandeis, Louis, 122
Brau, Salvador, 41
British law: colonial law in India and Sri Lanka, 240; Monarch-in-Parliament, 20; Palestinian passports, 125. *See also* England
British East India Company, 212
Brother Rashid (character), 133–34, 138
Brown v. Board of Education, 253
Brundtland, Gro Harlem, 281
Buddhism, 11, 199
Bunce, William K., 202, 203
Bureau of Non-Christian Tribes, 70
burial laws, Hawaii, 151
Burnham, Daniel, 63, 68–69
Bush, George W., 268, 291

California code of civil procedure, 66, 86n77
Calvin, John, 190
Canada, 210, 219, 310, 311
Caribbean territory, 38–39, 41–42, 45–47. *See also* Puerto Rico
Carroll, Henry K., 42–43
Carroll, Lewis, 177–78
Cassidy, Michael, 255, 256–57
Catholic Church (Puerto Rico), 4–5; adaptations in ecclesiastical administration, 46; church property disputes, 1898–1908, 41–45; juridical personality, 4–5, 38, 39–40, 44–45, 47, 49n24; *patronato real* (royal patronage), 41; two-tiered system, 41. *See also* Puerto Rico; Roman Catholicism
Catholic Extension Society, 46
The Catholic World, 46

Cavell, Stanley, 171, 174–77
Central Intelligence Agency (CIA), 11
"chain of memory," 276
A Challenge to the Church (South Africa), 256–57
chancery: English, 58, 62, 71, 79n15; origin of term, 64–65; *real audiencia chancillería*, 55, 63–65, 75. *See also* courts of equity (chancery); equity
Chang, Gary, 157
Charles I, 23
Chatterjee, Bankim Chandra, 213–14, 225n12
Chicago: case overload, 57–58; circuit court chancery, 51; city hall, 69; equity, 55–63, 70–75; equity jurisdictions, 57, 82n26; home rule campaign, 62–63, 76; Municipal Court of Chicago, 52, 69–75; naturalization to turn out vote, 58; plans for, 52, 69, 75; Progressive Era, 54; U.S. circuit and district courts, 82n27; World's Columbian Exposition, 1893, 62–63
Chicago Civic Federation, 51–52, 62–63, 69, 73
Chicago Juvenile Court, 62
Chicago Legal News, 60
Chicago Woman's Club, 61
Chikane, Frank, 257–58
Choudhury, Bikram, 218
Christ for the World Chapel (Protestant), 102–5
Christian Democratic Party (Norway), 284
Christianity: doctrines, 190; as export, 6; naturalization of, 7, 232, 304; presumed to be shared background, 173. *See also* evangelical Christians; protestant Christianity; Roman Catholicism
Christianity Today, 257, 261, 264
Christian Life Commission (SBC), 261–62, 266
Christian Slavery (Gerbner), 136
"Christian Slavery," 26
chronotopes, 92–94, 98–99, 107, 108–9n5, 108n2
The Church and Christian Education (Vieth), 202–3
"Churches Act to Thwart Apartheid" story, 266
Churchill, Winston, 214
Church of England, 21, 22–24, 208n27
Church of Norway (CoN), 276–80, 284–85; legal personality, 285–86
"churchstateness," 305
Circe (Miller), 171
The City of God (Augustine), 190
Civil Information and Education Section (Allied Occupation), 202–4
civilization, 1, 6, 9–11, 59, 64, 278, 300–301n4, 305
civil law, 53, 66, 70, 190

civil order, religion's challenge to, 191
civil religion, 12, 101–2, 106–7, 265, 306–7; apophatic gesture and, 94, 308; as "invisible religion" or "American sublime," 94
"Civil Religion in America" (Bellah), 306–8
civil rights legislation, 13
civil rights movement, United States, 250
civil society actors, 12; Norway, 275, 283–84
Civil War. *See* American Civil War; English Civil War of the 1640s
Clay, Cassius. *See* Ali, Muhammad
Cleland, McKenzie, 73
Coalition Against Genocide, 223–24n5
Código Civil (1899), 64, 67
COINTELPRO, 230
Cold War, 6, 105, 169, 260, 306; efforts to combat secularism and communism, 12; Japan and religious training, 205; Norway and, 284; "religious offensives," 11
colonialism: India, 211, 212–17; settler, 151, 162, 204, 211, 310
colonization: conversion inseparable from, 26; internal, of Indigenous and enslaved populations, 3; missionary work as justification for, 25; of yoga, 211, 221–22
Committee on Buddhism, 11
common law, 54, 57–59, 62, 70, 81n24
communism, 7, 11–12, 199, 202, 205, 259, 261, 283
Comprehensive Peace Agreement (CPA) of 2005 (Sudan), 291, 295, 298
Comte, Auguste, 274
Concerned Baptists, 266
Concerned Evangelicals, 266
Conference of Senior Circuit Judges, 75
Congo, 260
Congregationalists, New England, 23, 25, 32
conscience, 60–61, 67; equity and, 51, 54, 58; individual, 119, 262–65; Japanese State Secrets Law and, 199; liberty of, 23, 27, 37, 41, 199
Conservative Party (Norway), 273
Constantinian revolution, 190
Constitution, U.S., 21, 308; Article I, Section 8, 39; Bill of Rights, 4, 30; disestablishment in, 27; due process rights, 187–88; extension of into Caribbean, 39; Khan's use of in 2016 presidential campaign, 192. *See also* First Amendment; Fourteenth Amendment
constitutionalism, popular, 188, 193–94n9
Constitution of 1876 (Puerto Rico), 37, 41
conversion, 26, 29, 34, 35; Ali's, 130–31, 136–38, 140–45, 309; asylum seekers and, 234–35

Cook County. *See* Chicago
Corn, Joseph, 96
coronavirus pandemic, 179n14, 311
corporate law, 39–40
corporate legal consciousness, 188
corporation sole, 38, 40–41, 45
corporate trustee system, 40
La correspondencia (newspaper), 45
The Cosmopolitan Railway (Gilpin), 96–97, 109n9
Cost of Discipleship (Bonhoeffer), 254
Coudert, Fred, 47
Council of Europe, 281
Council of Trent, 37
"countering violent extremism" (CVE), 228, 229–33, 241n5, 290
A Course on Zionism (Sampter), 123
Court of Domestic Relations (Chicago), 74
courts of equity (chancery), 51; administrative bureaucracies, 57–58; appeals, 72; domestic affairs, 56, 66–67, 73; probation, 61–62, 73–74; procedural rules, 54, 59, 65–66, 71–75; undue delay eliminated by, 72. *See also* equity; Philippines
Crabbe, Kamana'opono, 153
Creole Catholics, 31
Criminal Act (Norway, 1842), 278
Cromwell, Oliver, 27
Cuba, 44, 70
cultural appropriation, 6, 210–12, 218–19, 221, 224n6, 310; as extractive colonialism, 211
culture industry, 169, 211
Cunningham, Charles, 65
Custer, George, 26

Daily Beast, 197
Dakota Access Pipeline, 152
Dalits (Untouchables), 215, 221, 225n19
El defensor cristiano (Methodist periodical), 45
democracy, 11, 31, 122, 174; religion and, 202, 228; teleological conception of, 231, 239
Democracy in America (Tocqueville), 174
Denmark, 280
Denmark–Norway, 278
Denver, Colorado, 96
Department of Hawaiian Home Lands, 156
Department of Homeland Security, 230, 241n5, 289–90
Department of Land and Natural Resources (Hawaii), 157, 159
Department of the Interior, U.S., 161–62

dependent populations, equity and, 54–57, 71, 76; children, 61–62
desamortización, 43
Devi, Indra, 216
Dinka ethnic subgroup (Sudan), 292
Diocese of Puerto Rico, 42, 44–46
disavowal, 176–77, 178n2
Discourses (Machiavelli), 173
disestablishment, 2, 305; Church of Norway, 276, 280; corporate legal consciousness, 188; first U.S. (1776–1865), 38, 39, 40; haphazard emergence of, 4; local and state establishments, 27; not a right, 20; religio-legal history of the evolution of modern law, 183–84
Doctrine of Discovery, 162, 309
domestic/foreign, 1–2, 5–8, 13, 178n6, 290, 300n3, 305; "foreign in a domestic sense," 229, 239, 311
double cross, 2, 131, 191, 308–9, 308–12
Downes v. Bidwell (U.S.), 39
due process (U.S.), 66, 70, 84n54; absolutist understandings of, 188, 194n11; in church proceedings, 183; ecclesiastical law and, 187–88; Hawaiian failures, 161; origins in Roman law in medieval Europe, 188, 194n16
Due Process Clause (U.S.), 84n54
Dukmasova, Maya, 243n18
Dunn, James, 262–67
Dutch Reformed Church, 191, 256
Dwight, Timothy, 32

Eastern Greenland, 281
East India Company, 29
ecclesiastical authority, 22, 24, 28, 183–84; "church discipline," 188; judgments, 186–87; overlap with secular law, 183–95
ecclesiology, 20
Eisenhower, Dwight D., 205
Elizabeth I, 22
Emerson, Ralph Waldo, 175–77
Employment Division v. Smith, 12–13
Enelow, Hyman Gerson, 120
England: America as "abroad" of, 20; chancery court, 55, 79n15; colonial policy, 4; judicature acts, 53; justice of the peace courts, 71; protestant hegemony, 23; Quebec Act (1774), 29–30; Reformation, 22–23; Restoration, 23–24; Roman Catholics, 22, 34. *See also* Britain
Engel v. Vitale (U.S.), 264
English Civil War of the 1640s, 23, 29

English Test Acts, 30
Enlightenment, 275
Episcopal Church, 261
equity, 51–90; alternative legal traditions, 59; as beyond letter of the law, 51, 53–56, 59, 77; Chicago, 55–63, 70–75; as contrary to rule of law, 52; defined, 53–54; dependent populations and, 54–57, 61–62, 71; labor disputes, 61, 82n36, 84n48; origins, 53–54, 78–79n5; used to suppress boycotts and strikes, 55; women, jurisdiction over, 56–57; women and, 59–61. *See also* courts of equity (chancery)
Equity Club (women attorneys' professional organization), 60–61
Ethical Culture, 118, 120
Ethics and Religious Liberty Commission (SBC), 267
Ethnologishes Museum in Dahlem (Berlin), 153–54
European Court of Human Rights, 279
European Parliament, 284
Evangelical Christians: Bible verses as actants, 251–52; Black churches, 260; church law, 185; *Evangelical Witness in South Africa* statement, 257–59, 266; global network of, 251–52; Left, 258, 260; Right, 261; Romans 13 and, 249, 252–55, 265, 267–68; Romans 13 and South Africa, 255–59; "sins" of racism and complacency, 259; Sudanese civil war, support for, 299; theorizing of state, 249–50; transnational networks, 5, 250–51, 255–57. *See also* apartheid, South Africa; Southern Baptist Convention (SBC)
Evangelical Lutheranism, 278
Evangelical Union of the Philippines, 9
Evangelical Witness in South Africa statement, 257–59, 266
Everson v. Board of Education, 11
exception, figure of, 174. *See also* American exceptionalism
expansion, territorial, 6, 10, 22, 24–29, 31–32, 51, 92, 178n2, 238, 281; Philippines and, 56, 63, 69. *See also* imperial America

Falwell, Jerry, 255, 270n18
Federal Bureau of Investigation (FBI), 230–32, 241n8
Federal Rules of Civil Procedure (1938), 75, 77
Federation of New Religious Organizations of Japan, 196, 199

Fetch Clay, Make Man (Power), 133–44, 146n15; boundary maintenance in, 137–40. *See also* Ali, Muhammad

First Amendment (U.S. Constitution), 211; free exercise protections, 2, 30, 231, 278, 301, 307; *Hosanna-Tabor v. EEOC*'s effect on, 13

First Provincial Council of Baltimore (Maryland), 40

"First Statement by John Garang to the Sudanese People on 10 August 1989; Following the Military *coup d'état* of 30 June 1989" (Garang), 297, 303n19

Foraker Act (Organic Act of 1900), 37–38, 39

"foreign in a domestic sense," 229, 239, 311

foreign policy, U.S, 2–5, 11, 205, 260, 289–92; "religion abroad," 277. *See also* Cold War; Japan

Foreman, George, 131

Fourteenth Amendment, U.S. Constitution, 30, 84n54

Frank R. Wolf Act of 2016, 200

Frazier, Joe, 144, 309

freedom, 12; anxious, 173–74, 176–78; to flourish, 92; international norms, 199; of religion, assumed for United States, 3–4. *See also* religious freedom

French Canadians, 29

French Code Napoleon, 64

French Empire, 21, 28

French Revolution, 31

Freund, Ernst, 69, 70

The Frontier Spirit in American Christianity (Mode), 97

Frost, Robert, 106, 167

Fuller, Lon, 189

Fuller, Melville, 44–45

fundamentalism: as misleading term, 185; Moody Bible Institute, 73. *See also* evangelical Christians

Fundamental Law on Education (Japan), 198, 203, 205, 209n34

G7 Summit, 2016 (Japan), 197

Gandhi, Mohandas K., 214–16, 217, 221n21

Gandhi, Vikram, 219

Garang, John, 292, 297, 303n19

Genesis, 263

genocide, 167; cultural, 210

Georgia, 24

Gerbner, Katharine, 26, 136

German asylum courts, 233–34

Ghose, Aurobindo, 225n21

Ghosh, Amitav, 108n2

"Ghosts of Yogas Past and Present" (Patankar), 221–22

Gilpin, William, 96–98, 109nn9, 10

Gingrich, Newt, 231

Global South, Christians in, 260

Glorious Revolution of 1688, 24

Goldberg, Michelle, 225n25

Goodnow, Frank, 56

Government Pension Fund Global, 282

grace, common, 191, 195n25

Graham, Billy, 256, 260–61

The Great Adventurer (Sampter), 120–21

Great Awakening, 24–25, 136

"greater United States," 238, *239*, 245n42

guardianship, 54, 57, 61; women and, 59–60

Gullestad, Marianne, 283

Hadassah (American Zionist women's organization), 121, 122, 123, 124, 127

Hae Hawaii (Kingdom of Hawaii flag), 154

Hale o Kuhio (House of Kuhio) encampment, 154–59, *155*; Prince Kuhio Day, March 26, 2018, action, 155; Puʻuhuluhulu camp, 156

Hale o Kūkiaʻimauna camp, 157–59

Hall, G. Stanley, 121

Harlan, John, 64

Harper's Weekly, 32, *33*

Haṭha Yoga Pradīpikā, 216

Hawaii, 3, 148–66, 207n12, 310; Akaka Bill, 161; Aloha ʻĀina (love the land) movement, 156–57; arrests of activists, 159; conflicting Native rights laws, 148–49; Department of Hawaiian Home Lands, 156; Hale o Kuhio (House of Kuhio) encampment, 154–59, *155*; immersion school movement, 160; Indigenous jurisdiction, 4, 149–52, 155, 160, 163n1; "inherent sovereignty," 149; iwi (bones) and ʻāina (land) in religious life, 150; jurisdictions of religion in, 150–52; Kingdom of, 151–52, 159; language, 159; Maui, 159; Mauna Kea Thirty Meter Telescope (TMT) protests, 151, 154, 157–63; media portrayals of activists, 158–59; militarization of, 155, 157; Pōhakuloa Training Area, 157

Hebron massacre (1929), 125

Heidegger, Martin, 176

Henry VIII, 22

Hermanos Cheos (lay network), 46

Hindu American Foundation (HAF), 211, 220, 223–24n5
Hinduism, 123
"Hinduphobia," 211
Hobby Lobby (*Burwell v. Hobby Lobby Stores, Inc.*) (U.S.), 119
Hobsbawm, Eric, 275
Hochberg, Gil Z., 245n44
"home," 8, 115, 117–18; in America, 24; projected onto distant land, 291–92; as frame for practice, 298–99; Hawaiians on Hale o Kuhio and Mauna Kea, 159; instability of categories, 290–91, 296, 299–300, 301n6; in Japan's religious freedom debates, 203–5; Sudan and, 289; United States as, 118–21. *See also* "abroad"
home/abroad, 1–7, 13, 91, 201, 304–12; Ali and, 130–32, 136–37, 141–45; borders and, 229–30; "border subterfuge" and, 236; courts of equity and, 53, 56, 76; Norway and, 283–85; rule of law and, 183–85, 191; scale and, 116–18; Sudan and, 289–91, 294, 297–300, 301n6, 302n10. *See also* "abroad"; "abroad of a different home"; "home"
Homeland Security Grant Program, 230
homemaking, 5, 124–26
Homeric Epics, 171, 176
home rule, 4, 51–90, 310; campaigns for, 62–63, 76; imperial expansion and, 63; as model for statecraft, 56. *See also* Chicago; courts of equity (chancery); equity; Philippines
Homo sacer (Agamben), 174
Hoover, J. Edgar, 230
Hoover Dam, 101
Horwitz, Morton, 52
Hosanna-Tabor v. EEOC, 13
Hudson, Winthrop, 263
Hui Mālama I Nā Kūpuna O Hawai'i Nei, 152–54
Hull House, 61, 62, 74
Humphrey, Hubert, 102–3, 105–6
Hussein, Saddam, 132

Ibrahim, Ahmed Sharif, 300n2
identity: repertoire of, 140–44; submersion, 228, 233–35
"Idol worship" (*Harper's Weekly* engraving), 32, *33*
If Christ Came to Chicago! (Stead), 63
Igga, James Wani, 288
Iliad (Homer), 171
Illinois General Assembly, 58
Illinois Juvenile Court Act (1899), 62
Illinois, Supreme Court of, 57, 73

Immerwahr, Daniel, 238, 245n42
immigration, 22; converts and, 34; European tradition of, 107; Indian diaspora in United States, 220–22, 226n31; internal, 31, 104; multiple ecclesiologies in, 190–91; naturalization to turn out vote, 58; Roman Catholics and, 31; from "Shithole Countries," 174; Trump's rhetoric, 174–75; xenophobic nationalism, rise of, 290
imperial America, 6, 9–11, 228–45, 305; "greater United States," 238, *239*, 245n42; Japan and, 200; religion as border subterfuge, 228–29, 236–38; World War I and, 122. *See also* expansion; Philippines; United States
Imperial Rescript on Education of 1890 (Japan), 197
"imposterhood," religious, 228, 234–35
incorporation doctrine, 11, 39
Independence for the African Church (Wakatama), 258
India, 29; Aundh, state of, 217; caste considerations, 212–14; colonialism, 211, 212–17; as commodity fetish, 218, 219–20; homogenized identity, 212, 216; Indian diaspora in United States, 220–22, 226n31; Mysore, state of, 217; "princely states," 216; social injustice, 220; upper-class Hindu archetype, 212–14. *See also* yoga
Indian Wars (U.S.), 25
Indigenous jurisdiction, 4, 149–52, 155, 160, 163n1
Indigenous peoples, 311; auto-jurisdiction, 149–50, 152–54, 160–61; "conversion" policies toward, 3; depopulation of, 170; global, 152; humanist reformers' views of, 9; jurisdiction, successes of, 152; Philippines, 63–64; Sami, 278, 286–87n11. *See also* Hawaii; Native Americans
individual, 168; as essential unit of religion, 119–20, 128; legal consciousness of, 187–88
in loco parentis, 62, 84n54
inside/outside, 1, 4–6, 13, 127; Norway, 276–79; overlap between ecclesiastical and secular law, 183–85. *See also* home/abroad
Insular Cases, 9, 245n42; *Downes v. Bidwell* (U.S.), 39; Taft's role in, 44, 55–56
International Court of Justice, 281
International Monetary Fund, 169
International Religious Freedom Act (1998), 3–4, 12, 306; "Countries of Particular Concern," 200–201, 206

In Whose Image? Political Islam and Urban Practices in Sudan (Simone), 293
Iraq, 201
Iraq War, 268
Ireland, 22
Irish Catholics, 31
Ise Shrines, Japan, 197, 199
Islam, 6; "good Muslim" mode, 132, 231; in Norway, 278–79; state-sanctioned, 296–97; U.S. fantasies about control of, 299. *See also* Muslims
Islam: An American Religion (Marzouki), 236–37, 243n20
iwi (bones) and *'āina* (land), 150, 156–57, 310; repatriation, 152–54
Iyengar, B. K. S., 216, 218

Jackson, Andrew, 28
Jamaica, 24
James, Henry, 99
James I, 22
Japan, 3, 11, 196–209, 310; Abe Shinzō administration, 196–97; Allied Occupation of (1945–1952), 196, 198, 201–4, 241n2; Anti-Conspiracy Law of 2017, 196–97, 198, 199; constitution, 198–99, 201; constitution of 1890–1945, 207n5; education and religious freedom in, 201–5; Fundamental Law on Education, 198, 203, 205, 209n34; as "hard to see," 200, 201; "home" and "abroad" in religious debates, 203–5; land deal with religious academy, 197; legal unit of society, proposed changes in, 199; liberal and religious minorities' concerns, 205; Liberal Democratic Party (LDP), 198–99, 201; morality education, 205; overseas observers of, 199–200; "Peace Constitution," 203; Peace Preservation Law (Chian iji hō), 1925, 196; religion defined, 197–98; religious freedom, 196; religious freedom rhetoric, 197–98; rule of law and, 201; U.S. alliance and international religious freedom, 200–202
Japanese Buddhist Federation, 199
Japanese Federation of Religions, 203
Jay-Z, 177–78
Jeffress, Robert, 268
Jesuits (Society of Jesus), 28
Jesus, 190, 250
Jewish International Synagogue (John F. Kennedy airport), 102–5
Jewish law, 190, 252–53

Joan of Arc, trial of, 184, 187, 193n8
John F. Kennedy Airport, 102–6, 111n30
Johnson, Jack, 134, 138–40, 140–41
Johnson v. M'Intosh (U.S.), 309
Jois, Pattabhi, 216, 218
Jones, Bishop, 46
Journal of the American Institute of Crime and Criminology, 68
Judaism: Ethical Culture and, 118, 120; Jewishness as communal belonging, 120; New York Board of Rabbis, 103–4; Reform rabbis, 120
juridical personality, 4–5, 38, 39–40, 44–45, 47, 49n24
jurisdiction, Indigenous, 152; "a'ole!" and "Ae," 161–62; auto-jurisdiction, 149–50, 152–54, 160–61; direct action, 156, 158; Hale o Kuhio and, 155; Hawaiian language, constitutional right to, 159–60; "Kanaka Rangers" program, 155–56; Kapu Aloha ("rule of love"), 158; *kia' i* (protectors), 151, 156, 158; occupation of land, 157–58; speaking law, 160–61
juryless criminal proceedings, 51–57, 61–62, 64, 66, 71; Panama Canal Zone, 70. *See also* courts of equity (chancery)
jury trial, 70, 72; disappearance of, 76, 79n10; reintroduction of in Chicago, 72–73
justice of the peace courts, 71
juvenile courts, 61–62
Juvenile Protective Agency (Chicago), 74

Ka'eo, Kaleikoa, 153, 159
Kagan, Michael, 234
Kahanu, Noelle, 153
Kaho'olawe, bombing of, 157
Kairos Document (South African Christians), 256–58
Kanaka (Native Hawaiians), 156
"Kanaka Rangers" program, 155–56
Kant, Immanuel, 120
Kaplan, Mordecai, 124
Kasemann, Ernst, 270n21
Kawaiaha'o Church burial dispute, 150–51
Keali'ikanaka'ole, Kauila, 153
Keio University, Tokyo, 68
Kelley, Francis Clement, 46
Khan, Khizr, 192
Khartoum (South Sudan), 288
kia' i (protectors), 151, 156, 158
kibbutz, 119, 127
Kibbutz Givat Brenner, 126
ki' i (carved statues), 153

Kindersley, Nicki, 300n1
King, Martin Luther, Jr., 133
King Lear (Shakespeare), 171
Kings College (later Columbia University), 25
Kishimoto Hideo, 203, 204–5
Kohler, Kaufmann, 120
Krishnamacharya, Tirumalai, 216
Krishnamurti, Jiddu, 119, 127
Kū (deity), 158
kuleana (obligation), 150
Kumaré (film, Gandhi), 219
Kyoto Protocol, 281

La Iglesia Católica Apostólica y Romana en Puerto Rico v. Municipio de Ponce (Puerto Rico), 44
Land, Richard, 267
Lathrop, Julia, 61, 62
Latour, Bruno, 251, 267
Lau, Lisa, 219
Lausanne International Congress, 260–61
Lautsi and Others v. Italy (ECHR), 279
law: civil, 53, 66, 70, 190; common, 54, 57–59, 62, 70, 81n24; as domain of life, 189; international, 291; Jewish, 190, 252–53; letter of, 51, 53–56, 59, 77; moral, 58–59, 61; "natural," 191; overlap of ecclesiastical and secular, 183–95; explanation of, 187–89; in perpetuity, 160–61; procedural rules, 54, 59, 65–66, 71–75, 189;
"real", 120; role in religious freedom, 191. *See also* Chicago; courts of equity; equity, home rule; Puerto Rico; rule of law; Spain
lay empowerment, 40
lay organizations, 40, 46
Lazarus, Emma, 92
Lazarus, Josephine, 120–21
League of Nations, 281
legacies of American exceptionalism, 167–79; intellectual, 176; looking away from, 167, 170, 177–78; racism, 176–77; religion and secularism, coming to terms with, 173–74; religious politics, 171–72, 178n6; tragic modes, 170–73, 175–77. *See also* American exceptionalism
"Legacy" (Jay-Z), 177–78
legal tutelage, 43, 47
Leirvik, Oddbjørn, 277
Lekhanyane, Joseph, 255
Lenape people, 20, 25
"Letter concerning Toleration" (Locke), 24
Letter to the Romans (Paul), 6

Levensohn, Lotta, 115
Liberal Democratic Party (LDP), Japan, 198–99, 201
Liberia, 6, 305
Lie, Trygve, 280
Lili'uokalani, Queen, 159
Linebarger, Paul, 66
Link, Jurgen, 274
Liston, Sonny, 131, 133–34, 138–39
The Lively Experiment (Mead), 98, 110n14
Lobingier, Charles, 64, 67, 68, 86n86
Locke, John, 24
Long, Charles, 106–7, 308
Longer and Shorter Catechisms, 185
Louisiana, 31
Louisiana Purchase Exposition, St. Louis, 1904, 69
Love the Sin (Jakobsen and Pellegrini), 8
Luther, Martin, 190
lynching, 188
Lyng v. Northwest Indian Cemetery Protective Association (U.S.), 151

MacArthur, Douglas, 11
Machiavelli, Niccolò, 170, 173
Mack, Julian, 62
Madison, James, 9
Magna Carta, 4, 194n16
Mahar v. O'Hara (U.S.), 57
"Make America Great Again", 175
mālama 'āina, 157
Malcolm, George, 66–67, 68
Malcolm X, 133, 134
Mangyans of Mindoro Province (Philippines), 67–68
Manifest Destiny, 28
Manto, Saadat Hasan, 295, 301–2n10
Mark 12:17, 190
Marshall, John, 309
Martinez, Anne M., 46
Maryland, 23, 40
Marzouki, Nadia, 231, 236–37, 240, 243n20
Massachusetts, 23, 26–27
Matthew. 22:21, 190, 250
Mauna Kea Thirty Meter Telescope (TMT) protests, 151, 154, 157–63
McBride, Keally, 240, 291
McKinley, William, 9–10, 11, 55
McLeary, James H., 44
Mead, Sidney, 98, 110n14
medieval metropolis, 53–54, 56, 62–63

Mehta, Uday, 290
Merriam, Charles, 69
The Message of Genesis (Elliott), 263
Methodism, 22; General Conference of the Methodist Church, 27; organizational and missionizing skills, 32, 34; Southern Methodist churches, 30
Miller, Madeline, 171
Miller, Perry, 101
Millerites, 22
minstrelsy, 134, 140, 141–42
miserabile personae, 54, 56, 59, 71
missionaries, 22; among Native Americans, 25–26; among people of African descent, 26; eastern states, 32; Methodist, 32, 34; New Englanders, 32; Norway, 278, 282–84; Roman Catholic, 32
Mode, Peter G., 97–98
modern postural yoga (MPY), 210, 216–17
Molebatsi, Caesar, 258
Monthly Religious Magazine, 56
Moody Bible Institute, 73
The Morality of Law (Fuller), 189
Moral Majority, 260
Moravians, 25
Moritomo Academy, 197
Mormons (Church of Jesus Christ of Latter-day Saints) 9, 22, 30–31, 34
Morris, Henry, 76
Moses, Bernard, 63, 70
Mowshowitz, Israel, 104
Mugler v. Kansas (U.S.), 61
Muhammad, Elijah, 131, 132
Muhammad, Warith Deen, 131
Mullins, Edgar Young, 249, 262
Municipal Court of Chicago, 52, 69–75, 88n99; state reductions of jurisdiction, 72
Museum fur Volkerkunde Dresden, 152
Muslim Brotherhood, 292
Muslims: CVE programs and, 229–30, 290; "good" *vs.* "bad," 132, 231; in India, 221; in Palestine, 124; in South Sudan, 6, 294–96; transnational solidarity and, 295–96; war on terror and, 12, 289, 300n2. *See also* Islam

Nansen, Fridtjof, 280
National Baptist Convention, USA, 261
national identity: American, 168, 174–75; India, 218; Norwegian, 174; two Sudans, 290
National Islamic Front (NIF), 292–93
National Security Council, 11
Nation of Islam (NOI), 131–34

Native American Graves Protection and Repatriation Act (1990), 151
Native Americans: in early republican America, 20, 25–26; Five Civilized Tribes of the Southeast, 25; Indian Removal policy, 25; Kiowa, 310; Lenape people, 20, 25; Ojibwe/Chippewa, 9; Quaker mission to the Senecas, 26. *See also* Indigenous peoples
Native Hawaiians, federal recognition proposals, 151, 161
Nauvoo, Illinois, 30–31
Nelson, Knute, 9
Nelson Act of 1899, 9
neo-Calvinists, 191
The Colossus (Lazarus), 92
New England: anti-Catholicism, 28; colonial, 19–20; disestablishment, 1833, 27; missionaries from, 32; "Praying Towns," 25; Puritans, 23
New Orleans, 31
New Oxford Annotated Bible, 253
New York: city skyline, 99–100; Port Authority, 103–5; Puerto Rican residents, 104. *See also* Tri-Faith Chapel Plaza (John F. Kennedy Airport)
New York Board of Rabbis, 103–4
New York Harbor, 99
New York Theatre Workshop, 133
New York World's Fair, 1964, 103
Nhial, Abdullah Deng, 292–94, 297, 302n15
Nidaros archdiocese, Norway, 276
Niebuhr, Reinhold, 27
Nijhawan, Michael, 233–34
Nippon Kaigi (the Japan Conference), 197
Nobel, Alfred, 280
non compotes mentis, 57
nones (nonreligious), 279
normalism, 274–76, 279–80, 285, 311
Norris, W. F., 86n81
Northampton, Massachusetts, 26–27
North Atlantic Treaty Organization (NATO), 281
Northern Baptist Convention, 261
North Korea, 196
Northwestern University School of Law, 68
Northwest Ordinance, 27, 81n23
Northwest Territory, 57
Norway, 7, 117, 273–87; Act Relating to Religious Communities, 276; approach to religion "at home," 276–80; assimilationist period, 278; Church of Norway (CoN), 276–80, 284–86; Constitution, 1814, 274, 276, 278;

disestablishment of CoN, 276, 280; as "do-gooder regime," 283; extractive industries, 281–82; foreign policy, 282–84; formative years, 275; inside/outside dynamic, 276–79; in international arena, 280–82; missionaries, 278, 282–84; normalism, 274–76, 279–80, 285, 311; Norwegian Labour Youth camp attacks (2011), 273; "othering" in, 277–79; "professor politicians," 275; religious education in schools, 277–78; Sami people, 278, 286–87n11; subsidies to religious communities, 275–76, 279; "us" and "them" debates, 273–74, 277, 285
Norwegian Humanist Association, 279
Norwegian Labour Youth camp attacks (2011), 273
Norwegian Ministry of Foreign Affairs, 284
Novak, William, 52
Nixon, Richard, 260
Nye, David, 100–102, 110n20

Obama administration (U.S.), 161–62, 230
occupation: Allied Occupation of Japan (1945–1952), 196, 198, 201–4, 241n2; of Puerto Rico, 37–38, 41–42
The Odyssey, (Homer), 171
Office of Religion and Global Affairs (U.S. State Department), 12
Ohman, August, 238, *239*
Olson, Harry, 71–72, 74
Organization for Economic Co-Operation and Development (OECD), 283
Orientalism, 125, 216, 218, 219–20; re-Orientalism, 219
Orr, Mark T., 202, 203
Osaka Prefectural Government, 197
Oslo Center for Peace, Democracy and Human Rights, 284
Othello (Shakespeare), 171
Our Common Future (United Nations), 281
Our Lady of the Skies Chapel, 102–5

Packard, Elizabeth, 60
Packard, Samuel, 61
Padilla, René, 258
Palestine, 115–29; as collective Jewish home, 124; Sampter in, 122–27; violence in 1920 and 1929, 125
Palestine Legal, 243n22
Palestinians, 232
parens patriae, doctrine of, 53

partition of India, 6, 290–91, 293–94, 297–300, 301n10
Patankar, Prachi, 221–22
paterfamilias, 54, 74
Paul, 6, 190, 249, 252–55, 264; Romans 13:1–7, 249, 252–55, 265, 267–68; theological industry around, 254
Peace Corps, 264
Peace Preservation Law (Chian iji hō), 1925, 196
peace processes: Norway and, 280–83; Sudan and, 290
Pennsylvania, 30
Permoli, Bernard, 31
Permoli v. New Orleans (U.S.), 30, 31
Perpina y Pibernat, Juan, 42–43
Perry, Lincoln, 134–44
Peterson, Eugenie, 216
Philippine Bureau of Justice, 66, 75
Philippine Commission, 51, 56, 63–66
Philippines, 6, 44, 49n24, 51; 1901 code of civil procedure, 66; *audiencia territorial*, 79n14; challenges to competency of judicial officers, 64, 65, 67; conversion of natives, 63–64; domestic relations law, 66–67; due process protections, 66; governors-general, 65; imperial legacy's effect on, 54–55; insular courts, 9, 63–68; local self-government, 69, 70; Mangyans of Mindoro Province, 67–68; *Plan of Manila*, 52, 63; *protector de indios*, 65; *real audiencia chancillería*, 55, 63–65, 75; reservations, 67–68; Spanish legal order in, 51, 54–55, 63–65, 70; U.S. annexation of, 9–10
Philips, Kevin, 29
Pinch, William, 212, 213
Plan of Chicago (Burnham), *52*, 68–69, 75
Plan of Manila (Burnham), *52*, 63
Pledge of Allegiance, 205
pluralism, 21; chronotopic aspects of, 108–9n5; early republican America, 19–21; as "hard to see," 93–94, 98–99, 106–8, 167, 178; as sign of cooperation, 97–98, 105
Political Theology (Schmitt), 174
Polynesian myths, 150
Pomeroy, John, 86n77
Ponce (Municipality of Ponce v. Roman Catholic Apostolic Church in Porto Rico, 1908, Puerto Rico), 44–47
Ponce, municipality of (Puerto Rico), 43–49
Ponce de León, 44
Popular Congress Party (Sudan), 293
popular constitutionalism, 188, 193–94n9

possession, 39–41, 305
Post-American, 260
Power, Will, 133–44, 146n15
Presbyterian Church: division of, 186; legalistic tradition of church governance, 189Presbyterians, 32
Prince Kuhio Day, March 26, 2018, 155
Princeton Seminary (New Jersey), 186
Princeton University, 25
probate court, 60–61
probation, 61–62, 73–74
Progressive Era, 54–55
"The Proper Organization and Procedure of a Municipal Court" (Olson), 72
property, 39–41; colonial lives of, 38; *desamortización*, 43; disputes in Puerto Rico, 38–49; human, 57; legal tutelage, 43, 47; not publicly registered, 42–43
Protestant Center (New York World's Fair, 1964), 103
protestant Christianity: American technological sublime and, 101; Christ for the World Chapel, John F. Kennedy Airport, 102–5; individual as essential unit of religion, 119–20, 128; lack of leadership in early republican America, 27; local and state establishments, 27; naturalization of, 9; in Puerto Rico, 46–47; supersessionist claims, 7; westward spread of, 31. *See also* Church of Norway (CoN); evangelical Christians; specific denominations
Protestant Council of New York, 103
Protestants and Other Americans United for the Separation of Church and State, 264
Protestant Supremacy, 26
Puerto Rico, 4–5, 9, 37–50, 305; aftermaths of *Ponce*, 46–47; "Americanization," 38; Autonomic Charter of 1897, 37; church property disputes, 1898–1908, 41–45; Constitution of 1876, 37, 41; disestablishment in, 37–38; Foraker Act (Organic Act of 1900), 37–38, 39; freedom of conscience in, 37; intellectuals and political leaders, 41; Ponce, municipality of, 43–49; *Ponce* ruling, 44–45; property disputes between Catholic Church and U.S. government, 38–49; protestant evangelizing in, 46–47; U.S. occupation of, 37–38, 41–42. *See also* Catholic Church, Puerto Rico
Puritans, 23, 174

Quakers, 26, 30, 310
Quebec Act (1774), 29–30

racism, 28; as American legacy, 176–77; apartheid stances of evangelicals, 250–51, 256, 259, 262
Rand McNally, 94
Reagan, Ronald, 144, 264, 309
real audiencia chancillería (Philippines), 55, 63–65, 75
reformations, 188, 191, 262; England, 22–23; Norway and, 276
refugee status determination, 234
Reinsch, Paul, 69
"The Relationship Between Religion and Education in America: A Comparative Glimpse at Japan" (Kishimoto), 204
religion/politics, 4, 305; CVE programs and, 228, 229–33, 290
religious freedom, 9, 19, 93, 119, 237–38; as American export, 1–4, 6, 11–12, 305–6; CVE and, 231–32; education in Japan and, 201–5; Hawaii and, 154, 159; international, 200–202; International Religious Freedom Act (1998), 3–4, 12, 306; Southern Baptist Conference and, 264–65; war on terror and, 12, 231–32
repatriation: Hawaiian items, 151, 152–54; South Sudan and, 288–89
repertoire, 137, 146–47n15, 146n13; of identity, 140–44
Report from the Capital (Baptist Joint Committee), 266
restorationist religious movements, 22
revolutions, political, 19, 24, 119, 278
Rhode Island, 23
Richland, Justin, 160–61
rights consciousness, 187
Rogers, Adrian, 264
Roi, Sonji, 133, 138
Roman Catholicism: Creole Catholics, 31; in early republican America, 21, 25–27; England, 22, 34; Indigenous mission communities, 25–26; "industrial chapels," 103; as intolerant internal other, 27; Maryland, 23; material pagan practices of, 7; organizational and missionizing skills, 32, 34; Our Lady of the Skies Chapel, John F. Kennedy Airport, 102–5; *Permoli v. New Orleans* (U.S.), 31; sex abuse scandal, 192–93; state-level disputes, 31; as state religion, Puerto Rico, 37. *See also* Catholic Church, Puerto Rico
Roman Empire, 190
Roman law, 188
Romans 12:10 (Paul), 253

Romans 13:1–7 (Paul), 249, 252–55, 265, 267–68; circulated in South Africa, 255–59
Roosevelt, Theodore, 44, 69
Rosenfeld, Paul, 99–100, 110n17
Rowe, Leo, 70
Royce, Josiah, 121
rule of law, 4, 45, 183–95; American dedication to, 187–88; equity as contrary to, 52; equity as cornerstone of, 56; Japan and, 201; as political goal, 185–86; in United States, 189–92

Sami people, 278, 286–87n11
Sampter, Elvie, 122
Sampter, Jessie, 5, 115–29; as binationalist, 125; homemaking in Palestine, 122–27; as pacifist, 122, 125; United States as home, 118–21; United States as not-home, 121–22; U.S. citizenship relinquished, 118; *Works: A Course on Zionism*, 123; *The Great Adventurer*, 120–21; "Nationalism," 125; *The Seekers*, 121
scale, 116–18, 131, 144
Schmitt, Carl, 55, 174
school prayer amendment proposal, 264, 267
Scotland, 22
secularism, 268n2; "American," 296; Catholic Church sex abuse scandal and limitations of, 192–93; Cold War efforts to combat, 12; French, 296–97; narrow religious interests and, 172; overconfidence in, 190; prejudice against possibility of religious justice, 189–90; South Sudan, 294–96
secularization, 7, 10, 132, 137, 143, 277, 296
The Seekers (Sampter), 121
Segal, Hyman, 121, 124
Self-Defense Forces, Japan, 198
Senate Judiciary Committee, 75
separation of church and state, 11, 38, 40, 187, 264, 306
settler colonialism, 151, 162, 211, 304, 310
sex abuse scandal, Catholic Church and, 192–93
Shah, Priya, 219
Shakaiken (journal), 204
Shakespeare, William, 171
Shintō religion (Japan), 197–200, 202, 205–6, 208n17
Shintō Seiji Renmei (Shintō Association for Spiritual Leadership, or SAS), 197, 198, 205
Siete Partidas (Castilian legal code), 64, 68
The Silence of the Girls (Barker), 171
Simone, T. Abdou Maliqalim, 293
Singh, Roopa, 221

slavery, 170, 306; Africans in early republican America, 20–21, 25–26, 170; Afro-Caribbean, 136; British Empire's economy and, 20–21; centering of, 175, 179n14; "conversion" policies and, 3; equity courts and, 80–81n22; "human property," 57; missionaries and, 26; Quebec Act and fears of, 29; Roman Catholicism associated with, 28
Slotkin, Richard, 109n10
Smith, Joseph, 30–31
Society for the Promotion of Buddhism, 11
Society for the Propagation of Christian Knowledge, 24
Society for the Propagation of the Gospel in Foreign Parts, 24
Song of Achilles (Miller), 171
"soul competency," 262–65
"soul freedom," 262–65
South Africa, Republic of, 5, 117; divestment from, 261, 266; evangelical Christians in, 249–72; Romans 13 circulated in, 255–59; Soweto uprisings, 258; "Terrorism" Act, 259; townships, 255–56
South African Baptist Union, 266
South African Council of Churches, 256–57, 266
South African Defence Force, 256
South Asian Americans Perspectives on Yoga, 221
Southern Baptist Convention (U.S.), 253, 261–63; Christian Life Commission, 261–62, 266; "creedalism," 263; Religious Freedom Committee, 267; Statement of Baptist Faith and Message, 263
Southern Baptist Theological Seminary, 266
South Sudan, Republic of, 6, 288–303; Abyei region, 294; "Ministry of Gender," 291; Muslims and transnational solidarity, 295–96; Muslims as internal foreigners, 294–95; reinvention of self in, 294–95; repatriation, 288–89; secularism, 294; USAID and, 291. *See also* Sudan
sovereignty, 310–11; equity and, 54–55; external to the United States, 151, 156; Indigenous movements, 311–12; in princely states of India, 217; settler, 304; of "we, the people," 189, 236–37
Spain: Castilian law, 64–65; concordats with Vatican, 38, 41, 43, 44, 47; *desamortización*, 43; Iberian law, 65; *patronato real* (royal patronage), 41; Spanish legal order in Philippines, 51, 54–55, 63–65, 70
Spanish-American War, 9, 37, 40, 51
Spanish Empire, 21, 28

Spanish Penal Code, 37
spiritual health, promotion of, 12
spirituality, 93–94, 106
Starr, Frederick, 70
State Department, U.S., 3–4, 12, 200–201, 289
State Secrets Law of 2014 (Japan), 199
Statoil (Equinor), 282
Statue of Liberty, 92, 99, 105
Stead, William, 63
Stepin Fetchit (Lincoln Perry character), 134–44
Stevens-Arroyo, Anthony, 38
Stiles, Ezra, 32
Stott, John, 252, 254–55
Suarez, Francisca, 41–42
sublime: European, 100; technological, 94, 100–101
Subrin, Stephen, 75
Sudan, Republic of, 6, 288–303; civil war, 289; civil war (second, 2013), 291, 292; civil war, U.S. evangelical support for, 299; Comprehensive Peace Agreement (CPA) of 2005, 291, 295; as "hard to see," 303n24; Sudanese Revolution of 2018–2019, 302n15; White Nile state, 293. *See also* South Sudan; South Sudan, Republic of
Sudanese Student Union (Al-Azhar University), 292
Sudan People's Liberation Movement (SPLM), 293, 297, 298
Supreme Court of the Philippines, 65–66, 70
Svalbard (Arctic archipelago), 281
Swaggart, Jimmy, 259
Sweden, 275, 280
Szold, Henrietta, 121, 122

Tafel, Edgar, 104–5
Taft, Alphonso, 10–11
Taft, William Howard, 51–52, 55–56, 63–65, 69, 70; 1908 presidential campaign, 72; California code, view of, 86n77; as president, 74–75
Taft Commission, 55, 63, 65–67
Tajik, Hadia, 273
"Take Back Yoga" campaign, 211, 220, 223n4
Taney, Roger, 31
Taylor, Diana, 137, 143, 146n13, 147n15
technological sublime, 94, 100–101
temperance, 61
Terrell, Ernie, 144, 309
El testigo evángelico (United Brethren publication), 46
Texas Baptist Convention, 262
Theologies of American Exceptionalism, 2

Thomas, Brook, 39–40
Thomas Aquinas, 54
Through the Looking Glass/Alice in Wonderland (Carroll), 177–78, 184
Tilak, B. G., 215, 225n18
"Toba Tek Singh" (Manto), 295, 301–2n10
Tocqueville, Alexis de, 174
tolerance, 24, 29
Toleration Act of 1689, 24
Tolman, Edgar, 75
TransAfrica, 266
transnational evangelical networks, 5, 250–51, 255–57
Treaty of Paris (1898), Article VIII, 9, 43, 44–45, 48–49n21
The Trials of Muhammad Ali (film), 131
Tri-Faith Chapel Plaza (John F. Kennedy Airport), 102–6
triumphalist exceptionalism, 174–75, 184, 200
Trump, Donald, rhetoric of, 168, 174–75; administration of, 230, 268
Tsukamoto Kindergarten, 197
Tuley, Murray, 51, 54, 57–59, 61, 82n28, 84n48; Municipal Court of Chicago and, 71, 73, 88n99
"Tuley Law" (1887), 84n48
al-Turabi, Hasan, 293
Tutu, Desmond, 255, 257
Tvedt, Terje, 283
Twain, Mark, 1, 290, 300–301n4
two kingdoms theology, 190

UN Declaration on the Rights of Indigenous Peoples, 153
UN Environmental Agency, 281
"unincorporated territories," 9
United Brethren, 46
United Nations, 152, 280, 301n7
United States: of America, as corporate body, 39–40; cultural politics of yoga in, 218–22; cultural trajectory, 169; economic style and set of possibilities, 169; ethnonationalism, rise of, 299; extrajudicial execution of Black males, 290; freedom of religion assumed for, 3–4; global context of, 229; as "hard to see," 91, 93–94, 106–8, 167, 178; hegemony reliant on allies, 200; as home, 118–21; Indian diaspora in, 220–22, 226n31; juridical standing, 168; noninterference at state level, 30–31; as not-home, 121–22; political form, 169; protestant pluralism as informally official religion, 27; proto-, 4; Puerto Rico, occupation of, 37–38, 41–42; racial domination by, 172; rule of law in, 189–92;

self-governing autonomy, 12–13; Sudan and, 291–92; as superpower, 174; wealth and power of as exception, 168–69, 172. *See also* American exceptionalism; imperial America; legacies of American exceptionalism
United States Agency for International Development (USAID), 291, 301n7
United States Commission on International Religious Freedom (USCIRF), 12, 196, 200–201
United States Education Mission to Japan, 202
United States v. Bastanipour (U.S.), 234
Universal Congress of Lawyers and Jurists (St. Louis exposition), 69
University of Chicago, 69–70
University of Khartoum (Sudan), 292
University of Oslo, 275
University of Ottawa, 210, 219
University of Wisconsin, 238
U.S. Army, on Hawaii, 157
U.S. Census, 108n4
U.S. Hall of Justice proposal (Burnham), 63
U.S. Operations Coordinating Board, 11
U.S. protectorates, 70. *See also* Cuba; Philippines

Valladolid, Castile, 64
van Buren, Martin, 30
Vande Mātharam (India's national song), 213–14
Vatican: Cold War era partnership, 11; concordats with Spain, 38, 41, 43, 44, 47
Vieth, Paul H., 202–3, 204
Vietnam War, 134, 306
Villamor, Ignacio, 68
violence: CVE deradicalization programs, 228, 229–33, 241n5, 290; "disengagement," 230–31; necessary to exceptionalist narrative, 92, 109n10; Palestine, 1920 and 1929, 125
Virginia, 23, 25, 27
"Visible People and Invisible Religion" (Long), 106–7
Vivekananda (yogi), 217
voluntarism, 4

Wakatama, Pius, 258
war on terror, 6, 12–13, 300n2; CVE deradicalization programs, 228, 229–33, 241n5, 290
"warrior ascetics," 212–13
Washington, George, 29
West, Geoffrey, 116
Westminster Confession of Faith, 185
Westminster Seminary (Philadelphia), 186

Wheaton College, 258
When We Were Kings (film), 131
"white," use of as term, 26; "white ways of life," 9
Whitefield, George, 25
Wigmore, John, 68, 74
Willard, Frances, 61
Williams, William Appleman, 238
Winthrop, John, 28
Wittgenstein, Ludwig, 176
Woman's Christian Temperance Union, 61
women: as Chicago attorneys, 60–61; equity and, 59–61, 74; equity's jurisdiction over, 57; female police force proposal, 63; guardianship and, 59–60; home rule and, 56; murdered in literature, 171; as "protective officers," 74
World Bank, 169
World Community of Al-Islam in the West (American Society of Muslims), 131–32
World Council of Churches, 255, 257
World Vision, 261
World War I, 122, 125

xenophobic nationalism, 290, 299

Yale University, 32
Yasukuni Shrine (Japan), 199
Yerushalmi, David, 231
yoga, 6, 210–27, 237, 310; *ahiṁsā* (not harmful), 215; *anāsakti* (nonattached), 215; as anticolonial tool, 212–16; asceticism, power of, 215; authenticity markers, 218–19; caste and class inequalities in, 213–18; colonization of, 211, 215–16, 221–22; criminalization of yogis, 212–13, 224n10; elite Sanskrit texts of, 213; Hindu American Foundation (HAF), 211, 220, 223–24n5; homogenization of, 212, 216; imbrication in colonialism, 212; industry, 219, 225–26n26; *karma yoga* political philosophy, 215–16; modern postural yoga (MPY), 210, 216–17; as political philosophy, 215, 224n6; *sūrya namaskār,* 216; "Take Back Yoga" campaign, 211, 220, 223n4; tourism in India, 218; uprising in Bengal, 1763–1802, 212–13; *vinyāsa* form, 216. *See also* India
Yogasūtras (Patanjali), 119, 215, 216
yogis: as alternate locus of authority, 213–14, 224n10; criminalization of, 213–14, 224n10

Zion Christian Church (South Africa), 255
Zionism, 115, 117, 121–25, 127–28
Zollmann, Carl, 45

RELIGION, CULTURE, AND PUBLIC LIFE
....
Series Editor: Matthew Engelke

After Pluralism: Reimagining Religious Engagement, edited by Courtney Bender and Pamela E. Klassen

Religion and International Relations Theory, edited by Jack Snyder

Religion in America: A Political History, Denis Lacorne

Democracy, Islam, and Secularism in Turkey, edited by Ahmet T. Kuru and Alfred Stepan

Refiguring the Spiritual: Beuys, Barney, Turrell, Goldsworthy, Mark C. Taylor

Tolerance, Democracy, and Sufis in Senegal, edited by Mamadou Diouf

Rewiring the Real: In Conversation with William Gaddis, Richard Powers, Mark Danielewski, and Don DeLillo, Mark C. Taylor

Democracy and Islam in Indonesia, edited by Mirjam Künkler and Alfred Stepan

Religion, the Secular, and the Politics of Sexual Difference, edited by Linell E. Cady and Tracy Fessenden

Boundaries of Toleration, edited by Alfred Stepan and Charles Taylor

Recovering Place: Reflections on Stone Hill, Mark C. Taylor

Blood: A Critique of Christianity, Gil Anidjar

Choreographies of Shared Sacred Sites: Religion, Politics, and Conflict Resolution, edited by Elazar Barkan and Karen Barkey

Beyond Individualism: The Challenge of Inclusive Communities, George Rupp

Love and Forgiveness for a More Just World, edited by Hent de Vries and Nils F. Schott

Relativism and Religion: Why Democratic Societies Do Not Need Moral Absolutes, Carlo Invernizzi Accetti

The Making of Salafism: Islamic Reform in the Twentieth Century, Henri Lauzière

Mormonism and American Politics, edited by Randall Balmer and Jana Riess

Religion, Secularism, and Constitutional Democracy, edited by Jean L. Cohen and Cécile Laborde

Race and Secularism in America, edited by Jonathon S. Kahn and Vincent W. Lloyd

Beyond the Secular West, edited by Akeel Bilgrami

Pakistan at the Crossroads: Domestic Dynamics and External Pressures, edited by Christophe Jaffrelot

Faithful to Secularism: The Religious Politics of Democracy in Ireland, Senegal, and the Philippines, David T. Buckley

Holy Wars and Holy Alliance: The Return of Religion to the Global Political Stage, Manlio Graziano

The Politics of Secularism: Religion, Diversity, and Institutional Change in France and Turkey, Murat Akan

Democratic Transition in the Muslim World: A Global Perspective, edited by Alfred Stepan

The Holocaust and the Nakba, edited by Bashir Bashir and Amos Goldberg

The Limits of Tolerance: Enlightenment Values and Religious Fanaticism, Denis Lacorne

German, Jew, Muslim, Gay: The Life and Times of Hugo Marcus, Marc David Baer

Modern Sufis and the State: The Politics of Islam in South Asia and Beyond, edited by Katherine Pratt Ewing and Rosemary R. Corbett

The Arab and Jewish Questions: Geographies of Engagement in Palestine and Beyond, edited by Bashir Bashir and Leila Farskah

GPSR Authorized Representative: Easy Access System Europe, Mustamäe tee 50, 10621 Tallinn, Estonia, gpsr.requests@easproject.com

www.ingramcontent.com/pod-product-compliance
Lightning Source LLC
Chambersburg PA
CBHW021931290426
44108CB00012B/800